For Don,

In the hope that you will find some nuggets of wisdom here!

Sláinte,

Aart De Geus, Eric Thode, Christiane Weidenfeld
Europe Reforms Labour Markets

Aart De Geus, Eric Thode, Christiane Weidenfeld

Europe Reforms Labour Markets

Leaders' Perspectives

With country notes by
John Martin

DE GRUYTER

ISBN 978-3-11-036577-1
e-ISBN (PDF) 978-3-11-036510-8
e-ISBN (EPUB) 978-3-11-038583-0

Bibliographic information published by the Deutsche Nationalbibliothek
The Deutsche Nationalbibliothek lists this publication in the Deutsche Nationalbibliografie; detailed bibliographic data are available on the Internet at http://dnb.dnb.de.

© 2016 Walter de Gruyter GmbH, Berlin/Boston
Cover image: Katharina Wanner
Photographers: Lucáš Piaček (Radičová); Benoit Granier (Fillon); Nordic Cooperation Website (norden.org)/Magnus Fröderberg (Rasmussen); Kaupo Kikkas-Riigikantselei (Ansip); private (Balkenende); Tony Blair Office (Blair); Europaparlament (Buzek); private (Papandreou); Marco Urban (Schröder); Businessfoto Hamburg (Schüssel); private (Zapatero); private (Monti)
Printing and binding: Hubert & Co. GmbH & Co. KG, Göttingen
♾ Printed on acid-free paper
Printed in Germany

www.degruyter.com

Contents

Foreword

In 2002, Aart De Geus was appointed Minister of Social Affairs and Employment in the Netherlands. Under the leadership of Prime Minister Jan Peter Balkenende, the Dutch government implemented an ambitious agenda to reform the labour market, social security, pensions and health. In 2004 the Netherlands held the EU presidency. By that time EU ministers were discussing reforms intensely and learning from each other. Most of the time, however, they were fighting their own battles. Some common wisdom existed about "where to go", but less was known about "how to get there". After serving in the Dutch government, Aart De Geus became Deputy Secretary General of the OECD. In this context, he had the opportunity to work on the international project Making Reform Happen, which dealt with the political economy of reform, that is, how to realise a successful process of reform, the very question addressed in this book. The project covered several areas, including product markets, labour markets, pensions, tax, health, education and the environment.

In 2001, Eric Thode was appointed labour market economist at the Bertelsmann Stiftung. In Germany, the Schröder government decided to reform labour markets and pensions substantially, and the Bertelsmann Stiftung supported these efforts with expertise, discussions and recommendations.

Around this time, Christiane Weidenfeld embarked on a career in academia, holding research and teaching positions at the Universities of Cambridge and Cologne, before venturing into the world of applied policy research at the Bertelsmann Stiftung, where she focuses on European integration and international economic policy.

Following the professional experiences described above, we, the authors, met at the Bertelsmann Stiftung in 2013 and considered writing a book on European reforms in the areas of labour markets, benefits and pensions. The idea gained momentum when we decided to include interviews with former prime ministers so we could share their perspectives. As the action platform for these reforms is mainly the nation-state, we chose 12 of the 28 EU member states and took a closer look at what happened in these countries. We asked John Martin, a former Director of the OECD with extensive international expertise, to provide country notes. We also are deeply grateful that we could benefit from his outstanding expertise and experience when we worked on the historical and conceptual framework and on our conclusions.

The 12 countries were chosen to represent not only a vast majority (80 per cent) of the EU's population, but also its economy (83 per cent of GDP). Moreover, we have tried to include examples of the different types of social market economies, social traditions and (current) roles in Europe. Thus, we selected Germany, France and the UK as large Western EU countries; Italy, Spain and Greece as Southern EU member states; the Netherlands, Austria and Denmark as midsized Continental/Nordic EU countries; and Poland, Slovakia and Estonia as Eastern EU member states. We were delighted that the most prominent prime ministers in office at the time these countries implemented reforms accepted our invitation to be interviewed for this book. In the three years we spent assembling it, it became clear that the need for structural reforms remains high on political agendas. Nonetheless, few lessons have been learned about the political economy of reforms so far. Our goal is to increase understanding in this area, not from an academic, but from a practical perspective, in order to be of help to actors and stakeholders during future reforms of labour markets, benefits and pensions – and thus increase the prosperity and well-being of those living in the EU.

Being surrounded by so many knowledgeable and dedicated colleagues at the Bertelsmann Stiftung has significantly added to the overall quality of this book. We express our sincere gratitude to all of them. While we have benefited greatly from the ideas and suggestions of far too many colleagues to mention them all, we feel that three deserve special mention. We are profoundly grateful to Stefan Empter, who often provided us with new vistas and with suggestions for additional avenues of research and lines of enquiry. We are also indebted to Klaus-Henning Groth, who provided continuous advice on the intricacies associated with framing, branding and publishing a book like this. Finally, we wish to thank Gabriele Horsmann, without whom we would not have been able to surmount the logistical challenges that came with conducting our research.

Last but not least, we wish to thank our families, whose patience and encouragement provided both an important element of reassurance and a constant source of inspiration.

Aart De Geus
Eric Thode
Christiane Weidenfeld

Chapter 1
Introduction

London, 1888. Angus McAfee struggles as he is descending the stairs to the damp, mould-infested one-bedroom flat he shares with three fellow workers from the steel factory. He came from rural Scotland to find the prosperity that was promised by the opportunities of the new Industrial Revolution. Work was hard, hazardous and certainly not good for his health, with the thick sulphurous air he had to breathe at the factory. But at least pay was fairly decent and he was confident to make a reasonable living. However, shortly after his 23rd birthday he got stuck in a railway junction on the factory premises, crushed his foot and has been permanently limping ever since this injury. He had difficulties standing the whole day at his former workplace, so he was transferred to a different task that was less strenuous, but only paid a meagre wage. Hardly being able to pay for his food and rent, he had to come to terms with the idea of going back to Scotland and living off the family he had left.

Amsterdam, 1890. Marlene van der Vlugt suffers an even worse fate. Her husband died in an accident, leaving her and the three children on their own with no financial means to make a living. At least, the widow receives food, clothes and a little money from a church-run charity, but that support is highly volatile because the church can only redistribute what the people in the parish are willing to give in alms. Marlene has to send her oldest son to work, instead of to school, and the two younger ones will have to follow soon in order to make ends meet.

Vienna, 1892. Hans Gruber, a watchmaker in the third generation, is opening up his small workshop in the morning. Aged 68, his back is aching and, with his gradually stiffening fingers and deteriorating eyesight, he finds it harder and harder to assemble the tiny gears, springs and spindles that bring his beloved pocket watches to life. But he is left without any choice because his marriage was not blessed with any children who could have taken over the workshop, thereby permitting him to retire. Hans knows he will have to work until he dies.

These three short stories are intended to illustrate important social risks workers, craftsmen and their family members faced at the end of the 19th century. Those were dire risks, often endangering the sheer existence of individuals and entire families. Invalidity, death of the breadwinner, unbearable working conditions, lack of access to health services and childlessness were among the most important social risks threatening the citizens in European countries of that time.

Fast-forward to the present. Thanks to the invention of the welfare state and to its extensive development over the past 120 years, most of those risks are no longer life-threatening. Regulations governing working conditions, the various branches of social security, basic income guarantees and redistributive public services have either substantially reduced the likelihood of conditions such as those mentioned above occurring or have at least managed to ameliorate their negative consequences.

However, new risks have emerged that from a present-day perspective in our generally much more secure world are just as relevant and might be perceived as just as scary. The new social risks of the post-industrialised world might be listed as follows (Bonoli 2005): The transition from the industrial to the service economy and accelerated structural change is making workers struggle to keep up with new technologies, new work environments and the acquisition of new knowledge. The growth of so-called 'non-standard' work calls into question former accomplishments of the welfare state: the financial base is eroding, benefit levels are declining and new societal divisions between 'insiders' and 'outsiders' are emerging. Women's increasing participation in the labour market is not reconcilable with the archaic male breadwinner model and calls for new forms of family support, labour market regulation and social security. Long-term unemployment, resurging poverty, increasing income disparities, permanent exclusion from participation in societal activities and intergenerational injustice are additional risks threatening individual livelihoods and societal cohesion.

For political leaders, it has always been one of the most important priorities to shape public welfare policies in such a way that the social risks of their time could be managed or controlled. Ideally, this can be achieved by curbing the negative results of new developments, while letting flourish the positive aspects that almost always come about.

Because of the complexity of the matter, policymakers have always struggled with accomplishing this task. In order to implement successful welfare state reforms, they have to master two challenges simultaneously: 'do the right things' and 'do things right' – create policies that properly address the problems and let them materialise in the political process so that they will be implemented and fully effective.

1 Aim of this book: providing success factors for labour market, benefit and pension reforms

The idea for this book was born in early 2013, when the EU's combined unemployment rate had just risen to over 12 per cent. The prospect of unemployment becoming increasingly structural underlined the pressing need for labour market, benefits and pension (LMBP) reforms, and yet even three years later the political climate is still not conducive for many EU countries to implementing LMBP reforms. Three reasons in particular account for this state of affairs. First, persistently high unemployment rates in some European countries make it difficult to generate sufficient consensus in favour of additional reforms, as they might have damaging effects on labour market performance in the short term, even if it is clear that in the medium and long term they would boost employment. Secondly, many countries see the pressing need for fiscal consolidation, which results in less public funding being available to compensate those who lost out because of structural reforms. Finally, various countries continue to call for relaxation of fiscal austerity, arguing that, until growth returns, it is harmful to embark on structural reforms.

In light of these trends, this book seeks to increase our knowledge of how to design, implement and communicate LMBP reforms in a successful manner as a means to overcome voters' and policy makers' general resistance towards taking action and embarking on a programme of structural reforms. At the same time, the book aims to contribute to the general discussion on the political economy of reform by adding the novel perspective of 12 high-level practitioners, who were at the helm of their respective national governments during times when some of the most significant LMBP reforms in recent European history were implemented. Combining these two endeavours, the book thus draws on the first-hand accounts of 12 former European heads of government as a basis for identifying factors that make for successful, or unsuccessful, LMBP reforms. The aim is to reveal the political aspects, namely the opportunities, challenges and impediments to designing labour market, benefit and pension reforms and to describe the conditions under which successful reforms can be advocated, adopted and implemented in terms of 'process', which is of course inextricably linked to the dimension of 'content'. The book also examines the lessons that can be drawn from unsuccessful reform efforts and, by analysing how to make reforms happen, it identifies the factors that make for healthy labour markets, benefit schemes and pension systems in Europe.

2 A brief recap of welfare state history

The framework of the labour market and the pension system constitute two important pillars of a wider concept of social policy known as the 'Welfare State'. The following paragraphs aim to provide a brief, necessarily sketchy, overview highlighting the most relevant features of the history and research of the welfare state. This will show how contemporary and future labour market and pension reforms can be successful. In welfare state analysis, and especially when looking at LMBP reforms, path dependency plays an important role. Virtually never are reforms constructed from scratch. Rather, they are most frequently incremental improvements of already existing laws and regulations, being implemented by long-standing institutions and established constellations of actors. And even if 'big bang' reforms occur from time to time, they are also very much related to the previously established paradigms which they try to overturn. Against this backdrop, it is important to take a brief look at the evolution of the welfare state in Europe from a historical perspective.

2.1 Origins of today's welfare states

The inception of the modern welfare state is typically associated with the introduction of different branches of social insurance schemes in the German empire in the late 19th century. The then chancellor Otto von Bismarck prepared the law on public health insurance, which was put forward by Emperor Wilhelm I and passed by the German parliament in 1883. Similar laws on public work accident insurance, as well as invalidity and pension insurance, followed in 1884 and 1889, respectively. Occupation-based relief funds existed well before then in conjunction with other elements that can be considered essential to a modern welfare state, such as compulsory schooling, which had already been in effect since 1825 in the German state of Prussia. However, this was the first time that national, all-encompassing and mandatory insurance schemes came into force. Another novelty was that, in organisational and structural terms, this body was largely autonomous. This approach – to have an insurance-based social security – has been inextricably linked to the name of Bismarck ever since (cf. Stolleis 2013).

Other countries implemented their versions of a welfare state shortly thereafter. In the United Kingdom, for instance, the welfare state was conceived by the reforms of 1906–14 under the Liberal Prime Minister Herbert Asquith. These included the Old-Age Pensions Act in 1908, the introduction of free school meals in 1909, the 1909 Labour Exchanges Act, the Development Act 1909, which heralded greater government intervention in economic development, and the National Insurance Act 1911, which set up a national insurance scheme against the risk of unemployment and sickness, with contributions paid both by employers and employees (Boundless 2015). In France, the earliest elements of a modern welfare state emerged in the last decade of the 19th century when, for the first time since the French Revolution, the formation of workers' associations was allowed again. Simultaneously, firms were held responsible for any work accidents, regardless of whether an employer was actually at fault or not. In contrast to the 'common law' (*droit civil*), this constituted a new type of law, the 'social law' (*droit social*), which detached the responsibility of the employer from any deliberate or negligent misconduct. In addition, firms had to compensate workers through the payment of a social contribution to a mutual fund devoted to the insurance against specific risks. 'This was the early germ for the French Welfare State' (Boyer 2000, p. 29).

In Italy, to conclude this brief spotlight, the first scheme of obligatory pension insurance was introduced between 1898 and 1919, replacing a system of locally based assistance offered by religious and non-religious charitable organisations (Davì (no date)). A few years earlier, in 1890, the Crispi Law (named after the then Prime Minister Crispi) had enabled charity and other support institutions to become part of the public sector and obtain a firm juridical standing in return. Larger and economically relevant institutions were state controlled (Barbetta 1993).

2.2 Causes for the creation of the welfare state

Even in terms of this very limited selection of welfare state origins, it becomes clear that country-specific circumstances played an important role in the concrete outset and initial implementation. However, it should be noted that the underlying reasons for the welfare states to emerge rather simultaneously around the turn of the 19th century into the 20th are quite similar. The Second Industrial Revolution with the introduction of steam power and mass production can be regarded as the main trigger. It sparked the creation of a new class, the industrial workers, who frequently suffered from strenuous working conditions, unhealthy and dangerous work environments and alienation from their work. The reorganisation from craftsmanship to production lines weakened guilds and other previously existing workers' associations. This was exacerbated by the need for workers to move, mostly by rural exodus into urban areas, so that traditional structures for providing support to the sick, injured, disabled or elderly rapidly disappeared. A new social risk of that time, mass unemployment, emerged. These developments in their entirety created a demand for new types of insurance against the principal social risks, which had to be independent from occupational, community or religious affiliation. On the other hand, administrative capacity had greatly improved across Europe following the Napoleonic era. Thus, the new need for public social insurance could be matched by the improved capabilities of the state authorities.

The arguments for creating the welfare state, however, were not purely economic or sociological. In Germany, for instance, fears were expressed that rising numbers of industrial workers would pave the way for social democratic and

Marxist theories, serious threats to the political system and to the rulers themselves. Bismarck consequently used his social insurance policy deliberately to buy the consent of the working class for the existing political system (Schmidt 2005). In a similar way, secular policy makers, especially in Southern European countries, regarded the welfare state as an effective tool for pushing back the influence of the Catholic Church from societal and individual life. In this sense, church-affiliated charities were crowded out by state-run institutions.

Thus, dealing with new social risks arising from the technological change in conjunction with political economy considerations aimed at stabilising or further expanding the existing political system were important drivers for establishing the welfare state.

2.3 Two conceptual approaches: Bismarck and Beveridge

Welfare states have evolved and expanded ever since. Over the course of time, their focal points have been influenced by general economic conditions, seminal trends and war times. In Germany, for instance, the public unemployment insurance scheme was introduced in 1927 when the Weimar Republic enjoyed an economic boom. Initially, it was a huge success with a coverage rate of 80 per cent of all unemployed workers at the beginning of 1929. However, it quickly came under severe stress during the Great Depression, culminating in a coverage of barely 30 per cent in 1932 with a total of six million unemployed.

Ten years later, in December 1942, the Beveridge Report was published in the UK, named after the Chairman of the Commission on Social Insurance and Allied Services, William Beveridge. Written against the backdrop of the economic consequences of World War II, it is commonly viewed as embodying principles opposed to the Bismarckian welfare state. It formed the basis for post-war reforms in the UK, e. g. the creation of the National Health Service.

Even today, the names of Bismarck and Beveridge mark a fundamental distinction between two archetypes of welfare states. They can be distinguished through the following five criteria: purpose, nature of benefits, eligibility, coverage and financing (Bonoli 1997). Bismarck, on the one hand, stands for the social insurance model. Its primary objective is to provide an income in the sense that a certain living standard should be maintained if a contingency of sickness, unemployment, etc. occurs. In such a system, benefits therefore need to be earnings-related. Eligibility is normally assessed by the amount of contributions made to the insurance scheme. Waiting periods, as well as minimum and maximum contribution levels, are commonplace. The coverage of the insurance fund is (ideally) restricted to its members. Typically, both workers and employers pay into the fund, albeit not necessarily on equal terms. Overall, strong emphasis is put on the equivalence between contributions and benefits, and the old model of guilds – occupation-based arrangements – is still reflected in this setting. Apart from creating the legislative framework, the government has in principle a very small role to play in such a welfare state model.

On the other hand, Beveridge is associated with a universalistic welfare approach. The main objective lies in the prevention of poverty for everybody. It provides flat-rate benefits regardless of the individuals' former living standards or contributions. Frequently, the Beveridge model is associated with means-testing, i.e. assessing if individuals are really in need of a benefit or if they have other sources of income.[1] Eligibility is based on either citizenship or residence in the country, a distinction that becomes increasingly relevant with rising cross-country migration. Coverage of welfare benefits extends to the entire population according to the eligibility criteria. Logically, financial resources are collected by general taxation. The main features of the two archetype welfare states are summarised in Table 1.

Table 1: Main features of Bismarckian and Beveridgean welfare states

	Bismarck	Beveridge
Objective	Income maintenance	Poverty prevention
Nature of benefits	Earnings-related	Flat-rate
Eligibility	Contribution record	Citizenship or residence
Coverage	Members	Population
Financing	Contributions	Taxes

Source: Bonoli 1997

In reality, no current welfare state is organised in a purely Bismarckian or Beveridgean fashion. Hybrid models combining elements of the archetypes, both between and within different pillars of welfare states, are the norm. Every regime, even the Bismarckian types, has a tax-financed basic income security scheme designed to prevent poverty. In most advanced economies, contribution-based pension schemes have redistributive elements in order to top up low pensions. In addition, many public pension systems, unemployment benefits and active labour market policies are partly subsidised by general tax revenues. Nevertheless,

---

1 Interestingly, William Beveridge himself took a negative stance on means-testing.

the general approach a country has adopted towards the welfare state substantially shapes the framework for labour market and pension reforms.

The end of World War II marks the starting point for the creation of many European welfare states that are still, more or less, in place today. Western Germany developed the 'social market economy', a concept that goes beyond welfare state politics, but is strongly Bismarckian in the relevant aspects. Already a decade earlier, the idea of 'the People's Home' (*Folkhemmet*) had materialised in the shaping of the Nordic welfare states, most notably with the Agreement of Saltsjöbaden in 1938, which is seen as the foundation of social partnership in Sweden.

In the first three decades after World War II (*Les Trente Glorieuses* or *The Golden Age*), European economies flourished and so did the welfare states. Pay-as-you-go pension schemes were introduced against the backdrop of the enormous destruction of capital during the war. Working conditions were gradually improved in terms of working-time reductions, increased work-safety provisions, but also enhanced employment protection legislation. Redistribution and the provision of new welfare services were entirely fuelled by economic growth. Governments were in the comfortable position of being able to redistribute the gains from economic growth. Benefits for one group did not have to come at the expense of another group.

2.4 The 1970s and 1980s: welfare states under pressure

All this came to an abrupt halt when the first oil price shock hit European countries in 1973. For a rough sketch of the macro-economic environment from the 1960s until recently see Figure 1, which depicts the quarterly growth rate of real GDP for the EU15 countries.[2] Quickly, unemployment soared to unprecedented levels after World War II, not only leading to individual economic hardship, but also putting severe strain on the financing of social services. Once again, the welfare state came under pressure. Reducing unemployment was the primary objective of governments at that time. Two main approaches were adopted in order to achieve this goal: (i) expanding public spending on active and passive labour market policies, in order to alleviate hardship for the unemployed; (ii) reducing labour supply by early retirement and pushing the long-term unemployed into other social security schemes, such as those for disability and long-term sickness. This was the entry into a vicious circle, where rising unemployment

---

2 Because of data limitations it was not possible to aggregate growth rates for a larger cluster of EU member states.

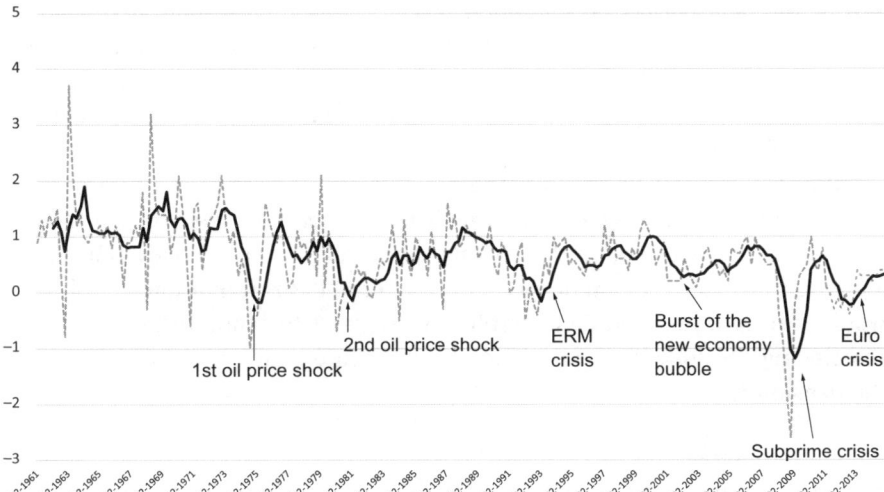

Figure 1: Quarterly growth rate of real GDP, EU15, 1961–2014
Note: The dotted line reflects the actual data, whereas the bold line depicts the five-quarter moving average.
Source: Eurostat.

leads to increased social expenditure and an increase in the dependency ratio,[3] implying rising contributions or taxes, further reducing employment and ulti-mately eroding the economic basis of the welfare state.

It was only after the second oil price shock in 1979, and the subsequent reces-sion, that economies in Europe embarked on a sustained recovery path. The specific developments of individual European countries, however, displayed more diversi-fied trends, experienced idiosyncratic shocks and became quite heterogeneous. In general, restored growth, reduced volatility and declining unemployment alleviated pressure on the welfare state at the beginning of the 1980s. However, new trouble was just around the corner. A new wave of globalisation brought about increased trading between the industrialised countries, but also the (at first tentative) integra-tion of emerging economies into the world markets. For the first time on a substan-tial scale, companies started to move production and the associated jobs from high- to low-cost countries. Domestic labour-intensive industries, such as shipbuilding or clothing and footwear, vanished altogether, because of the lack of competitiveness

---

3 The dependency ratio is defined as the number of inactive people relative to the number of people active in the labour market.

against the new players on the world markets. These developments spurred on structural change both within the industrial sector and also from industry towards services. At the same time so-called skill-biased technical change set in because of increasing use of computer technology and the educational expansion that had started in the 1960s and 1970s.

Rising structural unemployment, manifested by a growing share of long-term unemployed, as well as increasing income disparities, were the consequences in many European countries, posing serious challenges to the welfare state. Moreover, it became apparent – as early as in the 1980s – that lower birth rates would lead to a reversed demographic structure of the countries' populations, threatening the long-term sustainability of welfare state provisions, especially the pension and health systems.

2.5 Fall of the Iron Curtain and intensified globalisation

In contrast to these evolving trends, the fall of the Iron Curtain at the end of the 1980s was a disruptive event with serious consequences for European welfare states. Germany was at centre stage, when it integrated a population of 17 million into existing social insurance schemes and labour market policies. There are other examples: Finland also faced serious challenges, when the break-down of trade with the Soviet Union led to a deep recession and high unemployment in the early 1990s, and Sweden experienced a severe banking crisis with soaring public debt at the same time. The turmoil in the European Exchange Rate Mechanism (ERM) added to the turbulent times at the beginning of the 1990s.

Concerns for competitiveness, empty public coffers and persistently high unemployment prompted academics and political actors alike to develop a new approach to welfare state policies. The era of the ever-expanding welfare state that in some countries continued until the beginning of the 1990s had ended. Instead, a new paradigm of retrenchment, efficiency-enhancement and activation was created. Retrenchment in the sense of cost-cutting was the simple consequence of severe pressures on public finances and fears of losing international competitiveness, if taxes and contribution rates were to be further increased. Enhancing efficiency and cutting slack were mainly interpreted as intensified targeting of welfare services which was justified by the 'turning vice into virtue' approach (Levy 1999): Cutting benefits for those not really in need is perceived as a general contribution to greater justice and also frees up resources that can be used more effectively elsewhere. Redistribution became much more difficult than in the 'Golden Age' because declining growth rates and a tight public budget allowed new benefits for some, but only at the expense of others. The overarching goal of activation related to a fundamental finding: regardless of the general nature of the welfare state – Bismarckian or Beveridgean, generous or parsimonious – the services it provides have to be produced by the currently active generation. If the size of this generation is reduced by inactivity because of joblessness, long-term sickness, disability or early retirement, it implies the loss of economic output – not only at the individual level, but also for society as a whole and it affects the resources available for maintaining the welfare state.

The most recent challenge for European welfare states is still highly relevant at the completion of this book: the Great Recession and its serious consequences in terms of rising public debt, high and persistent unemployment in many countries raises once again the spectre of a lost generation and further increases inequality.

3 Worlds of welfare capitalism: a framework for assessing the need for reforms and their successful implementation

So far we have discussed broad challenges that have an impact on European welfare states in more or less similar ways. Globalisation, digital innovation or demographic change, as well as specific events such as the banking crisis, do not stop at borders. Unemployment, inequality and poverty exist in every country, albeit to varying degrees. While the effects are similar, welfare states have evolved in different directions when it comes to dealing with these challenges according to each country's individual history, culture, societal structure and political system. It is important to develop a deeper appreciation of these differences, in order to understand the motivations for the reforms discussed in the interviews published in this book and the processes undertaken by the political leaders to turn reform plans into reality.

3.1 General typology

Employing an up-to-date typology of modern welfare states is the appropriate filter for this task. It builds upon the seminal work of Gøsta Esping-Andersen, *The three worlds of welfare capitalism* (Esping-Andersen 1990) and subsequent refinements (Esping-Andersen 1999, Ferrara 1996, Arts and Gelissen 2002). In his initial typology, Esping-Andersen developed three dimensions to differentiate between welfare state arrangements: decommodification, stratification and the balance between private actors and the state in the provision of welfare services. Decommodification essentially describes the degree to which it is possible for the individual to participate in societal activities irrespective of the income from work or, put in simpler terms, if 'a service is rendered as a matter of right, and when a person can maintain a livelihood without reliance on the market' (Esping-Andersen 1990, p. 22). Decommodification will typically be more pronounced in Beveridgean regimes adopting a universalistic approach. Stratification describes the degree to which the welfare state itself leads to, or perpetuates, class structures in society. Stratification is more likely to occur in Bismarckian regimes that seek to maintain the living standards of certain groups. This is especially the case, if specific insurance schemes or labour market regulations exist for different groups of workers, e. g. blue-collar workers, white-collar workers and civil servants, as was the case in Germany up to the mid-1990s. The division of welfare service provision between the state and private actors depends on the perception of market failures in achieving societal goals. Relying on the market as the principal mechanism to allocate welfare services will inevitably assign a greater role to private actors.

Empirical assessments of appropriate indicators along those three dimensions led Esping-Andersen to identify three types of welfare states: (i) the liberal welfare state found in Anglophone countries, (ii) the social democratic welfare state of the Nordic countries and (iii) the conservative corporatist welfare state observable in many Continental European countries. Subsequent work by Esping-Andersen and his critics highlighted a fourth type of welfare state in the Southern European countries. While clearly related to the Continental European type, it is distinct from the rest in that the emphasis is on the family as an important provider of welfare services and as an insurance against low income of the individual.

Going beyond the four principal distinctive dimensions, the main features of welfare state models are summarised in Table 2.

Research on the nature of post-communist welfare states in the Central and Eastern European countries did not lead to a new type of welfare state. The general view is that these countries have developed hybrid models that combine elements of liberal and Continental European regimes in varying proportions. Thus, today's broad consensus on welfare state typology regarding the countries covered in this book is as follows:

Liberal model
– United Kingdom

Nordic model
– Denmark

Continental model
- Austria
- France
- Germany
- The Netherlands

Southern model
- Greece
- Italy
- Spain

Hybrid models of the Central and Eastern European countries
- Estonia
- Poland
- Slovakia

Table 2: Core principles and main features of welfare regimes

	Anglophone	**Continental**	**Southern**	**Nordic**
Core values	Equality of opportunity (basic needs-based social support)	Status preservation (equivalence principle)	Status preservation and differentiation	Equality of opportunity (socio-cultural needs-based social support)
Objective	Poverty alleviation	Income maintenance	Income maintenance	Participation in society
Entitlements	Residual	Employment-/contribution-based	Insider-biased	Residence
Employment	Liberal work ethic (self-reliance)	Ambiguous work ethic depending on religion	Weak work ethic	Protestant work ethic
Gender	Family servicing as private matter	Nuclear family as cornerstone of society	Extended family as core welfare provider	Active support for equal opportunities
Responsibility	Individual	Collective	Collective	Broad collective
Social security	Meagre transfers, residual services (means-tested and targeted)	Social insurance, high benefits, contribution contingent, long duration Separate public social assistance	Social insurance, fragmented benefits, long duration No additional safety net	Mixed models of universal transfers and contribution-based social insurance Generous public social assistance

Table 2 (continued)

	Anglophone	Continental	Southern	Nordic
Labour market policy/ regulation	Little regulation	Strong job protection, moderate active labour market policy	Strong job protection, little active labour market policy	Low job protection, otherwise high regulation, pronounced active labour market policy
Family support by the welfare state	Neutral	Passive, but generous	Passive, but limited	Active and generous
Beneficiaries	Poor	Male breadwinners	Labour market insiders	Residents
Actors in provision	Central role of market in welfare provision; state residual but with a monopoly over benefits provision and activation	State secondary to the social partners and family; intermediary groups	Central role of extended family, state rudimentary, voluntary (church) organisations	Central role of the state with secondary role of social partners
Industrial relations	Decentralised labour relations	Sector-wide inclusive labour relations (wide coverage)	Politicised sector- and firm-based labour relations (fragmented coverage)	Country-, sector- and firm-based labour relations (comprehensive coverage)

Source: Based on Hemerijck 2013, adapted and extended by the authors

3.2 Specific challenges to welfare state models

Apart from external challenges, welfare state models also face issues inherent in their designs. The next paragraphs discuss these challenges, in order to provide a better understanding why specific types of reform are more commonplace in certain welfare states than in others.

Liberal welfare state
Because of the low degree of decommodification in liberal welfare states, market incomes of economic actors largely determine disposable incomes of households. With the emphasis on poverty prevention and the absence of cushioning

redistribution in favour of the middle class, income inequality is normally comparatively high. Contributing to the high inequality is the typically rudimentary social partnership between business and labour, especially with a pronounced weakness of trade unions' bargaining power.

Since liberal models tend to rely on the markets and private actors as key providers of welfare services, they run the danger of excluding parts of the population from those services because of high income inequality. Thus, this formally universalistic model is, in reality, prone to yield inequitable outcomes. This can be observed primarily in the provision of old-age pensions which cannot guarantee a decent living standard for large groups of pensioners. Reliance on the market and a strong focus on targeting can also lead to underfunded government programmes that fail to address parts of the target groups originally aimed at.

Nordic welfare state

Nordic welfare states are typically characterised by a high degree of state activity financed by a high tax burden on companies and/or individuals, leading to high labour costs. This can negatively affect both international competitiveness and the ability of businesses to attract a highly skilled workforce. Staying afloat in times of globalisation is a major challenge for Nordic economies. Maintaining and improving high productivity is thus an important objective for those countries.

As a consequence of the 'people's home' paradigm, Nordic societies tend to be closed societies. While certainly not openly xenophobic, Nordic societies expect immigrants to assimilate rather than acknowledge the benefits of diversity. This may also prove to be a disadvantage in an increasingly globalised world, where many countries are competing to attract highly skilled immigrants. In addition, by its universalistic provision of welfare service with eligibility based on residence rather than citizenship, social insurance and basic income provisions might run short of financial resources if so-called 'welfare migration' occurs to a significant extent.

Against the backdrop of high taxation it is imperative to maintain equivalence between revenue and expenditure, in the sense that tax payers receive direct value for their money, e. g. free childcare service. This is also the reason why Nordic countries were the first to develop user-cost models of public provision. Maintaining public support for the welfare state by preserving, at the same time, performance incentives and solidarity between different groups is crucial.

Another potential problem for the Nordic countries, caused by universal and comparatively generous welfare services, is the supply shortage in service provision, for instance availability of appointments with specialist doctors. Since the market is virtually absent as an allocation mechanism and public finances give no further room for manoeuvre, situations of excess demand for such services can be long-lasting.

Continental welfare state

Continental welfare states replicate and produce a high degree of societal stratification. This leads to fairly low disparities within the different groups, but to comparatively high inequality between them. Furthermore, the transition from one tier to another frequently proves difficult. This is an impediment to upward mobility and to the development of a meritocratic society. The societal stratification also leads individuals to favour stable arrangements over flexible environments, e.g. job security is valued higher than employment security.

Frequently, the segmentation of society is reflected in duality on the labour market: around the core of stable, well-paid, full-time employment with indefinite contracts, high employment protection and comprehensive social security is a substantial margin of precarious employment characterised by fixed-term contracts, involuntary part-time work, reduced social security entitlements and/or low pay. Even further away from a stable employment situation are those who are not in work at all, especially the long-term unemployed and disadvantaged youth. This insider–outsider cleavage hinders future growth prospects by making it very difficult for many to acquire the skills and work experience needed to equip them for successful careers.

The role of social partners, especially trade unions in Continental welfare states, can go either way. This largely depends on the degree to which they are embedded in political processes and on how much responsibility they have in policy formulation which, in turn, hinges on the size and structures of unions and business associations. Higher numbers of small trade unions, who compete against each other, who have strong ideological convictions and who are hardly involved in the policymaking process through hearings, commissions and mandates in parliament, tend to play a confrontational, obstructive role. Bigger unions, who represent entire sectors or broad occupational groups and play a defined role in policy formulation, on the other hand, tend to a larger degree to take into account the consequences of their actions for the whole economy. Thus, it is important for Continental welfare states to maintain or develop a constructive social partnership.

Another distinct feature of this type of welfare state is the tendency for rising public debt. The objective of maintaining the living standards of its citizens put social security systems under severe pressure when unemployment soared at the beginning of the 1970s and has done so ever since. For instance, sending jobless older workers into early retirement, or keeping them on rather generous earnings-related benefits, is a particularly expensive policy. In order to keep up the ideal of income maintenance, tax-financed public budgets stepped in when social security funds ran deficits. Running continuous public deficits over decades presents a major challenge for debt reduction when decent levels of welfare services should be maintained at the same time.

Southern welfare state

As the Southern welfare state shares many features with the Continental variant, it also suffers from similar shortcomings: Dual labour markets, stratification of society, subdued flexibility and upward mobility as well as problematic social partnership are also faced by Mediterranean countries. When it comes to public debt, they displayed a heterogeneous picture up to the financial crisis. Whereas Italy had a long-standing record of high public debt, Spain had one of the lowest debt-to-GDP ratios in Western Europe. However, when the crisis hit Spain in 2007/2008, the government had to bail out the private sector from its high indebtedness so that public debt soared to unprecedented levels there as well.

A very distinct feature of the Southern welfare state derives from its strong emphasis on the family as a principal provider of welfare services. In this role, family tends to crowd out public welfare state institutions such as child care, the public employment service or pension systems. Consequently, those frequently appear less developed and functional than equivalent institutions in other welfare state models. Thus, the improvement of administrative structures and capacities to implement laws and regulation is an important challenge Southern European welfare states face.

Hybrid models of the Central and Eastern European countries

Because of the hybrid nature, the Central and Eastern European welfare states face similar challenges as the others – to varying degrees, depending on which 'pure model' they most resemble. Estonia, for example, has mirrored the Liberal type quite closely, and so it shares many of the United Kingdom's current issues. In contrast, Poland is closer to the Continental type, whereas Slovakia represents a more mixed picture. Regardless of their specific design, Central and Eastern European countries have clearly faced an additional enormous task, namely to achieve the transformation from a socialist to a market-oriented, politically democratic societal and economic structure. Building the appropriate institutions and implementing basic democratic principles, such as the rule of law or guaranteed property rights, has been a great endeavour and the process is still ongoing.

4 The LISC approach: legitimacy, implementation, stakeholders and communication

Students of economics and political economy have produced a considerable body of theoretically and empirically informed literature concerned with establishing factors that make for successful public policy reforms (and factors that make for unsuccessful ones, for that matter).[4] This section provides a short overview of this body of literature, which is aimed at offering a state-of-the-art account of what makes LMBP reforms work. Thus, rather than offering a critique of established wisdom, the summary provides a narrative account of what have been key facilitators of LMBP reforms. This exercise serves to prepare the ground for assessing the extent to which the perspective of government leaders responsible for some of the most major LMBP reforms Europe has seen over the past 15 years might resonate with, complement, or deviate from, the conventional wisdom.

For the purpose of this book, the factors existing scholarship identifies as being at the heart of successful LMBP reforms will be clustered under four main headings, namely:
- Legitimacy
- Implementation
- Stakeholders
- Communication.

These headings, and the factors they incorporate, are presented in the 'LISC diagram' below. The following sections will demonstrate how the individual enabling factors presented in the LISC diagram (Fig. 2) contribute to the success or failure of LMBP reform processes.

4.1 Legitimacy

In recent European history, the importance of political legitimacy as a building block of successful reforms has arguably never become as tangible as in light of the crisis that has affected significant parts of the global economy since 2008. With considerable parts of the populations in Southern Europe taking their

---

4 In undertaking research for this section of the Introduction, the authors have benefited in particular from the insights provided in the seminal works of Tompson (2009) and Galasso (2010).

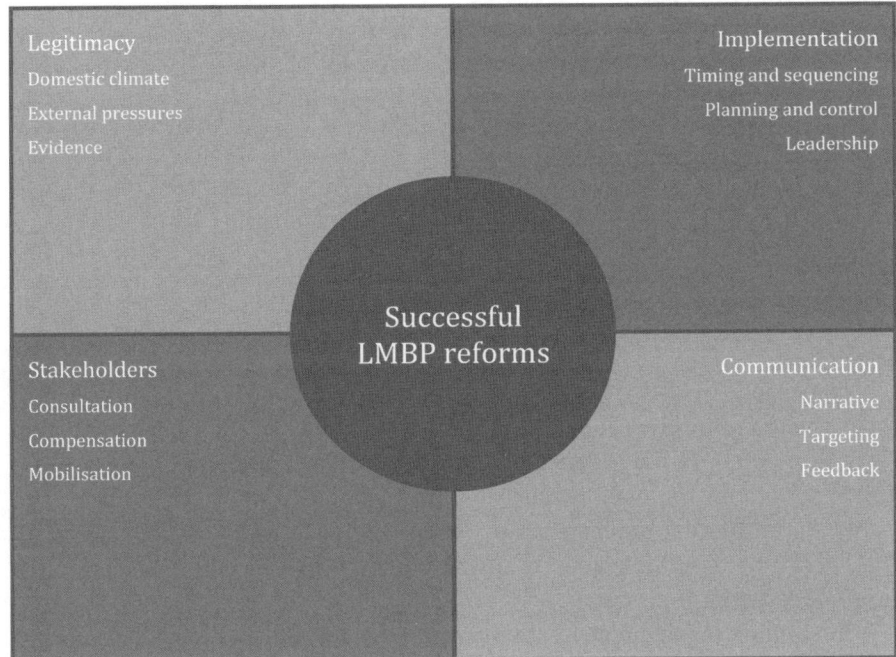

Figure 2: LISC diagram

anger over the impact of LMBP reforms to the street, it has become abundantly clear that governments need to underpin LMBP reforms with a clearly felt and widely shared sense of legitimacy, if they want to ensure the sustainability of these reforms. To create such a shared sense of legitimacy, governments will normally refer to a mix of justifying factors, namely domestic climate, external pressures and sound evidence.

Long-term orientation, sound preparation and a credible reform champion can contribute to a reform-friendly political and societal climate

An electoral mandate constitutes a key indicator of public approval of reform endeavours and hence a cornerstone of building a domestic climate conducive to the successful implementation of such reforms. In-depth OECD research into the role of electoral mandates in designing and implementing public policy reforms underlines that securing public approval of reforms by gaining a strong electoral mandate following a pro-reform election campaign is a vital precondition for making LMBP reforms a success (Tompson 2009). The European track record shows that LMBP reforms seem to produce the most visible and sustainable results when they have been widely advertised within the framework of a general election campaign. Political parties that have set their mind on a reform course therefore seem well advised to clearly communicate their reform intentions to the public before entering into office, if they want to ensure that their reform endeavours meet with success once they actually are in office. However, just like incoming governments, incumbent governments also critically depend on securing public approval before they start implementing LMBP reforms, if they want these reforms to become a success. In any case, LMBP reforms can only thrive when they are implemented in a reform-embracing domestic climate, created by public debate and deliberation sponsored by the political leadership.

Conversely, evidence suggests that reforms introduced 'overnight' seem to have severe limits when it comes to the sustainability of their implementation (Tompson 2009). In the absence of any prior public expression of approval for LMBP reforms in the making, such reforms generally only seem to meet with public approval after implementation when they yield widely visible effects almost instantly – an outcome not always easily achieved with what are often long-winded reform processes.

In securing public approval for reforms, incumbent or incoming governments have to first and foremost set out a compelling justification for the reforms to be introduced and the implications they entail. Specifically, senior decision-makers are well advised to justify the implementation of reforms on the grounds of long-term, structural goals. Unsatisfactory employment figures, in terms of levels, or in terms of sudden significant changes, are often the primary justification governments or campaigning parties present when pushing for LMBP reforms. Securing public approval for LMBP reforms is often a direct function of labour market performance. Indeed, high levels of unemployment or sharply rising joblessness tend to add to the number of those in favour of reforming the labour market.

In the European public eye, fiscal difficulties tend to constitute another compelling long-term structural reason for introducing LMBP reforms. This is especially clear in the case of pension systems, where concerns about the long-term financial sustainability are a main driver of reform, even though fiscal difficulties have been identified as rendering the implementation of such reforms more difficult at times. Thus, many structural reforms involve significant upfront fiscal costs and only yield tangible economic benefits in the long run, potentially resulting in a severe 'fiscal squeeze'. This imbalance of initial investments and short-term pay offs ultimately makes the justification and continued implementation of reforms more difficult.

One of the most robust findings to emerge from econometric work on the political economy of reform in recent years is that, rather than fiscal difficulties, the preservation, or the restoration, of sound public finances should provide the basis for the implementation, as well as any justification, of LMBP reform efforts being launched. After all, solid public finances allow decision-makers to provide the resources necessary for putting in place adequate compensation arrangements for those adversely affected by the implementation of reform. Hence, in countries with stable public finances, the maintenance of public finance should increasingly be advertised as long-term structural grounds that justify LMBP reforms.

In addition to long-term structural grounds, the portrayal of the government or campaigning party as a credible reform champion can contribute to a domestic climate conducive to implementing successful LMBP reforms. The 'Nixon-in-China' effect has been established as a particularly important amplifier of the legitimacy and credibility of political actors engaged in, or planning on, implementing LMBP reforms. Referring to a change of US foreign policy under former President Richard Nixon, who, despite his reputation as an anti-communist crusader, defied a generation-long edict against direct dealings with communist governments when he travelled to China in 1972 and re-established diplomatic relations, the Nixon-in-China effect denotes the pursuance of policies that are fundamentally opposed to the political ideology and convictions of the policymaker who pursues them. In the context of LMBP reforms, the Nixon-in-China effect translates into governments, which are less likely in the public eye to support and implement a specific type of reform, enjoying greater legitimacy when actually implementing such reforms. Evidence from Europe suggests that successful LMBP reforms were more often than not implemented under centre-left governments, which would be expected to be more likely to be opposed to such reforms, even if they were sometimes adopted with the cooperation of, or continued under, centre-right governments. In addition to making the implementation of reforms easier, substantial policy change also seems to be more easily sustained if implemented by parties that would appear *ex ante* to be ideologically opposed to it.

**External pressures can offer another source of justification
for implementing LMBP reforms**
Ever since the launch of the European integration process and certainly since the end of the Cold War, processes and actors external to the confines of the specific European country in which LMBP reforms are implemented, have gained in overall prominence when it comes to shaping the discourse on the need for reforms. Specifically, the effects of globalisation and European integration often provide European decision-makers with a powerful reform justification rationale. Thus, the pressures emanating from globalisation, such as trade liberalisation, international competition and international regulatory change, are routinely cited as le-

gitimate reason to overhaul LMBP policies. The implications for labour demand stemming from technological innovation are another frequently used line of justification. Finally, in the face of ever greater European economic and monetary integration, the European institutions and their policy outputs and recommendations have also increasingly served as a justification for implementing LMBP reforms.

However, recent years have also shown that instead of being an exclusive source of reform legitimisation, external pressure can unintentionally undermine the legitimacy of a government eager to implement reforms. The adverse impact of the Troika's calls for substantial LMBP reforms in Greece, which inter alia led to the defeat of the incumbent Samaras government in the 2014 general elections, offers a particularly vivid illustration of this point. Thus, significant parts of the Greek electorate considered the lack of (sustainable) economic growth and the severe economic hardship they suffered from as a result of the global economic crisis and the Eurozone crisis a product of ill-conceived LMBP reforms directly imposed by the Troika. Indeed, many even blamed the Troika for eroding the sovereignty and legitimacy of the democratically elected government.

Sound evidence is at the heart of any compelling justification of LMBP reforms

Governments and campaigning parties increasingly draw on external advice when trying to legitimise LMBP reform ambitions. Information and data provided by institutions external to government, such as international organisations, think tanks, research institutes, universities or consultancy firms, are used as evidence to underpin the virtues of specific reform packages or implementation approaches. Indeed, governments that are able to draw on what is – or is at least perceived as – high-quality, unbiased external expertise to justify the design of their reforms, as well as their reform implementation approach, usually benefit from a greater degree of legitimacy in the public eye and thus have a higher chance of successfully implementing the envisaged reform. An evidence base for reform therefore not only serves to improve the quality of the legislation to be implemented, but perhaps even more importantly it serves to publicly demonstrate the utility of the envisaged reform with regard to meeting the goals associated with the reform effort.

Not surprisingly, existing research suggests that the extent to which externally generated evidence can bolster the legitimacy of proposed reform efforts crucially depends on the actual source of evidence, as well as the conclusiveness of the evidence presented. Evidence provided by an authoritative, impartial institution that commands trust across the political spectrum generally has far greater impact, when it comes to creating support for reforms than the advice of a partisan actor who is known for representing the interests of a specific lobby (Douglas 2009, Head 2008, Mulgan 2005, Rosenstock and Lee 2002). For the same reason, it has been argued that permanent and independent public bodies with long established mandates are more likely to gain and keep credibility with the electorate than government-sponsored ad-hoc commissions or working groups, whose constituting members' interests might not always be as transparent as they arguably should be (Dyson 2005). In addition, the degree of scientific credibility of the evidence used to support LMBP reforms is a crucial factor in building public approval of the reforms.

However, once the impartiality of an external expertise broker is established beyond doubt, it can serve as an important one-stop shop for the 'depoliticisation' of otherwise difficult reform terrain. Notably, such an expertise broker does not necessarily have to reside within the state in which the reforms are implemented. Indeed, as mentioned earlier, international institutions, such as the OECD or the European Commission, have seen a steady increase in influence of their data and analysis in national discourses surrounding LMBP reforms.

Government strength plays no role in creating greater legitimacy of LMBP reforms

In the wider literature on public policy reform processes, a strong government majority has been identified as an opportunity to shape the public discourse in a way that makes arguments in favour of specific reform processes seem less contested and therefore more legitimate (Alesina, Ardagna and Trebbi 2006). However, an empirically informed OECD study into LMBP reforms suggests that government strength, as measured by its legislative majority, or lack thereof, is rarely a decisive factor in gaining legitimacy for reforms. Indeed, 'such factors as the government's command of a majority in parliament, the presence of a single-party government or a coalition with one strongly dominant party, and the strength of opposition parties are far from decisive' (Galasso 2010). Correspondingly, a weak or divided opposition is believed to have no visible effect on whether a reform is successful or not.

4.2 Implementation

Existing studies of reform processes fail to identify one single right strategy for the successful implementation of public policy reforms. Factors beyond the control of the stakeholders involved in reform implementation often play a decisive role. The success or failure of LMBP reforms, for example, seems often to be shaped by the existence or absence of a so-called 'reform ripeness'. Thus, individual LMBP reforms can be more easily pursued when they are part of a larger shift in structural policy settings, making them effectively part and parcel of wider economic policies. At the same time, successful reforms often appear to build on preceding smaller and piecemeal reforms or failed reform attempts, which have helped to challenge the status quo, nevertheless. Indeed, reform proposals do not always necessarily meet with success in the first place. Rather, successful reform plans often build upon past reform failures, revealing the importance of earlier reform attempts in making reforms happen. This argument follows the lines of the well-known 'path dependency' hypothesis. However, successful LMBP reformers are not entirely at the mercy of conducive external (pre-)conditions. Indeed, there are three elements that can help them to be successful, namely:
- appropriate timing and sequencing
- sound planning and control capacities
- willingness to assume and exert leadership.

Reformers need a sophisticated reform plan and administrative control capacities

Evidence suggests that successful European LMBP reformers have to take a long-term perspective, as the implementation of reforms takes over two years on average, including preparatory efforts associated with drafting the appropriate legislation and its actual adoption. Notably, this timeframe does not account for the considerable amount of 'pre-work' normally undertaken in preparation for drafting legislation. In contrast, unsuccessful reform attempts tend to be implemented hastily, often in response to a tangible crisis and resulting immediate pressures. Thus, the 'windows of opportunity' a crisis may open up with regard to pressing ahead with reforms are hardly ever successfully exploited when the appropriate preparatory work is not in place. In addition, governments need to be able to draw on strong administrative control capacities, if they want to make sure that reform proposals are not only adopted, but also successfully implemented, over time.

**Reforms are all about the right timing and sequencing –
a crisis can serve as a catalyst**

The existing literature on public policy reforms fails to establish a strong link between economic growth and governments' ability to successfully implement reforms. Indeed, evidence from past reform efforts across Europe suggests that public policy reforms seem as likely to be successfully implemented in times of economic growth as they are in times of economic decline. Yet, the general economic climate often seems to shape the timing of reform implementation attempts. Thus, LMBP reforms in Europe are typically initiated in periods of poor growth performance, if not outright economic crisis. Indeed, crises are often a necessary starting point for LMBP reforms.

However, the implementation of LMBP reforms seems to carry greater promise in times of economic upswing. Some therefore suggest that the best time for implementing LMBP reforms is immediately after a recession, when economic recovery kicks in (Saint-Paul 2002). In addition, it has been argued that an electoral cycle can determine whether a reform package meets with success or failure (Beck 1979, Haggard and Webb 1993, Haggard and Webb 1994). Thus, LMBP reforms implemented within the first two years of a government's term of office usually pay the highest dividends when it comes to orchestrating the re-election campaign. At the end of a four-year term in office, the reforming government might already be able to point to the first reform successes, enabling the head of government to create additional legitimacy for what might have been a difficult and challenging reform implementation process.

The success or failure of an LMBP reform process is also a product of appropriate sequencing. Tackling the least controversial reform issues first can generate a momentum for reform that facilitates further change. Thus, it has been suggested that initial reform steps successfully introduced may create pressure for further reform by changing the expectations of stakeholders and/or activating new support groups (Fernandez and Rodrik 1991). If early measures lead to an expectation of further reform, those affected by reform begin to adjust their behaviour in anticipation, and this itself may reduce resistance to subsequent measures. Indeed, changed expectations and the activation of new interests are among the ways in which reform setbacks sometimes lay the basis for subsequent success. For example, LMBP reformers often start their reform efforts by targeting labour market outsiders, leaving insiders unaffected – a classic 'take what you can get' strategy.

However, a strategy focused on harvesting 'low-hanging fruit' can also have its pitfalls. First, if very modest initial proposals are seen as overtures of deeper reforms to come, some stakeholders may oppose even relatively minor measures, in order to forestall the risk that the reform process will become more radical at a later stage.

Secondly, it can be difficult to ensure that a first wave of reform will indeed be followed by successive waves of reform. Thus, as the value of benefits enjoyed by exempt groups may increase as a result of reforms that target others, the unreformed insiders' incentives to protect their privileges might gradually increase.

Successful reformers take ownership of reforms and display leadership skills in seeing them through

A prominent finding in almost all studies on the factors underpinning successful LMBP reforms is the vital importance of political ownership and leadership. Thus, successful reforms always seem to be driven by highly visible individuals who are prepared to take ownership of the content of the reform package and who also have a considerable interest in seeing the package succeed. Significantly, political leaders who have career prospects outside politics are more prone to implementing reforms than those who are 'career politicians'.

A shared sense of ownership and strong leadership skills at the helm of a government are also crucial preconditions for establishing governmental cohesion, which in turn is key to successfully implementing LMBP reforms. It is vital that government members close ranks if they want to prevent reform opponents exploiting mixed messages about a reform sent out by different parts of the government. Indeed, reform opponents regularly capitalise on inconsistencies in the way government members portray reforms. Significantly, a 2009 OECD study found that in almost all cases in which disagreement within a government or the governing party over an LMBP reform became publicly visible, the reform was ultimately thwarted (Tompson 2009). This finding has prompted the OECD to suggest that government cohesion comes close to being a necessary – though by no means sufficient – condition for successful reform.

4.3 Stakeholders

For political leaders, managing opposition to an envisaged reform process and building alliances in favour of the reform package constitutes a top priority, as those losing out from LMBP reforms tend to be much more vocal, and therefore more instrumental, in shaping the public discourse than those benefiting from reforms. The reason for the heightened visibility of reform opponents, as compared to reform supporters, is that the costs of reform are not only usually incurred upfront, but they also often tend to have a highly tangible impact on specific groups who mobilise to oppose them as a result. In contrast, the economic benefits emanating from LMBP reform processes often only materialise in the long term and are allocated in a less predictable and more diffuse manner, which makes it difficult for governments to mobilise those who benefit from reforms. Accordingly, it has been suggested that governments should actively compensate those who incur a loss through the reform, consult influential stakeholders with a view to obtaining their support in the long run, and mobilise those who benefit from the reform.

Those losing out from reforms pose a considerable challenge to the success of LMBP reforms and might therefore need to be compensated

Various studies suggest that, in order to prevent the losers swaying public opinion in a way that hampers reform efforts, governments must engage directly with them and offer compensation (Atkinson and Micklewright 1991, Gerhart and Rynes 2003, Lodovici 2000). Indeed, a considerable part of the existing body of literature concerned with the examination of structural public policy reforms tries to discover when and how those who lose out as a result of reforms might best be compensated. Suggestions for compensation revolve around the outright exemption of those hardest hit by reforms from the actual reform, through temporal phasing in the reforms slowly, to paying financial compensation. The most appropriate strategy, however, depends on context and target group.

Consultation is another key means to overcome opposition to reforms

While existing research in the area suggests that failure to compensate those who lose out as a result of reforms may reinforce opposition to these reforms, it has also been pointed out that excessive compensation may often not be reconcilable with fiscal imperatives or that such compensation may pose a threat to the effects and/or the sustainability of the very reform package introduced (Sapir 2006). Therefore, engaging those who will be most tangibly affected by reform as part of consultative policy processes may pose a viable alternative, as such mechanisms might help to reduce opposition to reforms over time, even when no compensation is offered (Fernandez and Rodrik 1991). In the specific European context, governments are well advised to engage with the social partners. Indeed, evidence from past reform efforts across Europe underlines that in order to effectively manage opposition to a reform process, unions and employers' associations need to be continuously engaged (Galasso 2010). Another strategy geared at managing opposition to reform is to offer opponents a role in the post-reform system, thereby winning their approval for the proposed reforms.

In any case, the degree to which stakeholder cooperation is a requirement for the successful implementation of reform should be a factor in determining whether, and to what extent, the government should accept the constraints of corporatist bargaining when trying to succeed in the adoption of reform. In this respect, it is important to appreciate that a concertationist approach on the part of the government is unlikely to result in the successful implementation of a reform unless the government is in a position to reward (or sanction) cooperation (or non-cooperation) by the social partners or to make a credible threat to proceed unilaterally, if no accord with reform opponents is struck.

However, regardless of the efforts undertaken to ensure engagement of all groups affected, governments must be prepared to accept that reform processes may often result in the exclusion of certain stakeholder groups. After all, the general interest must prevail over the interests of specific groups. To attain this aim, even large groups may need to be wholly or partially exempted from a reform in order to secure its adoption. A case in point is the negotiation of pension reforms, which usually pays little or no attention to the views of younger workers, even though they will be responsible for paying for future pensions. Similarly, because of the long-term nature of their effects, labour market reforms often have only marginal effects for workers who are close to the legal retirement age.

Despite the difficulties involved, governments must always try to mobilise public support for reforms

With any notion of eradicating all political opposition to reform processes being utopic, it seems even more important to mobilise support for reforms to ensure a balance in public discourse. Somewhat surprisingly, the existing literature on reform processes has very little to say about the active mobilisation of interest coalitions in support of reform. In recent years, potential beneficiaries of LMBP reforms across Europe were often labour-market 'outsiders', who were not as well organised or as influential as labour market 'insiders'. In other instances, the potential beneficiaries of LMBP reforms were actually not in favour of reforms that were supposed to strengthen their participation in the labour market, such as those seeking a transition to early retirement. In particular, governments often fail to mobilise young people. Young people are very hard to mobilise and tend to vote less than their elders. Accordingly, there is little empirical evidence on how to effectively mobilise supporters of LMBP reforms. At the moment, therefore, it is only apparent that those losing out as a result of such reforms are more influential, as they tend to command greater organisational, political and financial resources.

4.4 Communication

In formal terms, communication may be seen as part of the approach that under-pins successful reform implementation, and there are indeed several crucial overlaps between the domains of implementation and communication. However, communication is of such crucial importance when it comes to the success of an LMBP reform endeavour that it merits being singled out. Governments often struggle to make a compelling case for reform because, as mentioned previously, reforms often involve substantial, and sometimes rather painful, upfront costs, while their benefits become only visible over time. Many governments have also had the depressing experience that it can be much more difficult to commu-nicate the link between a reform and its benefits, even *ex post*, than to establish the connection between a reform and its costs. Indeed, communicating the vir-tues of reforms effectively constitutes a considerable challenge, specifically in the field of LMBP, which is most effectively tackled when governments provide a strong and simple narrative, target the right stakeholders in the right way, and learn crucial communication lessons from these stakeholders' feedback.

The ability to communicate a strong and simple narrative is decisive with regard to successfully implementing reforms
Building a strong and simple reform narrative has repeatedly been identified as a key factor for implementing successful LMBP reforms. When communicating LMBP reforms, reformers must make sure to embed the need for reforms in a nar-rative that sets out a higher goal, promises a better future and stresses the com-mon good. Communicating reforms should be less about showing people what they will be deprived of and more about highlighting why the reforms are neces-sary for achieving and/or maintaining the common good. After all, a purely ra-tional approach to communicating the benefits of a reform tends to fail to cap-ture the imagination of those affected and ultimately their support.

Targeting the right audiences in the appropriate manner and communicating the costs of non-reform generates credibility
Accounts of successful LMBP reforms not only highlight the importance of com-municating reform components and aims as part of a strong narrative, but also the significance of communicating them in a tailor-made manner, so as to effec-tively address specific expectations and concerns of different audiences. Signifi-cantly, successfully communicating LMBP reforms should also always contain a

reference to the missed opportunity any failure to reform constitutes. Indeed, existing research on public policy reforms suggests that successful reformers not only continuously remind stakeholders of the need for reform, but that they also try to communicate the costs of non-reform (Matos 2010, Natali and Rhodes 2004, Stolfi 2008).

Effective communication entails elements of learning from stakeholders' feedback

The effective communication of reforms should not be confined to the dissemination of consistent and tailor-made narratives for different stakeholder groups. Real engagement with stakeholders also involves an element of consultation, in which their concerns are heard and digested. Such consultation efforts must thus result in the modification of messages about the purpose and benefits of the reform, and they might even result in some modification of reform proposals, including an element of 'learning by doing'. Continuous review of the messages sent out, and the way they are perceived by the recipients, can contribute to a decrease in the likelihood of a reform process being challenged or even reversed if the political situation changes.

5 Structure of the book

The book is guided by the endeavour to answer the question to what extent the experiences of the heads of government interviewed in the subsequent section confirm or disprove what the theoretical and empirical literature suggests to be true. This approach is premised on the view that, while the literature manages to determine some kind of ideal state for reforms, reality hardly ever lives up to this standard or, at least, deviates from it in various respects. Hence, why do reforms occasionally succeed although many framework conditions are unfavourable and why do reforms sometimes fail in a climate of propitious framework conditions? The interviews provide a new and different qualitative database to deduce those determinants of successful/failed reform processes that policymakers assess to be crucial. In this way, the book aims to help policymakers draw lessons for future reform efforts.

In line with the interviews conducted, the book examines labour market reform processes in 12 EU member states between 2000 and 2013.[5] Highlighting similarities and differences in the labour market reform processes of the different European countries under review based on extensive literature reviews, the book reveals the diverse labour market experiences across the EU in the run up to, and the aftermath of, the 2008 economic and financial crisis, and thus provides a comparative perspective which makes it possible to identify good and bad practice with respect to reforms.

In conducting and evaluating the interviews, the authors were supported by a steering group, comprising members of Bertelsmann Stiftung and external advisors. Between 2013 and 2015, the authors and the steering group held eight expert workshops to develop and review the questionnaire and to discuss the interview findings. Additionally, the authors were able to draw on the extensive body of the Bertelsmann Stiftung's former work on reform processes.[6]

Organisation of the book

Subsequent to this introduction, the following interviews enable the reader to make a sound assessment of important labour market reform processes that were carried out between 2000 and 2013. A major condition for such an assessment, however, is adequate and unbiased information about labour market trends. To this end, some general information and figures on labour market specifics, the development of the European labour market since the 1990s, and a short description of past labour market, benefit and pension reforms follow each interview. The interviews are followed by the authors' conclusions, summarising and evaluating the findings of the interviews and highlighting some of the lessons learned. The book closes with an epilogue providing an overview of current challenges for European labour markets and social systems and giving an outlook on how the lessons learnt from previous reforms help to take the necessary political actions of today and the future.

---

5 The country notes only cover the period up to late 2014, thus not accounting for reform effects and political developments that might have unfolded since.
6 See, for instance, the following works which were all edited and published by Verlag Bertelsmann Stiftung, Gütersloh: (2011) *It takes more than courage: guidelines for strategic policy reform*; (2010) *Making the European Union work: issues for economic governance reform*; Rüb, F.W., K. Alnor and F. Spohr (2009) *Die Kunst des Reformierens: Konzeptionelle Überlegungen zu einer erfolgreichen Regierungsstrategie*; Schumann, A. and E. Thode (eds.) (2006) *Fostering youth employment – current situation and best practices*: International reform monitor (Special Issue); (2005) *Social policy, labor market policy, industrial relations*: International reform monitor (Issue 10).

Chapter 2
Interviews with 12 heads of government

The book consists of interviews with 12 former European heads of government (in alphabetical order): Andrus Ansip (Estonia); Jan Peter Balkenende (The Netherlands); Tony Blair (United Kingdom); Jerzy Buzek (Poland); François Fillon (France); Mario Monti (Italy); Georgios Papandreou (Greece); Iveta Radičová (Slovakia); Anders Fogh Rasmussen (Denmark); Gerhard Schröder (Germany); Wolfgang Schüssel (Austria); José Luis Rodríguez Zapatero (Spain). All interviewees were heads of government over roughly the same time period (cf. Table 3, below) and responsible for overseeing important LMBP reforms. The reform countries chosen are representative of different European regions and different welfare state models. To ensure the impartiality of the book's findings, the interviewees have different political backgrounds.

It is important to note that the interviewees' roles as heads of government differed quite significantly. While the French prime minister's power, for instance, is balanced and ultimately severely limited in many policy domains by the President of the French Republic, the Italian prime minister we interviewed, Mario Monti, led a technocratic government which had been appointed by the Italian President rather than elected by the voters. In other words, he had not won an election to gain legitimacy.

Furthermore, it needs to be emphasised that the interviewees were not the only, and sometimes not even the leading, LMBP reformers in their respective countries. In effect, when writing this book, the authors were struck by the high degree of continuity in LMBP reforms, both preceding and succeeding the period under examination. Indeed, while some heads of government were able to draw on their predecessors' achievements, others lay the ground for their successors to build upon, and although some interviewees might have lost sight of their predecessors' or successors' work, the book demonstrates that the LMBP reforms reviewed have hardly ever taken place in a vacuum.

All former prime ministers were interviewed on the basis of a questionnaire that addressed the same general issues in order to ensure, as far as possible, that the results are comparable and allow for generalisation, while taking into account country-specific issues. The prime ministers were invited to give a personal, non-party political assessment. We focused on the general leadership perspective of the reform process rather than an assessment of the results in terms of party political electoral interests.

The authors recognise that there is a significant potential drawback to the methodology they chose in that interviewees are likely to display a cognitive bias

Table 3: Prime Ministers' terms in office

Andrus Ansip (Estonia):	13 April 2005–26 March 2014
Jan Peter Balkenende (The Netherlands):	22 July 2002–14 October 2010
Tony Blair (United Kingdom):	2 May 1997–27 June 2007
Jerzy Buzek (Poland):	31 October 1997–19 October 2001
François Fillon (France):	17 May 2007–15 May 2012
Mario Monti (Italy):	16 November 2011–28 April 2013
Georgios A. Papandreou (Greece):	6 October 2009–9 November 2011
Iveta Radičová (Slovakia):	8 July 2010–4 April 2012
Anders Fogh Rasmussen (Denmark):	27 November 2001–5 April 2009
Gerhard Schröder (Germany):	27 October 1998–22 November 2005
Wolfgang Schüssel (Austria):	4 February 2000–11 January 2007
José Luis Rodríguez Zapatero (Spain):	17 April 2004–20 December 2011

when assessing their time in office and the reform packages they introduced, producing the so-called 'halo effect'. The authors attempted to meet this methodological challenge in several ways. First, the evidence presented in the country notes is meant to serve as an objective measuring rod against which to judge the interviewees' own subjective perspective on reform processes. Secondly, the former heads of government interviewed for this book were explicitly asked about reform failures and their part in them. However, not surprisingly perhaps, they were somewhat hesitant to elaborate on unsuccessful aspects of reform attempts implemented during their time in government. Thirdly, the final chapter provides the authors' assessment of the interviewees' judgement.

1 Austria

1.1 Interview with Wolfgang Schüssel, 28 June 2013

'Elections are about the future, not about the past.'

In your capacity as Prime Minister of Austria you embarked on a number of reforms, such as the 2003 severance pay reform, the reform of the Austrian pension system and the tax reform in 2005. Could you describe the context that prompted these reforms?
The reforms started with Austria's alignment with the European Community. Until then, Austria was an overregulated, closed and small economy. In 1992, however, when the member states of the European Community and the European Free Trade Association (EFTA) agreed to establish the European Economic Area (EEA), the situation changed fundamentally. I was, at that time, Minister of Economic Affairs in Austria and President-in-Office of the Council of the European Free Trade Association. In this capacity I was assigned the task to finalise the EEA treaty with the then President of the European Commission, Jacques Delors. This proved to be an excellent 'training' for Austria's accession to the EU in 1995. EU membership signalled the real starting point: from that moment, Austria was fully integrated into the European market. In addition, the Iron Curtain had already fallen in 1989, resulting in the opening of the Eastern market. Thus, we first had the preparation for EU membership, from the establishment of the EEA to actual membership, and, secondly, the fall of the Iron Curtain and the opening up of the East – these two events shook up everything: it was no longer possible for Austria to have an overregulated, inward-looking economy with limited openness. Today, two-thirds of our economy is open to the international markets. Austria itself has a population of nearly nine million and with access to the new markets in the East our businesses reach about 60 million consumers with their products and services.

Before 2000, Austria's budgetary performance was very poor and if the budget had not been reformed and stabilised, also by means of our reforms, we would now find ourselves in the same position as the so-called 'crisis countries'.

What did you do to translate this window of opportunity into a political mandate? What did the political landscape in Austria look like at the time?
Austria's political elite was very enthusiastic about becoming an EU member and this was reflected in our negotiations with the European Community. In this we had the support of the majority of the public, the media and the social partners.

We had to prepare ourselves, as we wanted to become a really good member of the European Community, not the best in class, but a good student and a valued member state. The result of the national referendum on joining the EU, which was held in 1994, was extraordinary: 66.6 per cent of the population voted in favour of membership. This was a very good start, but the momentum for reform soon faded away. A general feeling emerged that it was enough to have become a member state and that there was no need to be overly ambitious, a view held particularly by the trade unions. Eventually, people started to feel that the government was not active enough and the trade unions were not interested in further reforms following the previous ones. As a result, there was a growing consensus in the campaign for the 1999 elections among the politically interested community – of course, not 100 per cent of the population, but the 20 per cent who are really interested in politics – that the time of the incumbent coalition between my People's Party, the Österreichische Volkspartei (ÖVP), and the Social Democrats, the Sozialdemokratische Partei Österreichs (SPÖ), led by Chancellor Viktor Klima, was up.

At that time, I presented my party and myself as an engine for reform. This was not always welcome: the average citizen does not want to be troubled with change; most people just want stability and prefer the status quo. Security is highly valued in Austria, and nobody wants to lose what they possess and give up any of their fortune and privileges. Our strategy in the 1999 elections did not pay off. The Social Democrats won, even though they lost nearly five per cent compared to the previous elections.[7] We also lost some votes[8] and came in third behind the right-wing Freedom Party, the Freiheitliche Partei Österreichs (FPÖ), who was able to increase support by 5 per cent and eventually beat us by 415 votes[9] – it was very disappointing.

Everybody knew that the old system had gone: from 1945 to 1966 and from 1989 to 2000, Austria had been governed by a grand coalition made up of Social Democrats and the People's Party. In 2000, the options were to form another coalition with the Social Democrats or to try something else. At the time, my party wanted to go into opposition. This was not possible. Public expectations forced us to review our intentions. In the end, however, the talks with the SPÖ failed – a final document for a future government was rejected by the party council.

We then formed a coalition with the FPÖ. At the beginning of my tenure as Chancellor, from 2000 to 2003, we were severely criticised both from the inside

---

7 The SPÖ lost 4.91 per cent of votes in the 1999 elections.
8 The ÖVP lost 1.38 per cent of votes in the 1999 elections.
9 In the 1999 elections, the FPÖ received 1,244,087 votes, while the ÖVP received 1,243,672 votes.

and the outside, but it was my ambition to convince everyone, especially our own citizens, that the government was reform-driven. Thus we agreed on the introduction of a new reform every week, following a precise timetable, and we presented all decisions publicly. Some people found this really breathtaking; the opposition could not decide which target to shoot. There were so many reforms being implemented that there was indecision among our opponents whether to criticise us for being a xenophobic, backward-leaning government or for being too keen on reforms.

As far as the labour market was concerned, some very important aspects of Austria's reform agenda had already been implemented in the early 1990s, with the Minister of Social Affairs, Josef Hesoun (SPÖ), and myself in the roles of chief negotiators. Hesoun was a very 'down-to-earth' former trade union leader, a tough politician and a very clever man. Negotiations with him could last through long nights before an agreement was reached, but after a deal was forged, he ensured that it was accepted by his own party. Josef Hesoun and I established a new organisational framework for the Austrian employment agency, the 'Arbeitsmarktservice'. Even changing the old name 'Arbeitsmarktverwaltung' to 'Arbeitsmarktservice' represented progress. The labour market reforms were very successful; for example, the current average period of unemployment in Austria is less than 100 days – half of the German figure.

The literature on the political economy of reform has long discussed the question of whether it is important to establish a strategic balance between a unilateral and a stakeholder-involving approach in putting through successful reforms. To what extent were you able to engage with trade unions in the pursuit of your reform endeavours, for instance with regard to the reforms of severance pay and of the pension system in 2003 and 2004?
These two approaches are, indeed, connected. The discussions about the 2003 severance pay reform started in the 1990s. Before 2003, employees, who were laid off after having been employed by the same company for at least 25 years, were entitled to a compensation equalling one year's salary. This had been an advantage for the long-term employed, but a disadvantage for those in their first three years of employment – they did not receive any compensation. In addition, employees were not compensated if they were simply moving to another job, but only if they were laid off. As Minister for Economic Affairs I tried to change this system, to transform it into a second pillar of the pension system, with annual wage contributions – paid by the company – of 1.5 to 2 per cent, so that everybody could benefit. My vision was to establish three pillars in the pension system: first, an individual pillar of savings with additional tax benefits;

secondly, the severance payment pillar, the business factor, so to say; and thirdly, the regular state pension, guaranteed against inflation.

In the 1997 to 2000 coalition, Chancellor Viktor Klima (SPÖ) was very much in
favour of such a system. However, he was blocked by the unions and parts of his
own party, and the business leaders were not very supportive either. The real debate started after 2000. The first step was a proposal for legislation by the ÖVP.
This was rejected by other parties with the claim: 'It is not enough, it is not fair
enough.' Then the social partners, especially the trade unions, stepped in, consenting to some aspects with proposals for changes. In 2002, we reached a compromise. The social partners agreed on annual wage contributions of 1.53 per
cent to the fund. However, we could not establish a fund representing the second
pillar in the pension system which included a mandatory element. The following
compromise was agreed with the trade unions: workers could choose themselves
how to use the money – they could either put it towards their pension or have it
paid out immediately. This option diluted the original idea of an additional pillar
in the state pension, which would have represented a big step forward. The next
phase was to be a fundamental reform of the public pension scheme, for which
I felt it important to involve the trade unions. We must have had between 20
and 30 meetings with the social partners, including the Minister for Social Affairs,
and we came very close to an agreement. In the end, however, the unions stepped
aside for political reasons: the SPÖ, at the time in opposition, blocked the process.

Concerning pension reform in general, it would have been preferable to calculate pensions on the basis of full lifetime salary contributions, instead of
counting only the ten years of highest contributions or the ten years immediately
preceding retirement. Nevertheless, I stuck to the compromise formula, although
I could have been more ambitious, which would have been better for Austria, but
politically it was important to have most of the social partners on board.

One important part of the trade union movement, the civil servants, agreed
with the government to harmonise their pension scheme with the general system
without a single minute lost to strike action. In hindsight, I would say that in
total it was a good reform package and broadly accepted. It was not a 100 per
cent success, but 80 per cent.

**How would you describe the relationship between government and trade
unions in Austria in general?**
In general, it is important to understand our system of *Sozialpartnerschaft*, of
employers and labour, in Austria. We have two associations on the employees'
side: the unions and the Chamber of Labour (*Arbeiterkammer*). Membership of
the Chamber is compulsory for employees. The Chamber's primary tasks include
involvement in the legislative process, providing a wide range of services to the

members and acting as a research institute devoted to the improvement of working conditions and to looking after the interests of consumers. In contrast to the trade unions, the Chamber is not involved in collective bargaining, but it acts, in effect, as the Social Democrats' think tank.

The Social Democrats also form the major fraction of union members; however, there are, of course, members from other parties as well. Normally, nothing happens in Austria without the agreement of the social partners. This can be a real advantage in decision making, but does also slow down the reform process. It is also important to note the differences between individual unions. For example, the service union has always shown a very stubborn resistance to reforms, in particular to the pension reforms, but the construction union and the metal workers' union are in general very constructively engaged. This has to do with the fact that these sectors are much more exposed to economic pressure.

The unions often represent very specific interests. Did you seek consensus with the unions in the pursuit of your reforms to compensate those who lost out as the result of the reforms?

My experience with pension reforms, on which my government embarked in 2000, is a good example in this respect. For the first time in our history, we calculated the effects of proposed reforms within a timeframe up to 2050. We assessed the effects of the reforms in all areas, for all ages and groups of citizens, for the next 45 years and conducted discussions with specific groups, for example about granting exemptions for strenuous work, which affects, say, 3 or 4 per cent of the labour force, mainly in the construction industry. Another group mentioned in these discussions were the steel mill workers. I always argued in favour of granting exemptions to groups of workers with known low life expectancy, if it was possible to establish who these groups were, but if there was a feeling that this was simply a pretext for a general reduction in the retirement age, I thought we should resist. The final compromise I was involved in was the so-called *Hacklerregelung*,[10] which was not targeted at specific groups, but making the stipulation that men who had contributed to unemployment insurance for 45 years and women who had contributed for 40 years were en-

---

10 The term *Hacklerregelung* comes from the colloquial Austrian word for a manual labourer or *Hackler*. While the exemption denoted by the *Hacklerregelung* generally applies to workers and employees regardless of their specific, strenuous or non-strenuous profession, it differentiates two groups of people: the *Hacklerregelung* for long term insured workers and employees applies to men born up to 1954 and women born up to 1959. The *Hacklerregelung* for hard labourers applies to men born up to June 1950 and women up to June 1955. According to the *Hacklerregelung*, these groups are entitled to retire at the age of 60 (men) or 55 (women), if they paid unemployment insurance contributions for 540 months (men) and 480 (women) months, respectively.

titled to retire in line with the previous pension scheme, at the ages of 60 and 55, respectively – but only for a transition period that was slated to end in 2010.

Did seeking a compromise with the trade unions help make the pension reform irreversible?
As I just said – my government granted the *Hacklerregelung* as a temporary exemption. But when I left office in 2007 it was extended – a big mistake. The temporary effects were understandable because, without these exemptions, some people would have lost 20 or 25 per cent of their pension, and this had to be taken into account: introducing temporary exemptions was thus an understandable action. Parliament voted for the prolongation in a famous session before Election Day 2008. Members of parliament were given a free vote and it turned out to be one of the most expensive sessions in history. Parliament decided on an annual package costing three billion euros that allowed for a prolongation of the exemptions to the pension scheme reform, the abolition of university fees and an increase in family benefits. It was a completely chaotic situation: parliament voted, with an overwhelming majority, for this package and de facto wasted money – an absolutely crazy moment. Even today we see the negative effects of this historic mistake.

Were you able to establish a consensus within the two coalitions you led as Chancellor to get your reform proposals through? If so, how did you manage to achieve it?
In my political career I have had experience with all possible forms of coalitions. Coalitions are never easy, because you have to compromise, you have complex negotiations within the cabinet, with parliament, with social partners and you have to deal with public opinion. In Austria we have a tradition of long and painstaking negotiations for a coalition treaty (*Koalitionsvereinbarung*). The more you can agree on from the outset, the better things work out in the years thereafter; and the faster you start the reforms – at the very beginning of a legislative period – the easier it is. If half of the period is gone, negotiations become very difficult, because the next election overshadows everything. It is therefore important to act fast and meticulously, starting with the coalition agreement. Some of my 'friendly' opponents and fellow negotiators complained about me, saying: 'He is so precise, he negotiates everything in detail.' Yes, but it is better to act in this way from the start.

In the first period, from 2000 to 2002, the climate in the cabinet was very good. Vice-Chancellor Susanne Riess-Passer (FPÖ) was excellent. I had not known her before and was a little bit sceptical at the beginning, but she proved to be thoroughly reform-oriented and a fantastic partner. There was always a spirit of change and reform, and we shared a strong sense of the need to serve the country. Looking neither left nor right, we did not know exactly how long we could work, how long we could survive demonstrations and international pressure, but we felt that we had to continue. A real team spirit, never seen in previous governments.

In the 2002 election, the FPÖ came down from 27 per cent in 1999 to 10 per cent.[11] That was a striking drop in support from the public, and the FPÖ was rather depressed and looking for ways to survive. Nevertheless, we continued the coalition, though it was much more complicated and difficult to keep the reform agenda alive in my second tenure. The effect was that it slowed down.

Did you draw explicitly on good practice from other countries, and how did you do this in reality?
I always found Danish, Swiss, and German labour market policies very interesting. Before becoming Minister of Economic Affairs I had served several years as Secretary General of the Business League ('Wirtschaftsbund') of Austria. We carefully studied privatisation processes in the USA, Great Britain and other countries. Representing the League, I explained the pros and cons of privatisation to the public: what we should avoid, what we could achieve, and what would benefit taxpayers, workforce and the competitiveness of companies. The second priority was research and development. Germany and Finland were our role models. Germany for its Max Planck Gesellschaft and Finland for its impressive 4 per cent R&D expenditure as a share of GDP. From 2000 to 2007 we doubled R&D expenditure and are now close to 3 per cent.

In addition, we had interesting discussions of Germany's Agenda 2010 and of Denmark's 'flexicurity' system. We organised guided tours for journalists to these countries to show them examples so that they could learn from them. This was positive, of course: the journalists wrote about it and thus helped pave the way to influence public opinion.

Did you use these trips to push the reforms or to campaign for reforms?
While in the Business League I had time, energy, interest and curiosity. As a medium-sized country, Austria cannot live in isolation, but embedded in the global economy, as we are, we have to look for good models and best practice. Some of the journalists who came on these trips were not the most important figures in their

---

11 In the 1999 national election the FPÖ achieved 26.9 per cent. In the 2002 national election the FPÖ achieved 10.0 per cent.

profession at the time, but some of them became very important and influential afterwards. At that particular time, they only wrote small articles and reports: not *the* big wave, but it paid off. I also wrote a few articles – with Johannes Hawlik – 'Mehr privat, weniger Staat',[12] for instance, and 'Staat lass nach'.[13]

What else did you do in terms of communications to sell your reform plans?
Before my term, the Chancellor and Vice-Chancellor used to hold separate press conferences after the weekly cabinet meeting. As Chancellor, I always gave a joint press conference with my coalition partner, Vice-Chancellor Riess-Passer. Immediately after the cabinet meeting we explained to the press what had been discussed, what had been decided, and we explained purpose and content. Everything was open for questions. This was completely new: open communication where everyone knew that questions were welcome and would be answered. As a result, the press had to write about our ambitions, even when they were sceptical. Some journalists were often critical, but they had to write about our plans and decisions. By the way, even the present government has continued with this tradition.

Nevertheless, most newspapers supported the reforms. They did not necessarily support the government politically, but they supported the reform agenda in principle. I cannot remember a single economist, political advisor, professor, scientist or important journalist who was against reforms at that time. Sometimes they criticised us for not going far enough, and I think they were right. Of course, reforms occasionally produce losers, not everyone is a winner. Some people criticised us, took to the streets and did not vote for us. That is okay, but in the end, the majority was more or less in favour of reform. Some 20 years ago Bruno Kreisky won his second general election as Chancellor campaigning with the slogan, 'Lasst Kreisky und sein Team arbeiten', and – following that – 'Let Schüssel and his team work' was the equivalent mood in 2002.

And what could other countries learn from Austria?
The dual apprenticeship system, the so-called *duales Berufssystem,* in Austria – as well as in Germany and Switzerland – could serve as a model for other countries on how to train well-educated and skilled young workers. In my opinion, it is a big mistake to promote all areas of academic study and disciplines as the

---

12 Johannes Hawlik and Wolfgang Schüssel, *Mehr privat, weniger Staat. Anregungen zur Begrenzung öffentlicher Aufgaben* (Vienna: Signum Verlag, 1983).
13 Johannes Hawlik and Wolfgang Schüssel, *Staat lass nach* (Munich: Herold Verlag, 1985).

only way out of the crisis. I think we need a good balance between academics and practically skilled workers – well, this is one thing.

Secondly, in times of crisis I would recommend the introduction of short-term work, the so-called *Kurzarbeit*. If a company faces temporary problems because of the growth cycle, it would be well advised to retain its skilled workers rather than lose human capital and face recruitment problems later on, once the economy has recovered. *Kurzarbeit* is a specific, unique work model in Austria and Germany, partly subsidised through labour market policies and partly paid for by the businesses themselves. In this context it is very important to note that 99 per cent of our companies are small and medium sized and with deep roots in the regions. Most of the owners of small businesses with, let us say, a workforce between 20 and 100, hold public positions in their local communities: they might be municipal councillors, actively engaged in sports, in culture or in their local church. As a result, employers find it difficult to lay off workers – because they know them personally – and they also know their workers' families personally. In short, everybody knows everybody. Supporting these workers through *Kurzarbeit* and such temporary measures is cheap and has a stabilising effect. This is the reason Austria today has the best employment figures in Europe: particularly when it comes to youth employment we are at the top, alongside Germany. This is not a given, but the result of our specific attitude: it is an Austrian mindset. This is what other countries could learn from us.

The general literature frequently poses the question as to whether reforming governments can be re-elected. Do you consider the outcome of the 2002 election, which was extremely positive for the ÖVP, to be a result of the reform agenda you had put forward?
Yes, absolutely. In the 2002 election the ÖVP gained 15 per cent, which I see as a strong support for our reform agenda. However, the positive outcome was also a result of the public's disappointment with our coalition partner.

After the reforms started to take effect, Austria was doing well economically and socially. Before the 2006 elections you must have thought that you had delivered on your promises and Austria was doing well. Research suggests, however, that it is often difficult to translate the success of reforms into electoral results. Could you elaborate on what happened in Austria?
It is true that nobody elects you because of past successes: the past is over. People elect you because they expect something; they hope for something or they fear something. Elections are always about the future, not about the past. Looking back, I think that l we did a good job overall: not everything was perfect

but – all in all – it was a professional performance. By 2006, however, our successes belonged to the past and people felt that the coalition's time was up; everybody knew it.

Incidentally, there was an additional factor: Austria held the Presidency of the Council of the European Union during the first half of 2006, and this was an absolutely exhausting challenge for us. It was a very difficult presidency by any standard, starting with the energy policy problems with Russia and Ukraine, followed by the cartoon crisis involving Denmark and the Islamic world, problems with the EU Service Directive, tough negotiations with the European Parliament on the 2007–13 budget and, finally, the United States and the Guantanamo affair. It was a really hard presidency. When Austria handed the presidency over to Finland, my team and I were really exhausted, honestly – and our general elections were coming up, which gave us no chance for a break in September. I had no energy left to tap into and neither did my staff. However, up to the very last moment the polls suggested that we were in the lead, alongside the Social Democrats. At the end, we both lost, but the Social Democrats' loss was a bit less severe than ours.[14]

How important do you consider strong leadership to be in order to secure successful reform processes?
It very much depends on the energy you invest in a reform project. From the very first moment of my political career, when I was elected into parliament, I stood for something. I agreed, for example, to the liberalisation of opening hours for shops. Later on, at the European level, I was known as an advocate for enlargement, integration and good neighbourhood policy.

I will never forget the spring 2003 convention of my party. I stood for re-election as party leader. Immediately after the victory in 2002, we announced a substantive pension scheme reform – very controversial, even in my own party. For two full days I sat at the party convention, my wife next to me, listening to 50 or 60 different speakers, intervening personally several times. I defended my reform proposal and was harshly criticised, especially by union members, but I stuck to the reform agenda. At the end I was re-elected with 95 per cent of the vote. Without my personal intervention, without my presence and commitment, the outcome would have been completely different.

---

14 The ÖVP and the SPÖ lost 7.97 percentage points and 1.17 percentage points, respectively.

In a very general sense, would you say that leadership is about taking the lead in the reform processes or is it more about the art of consensus building?

Both are necessary: you do not have to be an expert in something particular – this is not about leadership, but it is important to link yourself to a specific project and to have a team around you, both politicians and experts. I always had two or three ministers around me. I was never alone. Ten or twelve experts took part in the public debate, writing articles and giving interviews. A lone wolf is not a good leader. Leading is more about establishing a team – dedicated to a specific project and flanked by a group of experts, themselves armed with facts, studies and images. We always tried to link a reform project to a specific image and wording in the mass media, for instance *Zeit der Ernte*, harvest time. The government worked in a vineyard signalling that this was the time to harvest the reforms. Everybody had this picture in mind at some point. Importantly, in 2000, my government brought together economic affairs and labour into one ministry, something the German government copied later on. We felt that economic reform and labour should be in one hand, whereas social affairs, being different from issues relating to the labour market, should have their own portfolio. Such a separation clearly demonstrates the importance attached to social affairs, which after all includes issues such as care of the elderly, pensions and health.

If you were still in office, which measures would you take to reform your country's labour market in order to make it fit for the 21st century?

First of all, I would immediately get rid of all labour market limitations in Europe. For example, abolish all restrictions to the free movement of labour in Europe. Easing access for all EU citizens to labour markets depending on their professional skills. Today only seven of 800 professions are mutually recognised in all 28 member states – there should be more openness towards those who are willing to integrate into the society of another country. Giving people opportunities to work, especially in areas where we face a shortage of skills and labour, is important. It is strange that hundreds of thousands of young people from non-EU countries have the right to study in Europe and get degrees from European universities, without the right to work in Europe after graduation.

Secondly, it is important to encourage the younger generation to study more MINT subjects – mathematics, IT, natural sciences and technology. It is a pity that there are thousands of students of sociology, political sciences, journalism, theology and other arts and humanities subjects while we face shortages in MINT disciplines. Comprehensive information and incentives are needed to catch the interest of young people. When I was young we all knew a magazine called *Hobby*. Everybody read it, even those who were not thinking of a career as a scientist or mathematician. The ORF (Austrian Broadcasting Corporation) had TV series on science. Today, there is nothing like that. Upper Austria is the most industrialised province in Austria and they do not have a technical university. We should therefore establish a technical or IT university there.

Thirdly, the integration of migrants is a big issue. Austria is a country with one of the greatest varieties of cultures, languages, religions and cultural backgrounds. In my home city, Vienna, 50 per cent of the pupils attending the first class of elementary school do not regularly speak German at home and require additional language teaching. Integration into Austrian society is of utmost importance and this has always been underestimated. Immigrants should be compelled to learn the language, in order to be integrated. The population will grow, Austria does not just have an ageing, but also a growing, society. When I was young, Austria had a population of seven million, soon there will be nine million and the numbers are still growing with life expectancy going up.

In hindsight, looking at the labour market reforms your governments were responsible for, is there anything you would like to have done differently? Not with regard to the labour market reform, but I still believe it would have been better if we had been able to transfer the severance payment into a second pillar of the pension system; the pension scheme reform should have been more ambitious. Moreover, Austria needs more investment in research and development. Too much money spent on transfers – on the transfer of income – results in loss of capacity and resources for investment in the economic future. Money is not limitless.

1.2 A note on Austrian labour market performance over the past decade

1.2.1 The facts
Austria has been one of the best performers among EU and OECD countries in terms of overall labour market outcomes, especially if one focuses on the unemployment rate. Over the period since 2000, Austria's harmonised unemployment rate has fluctuated within the very narrow range of 3.6 to 5.2 per cent (peaking in 2005). Over a longer period, stretching back to the early 1980s, the unemployment rate has averaged around 4 per cent (see fig. 3). While the unemployment rate has increased slightly with the jobs crisis, the rise has been much lower than the hike in either the EU or the OECD area average unemployment rates. Indeed, at the time of writing, Austria had the lowest unemployment rate in the EU28: it

stood at 4.7 per cent in August 2014, compared with an EU28 average of 10.1 per cent and a eurozone average of 11.5 per cent (all rates are seasonally adjusted).

Evolution of the employment and unemployment rates in Austria, 1970–2014

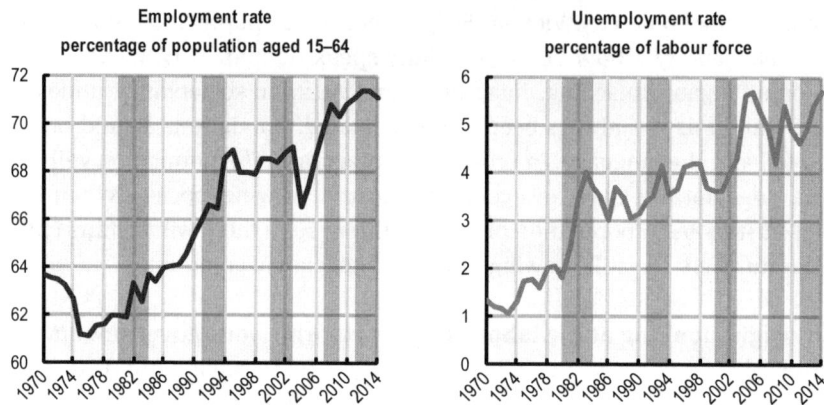

Note: Grey shaded areas refer to period of economic contraction (based on the output gap).

Source: OECD estimates based on the *OECD Labour Force Statistics*, *OECD Short-term Labour Market Statistics* and *OECD Economic Outlook Databases* (Cut-off date: 13 April 2015).

Figure 3: Labour market chart Austria

Employment growth has also been very buoyant over the period: the total employment–population rate rose from just under 69 per cent in 2000 to 73.7 per cent in 2013, compared with an increase of just over two percentage points in the EU average over the same period (cf. Austria's scoreboard). This is an impressive achievement, given that the 'Great Recession of 2008' hardly disturbed the trend of a rising employment rate in Austria, at a time when the EU average rate in 2013 was still almost one percentage point below its 2007 level. The good employment performance during the Great Recession owes much to the rapid response of the Austrian authorities in expanding the short-time work scheme (*Kurzarbeit*) and making it more attractive to employers, as well as to the speed with which they ramped up several other active labour market measures.[15]

---

15 For details, see OECD (2011b), pp. 14–15. Nevertheless, it should be noted that recourse to *Kurzarbeit* by Austrian employers during the Great Recession was much more limited than that by German employers to the equivalent scheme.

In terms of the composition of employment growth in Austria, the period since 2000 has witnessed rapid growth in part-time employment, especially among women. Whereas in 2000 the share of part-time employment in relation to total employment in Austria was only 12.2 per cent, i.e. below the EU average of 15.3 per cent, it had by 2013 increased sharply to 19.7 per cent, bringing it above the then EU average of 17.5 per cent. This period also saw an increase in the share of temporary jobs, up from 7.9 per cent of all employees in 2000 to 9.2 per cent in 2013; the share of temporary jobs, however, still remains well below the EU average now.

In terms of the demographic composition of employment, the youth employment rate has risen slightly since 2000, from 52.8 per cent to 53.8 per cent in 2013. Not only is the youth employment rate much higher in Austria than the EU average, the latter actually fell by 6 percentage points over the same period to just over 33 per cent.

Another indicator of Austria's good labour market performance is its relatively low incidence of long-term unemployment. In 2000, the share of long-term unemployment in relation to total unemployment was 25.8 per cent and it remained around this level throughout the subsequent decade, including the period after the Great Recession. It is striking that the share of long-term unemployment in Austria is well below that in neighbouring Germany: 24.3 per cent compared with 44.7 per cent in 2013, a year when the unemployment rates in both countries were very similar. The pattern of much less long-term unemployment in Austria than in Germany has persisted for a long period. This suggests that the Austrian public employment service (Arbeitsmarktservice (AMS)) has been relatively more successful in activating the long-term unemployed back into jobs than its German counterpart.

At the same time, Austria has managed to maintain below-average income inequality, as measured by the well-known Gini coefficient. Even though Austria has not escaped the almost universal trend of rising income inequality over the past two decades, the increase has been fairly moderate and much less than that recorded, for example, in Germany over the same period (cf. OECD (2011b)).

Indeed, Austria's very good overall labour market and social cohesion records have been recognised as such for many years by international organisations such as the OECD and the ILO.[16] Among the factors responsible for this good performance, three points are highlighted in OECD (2013a):
- a very successful export-oriented economy with close links to Germany and neighbouring countries to the East. Accession to the EU in 1995 and adop-

---

16 See, for example, Auer (2000), OECD (2006) and OECD (2011b).

tion of the euro in 1999 served to spur competitive pressures in the trading sectors and maintain high productivity, especially in manufacturing;[17]
- a well-skilled labour force, with a historically strong vocational education and apprenticeship system, serving to make the school-to-work transition system relatively smooth for most youth. This is reflected in the comparatively low youth unemployment rate in Austria – the latest rate of 8.2 per cent (seasonally adjusted) for the age group 15–25 in August 2014 was the second lowest in the EU28 after Germany, and far below the EU28 average of 21.6 per cent. Austrian firms are strongly committed to investing in training for their core workers. This is reflected in long-lasting relationships between prime-age workers and their firms;[18]
- a long tradition of social partnership, with the union and employer organisations taking major responsibility for the design and implementation of many labour market and social policy reforms in close and continuous dialogue with the government. For example, the social partners play a leading role in the governance of AMS and are key actors in the vocational education/apprenticeship system and in fostering on-the-job training.

Nonetheless, while Austria's overall labour market performance is the envy of most EU and OECD countries, it has a few weaknesses. Most notably, its employment rate among older workers is relatively low: in 2013, the employment rate for the age group 60–4 in Austria was only 23 per cent, compared with an EU average of 34.7 per cent; its employment rate among those aged 65–9 was also below the EU average. The employment rate among those aged 55–9, however, which in 2000 was almost 9 percentage points below the EU average, rose sharply over the subsequent decade to reach 63.7 per cent in 2013, just below the EU average of almost 65 per cent. In addition, employment rates are relatively low for low-skilled workers, many of whom are immigrants and women with young children.

These relatively low employment rates, especially among workers aged over 60, are a concern for the future. Faced with an ageing population, it will be vital for the Austrian economy to mobilise more of these underrepresented groups into work if Austria is to maintain future growth and current living standards.

---

17 OECD (2013a), p. 81 notes that Austria is one of the most deeply integrated OECD economies with global value-added chains: its upstream vertical integration indicator (proxied by the share of foreign value added in total exports) was 33 per cent, one of the highest ratios among OECD countries.
18 See OECD (2013a), Figure 1.17, for evidence that the average job tenure of Austrian workers aged 25–54 in 2011 was one of the longest in Europe.

As we shall see below, this particular objective has been an important driver of labour market and pension reforms in Austria over the past decade or more.

1.2.2 Major labour market and pension/early retirement reforms since 2000

It would be fair to conclude that, compared with some other EU and OECD countries, Austria has not been a major reformer in the labour market policy field, reflecting its relatively good performance noted above. Nonetheless, an important reform was introduced in 1994, when AMS was separated from the Labour Ministry and established as a separate public service agency. The aim was to increase its efficiency in the market for re-employment services. At this juncture, a culture of social partnership governance was established for AMS and the delivery of AMS services was decentralised. AMS operates as a so-called 'one-stop shop', responsible for the administration of benefit payments and the full range of re-employment services.[19] It also operates a strong culture of 'management-by-objectives', guided by an elaborate system of performance indicators, which are designed jointly with the social partners.

Since 2000, Austria has introduced one major innovation in the labour market policy field and it has engaged in a series of reforms to its pension and early retirement pathways with the explicit aim of raising its very low employment rates among older workers. It has also sought to increase the employment rates of the low-skilled and of women with young children through a series of incremental reforms.

A major innovation: the 2003 reform of severance pay[20]

Until 2002, Austrian employers paid severance pay to their workers when their job was terminated, if the worker had been employed by the firm for more than three years. The severance pay amounted to two months' wages and rose in line with the length of past employment up to one year's wages after 25 years of service. The severance pay system was believed to contribute to the strength of employment protection in Austria for permanent workers, thereby forcing more of the burden of adjustment to demand shocks on the short-tenure workers; it was also thought to inhibit

---

19 In the beginning, AMS was responsible for unemployment benefits while responsibility for employable working-age individuals receiving social assistance was delegated to the municipalities. However, from late 2010 on, AMS took over the responsibility for administering benefits and delivering re-employment services to this latter group. See Weishaupt (2011) for a discussion of the governance arrangements for the AMS.
20 This brief description of the severance pay reform draws heavily on Hofer (2007).

labour market mobility, as workers lost their entitlement to severance pay if they resigned from their job.[21] At the same time, the unions argued for the extension of severance pay to cover resignations and seasonal jobs.[22]

In order to overcome these problems, the Austrian government announced its intention in mid-2001 to reform the system of severance pay and it delegated the design of the new system to the social partners; the social partners reached an agreement and a law was passed in mid-2002, setting out the new system. Under this law, the severance pay system was replaced in 2003 by a unique system of individual savings accounts. An individual worker's account is funded by an employer payroll tax of 1.53 per cent of the gross monthly wage and is managed by an employee fund that invests the sum on the capital market. If employees with more than three years of tenure are dismissed, they can choose between taking a lump sum, further investing it in the same employee fund, transferring it to the employee fund of their new employer or putting it into their pension fund.[23] Under this reform, the severance pay entitlements could be cumulated by workers over a working lifetime, serving – if they so wish – as a form of extra retirement saving. If workers quit their job, or are dismissed within the first three years of tenure, no cash payment is made, but the savings account can be transferred to a new job.

From the worker's perspective, the reform made labour mobility a more attractive option, since severance pay was not tied to a particular employer, nor related to job tenure. It also extended entitlements to severance pay significantly, thereby satisfying one of the key union demands. From the employer's perspective, the reform reduced the uncertainty related to severance costs and the one-time costs of a dismissal. At the same time, the average severance pay is lower under the new system, compared with the old one, increasing its attractiveness to employers.[24] However, the additional payroll tax increased labour costs to the extent that it was not reflected in lower gross wages via collective bargaining. In

---

21 Stiglbauer (2006) shows that, if one leaves aside short-term flows, especially in seasonal industries, worker mobility in Austria is relatively low in international comparison.

22 Austrian data, quoted in Hofer (2007), suggest that, prior to the 2003 reform, only one-third of Austrian workers had entitlements to severance pay.

23 The original intention of the Schüssel government was that the account would function as a second funded occupational pillar of the pension system, but this proved to be unacceptable to the unions and a compromise was finally struck, whereby the choice of what use to put the funds to was left to the worker.

24 Hofer (2007) reports the results of simulations, which show that the severance pay is expected to be on average 35 per cent lower under the reform, compared with the average payout under the old scheme.

addition, the payroll tax is not experience-rated, i.e. high-turnover firms do not pay more in proportion to their layoff rates than low-turnover firms.[25] Thus, the new system provides an implicit subsidy to high-turnover industries, e.g. tourism and construction.

Given the innovative nature of this reform, it is surprising that no rigorous evaluations of its impact on the labour market exist. It is notable that in terms of the well-known OECD indicators of the strictness of Employment Protection Legislation (EPL), protection of permanent workers in Austria against individual dismissal exceeded the EU average in all years, while the opposite is the case for EPL for temporary workers (see table 4).

One of the stated objectives for the reform was to promote worker mobility. The evidence is ambiguous on this point. On the one hand, OECD (2013) highlights the fact that average job tenure is relatively high in Austria, compared with most other EU countries, and the number of times Austrian workers change employers is relatively low. This would seem to suggest that the reform did little to foster greater labour market mobility. On the other hand, it notes that the occupational mobility of the workforce with the same employer (so-called 'internal flexibility') is relatively high. The existence of the individual savings account and the possibility of using it as a form of pension saving may have helped bind workers more closely to their firms, thereby creating a more favourable environment for investment in firm-specific skills.

A series of reforms to facilitate working longer

An excessive culture of early retirement has been well entrenched in Austria for many years, as reflected in the relatively low employment rates for older workers and very low average effective retirement ages for both men and women. Despite a rise in older worker employment rates over the past decade, especially for the age group 55–9 (see above), they still remain well below the corresponding EU and OECD averages.

Beginning around the year 2000, however, and continuing to the present day, successive Austrian governments have sought to weaken the early retirement culture significantly, despite some backsliding. Major reforms to pension systems were made in 2000, 2003 and 2004–5. Part of the reason for these reforms was to put the pension system on a more financially sustainable basis for the future; another major objective was to raise the effective retirement

---

25 Experience-rating of firms' payroll tax rates in line with their layoff rates would serve to align the social and private costs of layoffs.

age. These reforms unified the rules for different occupational pension schemes. They raised the statutory retirement age for both men and women to 65 – though the increase for women was phased in very slowly (it will converge to that of men by 2033). They also reduced the possibility of early retirement through various special schemes and disability pensions, restricted the options for early retirement and reduced pension replacement rates through a shift from the best 15 years of earnings to the average of 40 years.[26]

However, there was some reversal of the main thrust of these reforms in 2004–5, when a path for early retirement was introduced for workers with long insurance records. Under this pathway (*Hacklerregelung*), workers who had contributed for at least 37.5 years could retire from the age of 62 instead of 65, albeit with a lower pension.[27] In addition, an early retirement option was introduced for heavy manual labour: the statutory retirement age was reduced by three months per year of such work. Again, in 2007, the 4.2 per cent penalty for early retirement was halved temporarily to 2.1 per cent and the special early retirement options were extended in 2008 as part of the initial response to the increase in unemployment in 2008–9.

Still, in response to the recovery in the Austrian labour market after 2009, eligibility for a disability pension was tightened in both 2011 and 2012, and the government has taken steps to tighten access to the special early retirement schemes. For example, the length of the insurance period for entitlement to the *Hacklerregelung* will rise from 37.5 years to 40 years for both men and women by 2017. The annual 4.2 per cent penalty, or bonus, for taking early, or later, retirement was raised to 5.1 per cent in 2012, in an effort to make it financially more rewarding to work longer.

In sum, there have been reforms to the pension system and various early retirement pathways over the past decade to raise the effective retirement age in Austria, and these reforms have borne some fruit, in terms of rising employment rates among older workers. Nonetheless, there is still a long way to go: OECD estimates for average effective retirement ages in 2012 of 61.9 years for Austrian men and 59.4 years for Austrian women were among the lowest in the EU.[28]

---

26 See OECD (2013a), Box 2.1 for a full description of the pension reforms.

27 The pensions were reduced by 4.2 per cent for each year of early retirement and a symmetric upward adjustment was applied for each year that retirement was postponed beyond 65.

28 The average effective retirement age relates to the five-year period 2007–12 and is calculated as a weighted average of (net) withdrawals from the labour market at different ages over a five-year period for workers initially aged 40 and over. In order to abstract from compositional effects in the population age structure, labour force withdrawals are estimated based on changes in labour force participation rates rather than labour force levels.

Make work pay for low-skilled workers

Recent OECD surveys of the Austrian economy have highlighted the high marginal effective tax rates for low-paid workers as a disincentive for them to seek work or to work longer hours. As an attempt to make work pay for such workers, the authorities introduced a wage top-up (*Kombilohn*) in 2006 and reformed it in 2009. It is targeted at workers aged over 50, at disabled workers and at parents with a period of unemployment lasting more than six months. It takes the form of a monthly wage top-up of 300 euros for full-time, or 150 euros for part-time, work; the aim is to encourage the target groups to accept low-paid jobs (paying a monthly wage of between 650 and 1700 euros). There is no evidence available yet to allow evaluation of the potential effectiveness of this in-work benefit.

1.2.3 Conclusion

Austria has been one of the star labour market performers among EU and OECD countries over the past two decades in terms of maintaining low unemployment rates and a steadily increasing employment rate. Unlike in most countries, the Great Recession hardly dented this excellent performance. Austria's success owes much to specific features of its economic structure and to its unique social partnership model.

At the same time, Austria has taken steps to reform some labour market policies and institutions over the past decade; particularly striking is Austria's innovative approach in transforming severance pay into individual savings accounts. Faced with an ageing population and a deeply entrenched culture of early retirement, much reform effort has focused on both changing the parameters of the pension system to make it financially sustainable in the future and seeking to close early retirement pathways. The latter reforms have had some clear effects in terms of raising employment rates for older workers and increasing the average retirement age, but there is still some way to go on these fronts. All these reforms were negotiated with the social partners, helping to build a consensus in support of reforms.

Table 4: Scoreboard for labour market outcomes and policies, Austria and EU, 1993–2013

	1993 AT	1993 EU	2000 AT	2000 EU	2007 AT	2007 EU	2013* AT	2013* EU
1. Employment rate (% of the working-age population)	**69.3**	61.2	**68.9**	63.6	**72.6**	66.7	**73.7**	65.9
– male	**79.0**	71.8	**78.0**	72.9	**79.9**	74.2	**78.8**	71.6
– female	**59.6**	50.7	**59.9**	54.4	**65.3**	59.2	**68.6**	60.2
– youth (aged 15/16–24)	**59.2**	39.5	**52.8**	39.4	**55.5**	38.2	**53.8**	33.4
– older people (aged 55–9)	**42.6**	47.6	**41.9**	50.6	**55.2**	57.3	**63.7**	64.9
– older people (aged 60–4)	**14.0**	22.3	**11.8**	22.3	**19.5**	29.4	**23.0**	34.7
– older people (aged 65–9)	**7.2**	9.2	**5.0**	7.4	**7.9**	9.5	**9.2**	11.3
2. Unemployment rate (% of labour force)	**3.5**	10.8	**3.5**	8.9	**4.4**	7.1	**4.9**	10.7
– youth (aged 15/16–24)	**5.0**	21.0	**5.1**	17.4	**8.7**	15.5	**9.2**	23.3
3. Incidence of long-term unemployment (% of total unemployment) (a)	**18.4**	42.0	**25.8**	44.4	**26.8**	41.6	**24.3**	46.5
4. Part-time employment rate (b)	**11.1**	13.8	**12.2**	15.3	**17.3**	16.0	**19.7**	17.5
5. Temporary employment rate (c) (temporary employees as % of total employees)	**6.0**	10.5	**7.9**	13.1	**8.9**	14.8	**9.2**	14.0
– youth (aged 15/16–24 as % of total youth employees)	**18.9**	28.8	**33.0**	38.0	**34.9**	41.8	**34.8**	43.0
6. Low-pay incidence (d) (% of employees)	**n/a**	n/a	**15.2**	15.7	**16.2**	16.5	**16.1**	15.0
7. Protection of permanent workers against individual dismissal	**2.8**	2.6	**2.8**	2.5	**2.4**	2.4	**2.4**	2.2
– Protection of temporary workers	**1.3**	2.3	**1.3**	1.8	**1.3**	1.6	**1.3**	1.8
8. Public spending on labour market policies (% of GDP)	**1.9**	2.9	**1.7**	2.0	**1.9**	1.6	**2.0**	2.0
– Spending on active measures (e)	**0.3**	0.9	**0.5**	0.8	**0.7**	0.6	**0.8**	0.8
– Spending on passive measures (f)	**1.6**	2.1	**1.2**	1.1	**1.2**	0.9	**1.3**	1.2
9. Net benefit replacement rate (g) (averaged over four family types and two earnings levels)	–	–	**64**	57	**64**	52	**68**	51
– initial spell (h)	–	–	**66**	71	**66**	71	**70**	71
– after 2 years of unemployment	–	–	**66**	69	**66**	67	**70**	67

* 2013 or latest available year.
(a) Persons out of work for 12 months and over.

(b) Part-time employment refers to persons who usually work less than 30 hours per week in "their 'main job'".

(c) Temporary employees are wage and salary workers whose job has a pre-determined end date as opposed to permanent employees whose job is of unlimited duration. National definitions broadly conform to this generic definition, but may vary depending on national circumstances.

(d) Persons with a wage less than 2/3 of the median.

(e) 'Active' measures cover categories 1 to 7 of the OECD/Eurostat data base on public spending on labour market programmes.

(f) 'Passive' measures cover categories 8 and 9 of the OECD/Eurostat data base on public spending on labour market programmes.

(g) Data on net replacement rates for 2000 refer to 2001.

(h) Initial phase of unemployment but following any waiting period. For married couples, the percentage of AW relates to the previous earnings of the 'unemployed' spouse only; the second spouse is assumed to be 'inactive' with no earnings and no recent employment history. Where receipt of social assistance or other minimum-income benefits is subject to activity tests (such as active job-search or being 'available' for work), these requirements are assumed to be met. Children are aged four and six, and neither childcare benefits nor childcare costs are considered. Unweighted averages, for previous full-time earnings levels of 67% and 100% of AW and out-of-work single and couple households with no children or with two children (children are assumed to be aged four and six, and neither childcare benefits nor childcare costs are considered). After tax and including unemployment and family benefits. Social assistance and other means-tested benefits are assumed to be available, subject to relevant income conditions. Housing costs are assumed equal to 20% of AW.

Sources: OECD Online Employment Database: www.oecd.org/employment/database; data on net replacement rates come from the OECD tax-benefit models (www.oecd.org/els/social/work-incentives).

2 Denmark

2.1 Interview with Anders Fogh Rasmussen, 16 January 2014

'You have to select your battles carefully.'

Could you give us a brief description of the main reforms you undertook when you were head of government?
I would point to three main strands of work during my term in office: first, we introduced stronger incentives to work; secondly, we intensified the activation of unemployment benefit recipients; and thirdly, we increased the retirement age.

As for introducing stronger incentives to work, we pursued a couple of tracks. One was to cut benefits for the unemployed and another to reduce taxation on lower incomes. Regarding benefit reduction, we took several measures as soon as we came into office, and they were specifically targeted at immigrants. However, as we could not discriminate against any group, we introduced the general rule that people who had worked in Denmark for less than seven years were only entitled to reduced social benefits if they became unemployed, with full entitlements after seven years of work. This was called 'introduction benefit' – 'start-help' would be the literal translation.

Of course, this measure was part of our policies to improve integration. It is interesting to witness the current debate in Europe on welfare tourism: it is exactly the same. How can you maintain a high level of free labour movement and, at the same time, protect your social security system against abuse? Personally, I believe that recipients have to qualify before they earn the right to get full benefits. If that is a general rule and not targeted at particular groups, then I think it is fair. I also met people who said: 'Yes, but I am a Dane...', to which I used to reply: 'Yes, but if you have lived abroad for ten years, and you didn't pay into the Danish welfare system, the rule applies to you as well. You have to qualify for social benefits.'

On top of that reduction of benefits for people who had worked in Denmark for less than seven years, we introduced a general ceiling on social benefits, in order to make sure that there was always an incentive to work. This was because we had examples of people who actually did not receive much more, or who even suffered a loss, when they went off benefits and moved into work, something that affected especially people on lower incomes. We introduced the general ceiling so that you could never, ever be in a position to get more out of the benefit system than if you worked, even if you were only on a low income.

An additional course of action consisted of a special tax deduction for those in employment. I do not remember the exact numbers, but in Denmark there were hundreds of thousands of people for whom it did not actually pay to work. Under the new system, if you turned from benefits to work, you got a special tax deduction. We thus used a two-pronged attack on the problem that, for low incomes, the incentive to work was insufficient. Creating strong incentives to work was one of the main reforms we introduced.

The second of the three main strands I mentioned at the start of this interview was that my government intensified, or advanced, the activation of unemployment benefit recipients. For those aged over 30, we made activation compulsory after nine months of unemployment. For those aged under 30, the young people, we made activation compulsory after three months of unemployment. By reducing social benefits for this age group, we strongly incentivised the young to opt for a solid education, instead of just living a passive life. In Denmark, we actually have quite generous state educational support grants, the so-called *Statens Uddannelsesstøtte*.

Furthermore, we made changes to local government funding. In certain cases, municipalities were better off handing out social benefits than investing heavily in active labour market policies and actually getting people back to work. Through the application of different incentives, we ensured that municipalities were encouraged to get as many people off benefits as possible. In my opinion this reform worked well, but it was a much disputed reform, because both the employers and the unions were sceptical – to put it mildly. As a result, it was not easy to get the bill through parliament. In general, we have a very decentralised system in Denmark, and municipalities are very influential. They have a great number of tasks and many tools at their disposal. This is why we felt that it would pay to focus on their efforts, when it came to activating the recipients of unemployment benefits. Local authorities have many opportunities to find the best jobs for people and I think this was the right thing to do. I am aware that this policy is still disputed, now and again, but it has not been reversed.

The third strand of action was, of course, that we made changes to the Danish Voluntary Early Retirement Programme (VERP) and increased the retirement age.

Just to complete the picture, as I see it, I shall add that one of the reasons why we managed to reduce unemployment to the lowest level ever in Danish history and, at the same time, keep inflation low – to everybody's surprise, by the way – was that we introduced quite a liberal migration policy. This may seem a paradox because, as you know, in parliament my government relied on the right-wing Dansk Folkeparti (DF), which promotes the tightening of immigration laws. However, we managed to get approval from them to introduce a green-card arrangement so that people looking for work could enter the Danish labour market on condition that they had a good educational background, vocational training or other skills. They could earn points through a system similar to the one in the

USA, Canada and Australia. We liberalised access to the Danish labour market under certain conditions. So, all in all, labour supply increased, as did employment, and this combination of increased supply and employment made it possible to keep inflation low, though unemployment had really been reduced to the lowest level ever – just before the financial crisis hit Denmark in 2008 and 2009.

Why did it prove so difficult for successive governments, including those you led, to implement reforms to halt the rise in disability pensions and the high rates of sickness absence?
Reforming the disability and sickness benefit schemes was not at the centre of our reform agenda. We were, of course, aware that sickness absence was quite high in Denmark. We do have a generous benefit system which allows people to get paid from the very first day of absence. We therefore discussed every now and then whether there should be something like a deferment or qualifying period of, say, two or three days, before people were actually entitled to such benefits. The main reason why it was not at the top of our agenda was not necessarily that we did not feel the need or urgency to get a substantial part of the working-age population off these benefits, but that there was very strong resistance from all kinds of stakeholders. Sometimes, you do what you can do. It is very similar to the tasks I faced during my time as NATO Secretary General: you have to select your battles carefully.

Looking back at the reforms your government introduced or continued, is there anything you would like to have done differently?
Retrospectively, as I just said, I think we did what was possible. Actually, it is not easy to introduce reforms when the economy is flourishing, when you are in an economic upturn; you do not have a 'burning platform' then, and this makes it more difficult to move forward on reforms. However, I think, taking this into account, we did as much as we could. With hindsight, I do not think we could have done more or could have done things differently. Of course, when the crisis hit Denmark, the then government – I had already stepped down to take up my next job – strengthened some of the tools my government had introduced, for example, by further increasing the retirement age. The crisis in 2008–9 created a new spirit which made it easier for my successor to carry out tough reforms. However, the first steps had already been taken before the crisis.

Given this lack of reform spirit due to the good economic conditions when you were in office, what drove you to set about carrying out reforms?
One obvious factor was that it became clear to us that there were too many cases where work did not pay. For us, this was a very strong argument. In general, I

think that most people expect the welfare state to correct such a situation. While we agree that we need a safety net if people become unemployed, it is also generally accepted that it must, of course, pay to work. That is what I call the 'welfare contract'.

To what extent were public finances a driver for your reform effort?
Public finances were not at the centre of the debate. Based on my experience as a politician, I also have to say that these general arguments about macroeconomics are very difficult to get across to the electorate, but if you can present concrete human examples, for instance people who would lose money if they went off benefits and moved into work, voters can be reached: something like this has an appeal. This is the way we proceeded in the 2001 campaign – we used concrete examples.

In 2001, when you were first elected head of government, did you explicitly campaign on the need to reform the Danish labour market?
Yes, my party, the liberal Venstre, campaigned on the pledge that work must pay. Immediately after we took office, we introduced the ceiling on social benefits and the introduction benefit I mentioned before, as well as other measures. One could actually say that when you want to implement reforms, the first step is to profit from the momentum created during an election campaign and following an election victory. It is, I think, a general experience that immediately after an election you have some opportunities. My advice would always be to grasp them. So that was the first step for us.

After that, challenges began to occur, of course, with the question on how we should move forward. At the time, we recognised that the Danish welfare state needed to be made fit for the future and, as a result, we established a welfare commission consisting of independent members – that is people who did not have any connections to the government, but 'free spirits', in particular from academia. That commission delivered a report in December 2005 with a number of very controversial suggestions. One idea was, for example, to increase the retirement age gradually, but there were also some suggestions on how benefits could be cut and activation policies strengthened. The commission was harshly criticised at first, but over time it created some kind of platform for debate and provided room for manoeuvre for my government.

It is interesting to see how we, that is those who were politically responsible, handled this commission's suggestions. In the first round, we left aside some of the more contentious suggestions because, in general, the commission's report was met with a lot of opposition. We decided to opt for a step-by-step approach and started by implementing only one part of the report. As a result, we managed to get approval from the opposition. Thus, in 2006, one year after the report was published, we reached a broad political agreement in the Danish parliament to raise the entry age to VERP from 60 to 62, albeit with a long introduction period. The agreement at the time was to phase in the change from 2019 onwards, thus offering quite a long period for employees to adapt to the new situation. In addition, by the way for the first time in the history of the Danish welfare state, we took back, so to speak, some earlier welfare arrangements. Some of the more controversial proposals that we had left aside in the first round were taken up and implemented after the crisis hit Denmark. In 2011, the start date of our VERP reform was brought forward by five years, as a result of which the increase to 62 years started in 2014 already. This is, incidentally, rather interesting because this had never been widely debated among the Danish public. You could therefore say that the commission lay the groundwork for the moment when the crisis hit. The ideas were on the table and could be seized when the climate was right. In addition to raising the entry age to VERP by two years, we also raised the state pensionable age to 67. We also introduced a special clause stipulating that from 2025 onwards the retirement age would automatically increase in line with an increase in life expectancy.

Would you say that the fact that you campaigned on a strong reform agenda contributed to your party's election victory in 2001?
I think, in general, it was time for a change in 2001. The former social democratic government under Poul Nyrup Rasmussen had been in office for eight years and there was a general lack of trust among the Danish public. The 2001 election campaign was dominated by very specific domestic issues, relating to immigration. People wanted changes in law, with immigration policies tightened, and the Venstre had a clear plan. Welfare issues played a role, too, for example the health policies. At that time, patients had to cope with very long waiting lists before they were treated, and we pledged to introduce more competition within the system. Among the points just mentioned, there was one which played an important role in the campaign, namely that one had to qualify for full benefits through having worked in Denmark for a determined period of time. Yet, in general, I think that most of the points talked about in this interview did not play a major role in the 2001 campaign.

To what extent was your implementation of the reform agenda backed by a general consensus in the government coalition?
Establishing a consensus in the coalition never posed a serious problem because the two coalition partners, the Liberals, my party, and the Conservatives, Det Konserva-

tive Folkeparti (K), had almost the same views on all of the issues discussed so far, which meant that there was never a problem – and this cohesion proved crucial. The opposition would not have hesitated to exploit any internal debates and frictions within the coalition. You have to demonstrate unity within the government, show clear leadership and set the course. That is a prerequisite, I think, for carrying through reforms. There are, of course, always certain limitations: in a coalition, each party wants to stand out, to demonstrate to their electorate that they are a bit more advanced or that they have a firmer position than the other party. Another limitation in my case was the fact that in all my three terms in office, I had to lead minority governments which depended on the right-wing Dansk Folkeparti.

In addition, Denmark is traditionally consensus-oriented and we were therefore always eager to reach a broad consensus in parliament. Generally, political action in Denmark starts with seeking to establish broad support for what needs to be done. That is how the Danish political system works: whenever we introduced new measures, we started negotiations with, practically speaking, all political parties represented in parliament. Sometimes, as was the case with the 2006 pension reform, we managed to get support from the opposition. On other occasions, we had to rely on the Dansk Folkeparti, whose positions and attitudes are, by the way, very similar to the Social Democrats when it comes to welfare policies.

In summary, I have to say that the cohesion in the government was good. The Venstre and the Konservative Folkeparti reached agreement on all the issues on the table and that, in my view, was crucial for our success. As for parliament, it was not always easy to have a sufficient majority to carry through our reform agenda. To be honest, there were certain limits on how far we could go and I have to say that, if it had only been up to the two coalition partners, we might have gone further. In the real world, of course, we had to negotiate and grant concessions – but we still managed to carry through what I would call substantive and effective reforms.

In light of your reliance on minority governments, where did you seek support for your reforms outside the political sphere – among the general public and with stakeholders?
All political processes start with seeking support from the electorate, the public. If you cannot get sufficient support from the public, or at least from your own electorate, it is difficult to get other political parties on board for your purposes. You therefore need to make a convincing case in public before you can reach an agreement in parliament. That is why, in terms of our reform agenda, we made quite an effort to make the case to our voters. As I mentioned, in 2001, we made the case about introducing incentives to work, about the need to qualify for social benefits – and I think we managed to get that message across. I

have already mentioned the establishment of the welfare commission as an instrument to, so to speak, create a 'burning platform' that enabled us to move forward with our reforms.

Speaking about stakeholders, I should add that in 2005 I created what we called a 'Globalisation Council' with membership from politics, i.e. some ministers, and including representatives from trade unions, employers' organisations, the community and businesses. I personally chaired this council. Its purpose was to ensure that the challenges of globalisation could be better addressed and to make Danish society 'fit for the future'. In this context it is important to note that our close interaction with the Danish collective bargaining powers in this council also helped a great deal in our efforts to implement many of the reforms. Although, in particular, Danish labour unions were sceptical about some of our reforms, the council provided an opportunity for us to talk with them on a regular basis. You know, even if you speak about competition from China – as, for instance, was the official purpose of a specific meeting – there is still an opportunity to discuss some current issues, including the welfare reforms, over lunch.

In general, were your attempts to reform the Danish labour market aided or hindered by the unions?
At the beginning, in 2001, we met with strong opposition from the labour unions. Traditionally, the unions in Denmark support the Social Democratic Party and they were therefore in natural opposition to my government, but we made a great effort to work with them in the spirit of good cooperation. For example, I had several personal meetings with the then leader of the biggest labour union in Denmark and, to the frustration of the opposition, we managed to get quite a good relationship with the labour unions eventually.

Of course, this good cooperation was the result of strategic deliberations in my government, but it was also helped by the pragmatic approach on the part of the unions. In today's world, the majority of labour union members are well off. Many of them are house owners and they, too, want to make sure that work pays. Nowadays, union members are much more pragmatic: they want their union to take care of their interests, their wages, their salaries, their working conditions – and all those matters. They do not feel particularly affiliated to one specific political party. Opinion polls confirm that many of them vote non-socialist and, as a result, union leaders have to pursue a more pragmatic approach. To sum up, my government was heavily criticised, but seen retrospectively, I do not think that we had difficulties in making the case. In the end, the labour unions acknowledged our positions.

Could you give us an example of when it proved particularly hard to convince the general public, the opposition or other stakeholders of a specific reform?
The most difficult welfare reform was the increase of the retirement age because, at that time, the Danish economy was really flourishing and people did not quite understand why it was necessary to work longer. We could make the general case that we all live longer. We had excellent calculations which showed, from a long-term perspective, how big the problem would be in a certain number of years because of the ageing population. We knew that we had to do something, but it proved very hard to make that case both to voters and to the opposition parties. I felt that was the most difficult challenge. There was also a point when I thought about making substantial compromises on the content in order to get the support of the opposition parties. Eventually, the welfare commission was useful: backed up by their work we approached the opposition and, because of the commission's sound arguments, we were able to reach a broad political agreement.

People tend to see the need for reforms in the long run, but do not want to experience the negative impact they might have on them; did you, as a result of this problem, explicitly target the younger generation when you introduced the changes to the Danish pension system from 2006?
Absolutely, we made a great effort to appeal to the younger generation. Opinion polls indicated that the young were very much more in favour of the reforms to the Danish pension system than the older generation was. This influenced our decision to have long introductory periods, which meant that we could tell people that they would not be affected: 'The entry age to VERP will not be raised before 2019; so you have plenty of time to adjust your retirement and pension plans.' The fact that the reform only affected those in favour of the change anyway proved to be decisive.

How can reform governments ensure their reforms' sustainability?
The best recipe to ensure a reform's sustainability is the establishment of wide-ranging political consensus. In fact, we are talking about reforms that are supposed to yield long-term effects. When we implemented the 2006 pension reform, we made every effort to get the broadest political support possible to ensure that the reform would not be reversed after the next election, in case we lost. In fact, in this particular case, the implementation of the pension reform was accelerated after a few years. The crisis helped at that time. So this example substantiates the well-known expression 'Every crisis is an opportunity in disguise'. We seized that opportunity. A reform which was less successful in terms of sustainability was the benefit reduction which my government introduced immediately after we took office in 2001: the Social Democrats, who succeeded us in government, made abolition of that reform one of the very first steps they took in office. In

2001, it had unfortunately not been possible for us to get sufficiently broad support and, as a result, the reform was reversed some years later.

Did reports by international organisations, such as the OECD, the EU or the IMF, influence your reform agenda?
Within the political establishment, if I may use that expression, analyses and recommendations by international organisations are, of course, read, and they have an impact – they really do. On the other hand, when I go to my electorate, having the support of an OECD report is not, with the greatest respect, the strongest argument. When I talk to political colleagues, however, or when I speak with unions or representatives of what I call 'the political and economic establishment', then such reports – whether from the OECD, the EU or any other international player – do of course have an impact, but they are not strong tools in shaping the debate with the general public. That is a hard fact.

Reforms always produce winners and losers. The reforms that were implemented in your time in office benefited mainly those who were in work. Did you compensate those who lost out as a result of the reforms?
No. Our argument ran as follows: 'It is better to have a job than to be on benefits. It is better to be in education than to be on benefits.' Regarding compensation, our reaction was: 'Yes, we will cut your benefits, but in exchange we will give you a job or an education.' That is the essence of the concept of active labour market policies. It is actually a strong argument, because that is also what people feel in general: of course it is better to have a job than just to get social benefits, and it is therefore relatively easy to make that case. That was the compensation we offered.

Would you, in the current debate on migration within Europe after the lifting of working restrictions, recommend to other European countries the kind of social security model your government introduced in 2001, including some general restrictions on access to benefits?
Yes, I think it is the only solution in the current debate on dealing with potential abuse of national welfare systems by immigrants from other European countries. I am generally strongly in favour of the European principle of free movement of labour and believe it to be an essential part of the single European market, a benefit for all of us. On the other hand, it is of course a matter of concern that countries with welfare systems mainly financed through taxation may be subject to abuse, if citizens from other, poorer, European countries can just move in and, from day one, claim generous social security benefits.

Actually, this leads to an interesting observation: in Europe, there are basically two different welfare state systems in terms of financing. In Scandinavia, the welfare state is to a high degree financed through taxation. In other countries, people have to pay specific fees, for instance by contributing to the national pension scheme, in order to qualify for benefits at a later stage. In this model, beneficiaries are not entitled to claim social benefits until they have paid a certain amount of money into the system. The problem is that if the welfare state is financed through taxes, as is the case in Denmark, there is no protection against abuse, which is why additional restrictions have to be introduced in such a system. Both models are based on the same premise, namely that rights have to be earned. In systems where rights have to be earned benefits of the welfare state can easily be combined with the principle of free movement of labour. I do not think that people are generally opposed to free movement of labour, provided that immigrants actually work. We should not forget that we need immigrants. However, people are opposed to free movement of labour if immigrants enter their country with the sole purpose of receiving welfare benefits.

In your view, which labour market reforms should European countries put on top of their agendas now?
Two issues are of utmost importance at the moment. First, reform of the retirement schemes to prevent future problems caused by ageing populations. In my view, it is evident that further reforms are needed in the area of retirement and pensions. Secondly, as mentioned just now, a solution must be found to deal with the conflict between free movement of labour in the single European market and the potential abuse of national social security systems: this poses a real challenge. I am concerned that the current debate on the influx of immigrants who might exploit a country's social security system will lead to strong opposition against what I think is vital for Europe: the free movement of people and the free movement of labour – we do have to address this issue and take people's concerns seriously.

2.2 A note on Danish labour market performance over the past decade

2.2.1 The facts
Danish labour market performance has followed a rollercoaster ride since the early 1990s. The economic crisis at the beginning of the decade hit Denmark hard and it saw the Danish harmonised unemployment rate peaking at over 10

per cent in 1993[29] (see fig. 4). Subsequently, as the economy recovered, there was a prolonged period of strong employment growth up to 2008 which was only briefly interrupted by the shallow slowdown at the beginning of the 2000s. As a result, when the Great Recession hit in 2008, the Danish unemployment rate was only 3.5 per cent, the second lowest in the EU after the Netherlands – a level last recorded in the mid-1970s. The total employment rate peaked in 2008 at almost 78 per cent, the third highest rate in the OECD area after Switzerland and Iceland.

Evolution of the employment and unemployment rates in Denmark, 1970–2014

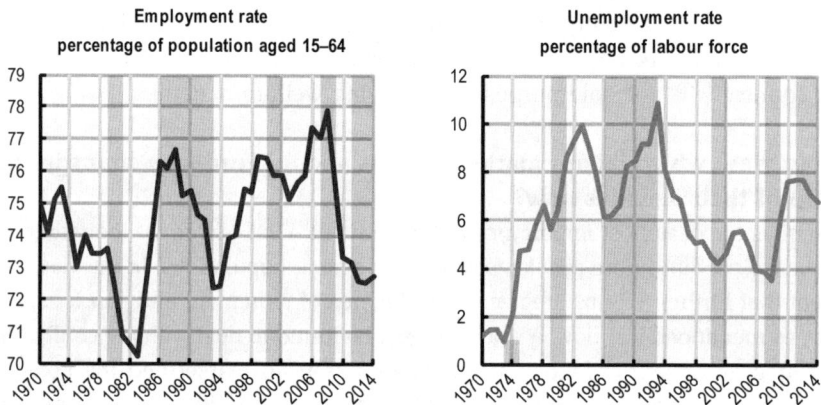

Note: Grey shaded areas refer to period of economic contraction (based on the output gap).

Source: OECD estimates based on the *OECD Labour Force Statistics, OECD Short-term Labour Market Statistics* and *OECD Economic Outlook Databases* (Cut-off date: 13 April 2015).

Figure 4: Labour market chart Denmark

This very successful period of Danish labour market performance led many observers to cite Denmark and its so-called 'flexicurity' model as the 'poster boy' for the European social model in terms of its apparently unique ability to balance a high degree of flexibility for firms in terms of the relative ease of hiring and firing workers with a high degree of job security for workers (cf. Box 1).

---

29 There are two main sources of data on unemployment in Denmark, one based on official register data and the other on the labour force survey. Most Danish analyses use the former, but OECD and Eurostat use the latter source, as it is more suited to international comparisons. In this note, we use the harmonised unemployment and employment data published by both Eurostat and OECD.

Box 1. The Danish flexicurity model

In response to its exceptional labour market performance over the period from the mid-1990s to the recent crisis, many observers have highlighted the Danish flexicurity model as a key ingredient in this success. Indeed, the European Commission endorsed the Danish model as good practice for other member states to copy as an inspiration for the European social model.

The Danish flexicurity model rests on three main pillars: (i) flexible hiring and firing regulations, as reflected in relatively low levels of the strictness of employment protection legislation (see table 5); (ii) a generous social safety net, as evidenced by the high levels of public social spending and the relatively high net benefit replacement rates; and (iii) a strong emphasis on active labour market policies (ALMPs), backed up by effective activation of unemployment benefit recipients (since the mid-1990s). The scope of the three pillars and interactions between them have always been negotiated between the social partners and the government, reflecting the long-standing Danish tradition of social dialogue on labour market issues.

The main features of the model predate the 1990s, but prior to that period, the balance between the pillars tended to favour the security dimension with very high benefit replacement rates, an exceptionally long duration of unemployment benefits being paid, compared to other countries (eight years) and weak activation of unemployment benefit recipients. The peak unemployment rate in the early 1990s was a real shock to the model, which forced a radical shift on the activation front. With the onset of the economic crisis in 2007–8, which hit the Danish economy relatively hard, labour market performance dipped sharply and this took the gloss off the flexicurity model for many observers. Indeed, the European Commission ceased to preach its virtues as loudly as they had done before the crisis. This has given rise to a debate in Denmark and elsewhere as to whether the flexicurity model is only good in 'fair-weather conditions' and that it will not be able to withstand the effects of a deep recession without fundamental modification. Madsen (2013) reviews this debate and argues that the Danish model has weathered the storm of the current downturn pretty well, even if this has necessitated some rebalancing between the flexibility and security pillars of the model. As we shall see below, this rebalancing is a continuing process.

The global economic crisis of 2008–9, however, hit the Danish economy hard and knocked some of the shine off the flexicurity model. Denmark, being the archetypical small, open economy, suffered disproportionately from the collapse in world demand for its exports, and this negative shock was amplified by the bursting of a major housing bubble. Despite fiscal stimulus to offset part of the negative impact on domestic demand, Danish GDP dropped sharply by 8 per cent from the pre-crisis peak to the trough. This large output drop was reflected quickly in large layoffs – the reverse side of the flexicurity model coming into play quickly in a steep downturn. As fig. 4 shows, this resulted in a sharp fall in the total employment rate between 2008 and 2013: in 2013, the employment rate was down to 74.3 percent and Denmark had slipped to the eighth highest rate in the OECD area, even though it remained well above the EU average of almost 66 per cent.

With the steep drop in employment, the unemployment rate more than doubled its 2008 level to peak at 7.6 per cent in 2011. More recently, however, there have been some signs of a recovery in the Danish economy and this has spilled over into the labour market – just as flexicurity leads to rapid layoffs in a downturn, hirings pick up quickly once demand recovers. This process appears now to be underway in Denmark and the harmonised unemployment rate has dropped slowly through 2013 and into 2014 to a seasonally adjusted 6.6 per cent in September 2014, the eighth lowest rate in the EU28.

Denmark's very strong labour market performance up to the crisis is highlighted in many of the indicators shown in the scoreboard. For example, the youth unemployment rate has consistently been one of the lowest in the EU, reflecting Denmark's strong tradition of investing heavily in vocational education and training and apprenticeships as a means of securing a swift and efficient school-to-work transition for many Danish youth. Even though youth unemployment almost doubled in the aftermath of the crisis, the situation has begun to improve recently in line with the drop in overall unemployment: by September 2014, it was down to a seasonally adjusted rate of 12.8 per cent, the fifth lowest in the EU28.

The share of long-term unemployment in total unemployment is relatively low in Denmark and this is a long-standing feature of the Danish labour market. Before the crisis struck, Denmark had the second lowest incidence of long-term unemployment in the EU after Sweden. Even though the incidence rose significantly after the crisis hit, reaching a peak of 28 per cent in 2012, it then dropped back to 25.5 per cent in 2013. In that year, Denmark's ranking within the EU had slipped slightly to the fourth lowest place after Austria, Finland and Sweden; however, it was still far below the corresponding EU or OECD averages. The high rates of job and worker flows in Denmark, which are one result of the flexicurity model, combined with reinforced activation since the mid-1990s, are partly responsible for the relatively low rates of long-term unemployment.

On the employment front, it is worth noting the relatively high and rising employment rates among older workers. All three five-year age cohorts shown in the Danish scoreboard have, first of all, employment rates significantly higher than the EU averages in all years since 1993 and have, secondly, recorded a strong trend rise over the past two decades.

Part-time employment is relatively well developed in Denmark. Its share in total employment has consistently outstripped the EU average and has risen steadily since 2000 despite the crisis, to a point where almost one in every five jobs in 2013 was a part-time position.

While the share of part-time employment is above average, the opposite is the case for temporary jobs. The share of temporary workers has been below the EU average since 2000 and the trend goes in the opposite direction: at 8.8 per cent in 2013, it was over 5 percentage points below the EU average. The high degree of flexibility in hiring and firing means that there is less segmentation in the Danish labour market between workers on permanent contracts and those on temporary contracts, and there is correspondingly less pressure on Danish employers to fill a disproportionately high number of vacancies through hiring temporary workers.

Another key feature of the current flexicurity model is a strong emphasis on activation of the unemployed and public investment in active labour market policies (ALMPs) to help offset the negative work disincentive effects arising from high net benefit replacement rates – the scoreboard shows that Danish benefit replacement rates for various durations of unemployment are consistently well above the corresponding EU averages.

Denmark has a long history of investing heavily in ALMPs as a vehicle for helping the unemployed find a new job and it also uses slots on ALMPs as a way of activating unemployment benefit recipients in periods when job vacancies are scarce. Spending on ALMPs plays the role of an automatic stabiliser in Denmark.[30] Indeed, Denmark spends the largest proportion of its GDP on labour market policies among OECD countries and also on ALMPs. In 2012, the most recent year for which comparative data are available from OECD, Denmark spent 3.8 per cent of its GDP on labour market policies compared with an OECD average of 1.4 per cent.[31] Out of this total, it spent 2.1 per cent of GDP on ALMPs, almost four times the OECD average.[32] So this key pillar of the flexicurity model is relatively costly in terms of the public finances in Denmark.

Thus far, we have emphasised the positive aspects of Danish labour market performance compared to other countries. However, all is not entirely rosy on this front in Denmark. While employment rates are relatively high, so is the proportion of the working-age population relying upon a range of inactivity benefits. In 2005, for example, 25 per cent of the population aged 18–66 were receiving various inactivity benefits.[33] Two of the largest such benefits were disability pension and sickness benefits (together they accounted for 8.9 per cent of the working-age population) and the Voluntary Early Retirement Programme (VERP), which accounted for a further 4.4 per cent of the working-age population. It is worth noting that recipients of unemployment benefits only accounted for 3.8

---

30 This point is emphasised by Madsen (2013).

31 See OECD (2014 g), Statistical Annex, Table P.

32 In terms of participant stocks in ALMPs as a percentage of the labour force, Denmark was ranked only fourth among OECD countries in 2012. When this fact is put alongside its very high public spending on ALMPs, it implies that the average duration of participation in an ALMP is relatively long in Denmark, compared with other OECD countries. This can be accounted for by the high share of ALMP spending devoted to relatively long education and training programmes in Denmark.

33 These data are expressed in full-year equivalents. For more details, see OECD (2008a), Table 3.2.

per cent of the working-age population in that year. While the share of unemployment benefit recipients in the working-age population fell sharply over the period from the mid-1990s to the onset of the Great Recession, this was offset by a trend rise in the numbers receiving other inactivity transfers, notably the disability pension and sickness benefits. As OECD (2013g) highlights, a worrying feature of the latter nowadays is the great number of people with a wide range of mental health problems who are receiving these benefits. It is proving extremely difficult in Denmark, as in other OECD countries, to develop effective policies to help workers with these specific difficulties to stay in work or to find a new job.

Having such a large part of the working-age population dependent on generous income support helps explain the relatively high tax burden in Denmark and this has been identified by the Danish Welfare Commission and other commentators as a threat to the future financial sustainability of one of the key pillars of the flexicurity model. As we shall see, attempts to tackle this challenge, notably in terms of reforming the disability and sickness benefit systems and the VERP, have dominated much of the labour market and social policy debates in Denmark over the past decade.

A final feature of the Danish labour market that stands out in international comparison is the relatively low level of average hours worked per year. Since 1990, Danes have worked between 1400 and 1500 hours per year on average, and there has been very little variation around this level. In 2013, the average Danish worker worked 1411 hours, well below the OECD (weighted) average of 1770 hours. Part of the explanation for this relatively low work effort are the very high marginal tax rates on salaries and wages, even at comparatively low earnings, which affect incentives for people to work harder. The high marginal tax rates are, of course, the corollary of the high tax burden and high public spending in Denmark, especially expenditure on the welfare state. Over the past decade, successive Danish governments have sought to 'make work pay' by either cutting marginal tax rates directly and/or by introducing in-work benefits to top up low earnings, but these reforms have always been at the margin and their impact on labour supply and work effort has been correspondingly rather limited.

At the same time, the redistributive power of the tax and benefit system is relatively high in Denmark. As a result, earnings and income inequality, while they have risen somewhat in Denmark over the past two decades, remain well below the EU and OECD averages. In addition, OECD (2008b) showed that intergenerational mobility is relatively high in Denmark by international comparison, suggesting that the flexicurity model not only delivered good labour market outcomes but contributed to good equity results, too, both from static and dynamic perspectives.[34]

2.2.2 Major labour market and welfare benefit reforms since the mid-1990s: activation of unemployment benefit recipients

When discussing the recent reforms under this heading, it is important to bear in mind that there is an element of continuity to them. As noted above, these reforms began in earnest in the early 1990s, when the unemployment rate peaked in double-digits. Starting in 1992, but especially from 1994 on, a series of reforms were introduced by successive Social Democratic governments led by Poul Nyrup Rasmussen, with the explicit aim of activating the unemployed earlier in their periods of unemployment so as to ensure that they searched for work more actively or that they took active steps to improve their employability. The main such reforms are listed in Box 2.

Box 2. Main reforms to the Danish activation strategy in the 1990s

1992: Job offers for youth, previously made after two-and-a-half years of unemployment, were brought forward.
1994: The so-called 'active benefit period' was introduced after four years of unemployment. Individual action plans were instituted. New data bases were developed to link the public employment service (PES) to the benefit agencies.
1995: Stricter supervision of the benefit eligibility criteria was introduced.
1996: The 'active benefit period' was applied after two years of unemployment.
1999: The unemployed were required to register with the PES from the first day of unemployment. The relaxation of the job availability rule, which had previously applied to the unemployed aged 50–9, was limited to those aged 55–9.

The list of reforms shows a clear and consistent pattern of putting more obligations on the unemployed earlier in their unemployment spell, giving a more active role to PES case workers and making better use of participation in ALMPs to assess job-search behaviour. At the same time, the threat of benefit sanctions in cases where the unemployed did not fulfil their obligations was reinforced. Evaluations of these reforms show clearly that they had a positive impact on the movement of the unemployed from benefit rolls to work.[35] It is also clear from

---

34 See OECD (2008b), Chapter 8, for the evidence on intergenerational mobility.
35 See, for example, OECD (2005b), Bredgaard et al. (2005) and Geerdsen (2006). A recent study by Fallesen et al. (2014) shows evidence that activation schemes for the unemployed who were not eligible for unemployment benefits yielded significant social benefits in terms of reduced crime rates, especially among young Danish men.

the evaluations that the threat effect of a possible benefit sanction was part of the explanation for the success of these activation measures, as was more intensive contacts with PES case workers and greater emphasis on job-search activity.

During the period from 2000 until the crisis struck, there was only fine-tuning of these measures, as they appeared to be paying off in terms of the trend decline in the unemployment rate. However, when the crisis hit, the Fogh Rasmussen centre-right government reacted quickly. In late 2007, it brought forward the 'active benefit period' to nine months instead of one year; full-time activation was required after two-and-a-half years of unemployment. The unemployed were required to have more regular contact with their municipal job centre and more responsibility for the delivery of employment services was decentralised to the municipalities grouped into four employment regions. In mid-2009, the succeeding centre-right government led by Lars Lokke Rasmussen tightened activation requirements for the young unemployed (under the age of 30): they were required to attend a first job interview and engage in compulsory activation after one month of unemployment.

The fiscal stimulus packages of 2009 and 2010, which aimed to cushion the economy from the adverse demand shock led to rising public deficits, and the Conservative–Liberal government negotiated a programme for fiscal consolidation, to be implemented in 2011 and subsequent years. The most controversial of the measures under the fiscal consolidation programme were the proposals for reform of the unemployment benefit system. They consisted of two main measures:

(i) A tightening of benefit eligibility: the conditions for renewal of benefit entitlements were aligned with the rules for qualifying for benefits for the first time. In both cases, the criteria were to be 52 weeks of full-time work during the last three years. Before then, the criteria for renewing benefit entitlement had been only 26 weeks of full-time employment in the previous three years.

(ii) A reduction in the duration of the benefit period: under the old regime, an insured unemployed could receive unemployment benefits for four out of the last six years. The reform cut this to a maximum duration of two out of the last three years.

Not surprisingly, these proposals to cut the generosity of the unemployment benefit system were strongly resisted by the unions. In response, the new coalition government, led by the Social Democrat Helle Thorning-Schmidt, which took office in late 2011, postponed the implementation of that particular reform by temporarily extending the duration of benefits for those who would have lost their entitlements under the new rules. The new rules came into operation at the beginning of 2013, but faced with continued union opposition and a slow recovery on the job market, the Thorning-Schmidt government introduced a temporary scheme for the unemployed who had exhausted their benefit entitlements; the temporary scheme is to be phased out gradually over the period up to 2017. However, under the temporary scheme, the benefit replacement rate during the final two years has been cut to 60 per cent of the benefit paid in the first two years. It also maintained the tighter benefit eligibility rules despite union pressure to reverse them, too.

A final contentious issue concerns the role of the municipalities which, since the 2007 local government reform, are currently responsible for the delivery of employment services, including the delivery of ALMPs, while the central government sets the framework for ALMPs, designs the broad activation strategy and provides much of the funds.[36] This decentralisation has been dogged by problems concerning the organisation, steering and financing of labour market policies. It has proved very difficult to design appropriate financial incentives for the municipalities to encourage them to get as many welfare recipients off benefits and into work as possible in a cost-efficient manner. This issue is a very 'hot political potato' in Denmark and an attempt to resolve it by tripartite negotiations failed in 2012. Since then, the coalition government has, for the moment, evaded the issue and set up an expert group to work in parallel with the social partners to develop new proposals over the next two years.

Voluntary early retirement programme (VERP)
The VERP was first introduced in 1979 during a period of high and rising youth unemployment. As was the case in other countries which introduced similar early retirement schemes in the late 1970s and early 1980s, the original aim had been to urge Danish firms to hire more young people by encouraging older workers to take early retirement. Under the scheme, Danish workers insured under the unemployment benefit system, who had paid their VERP contributions for 30 years, could retire at the age of 60 and receive a benefit similar to the unemployment benefit, until they reached age 65 and became eligible for the state pension.[37] While the original aim of stimulating youth employment was not fulfilled in practice, the VERP became very popular with the social partners and older workers. As a result, there was a steady trend rise in the share of the

---

36 Some observers have suggested that one of the reasons why the Fogh Rasmussen government pushed for this major reform was to weaken the role of the social partners in determining labour market policies.
37 When the VERP was first introduced, the state pensionable age was 67.

working-age population taking early retirement, up from around 1 per cent at the beginning of the 1980s to a peak of 5 per cent in 2004.

The steep rise in the number of older workers on VERP attracted much adverse comment, because of its negative effects on labour supply and the public finances. For example, both the OECD and the Danish Welfare Commission called for it to be phased out, but the social partners, both unions and employers, vigorously resisted such a radical step. Hence, incremental reforms have been made to the scheme over the past 15 years to reduce its scope and costs (cf. Box 3).

Box 3. Main reforms to the VERP

1999: The pension was cut during the first two years as an incentive to postpone entry to the scheme until age 62. The state pensionable age was lowered from 67 to 65.

2006: The entry age to VERP was raised from 60 to 62, to be phased in gradually from 2019 to 2022. At the same time, the state pensionable age was raised back to 67, to be phased in from 2024 to 2027 so that all older-worker cohorts could benefit from five years on the VERP.

2007: A special in-work tax credit was introduced for those aged 64, conditional on them having worked full-time from age 60 to 64. The credit could reach 28 per cent of average full-time earnings during the one year it could be received.

2011: The duration of receipt of a VERP pension to be cut from five to three years between 2018 and 2023. The increase in the entry age to the VERP to 62, agreed in 2006, to be brought forward by five years to 2014–23. At the same time, the increase in the state pensionable age to be phased in more quickly over the period 2019–22.

Some success has been achieved by the reforms of the mid-2000s: they broke the long-term upward drift in the share of the working-age population receiving a VERP pension. As a result, the share of the working-age population receiving a VERP pension declined from a peak of 5 per cent in 2004 to 3.5 per cent in 2010. It is likely that the latest reform of 2011, which phased in the increase of the early retirement age more quickly, will result in a further decline of workers aged over 60 on VERP, but when this development is seen in combination with the reforms to the activation/unemployment benefit system outlined above, unions fear that the security element of the flexicurity model has been undermined in recent years.

Disability/sickness benefits

While successive reforms over the past 15 years to activate the unemployed and the recent reforms to the VERP have paid off in terms of reducing the share of the working-age population on those benefits, there has been no similar success in terms of cutting the large numbers on disability and sickness benefits. This long-standing challenge can be described as the Achilles heel of Danish labour market reforms. It is a problem which Denmark shares with its Nordic neighbours.

In Denmark, disability benefits are flat-rate benefits which correspond to around 70 per cent of average earnings. Eligibility requires that the person is unable to work in an unsubsidised job, as determined by a resource profile based on health and many other factors. Sickness benefits are earnings-related with a low maximum threshold equal to about 55 per cent of average earnings. Benefits are paid for up to one year in 18 months, though this can be extended for up to six months. Employers pay the first 21 days of sick pay and then it is paid by the municipality. However, collective agreements often top up sick pay so that many workers, especially white-collar workers, have a sickness benefit replacement rate of 100 per cent.

A rather unique element in the Danish disability benefit system is provided by the so-called 'flexjob' scheme whose original aim was to reduce the high inflow to disability pensions. Flexjobs are targeted at individuals with permanently reduced work capacity who benefit from a generous and permanent wage subsidy paid to the employer. The municipalities, who administer the scheme, pay the subsidy to the employer in line with the individual's reduced work capacity, while the worker in question receives the normal wage for that occupation. The municipalities have a financial incentive to place people with health problems in flexjobs, as this way they are reimbursed more generously by the central government than if people are on a disability pension.

Since its inception, the flexjob scheme has proved to be very popular with workers with health problems, employers seeking to transform full-time into part-time jobs and with municipalities.[38] Indeed, so popular has the scheme become that there is a waiting list of people who are entitled to a flexjob, but who cannot get one immediately: while waiting, they are paid a waiting benefit at the same level as a disability pension.

High rates of sickness absence, a high rate of working-age people in receipt of a disability pension and a growing demand for flexjobs impose large economic costs on the Danish economy through reduced labour supply and high public spending. OECD (2008d), p. 14 summarised the challenge succinctly as follows, and this statement is as valid today as it was eight years ago:

'The main challenge in Denmark is the continuously high rate of dependence of the population on various health-related benefits despite a series of benefit reforms. A large and increasing share of this concerns people with mental health conditions, making up for almost one out of two new claimants. Related to this trend, the average age of new recipients is falling because more young people are successfully applying for disability benefits. The other side of the problem is, that once on disability benefit, people remain on it until retirement: the outflow from benefit into work is particularly low in Denmark.'

---

38 OECD (2008d) highlights the fact that often people with sufficient work capacity to do a normal job were transferred to a flexjob.

Danish governments of both the Left and the Right have attempted to tackle these challenges since the late 1990s, with the latest reforms introduced in early 2013 (cf. Box 4). Despite all this reform activity, it is hard to detect any real signs of success: the share of the working-age population on a disability pension remains rather stable and above the OECD average, the incidence of sickness absence is also above the OECD average and has changed little over the past decade, and flexjobs remain very popular. In addition, as part of the 2011 reform to the VERP, a new senior disability scheme was created for those workers aged over 40 with health problems. OECD (2014b) expresses concern that it could become a new pathway to early retirement. Thus, it remains to be seen whether the most recent reforms will fare any better than previous attempts to tackle the problem.

Box 4. Main reforms to the disability pension/sickness benefit systems

1998: Flexjobs introduced.

2003: Following an agreement with the social partners, the assessment of disability was shifted from a focus on incapacity to one of remaining work capacity; the partial benefits for partial disability were replaced by a single benefit in line with the unemployment benefit.

2006: Eligibility criteria for a flexjob were tightened and the maximum subsidy cut. Municipalities were required to follow up people on sickness benefits more intensively, profile them and prepare action plans for a quick return to work; failure to do so could lead to a cut in the state refund to the municipality.

2008: An action plan was introduced to cut sickness absence by 15 per cent by 2015. It aimed to promote early intervention by fostering active co-operation between the employers, the sick workers, medical professionals and municipal case managers.

2009: Controls on sick leave were reinforced and more emphasis put on rehabilitation.

2011: A new 'senior' disability scheme was introduced for those with health problems who were within five years of receiving an old-age pension.

2012: For those aged under 40 with health problems, access to a disability pension was replaced by a 'new rehabilitation' model with integrated health, social and employment services.

2013: Further reforms to the flexjob scheme were introduced. The largest subsidies are now targeted at those with the lowest wages and earnings capacity. The maximum flexjob subsidy was cut slightly. Flexjobs will only be granted temporarily, at least initially for five years. The temporary focus will be strongest for young people. The unemployed referred to a flexjob will be required to undertake active job searches. The new regulations will not apply to existing holders of flexjobs, only to those moving into a flexjob.

2.2.3 Conclusion

Denmark enjoyed a prolonged period of strong labour market performance from the mid-1990s up to 2008, when it was hard hit by the Great Recession. The subsequent sharp deterioration in labour market performance until very recently has taken some of the gloss off the unique Danish flexicurity model, with some observers arguing that it only works well in fair-weather economic conditions. However, the main pillars of the model have evolved over time, shifting the balance between flexibility for firms in terms of hiring and firing workers and security for workers.

The flexicurity model has worked less well, however, with regard to the trend rise in the share of the Danish working-age population on disability pension and sickness benefits, and the growing role of mental ill-health as a key driver of these trends. Many attempts have been made to reform these systems to date but they have been unable to replicate the success of the activation reforms for the unemployed. One part of the problem lies in the relative generosity of disability pension and sickness benefits, which have been defended strongly by the unions. It has proved impossible to lower these rates as part of a comprehensive strategy to tackle the problems.

Instead, current policies put more emphasis on early diagnosis and prevention, bringing together all the key actors (the sick workers, the employers, the medical professionals, the social and employment services caseworkers at the municipal level), investing more in rehabilitation and employment support and using financial incentives to encourage the municipalities to focus more on work-related outcomes. Given the past failures of reforms along these lines, it is hard to be optimistic that the most recent reforms will do the trick.

Table 5: Scoreboard for labour market outcomes and policies, Denmark and EU, 1993–2013

| | 1993 | | 2000 | | 2007 | | 2013* | |
	DK	EU	**DK**	EU	**DK**	EU	**DK**	EU
1. Employment rate (% of the working-age population)	**73.8**	61.2	**77.0**	63.6	**78.3**	66.7	**74.3**	65.9
– male	**77.9**	71.8	**81.4**	72.9	**82.6**	74.2	**77.5**	71.6
– female	**69.7**	50.7	**72.5**	54.4	**73.9**	59.2	**71.2**	60.2
– youth (aged 15/16–24)	**60.3**	39.5	**67.1**	39.4	**65.3**	38.2	**53.7**	33.4
– older people (aged 55–9)	**64.8**	47.6	**72.6**	50.6	**79.8**	57.3	**77.8**	64.9
– older people (aged 60–4)	**36.3**	22.3	**30.9**	22.3	**38.6**	29.4	**44.8**	34.7
– older people (aged 65–9)	–	9.2	**12.2**	7.4	**12.6**	9.5	**14.9**	11.3
2. Unemployment rate (% of labour force)	**10.7**	10.8	**4.5**	8.9	**3.8**	7.1	**7.0**	10.7
– youth (aged 15/16–24)	**14.6**	21.0	**6.7**	17.4	**7.5**	15.5	**13.1**	23.3
3. Incidence of long-term unemployment (% of total unemployment) (a)	**25.2**	42.0	**20.0**	44.4	**16.1**	41.6	**25.5**	46.5
4. Part-time employment rate (b)	**19.0**	13.8	**16.1**	15.3	**17.3**	16.0	**19.2**	17.5

Table 5 (continued)

	1993		2000		2007		2013*	
	DK	EU	**DK**	EU	**DK**	EU	**DK**	EU
5. Temporary employment rate (c) (temporary employees as % of total employees)	**10.7**	10.5	**10.2**	13.1	**9.1**	14.8	**8.8**	14.0
– youth (aged 15/16–24 as% of total youth employees)	**29.2**	28.8	**29.8**	38.0	**22.5**	41.8	**20.9**	43.0
6. Low-pay incidence (d) (% of employees)	–	–	**11.3**	15.7	**15.1**	16.5	**16.7**	15.0
7. Protection of permanent workers against individual dismissal	**2.2**	2.6	**2.1**	2.5	**2.1**	2.4	**2.2**	2.2
– Protection of temporary workers	**3.1**	2.3	**1.4**	1.8	**1.4**	1.6	**1.4**	1.8
8. Public spending on labour market policies (% of GDP)	**7.2**	–	**4.3**	2.0	**2.8**	1.5	**3.8**	2.1
– Spending on active measures (e)	**1.8**	–	**1.9**	0.9	**1.3**	0.6	**2.1**	0.8
– Spending on passive measures (f)	**5.5**	–	**2.4**	1.1	**1.5**	0.8	**1.6**	1.3
9. Net benefit replacement rate (g) (averaged over four family types and two earnings levels)	–	–	**84**	57	**67**	52	**66**	51
– initial spell (h)	–	–	**86**	70	**84**	71	**84**	70
– after 2 years of unemployment	–	–	**86**	66	**83**	63	**83**	57

* 2013 or latest available year.

(a) Persons out of work for 12 months and over.

(b) Part-time employment refers to persons who usually work less than 30 hours per week in "their 'main job'".

(c) Temporary employees are wage and salary workers whose job has a pre-determined end date as opposed to permanent employees whose job is of unlimited duration. National definitions broadly conform to this generic definition, but may vary depending on national circumstances.

(d) Persons with a wage less than 2/3 of the median.

(e) 'Active' measures cover categories 1 to 7 of the OECD/Eurostat data base on public spending on labour market programmes.

(f) 'Passive' measures cover categories 8 and 9 of the OECD/Eurostat data base on public spending on labour market programmes.

(g) Data on net replacement rates for 2000 refer to 2001.

(h) Initial phase of unemployment but following any waiting period. For married couples, the percentage of AW relates to the previous earnings of the 'unemployed' spouse only; the second spouse is assumed to be 'inactive' with no earnings and no recent employment history. Where receipt of social assistance or other minimum-income benefits is subject to activity tests (such as active job-search or being 'available' for work), these requirements are assumed to be met. Children are aged four and six and neither childcare benefits not childcare costs are considered.

Unweighted averages, for previous full-time earnings levels of 67% and 100% of AW and out-of-work single and couple households with no children or with two children (children are assumed to be aged four and six and neither childcare benefits not childcare costs are considered). After tax and including unemployment and family benefits. Social assistance and other means-tested benefits are assumed to be available subject to relevant income conditions. Housing costs are assumed equal to 20% of AW.

Sources: OECD Online Employment Database: www.oecd.org/employment/database; data on net replacement rates come from the OECD tax-benefit models (www.oecd.org/els/social/workincentives).

3 Estonia

3.1 Interview with Andrus Ansip, 23 March 2015

'Our refined and inclusive legislative process involving employers and employees had not been so common in Estonia before.'

It has been nine years since the government you led embarked on a number of important labour market reforms. In hindsight, to what extent and in which way do you consider the reform package a success? Which elements of the package have since then revealed shortcomings?
In July 2009, in the midst of the economic and financial crisis, we implemented a new Employment Contract Act (ECA), a major labour market reform aiming to increase labour market flexibility and to improve the administrative capacity of our labour market institutions. It compiled the individual acts governing Estonian labour law – the Employment Contract Act, the Wages Act, the Holidays Act, and the Working and Rest Time Act – into a single piece of legislation.

Before the economic and financial crisis, employment protection legislation for permanent workers in Estonia was significantly stricter than in other Central European countries and than the OECD average. An essential reform element was therefore the liberalisation of Estonian employment protection legislation (EPL), with notice periods shortened, severance pay cut, eligibility for re-employment of dismissed workers with their former employer restricted, and hiring and firing of workers eased. The new legislation also allows employers to cut the wages of their employees temporarily – in times of economic hardship – when employers cannot guarantee the contractually agreed amount of work to their employees and, as a result, it becomes unreasonably burdensome for employers to pay the contractually agreed wages. The overall goal was to reduce the direct and indirect costs of terminating an employment relationship.

Keeping in mind the principles of the flexicurity approach, also promoted by the European Commission, we agreed to balance workers' reduced employment protection by increasing the income protection for the unemployed. To this end, we raised the level of unemployment insurance benefits and eased the eligibility criteria to increase the share of people entitled to receive unemployment benefits. Implementation of these measures was, however, postponed until 2013, because of the need for fiscal consolidation.

Moreover, Estonia significantly increased expenditure on active labour market policies in order to facilitate a return of the unemployed to the labour market. Between 2008 and 2009, Estonian ALMP (active labour market policy) spending doubled from 0.1 per cent of GDP to about 0.2 per cent. In order to work against the massive rise in unemployment during the crisis, in 2010 we decided to cut expenditure on training allowances by 50 per cent – the major policy measure before the outbreak of the crisis – and instead we increased the spending on employment subsidies to keep people in work. When employment growth recovered, spending on wage subsidies was reduced and spending on training increased again.

Another important reform element was the merger of the Labour Market Board, i. e. the Estonian public employment service, and the Unemployment Insurance Fund. Through the integration of employment and benefit claims services within a single new agency, we aimed to increase the administrative capacity of our labour market institutions in general.

The labour market reforms that Estonia undertook at the end of the last decade are bringing benefits both for employees and for businesses. Employment and growth figures since then are evidence for the advantages of a more flexible and secure environment for labour relations and for public labour market services. A Eurofound survey conducted in 2013 also shows that a majority of employees were satisfied with the safety net labour market regulations in Estonia were offering at the time.

On shortcomings, I would point to the need for better public awareness about these issues. The same Eurofound survey also evaluated knowledge of employment rights among the Estonian population: more than one-quarter of employed and unemployed people assessed their own understanding of labour laws as poor, and more than three-quarters of them felt the need to know more about the rights and obligations related to employment regulations.

Were you able to plan your changes in a climate of reform? If not, what did you do to generate such a climate?
First of all, it should be noted that the existing labour legislation was outdated anyway and had been awaiting a review for almost a decade. The previous ECA dated back to 1992 and therefore needed substantial modification and amendment, in order to remain in line with the changed structure and operation of the Estonian labour market. Although the need for reform had already been recognised in the late 1990s, several reform attempts had failed because of disagreements between the social partners and the government, on the one hand, and among various ministries, on the other. Especially Estonian unions were very hesitant regarding the need to liberalise labour market legislation. In the end, however, the unions agreed to make the labour market more flexible, because we included social security issues in the package.

New labour laws and a more flexible labour market were clear promises made by my Reform Party in the March 2007 general elections, which we won. The subsequent coalition agreement was explicit on the reform and the need for a new law; as a result, the new Employment Contract Act was adopted in December 2008.

The reform was preceded by several studies, many of which concluded that the Estonian labour market had been comparatively flexible. One should not forget that, since 1992, Estonia had had a fixed exchange rate regime, which in itself prescribed labour market flexibility. Nevertheless, there was still a lot to be gained by doing away with any remaining rigidities and especially by making more use of active labour market policies. This was confirmed, for example, by the World Bank's *Doing Business* reports.

We explored the practices in other countries as well, especially the so-called flexicurity arrangements in the Nordic countries. The European Commission's Green Paper on modernising labour law, which was published in November 2006, was also a good reference point for reforms in Estonia. The Commission's Green Paper examined the role which a modernisation of employment legislation could play in advancing the flexicurity approach, i. e. a combination of greater labour market flexibility with improved employment security, in order to produce labour markets that are more responsive, but at the same time fairer and more inclusive. The Green Paper and the European debate that subsequently evolved around the flexicurity concept, as well as the lessons learnt from the Nordic countries, were highly relevant for the development of our labour market reform package.

To what extent could you rely on, or were you able to establish, a general consensus in your government – in other words: was there government cohesion?

There was a wide consensus on the general approach but, as usual, the devil was in the detail. Although the draft law did build on the outcome of consultations with stakeholders, the discussions to finalise the reforms in the government and parliament took quite a long time.

The real discussions happened during the negotiations for the coalition agreement, i. e. at an early stage. Although it was not easy to keep this line when under pressure from interest groups, the fact that there was an explicit description in the coalition agreement helped secure government cohesion.

When you were working on your reform plans, how did you engage with relevant stakeholders and the general public?

This was a legislative process where all stakeholders were involved from the very beginning. The consultations lasted for a year and eventually the main principles of the new law were laid down in a tripartite agreement between employers, employees and the government. Such a refined and inclusive legislative process had not been so common in Estonia before. There was also an extensive public information campaign on the new law.

In hindsight, I can say there were no clear losers because of this reform. The employers became more willing to hire people even in uncertain times and good use was made of the new enabling measures that the government created to provide for the unemployed and the underemployed.

The opposition parties voted against the reform along their party lines. Before then, there had been various attempts to engage them through seminars and similar events, but that turned out to be of little use.

Did you draw explicitly on good practice in other countries either at design or marketing stage of the reforms?
As mentioned before, we took account of the experiences other countries had had, especially the Nordic countries. Referring to the Nordic countries may have helped with the public perception of the reform. We also explicitly referred to EU public consultations on the Green Paper on flexicurity. All in all, the strongest argument we used when we made the case for change was that reforms were clearly in the interest of the Estonian economy and people. We never tried to hide behind any external influence when we talked to our electorate and stakeholders.

Would you agree that reformers should aim at striking a balance between unilateral and concerted actions in the design, adoption and implementation of structural reform?
Yes, this is generally true, but one has to remain open to adjustments, either made on the basis of sound arguments or necessary in the interest of the whole package. Implementation became swifter and the financial crisis prompted some last-minute changes to the draft law. Voluntary unemployment was excluded from the scope of unemployment insurance: the initial idea of insuring the unemployed who had voluntarily left their previous job was probably a step too far – and also unnecessary.

How important do you consider strong leadership in order to secure a successful reform process?
Good leadership is about winning consent, for sure. It has been a rule in all my cabinets to take decisions unanimously. Sometimes it took dozens of meetings to get somewhere; sometimes it took a change in the coalition. As for example in 2009, when the coalition partners of my second cabinet were unable to agree on a common position with regard to the budget cuts that became necessary in the wake of the economic and financial crisis. Eventually, the Social Democratic

Party left the cabinet, and as coalition talks with the People's Union of Estonia failed, my party, the Estonian Reform Party, and our coalition partner, the Union of Pro Patria and Res Publica, decided to continue as a minority government.

As for the policies we introduced, the trust in the government of Estonia and the outcome of the elections speak for themselves.

To what extent can the strong recovery of the Estonian economy following the 2008–9 crisis be attributed to your reforms in labour market and social policies?

The strong post-crisis recovery in Estonia was facilitated by policies that the government implemented during and, most importantly, also well before the crisis. Prudent fiscal policy was one of these policies. Estonia has had the lowest public debt level in the EU in this century. There were no government bills and bonds in the market when the crisis broke out. Indeed, the opposite was the case: Estonia was able to rely on public reserves accumulated in good times. This in itself was a factor of confidence for the private sector, especially during the crisis.

Labour market reform was an integral part of my government's handling of the crisis. We had to get rid of all inflexibility in labour relations and make public support schemes more effective. No doubt those changes contributed positively to the fast recovery of growth and employment in Estonia. Entrepreneurs became less hesitant to hire people and to venture into new businesses.

That said, fiscal responsibility and avoidance of excessive regulatory burden remained the key building blocks of Estonia's public policy during the crisis: the government's policies were widely understood and supported by the Estonian public, including the younger generation. Otherwise there would have been calls for a new government, as was the case in many other countries.

It is important to note that the government was trusted by 38 per cent of Estonians in the spring of 2009, and by 53 per cent a year later, as measured by the Eurobarometer. Thus, the year when the crisis and the policy responses hit the country hardest actually saw increased trust in the government. My Reform Party, which had been leading the coalition during the crisis, won the parliamentary elections in March 2011 with the highest ever support. Surely this would not have happened, if our handling of the crisis had been too unbalanced.

How can reformers ensure that their reforms are sustainable once labour market performance improves?

I cannot see any serious danger of the reforms being reversed. Recent studies, for example the Eurofound survey, to which I have referred above (page 81), show that both employers and employees were generally satisfied with labour regulations.

In other words: reform governments can be re-elected. Indeed, my party has won two consecutive general elections after the labour market reforms had been implemented.

Which challenges do you consider most pressing for the development of the European and Estonian labour market in the near future?
Europe in general could become much more competitive and have less unemployment, if the current, unnecessary, inflexibility and fragmentation in the labour market were lowered and the various governments' support measures were better targeted, similar to my government's handling of the situation in Estonia. Against the background of the rapid development of new technologies and the digitalisation of industry and society as a whole, we also need to get more young people, especially women, interested in digital careers. We need to show them that such careers can be challenging and creative as well as rewarding and fun. This is essential for our economy, as businesses face a critical shortfall of talented IT experts.

Employment performance since 2000 has been very good and convergence towards the EU average per capita GDP has continued, nonetheless income inequality and poverty risk in Estonia remain well above the EU average. Does this reflect a deliberate social preference by Estonians for growth over redistribution, to which the politicians have responded?
Indeed, both the economy and employment had been steadily growing from 2000 to 2007–8. No doubt this was the reason behind the continuous reduction in inequality and poverty levels. At the beginning of this century, the Gini coefficient stood at 0.362, and the income quintile share ratio was 6.3. By 2007, they had decreased to 0.309 and 5.0, respectively. Both these levels were exactly equivalent to the EU average at the time. One can hardly find any other EU country where the inequality was actually decreasing in these years. The level of absolute poverty was 14.3 per cent in 2004, and it dropped to 4.7 per cent in 2008, mostly because of a considerable increase in old-age pensions.

The recent crisis has somewhat reversed those trends. The belief that education, growth and employment are the main instruments for fighting poverty is pretty widespread among the Estonian people, because many of them had lived through the Soviet era, when inefficient redistribution of the modest resources played an important role.

The labour market performance of ethnic non-Estonians is significantly worse than that of their Estonian fellow countrymen. Why has it proved so difficult to tackle this gap?
Those differences have gradually become smaller. Recent data show that unemployment rates for both Estonian-speaking Estonians and Russian-speaking Estonians are well below the EU average, although Estonian speakers are, indeed, less likely to be unemployed. The employment rates for men are now almost equal. The main reason behind the remaining differences is the inherited structure of the labour force: for example, former miners and workers who had been employed in factories which used to be part of the state industry have often had to learn completely new skills to be ready for a different type of employment. In addition, many have been able to make use of various targeted services provided by the Estonian Unemployment Insurance Fund.

3.2 A note on Estonian labour market performance over the past decade

The Estonian economy is one of the most volatile in the OECD area, even when it is compared with other small open economies.[39] This volatility is reflected in the boom–bust pattern of GDP growth since the mid-1990s, after Estonia embarked on its transition towards a market economy. This pattern has been particularly pronounced since 2000. Real GDP grew strongly until 2008, outstripping most of its competitors and leading to convergence towards the EU average of real GDP per capita (measured in purchasing power parities, PPPs). This period of rapid growth came to a shuddering halt in 2008, when the combined effects of the bursting of the domestic property bubble and the global financial and economic crisis hit the Estonian economy with a vengeance. Real GDP dropped by almost 20 per cent in 2008–9 – the largest decline experienced by any OECD economy.

Nominal wages and prices, however, adjusted quickly to this very large shock, helping to restore cost-competitiveness, which had deteriorated during the boom period. This, in turn, helped spur foreign demand for Estonian exports, sparking off a recovery in 2010, which was then gradually supported by strengthening domestic demand. Thus, the steep downturn was followed quickly by a sharp rebound in output, though growth slowed in 2013, when export growth weakened

---

39 OECD (2012b), Figure 1 highlights that both the range and standard deviation of GDP growth rates were particularly large in Estonia over the period 2000–11, compared with a sample of other OECD small open economies.

because of declining activity in the main foreign markets (Finland, Russia, the eurozone). The OECD attributes this strong recovery post-2009 to a combination of structural strengths in the economy: a flexible labour force, a regulatory system which is business-friendly, EU membership and a successful transition from the currency board to eurozone membership and sustained credibility of fiscal policy.[40] Nonetheless, it should be noted that real per capita GDP has still not recovered to its pre-crisis peak.

This roller-coaster pattern of output growth over the period since 2000 has been reflected on an almost one-to-one basis in labour market performance (see fig. 5), more so than in other EU economies.[41] We shall now look at the main features of labour market performance in Estonia since 2000.

Evolution of the employment and unemployment rates in Estonia, 1970–2014

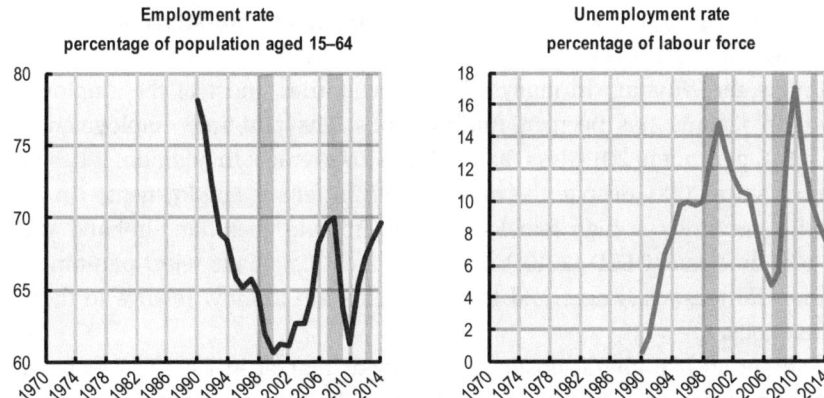

Note: Grey shaded areas refer to period of economic contraction (based on the output gap).
Source: OECD estimates based on the *OECD Labour Force Statistics, OECD Short-term Labour Market Statistics* and *OECD Economic Outlook Databases* (Cut-off date: 13 April 2015).

Figure 5: Labour market chart Estonia

---

40 Estonia adopted the euro as its currency on 1 January 2011. Previously, its currency (the kroon) had been pegged to the euro.
41 For example, OECD (2012b), p. 52 notes that the ratio of the drop in employment to the drop in real GDP in 2009 was 71 per cent in Estonia compared with an average of 43 per cent in the other EU economies.

3.2.1 The facts

In 2000, the total employment rate in Estonia was slightly below the EU average: 62.4 per cent compared with 63.5 per cent (see table 6), but the boom period up to 2008 witnessed very rapid rates of job creation in Estonia, which far outstripped those in most other EU countries. The net result was that, by 2007, the employment rate in Estonia was over 5 percentage points higher than the EU average. The employment rate then dropped sharply for the next three years, before beginning to recover in 2011. By 2013, it had rebounded to 71.3 per cent, still 1 percentage point below its pre-crisis peak but over 5 percentage points higher than the EU average.

This employment growth has benefited all labour force groups, but especially women and older workers. The female employment rate in 2013 was virtually identical to the pre-crisis peak and, at almost 69 per cent, was nearly 9 percentage points higher than the EU average. Older worker employment rates are significantly above the EU average for all five-year age groups shown in the table 6. The increases are particularly noteworthy for those aged over 60, e. g. the employment rate of those aged 65–9 was 27 per cent in 2013, nearly two-and-a-half times the EU average of 11.3 per cent.

Unlike the situation in many other EU countries, most of the employment growth in Estonia has been in full-time jobs. The part-time employment rate was only 8 per cent in 2013, less than half the EU average. In addition, it has hardly grown since 2000, despite the rapid growth in female employment – in many other EU countries, a high female employment rate goes hand-in-hand with a high part-time rate. OECD (2010f) notes that most Estonians reject part-time jobs for financial reasons: wages and fringe benefits are too low relative to those in full-time jobs.

Another special characteristic of the labour market in Estonia which sets it apart from most other EU countries is the very low temporary employment rate. It has hovered around the 3 per cent level in Estonia over the past decade, less than one-quarter of the EU average. It appears that employers in Estonia have little need for fixed-term contracts and find sufficient flexibility in hiring and firing decisions through the use of open-ended contracts. As will be seen below, this preference on the part of employers has in recent years been strengthened by changes to employment protection legislation (EPL) governing both permanent and temporary contracts.

The Estonian labour market is also characterised by a large share of ethnic non-Estonians, who are mainly ethnic Russians and who often have limited Estonian-language skills. They account for over 30 per cent of the total population and their employment rates are below those of their Estonian peers. Employment losses during the crisis also weighed more heavily on this group.

While, as noted above, the overall employment rate is relatively high in Estonia, it should be added that there is a relatively high rate of disability benefit (DB) recipients among the adult population aged 20–64. OECD (2012b) highlighted that the rate was the third highest in the OECD area in 2010 at almost 10 per cent, after Norway and Hungary. It also noted that the rate had risen since the crisis, arguing that disability benefits were fulfilling the role of a last-resort income support for those unemployed who were either not eligible for unemployment insurance or unemployment assistance benefits or who had exhausted their entitlements. At the same time, however, it has to be acknowledged that many recipients of disability benefits in Estonia are working, in contrast to the situation in most other OECD countries, and the average level of disability benefits is relatively low.[42]

When we turn to unemployment, the boom–bust pattern is clear cut. The harmonised unemployment rate dropped sharply during the boom period from 14.5 per cent in 2000 to a trough of 4.6 per cent in 2007. It then shot up to a peak of 16.7 per cent in 2010, before falling back as GDP rebounded. Since then, the unemployment rate has dropped significantly to 7.4 per cent in September 2014, well below the EU28 average of 10 per cent (both figures are seasonally adjusted). Even though it is still above its pre-crisis trough, this large drop of over 9 percentage points in such a short period is a remarkable achievement, and it has no parallel among other OECD economies in the post-2009 period.

During the boom period, Estonia recorded a sharp drop in youth unemployment: the rate more than halved between 2000 and 2007, from over 22 per cent to just under 10 per cent, well below the EU average of over 15 per cent. The rate then jumped sharply to nearly 22 per cent in 2011, before dropping back, in line with the rapid improvement in labour demand. By July 2014, the youth rate was down to 12.7 per cent, 9 percentage points below the EU average of 21.7 per cent (both figures are seasonally adjusted).

It is worth noting that, in the immediate aftermath of the crisis, OECD (2011c) expressed serious concern that Estonia was facing a high risk of a large increase in structural unemployment. It based its concern on two features of the unemployment response to the crisis: first, the very large hike in unemployment and secondly, the jump in the incidence of long-term unemployment. The latter rose from 49.8 per cent in 2007 to almost 57 per cent in 2011. The strong recovery in job prospects

---

42 See OECD (2010g), Figure 2.1 for evidence that Estonia had the third-highest employment rate among the disabled in the late 2000s of the 29 countries for which comparable data were available. One explanation for this is that disability benefits in Estonia, unlike in most other OECD countries, are not affected by the receipt of any income earned through work. In this way, disability benefits in Estonia operate like an in-work benefit with a zero withdrawal rate as wages are earned.

in recent years, however, has made significant inroads into the amount of long-term unemployment in Estonia. The result is that the incidence of long-term unemployment in 2013, at 44.5 per cent, was below its level in 2000, a year when the total unemployment rate was almost twice its current level. More recent OECD surveys of Estonia have acknowledged the strong labour market recovery and express less concern about the likelihood of a significant hike in structural unemployment.

Instead, OECD (2012b) highlighted the relatively high tax wedge on labour in Estonia, which weighs particularly heavily on low-wage workers. Not only does this harm their employment prospects, but it is also possibly a reason for the emigration of high-skilled workers from Estonia. The OECD has also called for greater activation of unemployment benefit recipients through a more effective public employment service (PES) and greater investment in more cost-effective active labour market policies (ALMPs).

Finally, income inequality in Estonia, as measured by the Gini coefficient, was above the EU27 average in 2013: 0.329 compared with 0.305.[43] It declined significantly during the boom period, but has widened slightly during the post-crisis period. Nonetheless, the level of inequality is currently less than it was in the early 2000s. The relative poverty rate, measured at 60 per cent of median income adjusted for household size after taxes and transfers, stood at just over 20 per cent of the population in 2011, slightly down on its level in 2004.

The tax/transfer system in Estonia plays a relatively modest redistributive role, which is unlike the situation in many other EU countries. This reflects both a relatively low public social spending effort (as a percentage of GDP) and the structure of the tax system – Estonia has a flat-rate income tax set at a relatively moderate rate of 21 per cent. The unemployment benefit system is not particularly generous by EU standards. The net benefit replacement rates shown in Estonia's scoreboard are always significantly below the corresponding EU averages.

In sum, the Estonian labour market has experienced a roller-coaster ride since 2000, but its performance in terms of both employment and unemployment rates has been significantly better than the EU average. This good labour market performance has gone hand-in-hand with a somewhat less favourable record on the income inequality and poverty fronts. We now turn to the major labour market and social policy reforms over the same period to see to what extent they have contributed to these outcomes.

---

43 These Gini values are based on the EU SILC and relate to the equivalised disposable income for the total population. The OECD's income distribution data base shows slightly different values for the same concept but identical trends over the period since 2004.

3.2.2 Major labour market and social policy reforms since 2000
Employment Protection Legislation (EPL)

A major reform of EPL was undertaken in mid-2009 during the financial crisis. The aim was to make it easier for employers to hire and fire workers on permanent contracts. As noted in Estonia's scoreboard, EPL for permanent workers in Estonia in 2007, as measured by the OECD's indicators, was significantly stronger than the EU or OECD average. Reforming EPL had been a continuous topic of debate between the social partners for almost a decade leading up to the crisis, which served as a catalyst to break the logjam, and a joint deal was struck around a new flexicurity package: the EPL reform was designed to increase labour market flexibility, while the security part was to be delivered by increased generosity of unemployment benefits. The latter part of the package was, however, postponed until 2013, to be dealt with as part of the large fiscal consolidation effort implemented by the authorities in an attempt to stem the growing public debt and to maintain credibility in the eyes of the international financial markets.

The EPL reform relaxed several key elements in the regulations governing permanent contracts. Notice periods were reduced, the possibilities for dismissed workers to be re-employed by their former employers, or compensated in lieu, were constrained and severance pay was cut significantly.[44] At the same time, the regulations governing temporary contracts were also liberalised: the range of tasks for which fixed-term contracts were acceptable was widened and temporary work agencies were allowed to operate as providers of labour services.

The scoreboard shows that the net effect of these changes to the law governing permanent contracts led to a significant drop in the OECD indicator from 2.7, based on the pre-2009 legislation, to 1.8 under the new regulations. There was a further reform to the EPL governing temporary contracts in mid-2012, which aimed to protect the rights of temporary agency workers. In particular, it aligned the rights of temporary agency workers for conversion of their contract to that of a permanent contract with those of ordinary fixed-term contracts. The scoreboard shows that this change in 2012 increased the OECD indicator for the strictness of EPL for temporary workers from 1.9 to 3.0 in 2013.

While there are no rigorous evaluations of the impact of these EPL changes on the Estonian labour market, it is plausible that they contributed to the high volatility in Estonian employment during the period of 2009 to 2012. Job destruction rates were extremely high and occurred quickly in the first two years of the crisis,

---

44 The amount of severance pay to be paid by the employer was cut and part of the remainder was to be paid by the new Unemployment Insurance Fund (UIF), which was created at the same time by a merger of the UI fund with the PES.

but once labour demand picked up in 2010, Estonian firms began to hire rapidly again. Employment growth has continued at a healthy pace and the vast bulk of the new jobs have been permanent ones.

Reform of the UI/UA system and the PES

It was noted above that the 2009 social partner agreement envisaged strengthening the social safety net in Estonia by making the UI (unemployment insurance) and UA (unemployment assistance) benefits more generous and enabling the PES to activate the unemployed into jobs. The increase in benefit levels was postponed for several years, but it did come into effect finally, as can be seen from the scoreboard, which shows higher net replacement rates for 2013, especially for the long-term unemployed.

The PES was merged with the UI fund in 2009 to create a new agency, which integrated benefit claims and re-employment services and enabled more effective activation of the unemployed, drawing on best practice from other OECD countries. Before the crisis, Estonia had spent very little on the PES and ALMPs, as the scoreboard shows. The crisis led to a significant increase in ALMP spending, most of which in the first instance went on wage subsidy measures. As employment growth recovered, spending on wage subsidies was scaled back significantly and spending on training was expanded in its place.[45]

PES resources were increased, in order to deal with the large increases in client numbers in the immediate aftermath of the crisis, and attempts were made to better target the limited staff resources at the more at-risk clients. In addition, the PES office network was modernised and greater use was made of IT, in order to free up resources for job-broking and counselling. Since 2009–10, PES staff caseloads have fallen back significantly, in line with the sharp decline in unemployment and with the expansion and restructuring of the service.[46]

Despite the increased resources devoted to activation in recent years, the intensity of the activation effort in Estonia still remains well below that in many other EU countries. One could argue that this is not unreasonable, given that the Estonian benefit system is relatively ungenerous by EU standards, so that con-

---

45 See Lauringson et al. (2011) for some evaluation evidence showing positive employment and earnings outcomes for participants in training programmes in Estonia.
46 Information supplied by the Estonian authorities to the OECD in late 2013 showed that the caseload in job-broking fell from around 400 on average in 2009–10 to around 210 in 2012–13; for case managers working with more hard-to-place clients, the caseload dropped from around 230 in 2009–10 to under 130 in 2012–13.

cerns about maintaining work incentives for the unemployed by relying upon strong activation are less warranted.[47]

Two caveats are in order here. First, inequality is above average in Estonia and the risk of relative poverty is high. This is partly because of the lack of benefit generosity and may well, of course, reflect the revealed social preference of the Estonian population, which seems to place a high premium on individual responsibility and work ethic. Still, if reducing inequality and poverty were to be assigned a higher priority in the future, one obvious way to achieve these goals would be through an expanded social safety net. In order to offset the potential disincentive impact of such a policy shift, however, it would be necessary for Estonia to design and implement a more effective activation system than the one currently in place.

Secondly, we highlighted above the large number of working-age adults drawing disability benefits and the risk that these benefits represent last-resort income support. Nowadays, this problem is less severe than in many other countries, notably in the Nordic countries, because so many of the disabled are working in Estonia. Nevertheless, there is, as OECD (2010g) emphasises, effectively no rehabilitation or activation of disability benefit recipients in Estonia. A further build-up in the numbers of recipients could pose a major challenge to Estonian policymakers in the future, as population ageing takes hold and there is a need to maintain the working-age population in order to sustain growth.

Family benefits

Family benefits consisting of child benefits, maternity and parental benefits and generous tax breaks are the one main type of social spending where Estonia matches the EU and OECD average expenditure as a percent of GDP. They have universal coverage and, unusually, are not means-tested. The aim of these policies is to boost the fertility rate and female labour force participation.

In order to achieve these aims, Estonia introduced one of the OECD's most generous parental-benefit schemes in 2004; the scheme's generosity was further extended in 2006 and 2008. The total length of maternity and parental leave can stretch to a period of up to 136 weeks in some cases and the replacement rates are extremely generous – from 100 per cent to up to three times the average wage.

Judged on the face of it, these very generous family benefits appear to have achieved their objectives. The fertility rate rose significantly from 1.3 in 2004 to 1.7 in

---

47 In addition to the relatively low levels of UI and UA benefits, eligibility conditions for entitlements to these benefits are relatively strict compared with other EU countries. For details, see Venn (2012) and Vork (2009).

2008–10 before dropping back slightly to 1.6 in 2011–12; the female participation rate rose from 63 per cent in 2004 to almost 69 per cent in 2013, despite the effects of the crisis. In the absence of hard evidence, based on proper evaluation, it is difficult to attribute all of these increases to the family benefits scheme, since other factors influence family formation and labour force participation decisions. Nonetheless, it is difficult to rule out generous family benefits as one determinant of these favourable outcomes, given the timing of the introduction of the various schemes.

OECD (2012b) argues that the existing scheme is not as cost-effective as it could be, given its heavy reliance on cash benefits, as opposed to provision of public childcare. Estonia spends relatively little on public childcare and the OECD recommends reducing the generosity of the parental benefit, in order to expand the number of public childcare places. It claims that this switch would help boost female labour force participation and strengthen child development.

Pensions

Following the transition to a market economy in the 1990s, it became apparent that the pension system inherited from the Soviet period was no longer fit for purpose. Legislation was introduced in 1998, 2002 and 2004 which established a three-pillar system that is being gradually phased in. For the moment, pension payments are still strongly dominated by the first pillar, but the institutional foundations have been laid for fully funded second and third pillars.

As a hangover from the Soviet era, workers in several occupations can retire early and on more generous pensions.[48] The statutory retirement age is 63 for men and it will rise to the same age for women by 2016. This is below the median retirement age of 65 in OECD countries, but can be explained by the relatively low life expectancy in Estonia, especially for men. The system offers a bonus of 10.8 per cent per year for deferring the pension beyond age 63, while there is a penalty of 4.8 per cent per year, if the pension is taken out at age 60. It is noticeable that very few pensioners take up the deferral option, whereas almost half of new pensioners opt for an early pension despite the penalty.[49]

The second pillar is a compulsory defined-contribution system. Since 2002, all new labour force entrants are enrolled in private funds chosen by the worker. Capital accumulation under the second pillar was partly suspended from 2009 to 2011, with those contributions being diverted to the first pillar as part of the fiscal consolidation

---

48 OECD (2010f) noted that early retirement applied to 18 per cent of the pensioners in 2009.
49 Praxis (2011) calculated that the penalty for early retirement would need to be increased to 5–7 per cent per year in order to ensure actuarial neutrality.

effort. There is a concern that returns in the second pillar are too low because the operating costs of the private funds are too high.[50] The voluntary third pillar consists of tax incentives for individual saving plans.

As noted above, older worker employment rates are relatively high in Estonia and have continued to rise throughout the crisis. It seems likely that the pension reforms have contributed to this favourable outcome, though, once again, in the absence of concrete evidence, it is impossible to quantify the magnitude of this effect.

3.2.3 Conclusion

Estonia is a very small, open economy, which is subject to very high volatility in output and employment. Nonetheless, it has achieved a significant recovery from the steepest downturn in the OECD area in 2008–9, with employment growing and unemployment having fallen to well below the EU average. Convergence towards real living standards in the EU is continuing, even if the gap is still large. The excellent performance reflects several structural features of the Estonian economy which have been strengthened by reforms to labour and social policies since 2000. The risks posed by high inequality and poverty, however, remain major challenges for Estonia, as does the need to maintain the size of the working population in the face of a serious ageing problem.

Table 6: Scoreboard for labour market outcomes and policies, Estonia and EU, 1993–2013

	1993		2000		2007		2013*	
	EE	EU	**EE**	EU	**EE**	EU	**EE**	EU
1. Employment rate (% of the working-age population)	**70.4**	61.2	**62.4**	63.6	**72.3**	66.7	**71.3**	65.9
– male	**77.4**	71.8	**65.8**	72.9	**75.7**	74.2	**73.8**	71.6
– female	**64.1**	50.7	**59.2**	54.4	**69.1**	59.2	**68.9**	60.2
– youth (aged 15/16–24)	**45.0**	39.5	**34.9**	39.4	**34.6**	38.2	**33.4**	33.4
– older people (aged 55–9)	**55.2**	47.6	**54.8**	50.6	**74.2**	57.3	**73.7**	64.9
– older people (aged 60–4)	**30.6**	22.3	**31.7**	22.3	**39.6**	29.4	**50.6**	34.7
– older people (aged 65–69)	**20.7**	9.2	**16.9**	7.4	**26.2**	9.5	**27.0**	11.3
2. Unemployment rate (% of labour force)	**6.5**	10.8	**14.5**	8.9	**4.6**	7.1	**10.0**	10.7
– youth (aged 15/16–24)	**10.9**	21.0	**22.2**	17.4	**9.9**	15.5	**17.9**	23.3

---

50 OECD Global Pension Statistics data for 2012 show that the operating costs of the Estonian funds, as a percentage of their assets, were the third highest among the countries for which comparable data are available.

Table 6 (continued)

| | 1993 | | 2000 | | 2007 | | 2013* | |
	EE	EU	EE	EU	EE	EU	EE	EU
3. Incidence of long-term unemployment (% of total unemployment) (a)	31.8	42.0	45.1	44.4	49.8	41.6	44.5	46.5
4. Part-time employment rate (b)	n/a	13.8	7.2	15.3	6.8	16.0	8.0	17.7
5. Temporary employment rate (c) (temporary employees as % of total employees)	n/a	10.5	2.7	13.1	2.1	14.8	3.5	14.0
– youth (aged 15/16–24 as % of total youth employees)	n/a	28.8	7.9	38.0	6.6	41.8	12.3	43.0
6. Low-pay incidence (d) (% of employees)	–	–	28.3	15.7	24.7	16.5	n.a.	15.0
7. Protection of permanent workers against individual dismissal	n/a	2.6	n/a	2.5	2.7	2.4	1.8	2.2
– Protection of temporary workers	n/a	2.3	n/a	1.8	1.9	1.8	3.0	1.8
8. Public spending on labour market policies (% of GDP)	n/a	2.9	n/a	2.0	0.2	1.6	0.7	2.0
– Spending on active measures (e)	n/a	0.9	n/a	0.9	0.1	0.6	0.3	0.8
– Spending on passive measures (f)	n/a	2.1	n/a	1.1	0.1	0.9	0.4	1.2
9. Net benefit replacement rate (g) (averaged over four family types and two earnings levels)	n/a	n/a	n/a	65	36	61	44	54
– initial spell (h)	n/a	n/a	n/a	70	58	70	59	70
– after 2 years of unemployment	n/a	n/a	n/a	66	33	63	41	57

* 2013 or latest available year. 2002 for data on temporary work and low-pay incidence. Data for the latter for 2007 relate to 2006. EPL data for 2007 relate to 2008.
(a) Persons out of work for 12 months and over.
(b) Part-time employment refers to persons who usually work less than 30 hours per week in "their 'main job'".
(c) Temporary employees are wage and salary workers whose job has a pre-determined end date as opposed to permanent employees whose job is of unlimited duration. National definitions broadly conform to this generic definition, but may vary depending on national circumstances.
(d) Persons with a wage less than 2/3 of the median.
(e) 'Active' measures cover categories 1 to 7 of the OECD/Eurostat database on public spending on labour market programmes
(f) 'Passive' measures cover categories 8 and 9 of the OECD/Eurostat database on public spending on labour market programmes
(g) Data on net replacement rates for 2000 refer to 2001. EU average refers to the median replacement rate.

(h) Initial phase of unemployment but following any waiting period. For married couples, the percentage of AW relates to the previous earnings of the 'unemployed' spouse only; the second spouse is assumed to be 'inactive' with no earnings and no recent employment history. Where receipt of social assistance or other minimum-income benefits is subject to activity tests (such as active job-search or 'being available' for work), these requriements are assumed to be met. Children are aged four and six and neither childcare benefits nor childcare costs are considered. Unweighted averages, for previous full-time earnings levels of 67 % and 100 % of AW and out-of-work single and couple households with no children or with two children (children are assumed to be aged four and six and neither childcare benefits nor childcare costs are considered). After tax and including unemployment and family benefits. Social assistance and other means-tested benefits are assumed to be available subject to relevant income conditions. Housing costs are assumed equal to 20 % of AW.

Sources: OECD Online Employment Database: www.oecd.org/employment/database; data on net replacement rates come from the OECD tax-benefit models (www.oecd.org/els/social/work-incentives).

4 France

4.1 Interview with François Fillon, 27 January 2014

'I have always been of the conviction that the French are much more reasonable with regard to reforms than those who are governing them.'

Looking back at your tenure as Prime Minister of France from 2007 to 2012, and maybe also at your role as French Minister of Labour and Social Affairs from 2002 to 2005, could you give us an assessment of your attempts at reform, in terms of what you think went well and what you think was difficult, or impossible, to achieve at the time?
Let me start by highlighting that France is a country with a very rigid labour market that has accumulated stronger and stronger protections for employees over the last 30 years. This hoarding of protective measures has resulted in a veritable wall against which those who want to enter the labour market have to bash their heads. To put it another way, our labour market offers great protection for those who are already inside, but is almost inaccessible for those outside.

Faced with this situation, what we mainly tried to do, or what I tried to do as Minister of Labour and Social Affairs, and then as Prime Minister, was to relaunch a social dialogue in France. We wanted to normalise the debate between the collective bargaining parties, in the way other European countries operate. France does, after all, have a very weak and conflict-based tradition of social dialogue. When I became Minister of Labour and Social Affairs, the number, and even existence, of trade unions had been fixed by decree after World War II – and not through elections – and it was more or less impossible to create new trade unions or to merge them. Successive governments put mechanisms in place to bypass the trade unions. This means, for example, that it was possible to come to a general agreement with the consent of only a minority of trade union organisations. In a company like Renault, for instance, you might have had a dialogue about a social problem and there were five trade unions around the table. One represented the majority, the Confédération générale du travail (CGT), another trade union, almost as powerful, was the Confédération française démocratique du travail (CFDT), and then there was a very small trade union, the Confédération française des travailleurs chrétiens (CFTC). At that time, if you managed to sign the agreement with the CFTC, it was valid for the entire company.

What we did to remedy this situation was that we broke the decree that had laid down the fixed list of trade unions. As a result, we now have trade union organisations whose role and power are linked to the results they achieve in professional elections within companies – a complete novelty. Beforehand, the hierarchy of trade unions was fixed for all time; it was as if we had decided that the political parties of the 21st century had to be the same as those of the 20th century.

We also got rid of a rule requiring that any agreement reached by the trade unions had to be more advantageous for union members than previously existing national agreements and legislation. Instead, we introduced a regulation stipulating that agreements have to be backed by a majority, meaning that they either have to be signed by a majority of trade unions or by a trade union that represents a majority of employees. These are very profound reforms, which have not had immediate results, because the culture and habits have to change as well. If we had not, however, removed that particular obstacle, I do not think it would have been possible to make any changes in France.

In addition, to give a certain substance and gravitas to the social dialogue, we brought in a new rule requiring the government to discuss any reform proposals in the social field with the collective bargaining parties before introducing legislation. This, by the way, continues to be not without difficulties. If, for example, the government wants to take very radical measures with regard to working hours and wants to act quickly, it is now bound to put the subject on the table first and discuss it with the collective bargaining parties. In the long run, however, I think it is a very good measure.

The other main thing we did, in addition to relaunching the social dialogue in France, was to modify French labour laws in 2008. I think we have the most complex labour laws in the world, certainly in Europe – there were thousands of pages of labour legislation – a nightmare. We tried to tackle the rigidity of it all, in part by approaching it 'sideways' rather than 'face on'. We introduced, for example, what we called the *rupture conventionelle*, an amicable way to terminate a contract. This was a completely new approach, because previously, if you wanted to end a contract in France, you had to dismiss a member of staff and enter into sometimes contentious negotiations, even if the employee had already agreed to leave. The new measure works quite well and is used frequently.

Given the rigidity of the legislation, however, what we have introduced is very modest compared with what we would have liked to introduce and what we would still like to do, namely reduce the sheer volume of labour legislation. As a matter of fact, the labour code is so complex that even companies that are quite powerful in terms of their legal resources get it wrong time and again. When they are up before a tribunal, employers almost always lose because of a procedural error, not because there is a genuine legal issue. Tribunals in France tend to create even tighter, more binding and more rigid laws than those already in the labour code.

In hindsight, is there anything you wish you had done differently?

In this respect, I would point to my government's intention to introduce a single employment contract, the *contrat unique*, in 2007 and 2008. This was supposed to reduce the strong duality typical for the French labour market and is a consequence of the existence of two kinds of contracts, namely the *contrat de durée indéterminée* (CDI) and the *contrat de durée déterminée* (CDD). Actually, introducing a single employment contract was one of the promises we made in the 2007 election campaign. We did not, however, achieve this in the end. We started discussions with trade unions to see how we could make it happen, but we quickly realised that, unless we engaged in a very hard power struggle, we would have ended up with a single contract effectively replacing the CDD, and that was not our goal. The aim was to relax the conditions of the permanent contract, to make the rules of employment and, most of all, those governing the dismissal of staff less complex. In the end, aware of the risks, we preferred not taking any action at all.

Perhaps we were not courageous enough. You have to understand that in 2008 we were getting to grips with the financial crisis, and we felt that this was not really the right time to introduce important social reforms. In a way, I also think we did not work hard enough to conceptualise the reform before we tried to launch it. We knew that we wanted a single contract – but the issue is not knowing *that* you want a single contract, it is knowing *what* you want to put into the single contract. We should have introduced this reform later on, say in 2010 or 2011, but by then we were approaching the presidential election. Introduction of a single contract is, however, a subject that needs to be tackled in the foreseeable future.

Another reform, which in retrospect I think we should have launched differently, is the *revenue de solidarité active*, the so-called RSA, which we created in 2009. In 2001 already, the then government had introduced a refundable, in-work tax credit, the *prime pour l'emploi* (PPE), for low-income households. It was introduced to make sure that people in work were better off than those on social benefits, i.e. to establish a difference between social assistance and salaries. The problem is that, in 2009, under President Sarkozy, we introduced the RSA in addition to the PPE. What we should have done, when introducing the top-up on low labour earnings, was to abolish the PPE, but we did not dare to do it, because we were afraid that too many people would lose out as a result. Looking back, I think we did not solve the problem of low earnings being too close to social benefits. In fact, I believe the situation has become worse – but that is how it is.

The process leading up to the RSA was remarkable. At the time, President Sarkozy wanted to open up his government to the Left in order to get broader support. Consequently, we appealed to the highly intelligent, but very left-wing Martin Hirsch, President of Emmaüs France, a powerful solidarity movement that looks after homeless people. Mr Hirsch agreed: 'I'll be willing to join you, but on condition that I help implement the RSA.' To be honest, we 'bought' left-wing support in exchange for a reform that we did not want to see enacted in that way. The RSA was supposed to prompt people to return to their jobs. Eventually, however, the reform led to an increase of social spending and has therefore been a failure.

This, too, is an area where future governments need to pursue reforms. I have some ideas on this issue, which I would like to share with you. First, we must modify unemployment benefits. These benefits are very high in France and people are entitled to them for quite a long time – two years. Oddly, many people consider this period a given right: you go on unemployment for two years and the need to start looking for work arises only after this time. My suggestion would therefore be to cut unemployment benefits.

My second idea is to link unemployment benefits with professional training for people who are unemployed for a reasonably long time. That means that we need to force the long-term unemployed to accept professional training, and if they do not agree, they will no longer receive benefits.

The third proposal would be to link aid for those with no income, for people who are really in dire straits, to undertaking a minimum number of hours of community service, which would turn granting these benefits into a sort of 'give and take'.

As to your question whether I wish I had done some things differently, I think in 2010 we should have decided on a legal retirement age of 65 instead of 62 only – that is for sure. I do not think there would have been a single additional demonstrator on the streets. President Sarkozy, however, was not tough enough, despite what you might have heard. A lot of people think of him as very hard, but I believe that he was quite consensual, and he was worried about his re-election. The problem is that Sarkozy, in his role as President, was inexperienced in dealing with the trade unions. He held discussions with union leaders in the way one would with political partners – he believed that he could 'score points' against them. As a lawyer, he thought that he would be able to persuade them by force of character, but experience shows that syndicalism just does not work like that. It is not about personalities, but it is essential to consider serious sociological factors. In the end, we did not raise the retirement age to 65, which I regret now.

What is your general assessment of the two big pension reforms you embarked on, first as Minister of Labour and Social Affairs, in 2003, and then as Prime Minister, in 2010?
One of the objectives of the first reform was to match the contribution period of civil servants to that in the private sector, because before 2003, a civil servant could retire after making contributions for 37.5 years, whereas a private-sector employee needed 40. We aligned these two periods and, very importantly, introduced a mechanism that the contribution period would automatically increase with rising life expectancy – starting with an increase to 41 years of contributions.

In 2010, we reformed several special retirement arrangements in the public sector, such as that for railway workers and police officers, among others. At the time, a railway worker, for example, was entitled to retire at 50. My government felt that these public sector groups should share the burden of all French pensioners. However, we could obviously not raise their retirement age from 50 to 60, or to 62. Instead, we raised it by exactly the same number of years as we had done for other groups. Since we moved the contribution period from 37.5 years to 40 years for civil servants, i.e. by 2.5 years, we raised the retirement age for this group by 2.5 years, from 50 to 52.5. To be honest, it was not really a spectacular reform, but the President of the Republic wanted to avoid confrontation at that time, because he was very afraid of a conflict.

As I mentioned earlier, in 2010 we raised the minimum legal retirement age from 60 to 62. It is a matter of public knowledge, not to say 'notoriety', that I fought for 65 and Nicolas Sarkozy cut it off at 62, because he did not want to create a public drama. As I said, I think that we will be forced to move towards 65. There are still a lot of things to do regarding retirement in France. We have yet to harmonise the public and private sectors completely, as there are still differences, most notably in the manner of calculating the level of pension payments. In the private sector it is based on the average of the 25 highest paid years, while in the public sector it is the average of the last six months in work. This is an important point and, at the same time, a tricky one. It is difficult to decide whether we should place everyone at the same level, because some groups of civil servants receive bonuses, which are not part of their salary, with the result that their pensionable salary is, in effect, less than their real income. As soon as we place everyone at the same level, we have to reintegrate bonuses into salaries, resulting in a considerable salary increase in the civil service, which is something that definitely needs to be taken into account when these matters are further considered.

Sometimes I wonder whether, in 2003, instead of simply improving the pension system by means of distribution, for example changing the cost of the pension scheme by adding years of contribution before payments are made, we should have put in place a comprehensive reform, a points-based retirement system which would have been the same for everyone – public and private – by introducing a larger proportion of capitalisation into the system, roughly like the Swedes have done it. This, too, is something I regret from time to time. But then again, I often ask myself: 'Would it have been possible, given the departure point, to go that far?' I do not think so, because the French pension system consists of a multitude of pension arrangements. We would have had to abolish all supplementary arrangements and merged them into one. The supplementary arrangements are managed by the trade unions, which is a real problem, because it is one of the major sources of income for them. The interesting thing is that the trade unions fight to stop the general pension system from increasing the contribution periods, but when they need to balance their own systems, they do not hesitate to do so.

Could you describe the groundwork your government undertook to pave the way for the pension reforms, to create a climate in favour of reforms with important stakeholders?
In 2000, the then government established a forum to which all relevant stakeholders were summoned to discuss the country's future pension reforms. The *Conseil d'orientation des retraites* allows us, every year, to take a clear and independent view on the current pension arrangements. This mechanism is very important in France, because there is a total lack of faith in political debates. You have people who explain to you that this country has no pension problems whatsoever, that it rather is the companies not making sufficient contributions to the pension schemes. There really is a huge capacity out there to obscure reality. I remember that in the debates I organised before the introduction of the pension reform in 2003, there were some extremely left-wing economists who explained to me that there was no problem in France with financing pensions, that it was all made up by the bosses of big companies. The *Conseil d'orientation des retraites* is made up of totally independent people: there are trade union representatives on it, as well as managers of pension funds, which makes it a forum that is respected by everyone. Nobody contests the annual reports made by the *Conseil*. It is an extremely helpful platform to establish a broad consensus.

In my capacity as Minister of Labour and Social Affairs I organised debates with the French trade unions over a six-month period. I also took trade union members with me on trips to other European countries, such as Germany, Finland, Sweden and Spain to enable them to learn from best practice abroad. I think that the trade unions were all astonished that pension reforms had taken place consensually elsewhere, while France was the only country where there had been perpetual conflict. In this respect, I remember in particular the representative from Force Ouvrière (FO), who had been persuaded by the harmonious climate in other countries, particularly in Germany, Finland and Sweden. In the end, when we spoke after our return to Paris, he said to me: 'It's what we ought to do, but we'll never manage it.'

I think adopting these measures made it possible, for the first time, to have the support of a major trade union in a matter concerning pension reform. I am referring to the CFDT's backing of the 2003 reform – they signed an agreement with us, which was quite spectacular; something like this was unprecedented in the area of French pension reforms. Unfortunately, the experience remained unique. As all other trade unions considered the CFDT a traitor and the union lost many of its members because it had backed our reform, it abstained from lending us its support in subsequent reform endeavours in 2008 and 2010. I will always remember the day we signed the final agreement with the CFDT. The then CFDT representative, François Chérèque, looked at me and said: 'Bon, maintenant, il faut que je me procure des gardes du corps.' ['Well, now I'd better get some body guards.'] This gives you quite a good idea of the violence that accompanies social debates in France.

As for the French Left, they played a despicable role in my view. The Socialists had opposed all pension reforms until 2014, when, for the first time in their history, they finally voted for one. In 1993, when Édouard Balladur raised the salary contribution period to 40 years, the Left took to the streets; in 2003, they opposed the reform with all their strength and obstructed me in parliament for more than three weeks. I stayed three weeks in parliament, night and day, defending the reform. In 2010, they started again. Compared to the situation in other European countries, there is no social and no political consensus in France. There is a lot of violence in the political confrontation regarding the issue of pension reforms. Will that change in the foreseeable future? Maybe – one does get a sense that the issue of pensions has become a little less contentious recently in France.

Could you tell us, in general terms, about your government's collaboration with the French trade unions, especially given your intention to relaunch social dialogue?
Collaborating with the unions has proved quite difficult in France. The French trade unions are small organisations, with very few members, among which the number of civil servants is very influential. I think, the Force Ouvrière

(FO), for example, has more members in the public sector than in the private, with the result that they are completely intransigent when it comes to cutting benefits for the public sector.

Let me highlight this with a short anecdote: in 2003, the then leader of FO told me: 'You can't touch civil servants' pensions because they have a contract for life.' When French civil servants are hired aged 20 or 25, they sign a contract – with society, as they see it – that lasts until their death. Moreover, in this contract, there is supposed to be no financial difference between the time of service and the time of retirement. As a result, FO, which is a moderate trade union, by the way, refused to sign the 2003 pension agreement with us and participated in the demonstrations. I have a very vivid memory of one episode, in June, I think, when there was a large demonstration in Marseille and the supposedly moderate leader of FO appealed for a general strike. A general strike – to paralyse the entire country. Even the CGT realised that this was a little excessive. Eventually, a general strike was prevented, the reform was passed by parliament in July, and the leader of the FO wanted to see me. I kept him on hold a little and waited until the end of September before receiving him, because I was still a bit angry. When I eventually saw him, he said: 'You're angry!' to which I replied: 'Well, yes, because a general strike is a bit excessive, don't you think? That wasn't reasonable.' He looked at me, smiled, and said: 'But you didn't listen properly. I appealed for a general strike, but not an unlimited one.'

This episode casts light on a general problem in France. What had made governments pull back in the past was the threat of obstruction to public services, for example the one-week strike by the railways, the shut-down of the Paris Métro for a week and school closures – events always reached a point where the government was obliged to back down.

Having said that, French governments need to quash the idea that it is impossible to have an agreement with the trade unions. During the five-year presidential period of Nicolas Sarkozy, we never had any labour disputes leading to stoppages. We managed to reach a great number of agreements with the trade unions on professional training and on the termination of employment contracts, among others. Moreover, under President Sarkozy, we introduced a reform requiring public service providers in education and in transportation, for example, to guarantee a minimum of service at any time. Public transport, for instance, is therefore legally forbidden to block the railways during a strike. Thus, while we are still far from the culture of social dialogue that exists in Northern Europe, I think we are heading in the right direction. There is a slow, but very real, modernisation of social dialogue in France.

In your reform activities, were you able to rely on a general consensus in the cabinet or in the government, maybe in particular between the government and the President?

In 2003, everyone thought that reform was impossible in France. Most French believed that I was going to get the sack, that there would be huge demonstrations and that the reform agenda would be ditched. Jacques Chirac, the then President of the Republic, never got involved in the 2003 pension reform discussions and never gave me the slightest public support, not ever! He waited to see whether everything that my government department aimed for would happen, and if things had taken a turn for the worse, he would have changed the Minister of Labour and Social Affairs. While the Prime Minister of the time, Jean-Pierre Raffarin, gave me plenty of support, a majority of members of the government thought at that time that we were going to fall flat on our faces and that we were headed for defeat.

Between 2007 and 2012, when I was Prime Minister, the difficulties came from President Sarkozy, who, after having announced that there were going to be some profound changes, in reality did not support any substantial change. In my view, there were two reasons for this. The main reason was, I think, that he was really afraid strong opposition forces would develop in French society. He was frightened of all sorts of public protest. The second reason was that he was a man who always wanted to do everything himself, on his own. He would, for example, speak directly to the trade unions, bypassing the Prime Minister and the government. I think this was a very bad course of action, because when the President of the Republic holds direct talks with the unions, there is no exit route – no way to escalate. Once the talks have taken place, you are stuck with the result! Whereas if a minister conducts the talks, he or she can be overruled by the Prime Minister, and if it is the Prime Minster, he can be overruled by the President. President Sarkozy, however, did not understand that.

In general, one has to understand that political change and reforms are issues which are incredibly ideologically charged in France. The first thing the Socialists did when they came into office in 2012 was to water down the pension reform by deciding that everyone who had started working at 18 could retire at 60. This, obviously, resulted in a contribution increase both for companies and employees to ensure that the pension system was financially secure. Later, they carried out a slightly different reform by increasing the duration of contribution periods, but in France there is still a general idea that social progress means working less and less. This idea is very strong on the Left and, of course, with the trade unions, but it is also found occasionally on the Right. It is very difficult to argue against this notion. In the last 200 years, the number of working hours per week went down from 60 to 50, 40, 37 and 35.

In my view, this attitude is outdated. As for the general public, I have always been convinced that the French are much more reasonable with regard to reforms than those who are governing them. I mean that most politicians in France still think that change inevitably causes violent opposition, but they do not realise that society has changed and that people have thought deeply about things. Concerning pensions, for example, there are a lot of people who now realise that they do have to work longer, that there is no alternative. As far as labour laws go, the same applies: the 35-hour week, for example, we never touched that. I may be wrong, but I think that the French population is more mature regarding these subjects than the politicians, who have developed reflexes based on past experiences. One of the reasons may be that French politicians have very long careers and very little experience of life outside politics, which makes them isolated from the real world.

As for your question about the collaboration of different government institutions, I would like to highlight another quite problematic feature of the French political system. The head of government is the Prime Minister, who directs the country's policy. The difficulty is that the election of the President of the Republic is conducted on the principle of universal suffrage, which gives him stronger legitimacy. Right now his mandate and the duration of his time in office are exactly the same as that of the parliamentary majority, which means that, in effect, the President has become the Prime Minister of this country. This is the case with François Hollande and it was already the case with Nicolas Sarkozy. As a matter of fact, we have a sort of monarch, who plays both the roles of head of state and head of government, with one of the greatest problems being that he is not accountable to parliament. The President of the Republic is, in effect, accountable to no one, while the Prime Minister has to go to parliament every day to answer questions – a constitutional problem, which needs to be solved. I do not know how it could be solved, because it would be very difficult to abolish the office of the President of the Republic, but we have a fairly serious constitutional problem on our hands. I once favoured the American system with a president who governs directly, controlled by parliament. A great number of people feel that France is too conflict-oriented a country to allow a system like that to work; we would always have a right-wing president and a left-wing majority, or vice versa. In any case, I do not think that we shall achieve constitutional change in the next decade.

What role was played by international organisations, such as the European Union, applying pressure to your reform plans?
The 2003 pension reform was decided over public finance issues. It was a purely national matter.

The 2010 reform was not part of our 2007 election campaign manifesto. At that time, in 2007, we thought that we had already done everything that was necessary in 2003. What, then, moved us in 2010 to carry out new reforms and to increase the retirement age to 62? It was, again, the national deficit, of course, but it was mostly the pressure of the international markets: the risk of being downgraded by rating agencies. In addition, the European Union played an important role. In other words, the 2010 pension reform was primarily done to show the outside world that France was carrying out reforms.

One year later, in 2011, the European sovereign debt crisis and the attacks on the European currency kicked in. In 2011, rating agencies exerted very strong pressure on France, and we were downgraded for the first time. We reacted, among other things, by taking a whole series of measures to reduce the deficit, some of which were tax increases, but also by accelerating the phasing in of the new retirement age. The initial reform had planned to phase in the increase by 2018, but we shortened the schedule to show the market and the outside world that we were serious about taking action, and it turned out that this worked relatively well.

What is your understanding of leadership, in light of what you described as a culture of conflict and ideological complexion in France?
I would start with the thought that leadership is a question of conviction and character.

In addition, it could perhaps also be about transcending the narrow boundaries of Left and Right. Given my party affiliation, I have obviously never been a man of the Left, but I would say that I have always had quite a 'social' and open view of society – this is how I would describe my political perspective. Given that the question is about leadership, I feel it is important that I have always been frank with the trade unions and that we have always had a relationship which allowed us to speak with each other openly. There were never any 'manoeuvres' in my times as minister or as head of government, even though French political life is full of examples of governments trying to find what I would call 'shameful' compromises with the unions. There has always been an element of give and take, but sometimes a slightly dishonest element of give and take, if you know what I mean. In France, unions used to be bought, but I have always refused to go down that road.

One exception may have been our dealings with the trade unions during the introduction of the RSA. I have to admit that we then fell back into the errors of the past. At that stage, however, I was very enthusiastic about the idea of opening up the government to the Left and it was really the first time that we even attempted to overcome the sterile antagonism between the Right and the Left.

We were inspired by Germany, where there was a real Left–Right coalition at the time. In the course of the process, however, I rapidly realised that our objective proved to be illusionary, and that, in reality, we had ended up with a bad reform, having swapped it for political support that was not worth very much. It was some kind of fool's bargain.

Moreover, as I have always been convinced that French society was ready for change, I was never afraid. I think that a lot of French politicians used to fear that they would be thrown out or side-lined and therefore adopted an approach which was much too prudent, but I myself was never afraid.

How can reformers ensure the sustainability of their reforms when election cycles might produce political change?
This is a very significant problem, especially in France, where policies undergo constant revision and reversal with changing governments. I have no definite answer as to how to solve this problem. At the moment, we are facing a very serious crisis of confidence between French society and the French economy: markets are hostile to France, as are investors. If I were a foreign – or even a French – investor, I would first ask myself if the current policy was going to be continued for several years or if it might change, and if I was not sure, I would think twice before investing my money in France.

How can one tackle this problem? My initial response would be to strengthen social dialogue. If a reform is backed by a broad social consensus, it is very difficult for any successor government to return to that subject, but this may not be sufficient.

At the moment I am working on another idea of how to deal with the challenge of sustainability, relating to the possible introduction of a requirement into the constitution that all governments must balance the budget, with certain conditions.

Beyond that, the issue of European harmonisation is being discussed at the moment, and this is even more complicated. Suffice it to say that I am in favour of the suggestion that the eurozone countries need to consider fiscal harmonisation a long-term objective, but for France it is difficult to raise this question at the moment, because it may look as if France were not capable of achieving its own reforms without the imposition of European constraints.

4.2 A note on French labour market performance over the past decade

4.2.1 The facts

France's labour market performance has been relatively disappointing over the past decade; since the mid-2000s, it has seen a marked deterioration in its performance relative to Germany, its nearest and largest neighbour and trading partner. The French harmonised unemployment rate dipped from 9 per cent in 2000 to a low of 7.5 per cent in 2008, before the Great Recession hit the economy hard (see fig. 6).[51] Since then, the unemployment rate has risen steadily to a seasonally adjusted level of 10.5 per cent in 2015, above the EU28 average of 10.1 per cent. This level is more than twice the German seasonally adjusted unemployment rate of 5.0 per cent. It is a striking illustration of the deterioration in French labour market performance compared to that of Germany that, as recently as 2007, the German unemployment rate had exceeded the French rate.

The total employment rate dropped from around 68 per cent in the early 1970s to just under 60 per cent in the mid-1990s, before rising steadily to over 64.6 per cent in 2007. In the immediate aftermath of the crisis, the employment rate dropped, as output declined. There has, however, been some small growth in the employment rate over the past two years: by 2013 it had recovered to its 2007 level (see table 7). In terms of the structure of employment in France by age groups, compared with other EU and OECD countries, it is well known that employment rates are relatively low in France for both youth and older workers, whereas they are relatively high by international comparison for the 'prime age' group.

The youth employment rate rose by almost 3 percentage points between 2000 and 2007, but it has dropped back again, because of the crisis, to under 29 per cent in 2013, below both the EU and OECD averages of 33 per cent and 40 per cent, respectively. The older worker employment rates are also below the corresponding EU and OECD averages. It is noticeable, however, that there has been a significant increase in the employment rate for the 55–9 age group since the beginning of the 2000s: the employment rate for this age group in

---

51 It is important to note, however, the prolonged trend rise in the French unemployment rate across business cycles since the first oil price shock of the 1970s. Thus, it rose from just over 2 per cent at the beginning of the 1970s to a peak of almost 12 per cent in the mid-1990s. The subsequent decade saw a drop of 4 percentage points in the rate, but most of this improvement was reversed after the Great Recession and the upward drift in unemployment shows no signs of being reversed at the time of writing, despite the promise made by President Hollande to reverse the rising trend during 2014.

Evolution of the employment and unemployment rates in France, 1970–2014

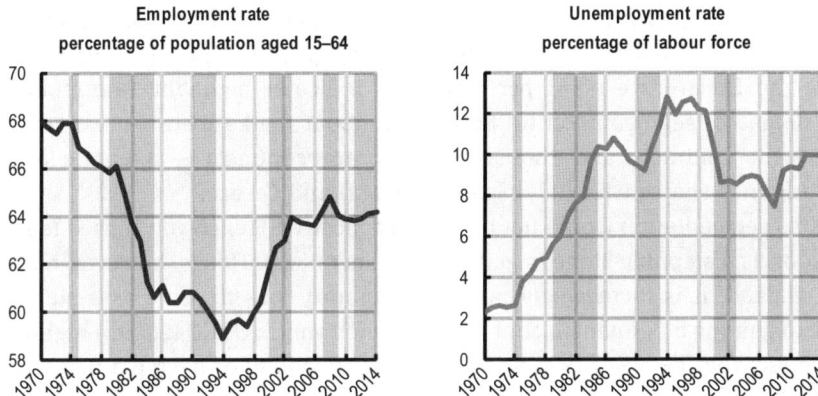

Note: Grey shaded areas refer to period of economic contraction (based on the output gap).

Source: OECD estimates based on the *OECD Labour Force Statistics, OECD Short-term Labour Market Statistics* and *OECD Economic Outlook Databases* (Cut-off date: 13 April 2015).

Figure 6: Labour market chart France

France in 2013 was almost 20 percentage points higher than in 2000, and it exceeded the EU average. Employment rates for those aged over 60 have also risen significantly. The rate more than doubled between 2000 and 2013, but it still remained well below the EU and OECD averages. While the employment rate for those aged 65–9 has also risen over the period since 2000, it is still extremely low in France: only 5.6 per cent of this age group were employed in 2013, compared with an EU average of 11.3 per cent. It is noteworthy that in France, as in most other EU countries, the trend rise in older worker employment rates was not interrupted by the Great Recession. Part of the explanation for this trend rise in older worker employment in France is a series of reforms to the pension system with the aim of encouraging longer working lives and the gradual elimination of early retirement measures (for details see below).

As for the type of jobs being created in France, it should be noted that there has been no increase in the share of part-time jobs in total employment since 2000, and this share is lower in France than the EU and OECD averages. As part-time jobs are predominantly held by women, who often find them a convenient means of combining caring responsibilities with work, the below-average share in France may be partly accounted for by the relatively generous family benefits, especially for families with more than one child.

With regard to temporary jobs, there has been some increase in their share of total wage and salary employment since the 1990s, especially since the crisis. By 2013, temporary jobs accounted for 16.5 per cent of employees, compared with an EU average of 14 per cent. It is also noticeable that almost 60 per cent of all temporary jobs in France in 2013 were occupied by young people, significantly above the EU average of 43 per cent. This indicator highlights the relatively high degree of segmentation in the French labour market between workers on permanent contracts and those on temporary contracts – a characteristic which France shares with Italy, Spain, Portugal and Greece.

This segmentation would not be such a concern if French youth used temporary jobs as a stepping-stone to getting permanent jobs. This is, however, not the case. Indeed, it is increasingly rare for temporary jobs to serve as a stepping stone to gaining a permanent contract for French youth: OECD (2009b) highlighted the fact that between 1996 and 2006 the probability of having a permanent contract one year after a fixed-term contract fell for French youth aged 15–24 from 43 per cent to 18 per cent.[52] The strong duality in the French labour market and the increasing difficulties French youth face in getting onto good career ladders are linked to the high degree of employment protection which workers on permanent contracts enjoy in France. A relatively high statutory minimum wage in France – the so-called SMIC[53] – also hinders the job prospects for many youth, especially those with low educational qualifications and little or no work experience.

As in other EU countries, the crisis has hit the French youth labour market hard. The youth unemployment rate has exceeded 20 per cent in every year since the crisis began. The latest seasonally adjusted rate for France was 24.4 per cent in September 2014, above the EU28 average of 21.6 per cent and over three times the German rate of 7.6 per cent.

The incidence of long-term unemployed (defined as those out of work for 12 months or more as a proportion of total unemployment) has remained rather stable at around 40 per cent since the crisis began. This indicator for France was 6 percentage points below the EU average in 2003.

Another specific factor of the French labour market which has been identified by many commentators as a source of weakness is a relatively high average and marginal tax wedge on labour. OECD data show that the average labour tax

---

52 Other data from the EU-SILC panel show a similar low transition rate from temporary jobs to permanent ones. Indeed, over the period 2003–9, the transition rate for France of only 14 per cent per year was the lowest in the EU. See OECD (2013i), Table 3.2, for details.
53 *Salaire minimum interprofessionelle de croissance.*

wedge in France was the second highest in the EU, after Belgium, in 2011.[54] This has an impact on both labour demand and supply. When it is coupled with a relatively high minimum wage, it hinders hiring prospects, especially for low-skilled workers and youth.[55]

In order to offset this negative impact on labour demand, successive French governments since the early 1990s of both the Left and the Right have cut employer social security contributions for low-paid workers.[56] The payroll tax cuts, however, have to be phased out not too far up the earnings distribution, otherwise they prove to be too costly to the public purse. In combination with the withdrawal of social benefits and other taxes that have to be paid when a previously unemployed or inactive person takes a job or seeks to work more hours, this can generate very high marginal effective tax rates (METRs), which can have a negative impact on labour supply, by dissuading people either from entering the labour market in the first place or from putting in a greater work effort. For example, OECD (2013i), using the OECD's tax-benefit models, shows that the METRs in France can be as high as 80 per cent for the transition from unemployment benefits to full-time work. Low-paid workers and single parents with children are particularly vulnerable to high METRs in France. In order to lower such high marginal tax rates, French governments have put in place several in-work benefits targeted to low-income households (for details see below).

A final specific aspect of the French labour market which is noteworthy is the very weak state of social dialogue which distinguishes France from Germany, the Netherlands or the Nordic countries. This, in turn, reflects the weak bargaining power of the trade unions, except in the public sector, and the fact that there are strong and continuing ideological divisions between the main union confederations.[57] The employers, for their part, are also divided and the power of the main confederation (the MEDEF) is weak. The poor quality of industrial relations in France has hindered attempts to establish consensus among the social part-

---

54 Labour taxes include personal income tax and employee plus employer social security contributions and any other payroll tax less cash transfers. For more details, see the OECD's *Taxing Wages* data base.

55 The level of the SMIC relative to the median wage in France is around 60 per cent, the highest level in the EU. See OECD (2013i), Figure 2.32.

56 Since 2007, a cut of 26 percentage points (over 28 for firms with fewer than 20 employees) has been applied to those earning the SMIC, with the tax exemption dropping to zero for those earning 1.6 times the SMIC.

57 The unionisation rate in the French private sector is well under 10 per cent. However, more than 90 per cent of French workers are covered by the provisions of collective agreements under a law which dates back to the early 1980s and guarantees the extension of any sectoral collective agreement to all other firms and workers in that sector.

ners on the reasons for relatively poor labour market performance in France and possible solutions.

Shortly after taking office, President Sarkozy tried to assign a priority to social dialogue as a route towards labour market and social policy reforms: only if the social partners failed to reach an agreement would the government pass a law. This had some immediate effect in terms of the important reform of dismissal legislation struck in 2008. Subsequent attempts to foster social dialogue under the Sarkozy Presidency, however, were less successful. President Hollande, after his election in 2012, made a renewed attempt to relaunch social dialogue, beginning with a national social summit and then a major labour market agreement struck by the social partners which the government passed into law in early 2013. These early successes have, however, not been sustained under the twin pressures of rising unemployment and plummeting popularity ratings for President Hollande. The two most recent attempts at social dialogue – the social summit of July 2014 and the negotiations on enterprise-level bargaining – failed.[58] Social dialogue is a fragile plant and it seems that the conditions and trust required for it to prosper do not exist in France.

In sum, the main structural weaknesses of the French labour market are fourfold: (i) relatively low employment rates among youth and older workers; (ii) high average and marginal tax rates on labour; (iii) a high degree of duality reflected in a large gap in the protection afforded to permanent compared with temporary contracts; and (iv) the poor quality of industrial relations.[59] Successive French governments have sought to deal with these weaknesses over the past two decades; in the next section we review these efforts, leaving aside the fourth since little has been done on that front until very recently and, as noted above, there are very few concrete outcomes to report.

---

58 See Martinot (2015) for a discussion of the recent attempts to foster social dialogue in France.
59 One could probably add to this list of structural weaknesses the lack of effective activation of the unemployed. The major reform on this front occurred at the beginning of 2009 when the French public employment service (ANPE) was merged with the unemployment benefits agency (UNEDIC) to create a new one-stop shop (Pole emploi), a reform which had been urged on France for many years by OECD. However, the reform coincided with the crisis and rising unemployment, and it has proved difficult to merge the two agencies which had very different organisational cultures and governance arrangements prior to the merger.

4.2.2 Major labour market and pension reforms since 2000

Pension reforms

The French pension system is characterised by a high degree of occupational segmentation with many separate schemes. While there is a general regime for workers in industry and commerce, there are many special regimes for public-sector workers. It is based almost entirely on compulsory social insurance operating on a PAYG basis. The system is relatively generous: for those who have contributed for the full minimum contribution period (MCP), it offers a net pension replacement rate in the range of 60–70 per cent. For many years, France also had a culture of early retirement.[60] This, in turn, contributed to a relatively low average effective age of retirement compared to other countries – 59.1 years for men and 59.5 years for women in 2011, according to OECD estimates.[61] The combination of these two factors results in very high public expenditure on pensions in France. Indeed, in 2010, France spent almost 15 per cent of GDP on pensions, the second highest share in the EU, after Italy.

Thus, concerns about the future financial sustainability of the pension system in the face of an ageing population and the need to foster longer working lives have been the main motivators for a series of pension reforms stretching back over three decades. The first reforms in the 1980s and early 1990s focused on raising social insurance contributions to plug the financial deficits in the system. This approach, however, raised the tax wedge on labour and hurt employment.

The first systematic attempt to reform pensions was made in 1993 by the centre-right government of Edouard Balladur. The reform was limited to the private sector.[62] While it left the official retirement age of 60 untouched, it raised the

---

60 This dates back to the 1970s and early 1980s. Indeed, the official retirement age was cut from 65 to 60 in 1983 with the ostensible aim of cutting rising unemployment. It failed miserably in terms of this aim but it did succeed in fixing age 60 as the date of retirement in view of French public opinion even though most other EU countries had higher official retirement ages or had announced plans to raise them.

61 For details on how the OECD estimates average effective retirement ages, see fn. 28 in the Austrian country note.

62 The omission of the public sector from the Balladur reform was a deliberate decision to minimise opposition to the reform. Public-sector workers were better organised than private-sector workers and their special pension schemes were more generous. The bargaining power of public-sector workers in this field was demonstrated when the Juppé government attempted in late 1995 to extend the scope of the Balladur reforms to cover the public sector and to eliminate the special pension regimes in the public sector. The proposals triggered a major wave of strikes which forced the government to withdraw the proposals. See OECD (2009b), Chapter 3, for details.

MCP for entitlement to a full pension to 40 years from 37.5 years, and this increase was phased in slowly over the period 1993 to 2003. In addition, the calculation of the reference wage on which the pension was based was extended gradually from the best ten years of earnings to the best 25. The Balladur reform, however, was only a stop-gap, which failed to ensure financial sustainability of the system in the long run.

In 2000, the Jospin government created the Conseil d'Orientation des Retraites (COR) as a forum at which all the key stakeholders could discuss future pension reforms. The COR rapidly established itself as a forum which could help the central actors reach some consensus on the issues at stake, even if it did not reach agreement on the precise reforms needed. It has continued to play this role under successive governments of the Left and Right.

Since 2000, there have been two major pension reforms, beginning with the Fillon reform of 2003 and continuing with the Ayrault reform of 2013. The main features of these reforms are highlighted in Box 5.

Box 5. Main features of pension reforms since 2000

2003 (the first Fillon reform): The provisions of the 1993 reform of private-sector pensions were extended to the public sector. Public-sector pensions were to be indexed to prices instead of wages, which had been the practice in the private sector since 1987. Incentives to extend working life were raised through a phased increase in the MCP for receiving a full pension by one year, bringing it to 41 in 2012 and 41.5 years in 2020. A bonus benefit accrual (*surcote*) of 3 per cent per year was introduced for those who had reached the MCP and worked beyond the age of 60. Early retirement before reaching the MCP was to be penalised by the introduction of an additional reduction (*décote*) of 1.25 per cent per quarter for each missing quarter up to a maximum of five years.

2010 (the second Fillon reform): The minimum legal retirement age was increased from 60 to 62, to be phased in by 2018. A link was established between the MCP and rising life expectancy, but the adjustment was not automatic. Entitlement to early retirement for civil servants with more than three children was abolished. A subsidy of up to 14 per cent of gross wages was offered for hiring unemployed people over 55.

2012: The increase in the legal retirement age to 62 was reversed for a minority of older workers who had begun working at an early age.

2013: No increase in the legal retirement age. The MCP will be increased gradually from 41.5 to 43 years, but only for those born after 1973. No change to public-sector pensions.

It should be noted that the social partners did not play a major role in these reforms. They were, of course, consulted extensively about them and participated in the debates in the COR. The unions did not have a common position on all of the reforms: some of the confederations were supportive of all or part of the proposed reforms, while others (notably the left-wing CGT) opposed most of the reforms. They organised protests and strikes against both of the Fillon reforms in 2003 and 2010, but they were unable to prevent the passage of the laws.

Public opinion, shaped in part by the work of the COR, has come to see the need for pension reforms, if the future financial sustainability of the pension system is to be assured, and the need to work longer, as life expectancy increases. It is noticeable, however, that all of the reforms to date have been parametric in nature rather than systemic, i. e. they have focused on changing key parameters, such as, for example, the legal retirement age, the MCP and the size of the *surcote* or *décote*, rather than attempting a fundamental reform of the system, as would be entailed by a shift to a points-based system (as in Germany) or a notional defined-contribution system (as in Italy and Sweden). While the latter has been discussed from time to time, no politician has been willing to grasp this nettle, even though the complexity of the current system and the inequities arising from it are crying out for reform. Instead, the politicians prefer to opt for 'band-aid' solutions, seeking to plug temporarily the financial gaps as they appear.

The latest reform of August 2013 is a perfect illustration of this approach. The stated aim was to fill the financial shortfall by 2020. It aims to achieve this by raising the MCP slowly, from 41.5 to 43 years in 2035. It also raises payroll taxes on both employers and workers which, in turn, could feed into higher labour costs, thereby hurting employment prospects, unless the higher taxes are offset by lower wages. OECD (2013f) estimates that the reforms are unlikely to plug the financial gap by 2020, unless economic growth recovers more strongly than the official projections anticipate it will. Thus, it seems safe to predict that the coming decade will witness further reforms to the pension system to ensure its financial sustainability.

On the other hand, it must be admitted that the reforms have succeeded in promoting employment of older workers. Most of the early retirement pathways have now been closed down.[63] The Fillon government also introduced a requirement that sectors and firms not covered by collective agreements with more than 50 employees had to reach collective agreements or develop action plans to promote older worker employment.

Firms that did not have such agreements or action plans in place by the beginning of 2010 were to be liable to pay a penalty of 1 per cent of their payroll to the old-age insurance fund. When the crisis hit hard, however, the penalty was waived, at least temporarily at first, though this seems now to have slipped into abeyance. In any event, most of the plans or agreements say little about meas-

---

[63] One recent example of such a reform concerned the exemption from job-search requirements for the unemployed aged 57 and over. When this was combined with the longer duration of unemployment benefits for the older unemployed, it meant that many of them could, effectively, retire at age 57. This exemption was closed in 2008 and phased in by 2012.

ures to boost the hiring of older workers, as distinct from measures to promote the retention of older workers.

A novel measure, which was introduced in 2013 by the Ayrault government, is the so-called 'generational contract'. Under this measure, firms with fewer than 300 employees receive a lump-sum subsidy if they sign a permanent contract for a young worker under the age of 26, while retaining an older worker aged over 57. The subsidy amounts to 2,000 euros for the youth and 2,000 euros for the older worker, and it is paid for a maximum of three years; the amount of the subsidy is doubled to 8,000 euros a year if both a youth and an older worker are hired by the firm. While it is too soon to pass a judgement on the effectiveness of this new wage subsidy, it is potentially vulnerable to large deadweight and substitution effects,[64] which would reduce its cost-effectiveness.

Labour cost subsidies and 'making-work-pay' reforms
Above, we emphasised the problem of high average and marginal tax rates on labour, especially for low-paid workers. The potential negative effects on labour demand are compounded by the relatively high level of the SMIC and its automatic indexation to earnings growth.

To help offset these negative effects, successive governments over the past 20 years have given generous employer payroll tax exemptions targeted at low-paid workers. These payroll tax cuts are a degressive function of the gross wage: they apply to employees of private-sector firms who are paid between 1 and 1.6 times the SMIC. Carbonnier et al. (2014) point out that about 50 per cent of the workforce is covered by such payroll tax cuts to some extent. They highlight that, in 2014, thanks to these payroll tax cuts, the tax wedge at the SMIC was only 34 per cent of total labour costs, as opposed to 46 per cent in the absence of the exemptions. At the same time, the payroll tax cuts are costly for the public purse: Carbonnier et al. (2014) state that they amounted to more than 1.3 per cent of GDP in 2011.

There have been many evaluations of these exemptions. There is a consensus that they have saved or created many jobs.[65] There is, however, less agreement about the 'cost per job created' associated with the payroll tax cuts. A recent review by Bunel et al. (2012) concluded that the cost per job created ranged very widely between 10,000 and 70,000 euros, with an average estimate of 24,000

---

64 Allegre et al. (2012) estimate, on the basis of a similar measure, that the net employment gains from the generational contracts are likely to be of the order of 20 per cent.
65 Ourliac and Nouveau (2012) estimate that the payroll tax cuts created or saved between 600,000 and 1.1 million jobs between 1998 and 2009.

euros. Drawing on this study, Carbonnier et al. (2014) argue that it would have been more cost-effective in terms of jobs created to have diverted at least 6 billion euros from the payroll tax cuts to public social investments. The results are, however, heavily influenced by specific design features of the payroll tax cuts and the degree to which they are targeted to low-wage workers or sectors. For example, Cahuc et al. (2014) evaluate the impact of an unanticipated and temporary hiring subsidy targeted at workers earning less than 1.6 times the SMIC in very small firms (with fewer than ten employees). The subsidy took the form of full exemption from the employer payroll tax for any hires made during the period from December 2008 to December 2009. Their results suggest that the subsidy had a significant effect on employment and that the net cost per job created was close to zero.

The latest step in this domain concerns the 'Tax Credit for Employment and Competitiveness', introduced by the Ayrault government in 2013. This measure takes the form of a corporate tax credit of 6 per cent of the gross wages of employees earning up to 2.5 times the SMIC. Unlike previous payroll tax cuts, it is less targeted at low-wage workers, thereby raising the likelihood of significant deadweight and displacement effects. Carbonnier et al. (2014) estimate that it is equivalent to a payroll tax exemption of between 25 and 30 billion euros, representing over 1 per cent of GDP. Thus, the net cost per job created of this new scheme could be very high.

The alternative possibility, namely encouraging the hiring of low-paid workers by lowering the SMIC or modifying its indexation method, has up to now been ruled out by the politicians, because of the 'totem-pole' status of the SMIC in France. The politicians were traumatised by the failed attempt of the Balladur government in 1994 to introduce a significant youth differential into the minimum wage – the so-called 'SMIC-jeunes'.[66] In 2009, an independent commission was set up to advise the social partners and the government on future increases in the SMIC; in general, its advice to limit the annual increases to the minimum legal amount has been followed to date.

In addition to a prolonged debate on how best to stimulate the hiring of low-paid workers, there has also been a long debate in France about financial incentives to work – the so-called 'making-work-pay' issue exemplified by high METRs facing individuals and households. To tackle the problem of high METRs facing

---

66 Strictly speaking, the proposal was to create a new form of employment contract for young workers –– the *contrat d'insertion professionelle* –– which would pay 20 per cent below the SMIC rate. It rapidly became known as the *SMIC-jeunes* and gave rise to massive student and union protests which forced the government to back down on the proposal. See OECD (2009b), Chapter 9, for an analysis of why this reform failed.

low-income households, two policy instruments are used in France. The first is a refundable, in-work tax credit – the *Prime pour l'emploi* (PPE) – for low-income workers, which was created in 2001. The second – the *Revenue de solidarité active* (RSA) – was created in 2009.[67] RSA provides a financial top-up to low labour earnings.[68] PPE and RSA are designed to be complementary: RSA tops up social benefits and wages to enhance work incentives, and PPE is added to this at higher, but still modest, income levels.

The available evidence suggests, however, that neither instrument is very effective. PPE is paid to a very large number of households, but the average amounts are very small and appear to have little or no impact on behaviour. Take up of RSA has been very disappointing: Bourguignon (2011) highlighted that almost 70 per cent of the target population for RSA did not claim it. As a result of these concerns, the Ayrault government announced its intention in January 2013 to reform the RSA and link it more effectively to the PPE. Such a connection is, however, difficult to design in a way that generates a maximum number of winners and a minimum number of losers without spending significant public funds on the measure. For this reason, the reform of the PPE/RSA has proceeded at a snail's pace. The latest news dates from November 2014, when Prime Minister Valls announced that the PPE and the RSA would be replaced by 'une prime d'activité' which would come into effect on 1 January 2016 and would be reserved for those earning less than 1.2 times the SMIC and whose household income would not exceed an (as yet undefined) threshold.

Finally, in 2007, in an attempt to increase hours worked by boosting workers' earnings, overtime pay was exempted from social insurance contributions and income taxes. An evaluation of this reform by Cahuc and Carcillo (2011) showed, however, that it had no significant impact on hours worked. The Ayrault government cancelled this exemption of overtime pay in 2012.

Tackling labour market duality

As noted above, the French labour market is characterised by a marked duality between those with permanent contracts (*Contrats à durée indéterminée* (CDI)) and those with temporary contracts (*Contrats à durée déterminée* (CDD)). The latter accounted for almost 17 per cent of wage and salary employment in 2013 and

---

67 RSA is embedded in a more general anti-poverty programme. Its creator was Martin Hirsch, who had previously been an anti-poverty activist, before joining the Sarkozy government as a junior minister.

68 Strictly speaking, there are two components to the RSA: (i) the RSA *socle*, which is the minimum-income benefit; and (ii) the RSA *activité*, which is the earnings top-up paid to those in work.

over 90 per cent of new hires. Workers on CDI benefit from relatively strong employment protection: the OECD's index for France is fairly high, compared to other countries (see France's scoreboard). Firms prefer to hire on a CDD, especially for young workers and, as noted above, it is very hard to move from a CDD to a CDI in France.

In order to reduce this duality, there has been much debate in France among academics about the merits of moving to a single employment contract (the so-called *Contrat unique*) which would apply to everyone with severance pay accumulating during the tenure of a job, while internalising the social costs of layoffs by linking firms' payroll taxes to their past dismissal behaviour.[69] The 2014 Nobel Prize in Economics was awarded to Jean Tirole, who has argued the case strongly for the urgent need in France to tackle labour market duality through the single contract route. Indeed, President Sarkozy, having included this as one of his campaign promises, proposed to reform employment protection along the lines of a single contract in 2007. This proposal was, however, swiftly rejected by both the unions and the employers, and the government therefore dropped it. Instead, it opted to introduce legislation relating to the agreement which was reached by the social partners in 2008 on amicable termination of an employment contract (*rupture conventionelle*). A similar approach was followed by the Ayrault government in 2013 relating to the latest agreement on employment contracts struck by the social partners. Details on these two agreements are shown in Box 6.

The 2008 reform proved to be very popular with both workers and employers, and there has been a sharp rise in the number of dismissals under the *rupture conventionelle*. This has made for more harmony concerning layoffs, but it has had little or no impact on lowering duality. As for the 2013 reform, it is impossible to assess yet whether it will have much impact in terms of lowering duality. However, it is noticeable that this reform is much more marginal than the reforms which were made to employment protection legislation and judicial practices governing unfair dismissals in Spain, Italy, Portugal or Greece in recent years and which cut dismissal costs much more significantly. Recently, Prime Minister Valls floated the idea of a single contract again, but this was immediately dismissed by the social partners. That being the case, it seems unlikely that the 2013 reforms will contribute much towards reducing labour market duality in France or boosting the chances of young workers getting a permanent contract.

---

69 See Blanchard and Tirole (2003) and Cahuc and Kramarz (2005) for arguments in favour of the single contract. A more sober assessment of the proposal is presented in Lepage-Saucier et al. (2013).

Boosting youth employment prospects

There is widespread agreement that the French education system is unsatisfactory in terms of preparing many young people for the transition from school to work. It is especially unsatisfactory for the least-educated young people. Detailed diagnoses of the weaknesses of the French educational system and recommendations on how to remedy them are contained in OECD (2009b) and in OECD (2013i), Chapter 2. In this note, we will therefore focus on recent reforms to employment and training measures designed to improve the school-to-work transition for French youth.

Box 6. Main reforms to employment protection legislation

2008: A new provision was established for amicable termination of a work contract – the so-called *rupture conventionnelle* – other than through a resignation or a layoff. This procedure gave rise to higher severance pay and entitlement to unemployment benefits. A new fixed-term contract was introduced for specific projects.

2013: The possibility was created to negotiate legally secured firm-level agreements that would allow, in the event of a serious economic downturn, wages and working-time schedules to be adjusted for up to two years in order to protect jobs. Once such an agreement is signed, a worker who refuses it can be dismissed fairly for economic reasons. The rules governing short-time working are simplified. Regulations governing collective dismissals are made simpler to lower the uncertainty surrounding dismissal costs. A non-conversion tax – in the form of higher employer social security contributions – is introduced for fixed-term contracts, if they are not converted to a CDI when the fixed term is up.

Source: OECD (2013b), Chapter 2.

Since the failure of the attempt to create a significant sub-minimum wage for youth in 1993–4, no French government has ventured down the track of seeking to boost hiring opportunities for youth.[70]

Instead, the main approach followed by successive French governments has been twofold: (i) developing vocational education and apprenticeships; and (ii) offering subsidised job opportunities in both the public and private sectors – the latter is often referred to in the French media as 'le traitement social du chômage'. Such subsidised jobs (including apprenticeships) currently account for about 25 per cent of all youth jobs in France, down somewhat from a peak of about one-third in the late 1990s, but well over twice the employment shares recorded in the early 1980s, when youth unemployment soared.[71]

---

70 There is provision for a youth differential in the SMIC, but it is extremely restrictive (limited to those aged under 17 with less than six months experience) and the gap to the adult rate is very small.
71 See OECD (2013i), Figure 2.34.

There has been a significant growth in vocational education and apprentice-ships, especially since the mid-1990s. However, if one compares France with well-known apprenticeship countries, such as Germany, Austria and Switzer-land, the latter have two to three times as many apprentices as a share of em-ployment. Apprenticeships in France tend to be of shorter duration, and comple-tion rates (around 50 per cent) are relatively low compared with the traditional apprenticeship countries. At the same time, there has been a trend for French firms to offer apprenticeships to those with higher levels of education, which makes it harder for less-qualified young people to make use of this effective pathway from school to work and thus to the better earnings and employment prospects, which are open to qualified apprentices.[72]

Two recent initiatives taken by the Ayrault government to boost youth em-ployment are (i) the generational contracts; and (ii) a significant expansion in the number of subsidised jobs, mainly in the non-profit sector (*emplois d'avenir*) targeted at the least-educated youth. The stated aim for the latter is to create 100,000 such jobs in 2013 and a further 50,000 in 2014.

In sum, it is hard to envisage a significant improvement in the youth labour market without a sustained economic recovery, more effective school-to-work pathways and a determination to tackle the duality challenge.

4.2.3 Conclusion

French labour market performance has been relatively poor in recent years, especially when compared with the stellar performance of Germany. This is linked to the decline in competitiveness of the traded sector. There are a num-ber of long-standing structural weaknesses in the French labour market which have so far resisted serious reforms. One area which has shown signif-icant improvement over the past 15 years is the labour market prospects for older workers which have been boosted, in part, by a series of reforms to the pension system and the elimination of most early retirement pro-grammes. These reforms have, however, been stop-gap in nature and have not ensured the long-term financial sustainability of the pension system in the face of an ageing population.

Other structural weaknesses have proved to be more difficult to crack. High tax wedges on labour use continue to weigh on labour demand and sup-ply, as does a relatively high minimum wage. Little or no progress has been made in reducing the duality in employment protection for permanent, as op-

---

72 See Abriac et al. (2009) for evidence on the rates of return to apprenticeships in France.

posed to temporary, contracts which hits young workers particularly hard. Instead, successive French governments of either political hue have tended to rely upon expanding active labour market policies to help the young unemployed. Many of these measures are probably not cost-effective, though the absence of rigorous evaluations of a great number of them hinders decision-making in this area.

Table 7: Scoreboard for labour market outcomes and policies, France and EU, 1993–2013

| | 1993 | | 2000 | | 2007 | | 2013* | |
	FR	EU	**FR**	EU	**FR**	EU	**FR**	EU
1. Employment rate (% of the working-age population)	**60.0**	61.2	**62.0**	63.6	**64.6**	66.7	**64.7**	65.9
– male	**68.3**	71.8	**69.1**	72.9	**69.5**	74.2	**68.6**	71.6
– female	**51.9**	50.7	**55.0**	54.4	**59.8**	59.2	**60.9**	60.2
– youth (aged 15/16–24)	**28.4**	39.5	**28.3**	39.4	**31.0**	38.2	**28.6**	33.4
– older people (aged 55–9)	**47.6**	47.6	**48.1**	50.6	**55.3**	57.3	**67.6**	64.9
– older people (aged 60–4)	**12.0**	22.3	**10.2**	22.3	**15.7**	29.4	**23.3**	34.7
– older people (aged 65–9)	–	9.2	**2.1**	7.4	**3.1**	9.5	**5.6**	11.3
2. Unemployment rate (% of labour force)	**11.4**	10.8	**9.0**	8.9	**8.0**	7.1	**10.3**	10.7
– youth (aged 15/16–24)	**25.6**	21.0	**20.6**	17.4	**19.1**	15.5	**23.9**	23.3
3. Incidence of long-term unemployment (% of total unemployment) (a)	**33.3**	42.0	**39.6**	44.4	**40.2**	41.6	**40.4**	46.5
4. Part-time employment rate (b)	**13.2**	13.8	**14.2**	15.3	**13.3**	16.0	**14.0**	17.5
5. Temporary employment rate (c) (temporary employees as % of total employees)	**10.9**	10.5	**15.5**	13.1	**15.1**	14.8	**16.5**	14.0
– youth (aged 15/16–24 as % of total youth employees)	**39.4**	28.8	**55.0**	38.0	**53.5**	41.8	**58.6**	43.0
6. Low-pay incidence (d) (% of employees)	–	–	–	15.7	–	16.5	–	15.0
7. Protection of permanent workers against individual dismissal	**2.3**	2.6	**2.3**	2.5	**2.5**	2.4	**2.4**	2.2
– Protection of temporary workers	**3.6**	2.3	**3.6**	1.8	**3.6**	1.6	**3.6**	1.8
8. Public spending on labour market policies (% of GDP)	**2.9**	2.9	**2.6**	2.0	**2.2**	1.6	**2.4**	2.0
– Spending on active measures (e)	**1.2**	0.9	**1.2**	0.8	**0.9**	0.6	**0.9**	0.8
– Spending on passive measures (f)	**1.7**	2.1	**1.4**	1.1	**1.2**	0.9	**1.5**	1.2

Table 7 (continued)

	1993		2000		2007		2013*	
	FR	EU	**FR**	EU	**FR**	EU	**FR**	EU
9. Net benefit replacement rate (g) (averaged over four family types and two earnings levels)	–	–	**65**	65	**60**	61	**60**	54
– initial spell (h)	–	–	**72**	70	**68**	71	**67**	70
– after 2 years of unemployment	–	–	**74**	66	**69**	63	**70**	57

* 2013 or latest available year.
(a) Persons out of work for 12 months and over.
(b) Part-time employment refers to persons who usually work less than 30 hours per week in "their 'main job'".
(c) Temporary employees are wage and salary workers whose job has a pre-determined end date as opposed to permanent employees whose job is of unlimited duration. National definitions broadly conform to this generic definition, but may vary depending on national circumstances.
(d) Persons with a wage less than 2/3 of the median.
(e) 'Active' measures cover categories 1 to 7 of the OECD/Eurostat data base on public spending on labour market programmes.
(f) 'Passive' measures cover categories 8 and 9 of the OECD/Eurostat data base on public spending on labour market programmes.
(g) Data on net replacement rates for 2000 refer to 2001.
(h) Initial phase of unemployment but following any waiting period. For married couples, the percentage of AW relates to the previous earnings of the 'unemployed' spouse only; the second spouse is assumed to be 'inactive' with no earnings and no recent employment history. Where receipt of social assistance or other minimum-income benefits is subject to activity tests (such as active job-search or being 'available' for work), these requirements are assumed to be met. Children are aged four and six and neither childcare benefits nor childcare costs are considered. Unweighted averages, for previous full-time earnings levels of 67% and 100% of AW and out-of-work single and couple households with no children or with two children (children are assumed to be aged four and six and neither childcare benefits not childcare costs are considered). After tax and including unemployment and family benefits. Social assistance and other means-tested benefits are assumed to be available subject to relevant income conditions. Housing costs are assumed equal to 20% of AW.
Sources: OECD Online Employment Database: www.oecd.org/employment/database; data on net replacement rates come from the OECD tax-benefit models (www.oecd.org/els/social/work-incentives).

5 Germany

5.1 Interview with Gerhard Schröder, 24 June 2014

'Political leadership means being willing to risk losing an election if the country's future is on the line.'

Mr Schröder, now that several years have passed, to what extent do you think the reform programme known as 'Agenda 2010' has succeeded? What parts of it need improvement?
Few would dispute the fact that Agenda 2010 has contributed to Germany's success. However, the Agenda is not the only factor contributing to the positive economic situation in Germany, which is clearly better than that of the other members of the European Union. There are three main reasons for Germany's relative strength.

First, we have always sought to maintain Germany's position as an industrial country, not only during my Chancellorship. The crucial factor is the structure of the German economy, which differs from the French and UK economies, for example: industry accounts for more than 20 per cent of Germany's gross domestic product, but only 11 and 12 per cent of the GDP in France and the UK, respectively. Germany has a structure, in which medium-sized businesses play an important role and this has kept the country economically strong even in times of crisis, compared to countries where the emphasis lies in the service sector and, most of all, in the financial services, as is particularly the case in the UK.

Secondly, we take a unique approach when it comes to negotiating working conditions, as you know: negotiations are held between very strong unions, who are, at least for the most part, genuinely interested in the common good, and strong business associations, who recognise the need for compromise.

The third factor is, indeed, Agenda 2010 – our attempt to respond to what has come to be known as 'globalisation'. Agenda 2010 considerably predated similar efforts in other countries. There was a realisation that the German industry was facing increased competition, in large part because of globalisation, and that dramatic steps were called for to maintain our competitive edge. That factor, coupled with the ageing of our population, forced us to think about ways to reform our social security systems.

Thus, Germany's strength today is a result of its industrial structure, its method of negotiating working conditions and Agenda 2010. In these respects, Germany differs from many other European countries, where the following observations can be made: first, a failure to understand how important the industrial sector and processes are for a country's economy, not least for employment; secondly, a failure to recognise the importance of what we refer to as a 'social partnership' and 'codetermination', a system of labour and management sharing responsibility and decision-making, which has been sharply criticised, particularly in the English-language media; thirdly, the realisation that merely discussing reforms is not enough – they need to be implemented, too. In this context, we can only hope that Prime Minister Matteo Renzi will be successful in Italy. For the first time, someone in Italy is actually seeking to accomplish something, rather than just talking about it. The Berlusconi years in Italy were wasted. Of course, we also hope that France will be successful. One thing is certain, if things go wrong in Greece, Germany can do a great deal to compensate. Greece accounts for 3 per cent of Europe's gross domestic product, which is small change for us. However, if a country like France does not become more competitive, even Germany will not be able to make up for it. That is a real threat.

Agenda 2010 is therefore one important factor in Germany's success. Ultimately, the Agenda was an attempt to revamp the social insurance systems to keep them affordable even under changed conditions, namely globalisation and an ageing society. In addition, it was also intended to change expectations towards the welfare state: we had to send a clear message. People need to be encouraged to take responsibility for themselves as much as possible. We had to point out that living in a welfare state does not mean being taken care of in every conceivable situation, but that it means, first of all, being responsible for our families and ourselves. Only when that is not possible, because of age, illness or unemployment, can society, in the form of the welfare state, be expected to step in. We called that approach *Fordern und Fördern* – 'Challenge and Assist'. It actually means expecting people to do what they can, but no more than that, as the old Latin saying has it: *Ultra posse nemo obligatur* – 'no one is obliged to do more than they are able to do'. However, if people are indeed capable of more, we need to assist them in their efforts. It is only when that is not possible that the welfare state has a responsibility to ensure that people can live in dignity, even in situations of existential difficulty. This is the philosophy behind the Agenda, and it has clearly been a success.

Another purpose of the reforms was to save money – which they did – and those savings could be invested in research and development, and also in education. For the first time, the federal government devoted its attention to all-day schools, investing considerable resources in that sector. In total, the federal government allocated four billion euros to the Bundesländer. These two goals, keeping the welfare state affordable and freeing up resources to invest in the future, were the motivation for Agenda 2010. The Agenda is not the only reason that Germany was able to regain its economic health after having been dubbed the 'sick man of Europe' by *The Economist* back then, but it is certainly one reason.[73]

As for its weak points, of course some things went wrong: the Agenda is not the Ten Commandments, and I have never claimed to be Moses. I shall not go into too much detail; the problems are sufficiently well known. For example, we had to address the issue of what a single mother with childcare duties can contribute and whether it might be necessary to offer some other kind of support, such as providing day-care centres. This was something that did not work out. I am sure there were also technical problems. When you design such a comprehensive reform process, it is purely theoretical at first – a legislative proposal. When it then turns out that the plan is incompatible with reality, you have to consider the possibility that the plan or some of its components are faulty – rather than reality itself. There were no ready-made plans to work with for first-time leaders of an industrialised country like Germany, at the head of a red–green coalition, a coalition consisting of the Social Democratic and the Green Party: plans needed to be developed first.

One of our mistakes concerned the pension policy: the previous government, led by Helmut Kohl, had introduced a so-called 'demography factor' into the pension system – we reversed that decision for the years 1999 and 2000, but in the course of pursuing our own reform, Agenda 2010, we found it necessary to reintroduce an even harsher version of what we called a 'sustainability factor'. We raised the retirement age and reintroduced the sustainability factor. We had made a political, a beginner's, mistake, which clearly had to be corrected as Germany began to face increasing competition.

You were elected Chancellor in 1998. What was it, exactly, that led to the drafting of Agenda 2010 at the beginning of your second legislative term?
During my first term, the government was faced with a number of foreign policy issues, such as the wars in Kosovo and other Balkan countries, naturally major concerns at the time. During the first four years of my Chancellorship, we believed that making a few adjustments in our social and labour policy would be enough, but this turned out to be wrong.

What ultimately led to Agenda 2010 was the failure of the so-called 'Jobs Alliance'[74] in the spring of 2003. After the 1998 election, we created a Jobs Alliance,

---

73 See "The Sick Man of the Euro", in *The Economist* 3 June 1999. http://www.economist.com/node/209559

74 The Alliance for Jobs, Education and Competitiveness was established in 1998 by the Schröder government after the electoral victory of the Social Democrats and Alliance 90/The Greens. Within the framework of the Alliance, the federal government and top representatives

in an effort to duplicate what the Wassenaar Accord had achieved in the Nether-lands. The Wassenaar Accord was a consensus-based model that accounted for the strength of the Dutch economy during that period, but this approach proved un-workable in Germany. We gave it a try, for a considerable amount of time, but it did not work, because we had the interesting situation – it is hardly surprising, looking back – that our partners in the Jobs Alliance, the unions on the one side and the employers' associations on the other, were focused on making de-mands on the government and pursuing their own interests at the same time. They were incapable of dealing with each other or of making concessions. The un-ions insisted that the government meet as many of their demands as possible and the employers' associations did the same. Neither side was willing to say: 'Collec-tive bargaining is our responsibility, and things need to change.' With the federal government as a moderator, we were willing to communicate with the other side, but for understandable reasons neither side wanted to take part in such a scenario. Before the Agenda was drawn up in 2003, and even prior to that, we, in the gov-ernment, had for our part reached the conclusion that this would not produce the reforms Germany needed. Both parties in the Jobs Alliance were unwilling to aban-don their strategy of using the government as a tool for their own ends.

That is why we decided to dismantle the Jobs Alliance and instead tackle the problem ourselves. After all, we were the ones who had been elected to defend the common good. With all due respect for the basic willingness of both groups, the unions and the employers' associations, to consider the public interest, I have to say that they did not do enough in the Jobs Alliance to achieve reform. That marked the beginning of the discussion of a new agenda – the Agenda 2010.

Following the failure of the Jobs Alliance, our reform agenda was criticised by both sides: the employers' associations felt that it did not go far enough, while the unions believed that it went much too far. We were asked, again and again: 'Why did you not involve them in the process?' It was not possible. We had worked long and hard to involve them in the framework of the Jobs Alliance.

What role did the European context play for the Agenda?
None at all, in the beginning. What did play an important role, however, was the fear of losing our ability to compete, which would have meant higher unemploy-

---

of the employers' associations and the unions agreed on measures to (a) reduce unemployment and bolster employment, (b) create more jobs and (c) make German companies more competi-tive. In the history of the Federal Republic of Germany, the Alliance is seen as an example of a tripartite corporate arrangement that includes the unions, the employers' associations and the federal government.

ment. We knew how dependent Germany is on exports and that inability to compete would have had serious consequences for Germany's business, which in turn would have affected employment.

The European debate occurred later, when the EU was hit by the financial crisis, which led people to ask why Germany, at the time governed by the first Grand Coalition, was more successful than other countries at coping with the crisis. They eventually realised that we had begun, some eight years earlier, with Agenda 2010, to make sure that we remained competitive. The European discussion of the Agenda was, thus, triggered by the crisis and the search for an explanation of Germany's relative strength.

Why did you choose to announce Agenda 2010 in your March 2003 government policy statement? You could have done so in the winter of 2002, during your coalition negotiations with the Green Party, putting the emphasis on the democratic coalition rather than on the power of the Chancellor.
If you look at the distribution of seats in the Bundestag during the second red–green coalition – with a government majority of four seats[75] – it was clear that it would not be possible to push through Agenda 2010 without considerable risk. Indeed, it turned out that several parliamentarians, some of them members of my own party, but also some from the Green Party, would never have agreed to the Agenda in its final form. Only the government was in a position to make the Agenda happen. It would have been much too risky to include the Agenda in our coalition agreement, and then to sit back and wait for the results of the secret vote to elect the Chancellor. That course would not have been very responsible, and that is why we did not go down that road.

To what extent were you able to reach a consensus on Agenda 2010, in your party and your government?
The Greens were not the problem; we were able to convince them fairly quickly. Ultimately, the Social Democrats were not a problem either; the reform programme was approved, after all – that was not the issue. But the resistance we encountered made it more difficult to sell Agenda 2010 to the public. The criticism from our own people obviously made it easier for the opposition to discredit our reforms than if we had presented a united front.

---

75 Distribution of seats in the 15th German Bundestag: Social Democrats (SPD) 251, Christian Democrats/Christian Social Union (CDU/CSU) 248, Alliance 90/The Greens 55, Free Democrats (FDP) 47, Party of Democratic Socialism (PDS) 2.

I later pointed out that if the SPD, the German Social Democratic Party, had had the strength to take ownership of the Agenda and to defend it – although I understand why that did not happen, as it was not in keeping with the party's tradition – they would now be the strongest, most forward-looking group of social democrats in Europe. No one can seriously dispute that.

What difficulties did you encounter from your party, the unions and the public at large when you were pushing through and implementing the Agenda?
How best to achieve reforms is an intriguing question. I think it is only possible from the top down, rather than from the bottom up. Why? Take a look at how democratically elected governments work. If you try to set a process in motion from the bottom up, with the ultimate decision preceded by a long, drawn-out discussion, then the question is whether this will yield an acceptable result, or whether the issue will simply be talked to death. We can observe that right now in France and other countries. In my experience, if you are trying to carry out an ambitious programme of reforms that are sure to cause difficulties for certain groups, including those that might be expected to support you – your party, the unions, your coalition partners – you are unlikely to succeed, if you start off by engaging in a broad-based debate, with every minor aspect of reform endlessly discussed and picked apart. You therefore cannot simply say to your party and the unions: 'Let's discuss what needs to be done.' The result will always fall far short of what is needed.

The problem is that Germany is still a rich country, despite all of its problems, and as a consequence, there is a strong interest in maintaining the status quo. You can expect people to ask, for example when comparing Germany with other countries: 'Why should we change anything? It is all working.' And that is the real problem. In contrast to that, if you ask people, theoretically, referring to a possible reform, whether change is needed in Germany, 90 per cent of them will say 'yes'. They will say that we need even more changes. 'What you are planning does not go nearly far enough.' The situation is reversed, however, when individual groups are actually affected. That is what makes it so difficult.

There is another reason why policymakers often fail to seek reform, and that is the gap between the time when a reform is initiated, with negative effects on certain groups, and its desired effect. Two, three, and sometimes even five, years may pass before a reform shows a positive impact. This delay can spell defeat for democratically elected politicians. Believe me, I know what I am talking about. That is why – you see this in the current government – many people say: 'Let's not rock the boat, things are running smoothly, we're in good shape. Let's rather do a pension reform because its negative consequences won't show up for another ten or fifteen years.' By 2030, the Grand Coalition's pension reform will cost 160 billion euros, since it allows some workers to retire earlier. That is the wrong political signal to send, particularly at a time when we are – quite rightly – asking our European partners to undertake structural reforms.

This raises the question: what does political leadership mean to you?
You cannot expect a politician to lose an election deliberately: no one wants to do that. I understand this – I did not want to either. However, political leadership today means being willing to risk losing an election, if the country's future is on the line. Ultimately, the question is not whether someone will voluntarily give up public office or pursue a policy that is certain to produce the same result; you cannot expect that. It is really about whether there comes a time when a government has to say that this is necessary. If it means losing the next election, then that is the price that has to be paid for holding a position of national responsibility. For us, this was that time. With all of the criticism we faced from the unions and from our own party, we knew that we might fail. In the end, we fared better than we had expected: the 2005 election was very close. The Agenda cannot have been the only factor contributing to our defeat. We still received slightly over 34 per cent of the vote.[76] Those are numbers today's Social Democrats can only dream of. In 2005, we campaigned on our support for the Agenda. One cannot, therefore, necessarily conclude that our determination to implement Agenda 2010 inevitably caused us to lose the election.

Today I look at Italy, where the results of the latest European elections have been particularly interesting. Making it absolutely clear that he was determined to achieve reform, Prime Minister Renzi was able to keep the country's populist groups in check. Contrast that with France, where there is a widespread sense that politicians are all talk and no action, and as a result the right wing has gained strength. This is my explanation for why the recent election results in France and Italy were so different.

How important is a window of opportunity – like the failure of the Jobs Alliance – for achieving reform?
The failure of the Jobs Alliance was not a 'window of opportunity': to call it that way would be a euphemism. It rather meant that we found ourselves on our own

---

76 Results of the 2005 Bundestag elections: CDU/CSU 35.2 per cent, SPD 34.2 per cent, FDP 9.8 per cent, PDS 8.7 per cent, Alliance 90/The Greens 8.1 per cent, NPD 1.6 per cent, other 2.3 per cent.

in confronting the difficult task of achieving reforms that were important for Germany.

Generally speaking, I do not believe that windows of opportunity play a particularly important role. You can see that in the case of Agenda 2010, which we initiated at a very unfavourable time. Normally, or rather ideally, significant reforms should be tackled during an economic upswing, when the economy is healthy and stable. That makes it much easier. We pushed the Agenda through at a time of crisis, and under such circumstances reforms can make a crisis worse. We realised this when we were criticised for violating the Maastricht criteria in 2003–4. As a matter of fact, if we had not done so, the Agenda could not have been introduced. If we had not violated the Maastricht criteria, we would have had to find a way to save another 20 billion euros, in addition to the pain caused by the Agenda. That would never have been possible. While the Agenda was under discussion, Hans Eichel, my Finance Minister at the time, asked me whether we could not find some way of complying with the Maastricht criteria after all, to which I replied: 'It won't work, Hans, you'll see. It can't. The Maastricht criteria can't be set in stone. They're economically based assumptions, but no more than that. And if we have to abide by them, it will jeopardise the Agenda.'

The same argument is made in the current debate about the euro crisis. Based on Germany's experience, I would say that if people are serious about reform, if they are not just talking about it, but actually doing something, then it should be possible to extend the Maastricht criteria. There is no need to fundamentally question the criteria, and there is no need to talk about whether countries should generally be allowed to go deeper into debt. We should say: 'If you are willing to implement structural reforms, if you are willing to consolidate your budget, you can have a little more time.'

If, for example, France and its current president were to get serious about developing a French version of the Agenda, which would have to be different from the German model, of course, and if he were to explain and actually implement it, then our response should not be: 'Now we are going to make it difficult for you, you must strictly adhere to the 3 per cent limit.' The question, for me, would be: 'What's the difference between 3 and 3.2 per cent, from an economic perspective?' That is hard to define. I understand why some people say that we must not allow the infringement of the criteria become the rule, and it does not need to be so. No one is suggesting that the criteria should be changed, but we should be more flexible in how we interpret them. You have to be able to say to a government: 'Okay, you can let your public debt increase to 3.5 rather than 3 per cent of GDP. But we want to see what you're doing with your labour market, your pension system, and so on. And if you're actually doing something, then we can be tolerant, for a limited period of time.' Then, we should indeed be tolerant.

People raise the idea of moral hazard, however, and talk about how we were the ones who allowed the Greeks to accumulate such massive debts, which is ridiculous. The situation is very different. Things have worked out in Spain, and clearly Prime Minister Mariano Rajoy has had some success. If I am remembering correctly, the Spaniards were allowed twice to let their public debt increase to considerably more than 4 per cent of GDP, and no one made a big fuss about it. That was probably true of the Portuguese, as well. There is no way around it.

I think this is a very important insight. Unfortunately, it is getting lost in the midst of highly ideological debates driven by various interests. Ideology is found not only on the Left, after all; there is also ideology on the democratic Right, as we can see when we look at the economic debate.

It is particularly striking that your Agenda policy was opposed by certain interest groups and your own party, but supported by the CDU/CSU opposition, with the government alone taking public responsibility. What were the advantages and disadvantages of that situation?
This raises the question of how to communicate policy decisions. I have always wished that I could have had 45 minutes of airtime on television, once a week after the evening news, to explain to people why all of this was necessary. That was, unfortunately, not possible, though.

The problem with what we call 'political communication' – informing the public about our policies – is that it takes place through the media, except during election campaigns. As a politician you are not able to do that to the extent you would like, since the journalists' perspective always finds its way into the message. That is how it is in a democracy.

There is another problem that makes political communication very difficult: if your own side, in this case my party and the unions, is sharply critical of the reforms you are trying to introduce, then you are arguing against your own supporters, while the other side, the opposition, which is constantly fighting to regain power, is quite happy to pick up on that criticism.

Thus it is enormously difficult to communicate with the public about a challenging programme of reforms. On the one hand, you have the media, and on the other, opposition from your own supporters.

What role does media pressure play? During your first legislative period, various prominent newspapers complained about the backlog of reforms needed in Germany.

Obviously, policy decisions are not made in a vacuum: what really prompted the Agenda was that unemployment was rising. It was approaching the five million mark, and we simply had to act – it would have been irresponsible not to. It was not so much the editorial writers, though I do not want to downplay the impact they had, but rather the situation itself. If we had not done anything, nothing would have changed or matters would have got even worse. Given the situation, the media did play a role, of course, but it was not the main factor – at least as far as I can tell.

There was a great deal of discussion and criticism in the literature about the idea of calling it 'Agenda 2010'. One objection was that 2010 was too far in the future; another was that the terms used – Agenda, SLG, ALG,[77] the Hartz reforms – were too technical. Why did you choose Agenda 2010?
When the time came to select a name, the speechwriters at the German Federal Chancellery offered a variety of suggestions. I do not remember all of them; they included the usual catchwords you can find in any political platform, 'Innovation and Justice', for example. There were all kinds of ideas. It was shortly before I was to give my government policy statement, the speech that introduced Agenda 2010. My wife is a journalist. We discussed it. She did not get involved with the content of the speech, of course, but she did ask me whether I was sure that we had given the baby the right name. I asked her why. I think we had chosen one of the familiar slogans, like 'Moving towards a Modern Society' or something along those lines. Her response was: 'No, that's definitely not right.' So I asked her to come up with a better idea and she said: 'Call it "Agenda 2010".'

I took the text and went back to the Chancellery, where all of my colleagues and staff were waiting, and asked them what they thought of it. No one liked it: they thought it sounded too technical, but I overruled them because I had decided it was the right name. It is a short name, not just the same old slogans we had heard in the past. As soon as my wife said it, I realised that it would be understood, not only in Germany, but internationally, too. It works in Singapore and just about anywhere else. It was the right name. It was also the right decision to convey the message that a reform like this takes time.

As for the other terms you mentioned, ALG, SLG, Hartz reforms and various others, I think it was a mistake to use Peter Hartz's[78] name in referring to the la-

---

77 SLG is the abbreviation of Sozialleistungsgesetz, the German law determining social benefits; ALG is the abbreviation of Arbeitslosengeld, unemployment benefits.
78 In 2002, Peter Hartz, Head of HR at Volkswagen AG, was appointed Chairman of the Commission for Modern Services in the Labour Market, which was charged with finding ways to reform the labour market.

bour-market laws. The debate was already underway before I realised that we should not have used the name of the commission's chairman to refer to the laws, but by that time it was too late to change it. ALG II and similar names are what we call 'legalese' and therefore difficult to remember. The words Agenda 2010 would have been enough, but I suppose the name of every law is eventually abbreviated.

I think the real problem was the initiative's association with one person. After all, Mr Hartz certainly was not responsible for the entire Agenda. The unions were involved with the commission's work, which had been done under Mr Hartz, and they approved its results, although they lacked the courage to support the laws publicly. I am sorry that Peter Hartz, who is still a good friend of mine, has had to bear the brunt of this. It was not fair on him, but that is the way it happened. These were PR mistakes that should not have been made – there is no doubt about it.

To what extent is it possible to correct or fine-tune reforms that have been pushed through against considerable opposition?
This is something people, especially the media, will have to think about. During the last phase of my term as Chancellor, the word *Nachbesserung* (correction) became something of a dirty word, and it was a huge mistake on the part of our communication efforts to allow that to happen. Correcting mistakes should really be regarded as a good thing. Why? When you are implementing a reform programme like Agenda 2010, things never work out exactly as planned. If the theoretical model proves to be unworkable or the goals you have set cannot be achieved, you have to make modifications. Reform is an ongoing process that requires adjustments to changed circumstances, no matter what the cause of those changes is – external shocks or whatever else. If a government says that there is a problem that it needs to correct – if a government actually admits that some aspect of its plan has not worked out – the appropriate response should be: 'Yes, you finally get it!'

In a democracy, people should not be afraid of politicians who say: 'I have made a mistake, and I am going to fix it.' The ones they should worry about are those who never make mistakes, or who think they do not. The idea that correcting a mistake should be considered negative was one of the craziest things which happened during my term in office.

I am not saying that no administrative errors were made; certainly some were, and they do, of course, deserve criticism, but correcting aspects of a plan that has not worked in practice – that should really be considered a positive thing in a democracy. It is no different in private industry: if you launch a product only to discover that it is a flop, you have to change something. Politicians need to be allowed to learn on the job, otherwise nothing will improve.

In your latest book, *Klare Worte*,[79] you talk about the conflict many reformers experience between a desire to make the world a better place and the need to retain power. One might conclude from your defeat in 2005 that it is better not to pursue reforms, but rather to concentrate on staying in office. What advice would you give those who want to be re-elected despite pushing for unpopular reforms?
I would never give advice to Germany's current government.

Would you give advice in general?
My only piece of advice would be this: it will pay off, perhaps not immediately, but eventually, to accept the risk of losing an election, if necessary. Right now, it appears that no one in Germany thinks it is necessary. In that regard, the crisis in 2003, with growing unemployment and a weakening of our ability to compete, was perhaps the kind of window of opportunity you mentioned earlier.

The literature on the political economy of reforms teaches us that, if reformers want to be re-elected, they may need to get the groups most affected by their reforms involved in the process or, alternatively, provide compensation. Was that a problem for the Agenda or do you think enough was done in that regard?
I do not know how the literature you are referring to arrived at that alleged fact. It has little to do with practical politics. Once again, there is no way to communicate directly with those who lose out in a reform. You have to communicate through the media, some of whom will tell the public that everything is as it should be, some that it is right to resist and some that 'they still have it too good'. Most policymakers are somewhere in the middle, but they have no way of communicating directly.

During the past few years, you have repeatedly called upon policymakers to show courage and continue to pursue a reform agenda. What should an Agenda 2020 look like?
Right now, we need genuine reform of the laws relating to foreigners. I read recently about a 19-year-old who passed the Abitur, the equivalent of a German

---

79 Gerhard Schröder (2014): *Klare Worte. Im Gespräch mit Georg Meck über Mut, Macht und unsere Zukunft* (Herder, Freiburg).

university entrance examination, with the highest possible marks. When this student applied for German citizenship, he was told that, because the law required it, he had to take a six-month German language course – and that, despite the fact that he had got top marks in the Abitur, including in German. We need well-educated people like this young man. There is a similar problem, when it comes to recognising foreign qualifications. At the moment we are not making any progress in this respect in Germany. We focus on the issue of asylum, instead of looking at people as individuals. That is one point.

The second point is pension policy. The current retirement age of 67 is appropriate, and we must not make further exceptions. A contemporary welfare state needs to address the challenges of demographic trends that are leading to a rapidly ageing society.

Thirdly, we need to increase the level of public investment – particularly in infrastructure, education and research.

Fourthly, our energy policy must be designed to strengthen, rather than weaken, our position as an industrial nation. Energy must remain affordable.

Finally, we need to take advantage of the potential of young and well-educated women in the labour force. That is only possible if we make sure that there are good childcare facilities; child allowances will not solve the problem. Working women need to be able to say: 'I'm employed, and I'm capable of doing my job, but I also know that my child is well taken care of while I'm at work.' I always try to explain that a society can never ever succeed if it does not take half of the population seriously, or if it does not provide enough jobs. I like to quote Mao in this context: 'Not only half the sky, but half of the earth belongs to women!'

All of these reforms should be part of an 'Agenda 2020'. The emphasis should, however, not be on the term 'agenda'. Instead, we need to outline the reforms that are needed to equip our society to meet the challenges of the future and to ensure prosperity and security in 2020 and beyond – in Germany, as well as in Europe as a whole.

5.2 A note on German labour market performance over the past decade

5.2.1 The facts

German labour market performance, and its perception by outside commentators and the media, has undergone a miraculous transformation over the past 15 years. Whereas *The Economist* called Germany 'the sick man of Europe' in

1999, it published a special report in 2013 highlighting Germany's economic predominance in Europe.[80] Many commentators and academics now hail the so-called 'German job miracle' and cite it as an example for the rest of Europe to imitate.[81]

Both the labour market chart (see fig. 7) and scoreboard (see table 9) for Germany illustrate the size of the transformation in German labour market performance, especially from the mid-2000s onwards. The German harmonised unemployment rate more than doubled from 5.5 per cent in 1991 to a peak of 11.3 per cent in 2005, before declining steadily to 5 per cent (seasonally adjusted) in September 2014 – the lowest rate in the EU28 for that month, and less than half of the EU28 average of 10.1 per cent. It is noteworthy that the Great Recession hardly disturbed this trend decline in unemployment over the past decade, in contrast to the situation in almost all of the other major EU economies. German output growth has consistently performed better than the EU average since the mid-2000s, on the back of a strong external demand for German products and a buoyant domestic demand, which has been partly supported by the greatly improved labour market performance.

In terms of employment, the overall employment rate varied within a very narrow range around 65 per cent between 1993 and 2005, before it climbed steadily to 75 per cent in 2013, almost 10 percentage points higher than the EU28 average. This very good employment performance has been reflected across most of the major labour force groups, particularly among youth and older workers. A further factor contributing to this strong employment growth has been a significant increase in immigration of foreign workers, mainly from Central and Southern European countries.

The youth employment rate has remained very stable at around 47 per cent since 2000, while the EU average has fallen by more than 6 percentage points over the same period. The relatively good performance of the German youth labour market is a long-standing one: in virtually every year since 1993, the German youth unemployment rate has been less than 10 per cent, while the EU average has always been in double digits, often exceeding 20 per cent. Indeed, the seasonally adjusted youth unemployment rate in Germany in September 2014 was 7.6 per cent, the lowest rate in the EU28, and just over one-third of the EU average of 21.6 per cent. It is well known that the consistently low youth unem-

---

80 See The Economist (2013).
81 See Rinne and Zimmermann (2013). It is salutary in this regard, however, to remember that in the early 1970s Germany was also often cited as a model of labour market performance for other EU countries to emulate. Nevertheless, that lustre wore off in the 1980s and 1990s as German unemployment soared and the 'sick-man' analogy became commonplace.

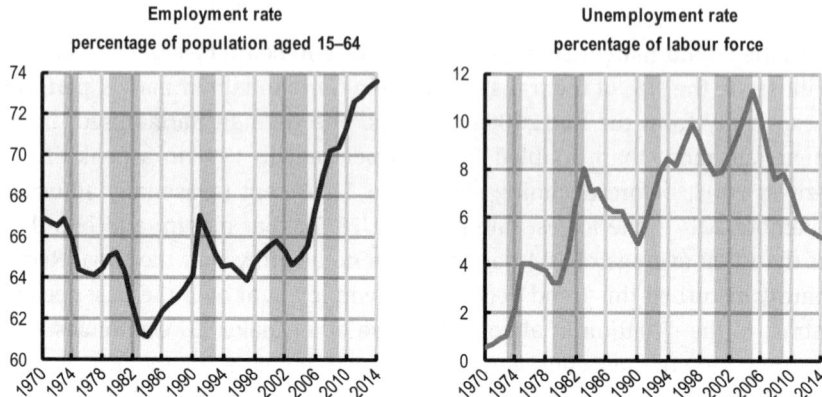

Evolution of the employment and unemployment rates in Germany, 1970–2014

Note: Grey shaded areas refer to period of economic contraction (based on the output gap).
Source: OECD estimates based on the *OECD Labour Force Statistics, OECD Short-term Labour Market Statistics* and *OECD Economic Outlook Databases* (Cut-off date: 13 April 2015).

Figure 7: Labour market chart Germany

ployment rate in Germany is attributed to the so-called 'dual system' of apprenticeship which combines vocational education in school with on-the-job training in firms. This system facilitates a relatively smooth transition, first, from school to work for the vast majority of young apprentices and, secondly, from a fixed-term contract as an apprentice to a permanent contract, once qualified, often with the firm that provided the training. As a result, the German dual system is rightly viewed as best practice for the school-to-work transition for other EU and OECD countries to emulate, though its unique history and specific German institutional setting do not make it easy to replicate in other countries.[82]

Another distinctive feature of the German employment record, which is more recent, is the strong growth in older worker employment rates. The scoreboard shows this clearly for the three age groups in question (55–9, 60–4 and 65–9): in all three groups there have been very sharp increases in the employment rates in Germany, which have overtaken similar increases in most other EU countries. As a result, the gap in the German employment rate for the age group 55–9,

---

[82] See Eichhorst (2013) for a succinct summary of the core elements of the German dual system.

compared with the EU average, increased from 6 percentage points in 2000 to 11 points in 2013. For the age group 60–4, the German performance is even more remarkable. Germany had a below-average employment rate for this age group in 2000, but by 2013 their employment rate exceeded the EU average by over 15 percentage points. Even among the age group 65–9, whose employment rate in Germany in 2000 was over 2 percentage points below the EU average, the rate had more than doubled by 2013 to exceed the EU average.

With regard to the types of jobs created since 2000, there was a strong growth in part-time jobs between 2000 and 2007, but the part-time share remained constant at around 22 per cent between 2007 and 2103 which, however, was significantly higher than the EU average of 17.5 per cent in 2013. This relatively high degree of part-time working is linked to the relatively low level of labour input in Germany: average annual actual hours worked per person employed were the second lowest in the OECD in 2013, at 1,388 hours, after the Netherlands.[83] The main factor behind this is the relatively low incidence of full-time work among women, especially among married women and mothers. Indeed, OECD (2012c) highlights the fact that one-fifth of German female workers work fewer than 20 hours a week, the third highest such share after Switzerland and the Netherlands, twice the OECD average. Such part-time work is associated with a high risk of poverty.

One factor behind the recent growth in part-time work is the fact that women account for many of the so-called 'mini-jobs', which were created as part of the Hartz reforms – these are jobs which currently pay less than 450 euros per month and which are exempt from tax and social insurance contributions on earnings up to the threshold; employers pay lower payroll taxes for such jobs than for regular jobs.[84] As the tax and social insurance exemptions are not targeted at low-paid workers, many mini-jobs are held by second earners and students.[85] Other factors which contribute to the high share of female part-timers, especially those working short hours, are: (i) the joint taxation of income for married couples, which imposes a high marginal tax rate on the second earner (mainly

---

83 See OECD (2014g), Table K.

84 When mini-jobs were first introduced in 2003, the earnings threshold was set at 400 euros per month. The tax and social insurance exemptions are phased out on earnings between 450 and 850 euros per month – so-called 'midi-jobs' – which, in turn, contributes to relatively high effective tax rates for workers with such earnings, acting as a disincentive for them to work more. OECD (2014c) notes that there were almost 1.4 million midi-jobs in 2011.

85 OECD (2014), Box 3.3 shows that second earners and students accounted together for 55 per cent of all mini-jobbers in 2010. Mini-jobs also favour multiple job-holding, as the income from other jobs does not count towards the mini-job earnings ceiling.

women); and (ii) the lack of affordable childcare for children under three years of age.

The period between 2000 and 2007 also saw some increase in the share of temporary jobs, which coincided with the liberalisation of regulations governing temporary agency work under Hartz I (see below). Germany has relatively strict employment protection for permanent workers, while its protection for temporary workers is relatively lax (see Germany's scoreboard). The relaxation of protection for temporary workers in the early 2000s probably contributed to its increasing share in the run-up to the Great Recession. The share dipped slightly between 2007 and 2013, however, though it remains very close to the EU average. Much of the recent employment growth has been in permanent jobs, and it has to be acknowledged that temporary jobs serve as a stepping-stone to a permanent job for many Germans, in contrast to the situation in other major EU economies such as France, Italy or Spain.[86]

The German job miracle has some black spots associated with it. For example, the first decade of this century witnessed a significant increase in the incidence of low-paid jobs (defined as jobs paying less than two-thirds of the median wage). The scoreboard shows that by 2013 such jobs accounted for almost one in five of all paid and salaried jobs in Germany compared with an EU average of 15 per cent. The increasing incidence of low-paid work in Germany is linked to the rising shares of part-time and temporary jobs which, in turn, are a significant driver of the widening earnings and income inequality in Germany that began in the mid-1990s and continued over the following decade. These labour market drivers of rising inequality owe something to the Hartz reforms implemented between 2003 and 2005, as well as changing demographic and workplace patterns.

Nonetheless, income inequality in Germany, as proxied by the well-known Gini coefficient, remained consistently below the OECD average throughout the period and even declined slightly in the period after the Great Recession.[87]

A second black spot is the persistently high share of long-term unemployment as a proportion of total unemployment numbers, despite the sharp fall of the overall unemployment rate in recent years. In line with the steep drop in overall unemployment since 2007, the incidence of long-term unemployment has also declined significantly. Notwithstanding this recent improvement, the in-

---

86 Walwei (2013) shows that almost 40 per cent of German workers on a temporary contract shifted to a permanent contract within one year.

87 For details on the trends and determinants of poverty and inequality in Germany since the mid-1990s, see OECD (2014c), Chapter 3. This highlights the fact that market-income inequality is higher in Germany than in many other OECD countries, but the redistributive effect of the tax/ transfer system is above average so that disposable-income inequality is below average.

cidence of long-term unemployment was still almost 45 per cent in 2013, almost 10 percentage points higher than the OECD average and only slightly below the EU average. The high incidence of long-term unemployment persists, despite the fact that one of the aims of the Hartz reforms is to lower it by activating more of the long-term unemployed into jobs.

A final concern is the relatively high tax wedge on labour. This reflects the comparatively high reliance on social security contributions as a source of tax revenues. OECD (2014c), Table 3.4 shows that the tax wedge in Germany is, on the one hand, significantly higher than the OECD average for a wide range of household types and earnings levels, and, on the other hand, bears heavily on low-income families and single parents.

Nonetheless, the very favourable German labour market performance during the Great Recession and the subsequent recovery suggests that it has passed an extremely difficult 'stress test' with flying colours. Perhaps the best indicator of this is the fact that the historical experience of the link between the business cycle and unemployment – the so-called 'Okun coefficient' – would have predicted an increase of almost 3 percentage points in the German unemployment rate following the steep drop in output in 2008; the actual increase was only 0.5 per cent.[88] The harmonised unemployment rate is at its lowest level in over 20 years, while the unemployment rates in most of the EU countries are still rising. In addition, OECD (2012a) shows that the Beveridge curve – the relationship linking the job vacancy rate to the unemployment rate – shifted inwards in Germany in the period following 2008, indicating a continued improvement in the process matching available jobs to job seekers.

There has been much discussion of the reasons for the recent German 'job miracle'.[89] One point is clear: much of the adjustment to the initial large drop in output in 2008–9 occurred when firms cut working hours rather than laying off workers. The explanations for this shift in employer behaviour, compared with past trends, sometimes put the emphasis on different determinants, but there is general agreement that this working-time flexibility reflected an increased willingness by firms, unions and workers to trade off job security against working time and wages. This willingness, in turn, was spurred on by policy in the shape of an expanded and more generous short-time work scheme (*Kurzarbeit*), which was taken up by many export-oriented manufacturers who were hit hard by the initial

---

88 For the empirical evidence on the Okun coefficient, see OECD (2012c), Box 1 and Annex 1.A1.
89 For good discussions, see Burda and Hunt (2011), Eichhorst (2012), Rinne and Zimmermann (2013), Caliendo and Hogenacker (2012) and OECD (2012c).

drop in world demand for their products in 2008–9.[90] Another factor behind the job miracle is the significant degree of wage moderation in Germany, compared with its major trading partners: relative unit labour costs fell in Germany post-2002, thereby helping to maintain the cost-competitiveness of the traded sector.

It is hard to attribute much of the recent job miracle to greater public spending on labour market policies. The scoreboard shows that before 2007 Germany spent more than the EU average on both 'passive' unemployment benefits and active labour market policies (ALMPs). Since then, however, its spending effort on both has fallen back to below the corresponding EU averages in 2013.

At the same time, most commentators agree that the Hartz reforms undertaken before the Great Recession also played a prominent role in enabling the German economy and labour market to pass this major stress test with flying colours. We now turn to consider these and other social policy reforms.

5.2.2 Major labour market and social policy reforms since 2000

Most of the reform activity in Germany over this period was concentrated in the years 2002 to 2005 and these reforms are collectively known as the Hartz reforms, named after Peter Hartz, the Director of Personnel at Volkswagen, who chaired the Commission which drew up the initial reform proposals for consideration by the government and parliament. In addition, there were a number of reforms to the pension system and to early retirement pathways, some of which predated the Hartz reforms and which were complemented by some of the Hartz reforms and continued after they had been completed. Since these reforms played an important role in spurring on the exceptionally rapid growth of older worker employment in the period after 2000, they will also be discussed below.

The Hartz reforms

It is important to consider the starting point for these reforms which the OECD described 'as the single biggest change in German labour-market policy in a generation'.[91] Three factors seem particularly important:[92] first, there was a general

---

90 At its peak, around 1.5 million workers were on the scheme in mid-2009; since then the number has fallen drastically as the economy has recovered. Hijzen and Venn (2011) publish an evaluation of the scheme, controlling for the deadweight and displacement effects associated with such subsidies. They estimate that it saved almost 240,000 jobs in Germany (0.6 per cent of employment). See also Hijzen and Martin (2013).
91 See OECD (2009c), p. 223.

election looming and unemployment was rising sharply. The Schröder government had been elected on a promise to cut unemployment and it had to be seen to be doing something to meet this promise, before it faced the electorate again. With the impending election on the horizon, the left wing of the SPD and their union allies had little choice but to endorse the reform proposals.

Secondly, the scandal surrounding large-scale data falsification at the Federal Labour Office (BA) – the German public employment service – put the social partners, who oversaw the workings of the BA, on the defensive. This scandal enabled Chancellor Schröder to set up the Hartz Commission with the ostensible mandate to prepare proposals to reform the BA. As will be seen below, the Commission interpreted this mandate very broadly.

Thirdly, the choice, and sequencing, of the reforms was carefully considered. The reforms focused on reforming the BA's operations and governance, activating the unemployed more vigorously and changing the unemployment benefit system to enhance work incentives. They ruled out changes to more contentious issues which would have provoked more serious opposition from the unions and from the left wing of the SPD. Hence, despite calls from the IMF, the OECD and the European Commission to tackle other issues, such as the collective bargaining system and the strictness of employment protection legislation (EPL) for permanent workers, these calls went unheeded. At the same time, the easier aspects of the reform proposals were pushed through first, leaving the more politically contentious ones to the end. In addition, the leading employer associations (the BDI and the BDA) and the main umbrella union confederation (the DGB) were consulted during the negotiations over the reforms, even if they were not formally represented on the 15-member Commission.

A noticeable feature of the reforms is that they tended to focus on the supply rather than the demand side of the labour market. This reflected a growing consensus that there was little or no effective activation of the unemployed or social assistance beneficiaries by the BA or the *Länder*, i. e. the regions, and the municipal authorities. Instead, the latter put their main emphasis on paying out benefit entitlements. The scoreboard shows that the net benefit replacement rates for the newly unemployed or for the very long-term unemployed (with a period out of work exceeding two years) were of the order of 66–70 per cent in 2000. When this was combined with a high marginal tax wedge on labour, it meant that there was little incentive for the unemployed or those able to work, but relying

---

92 See OECD (2009c) for a full account of these factors and their crucial role in the political economy of the Hartz reforms. It argues that the reforms were partly inspired by the 'New Labour' approach adopted by the Blair government in the UK when it came to power in 1997.

on social assistance, to find a new job quickly. At the same time, neither the BA nor the *Länder* and municipalities put much pressure on them to search actively for a new job or to take steps to improve their employability.

Table 8: A summary of the Hartz reforms

Reform	Implementation date	Main measures
Hartz I	January 2003	Establishment of public–private partnership temporary work agencies to help the unemployed find work; reform of the law on temporary agency work; tightened conditions for accepting job offers; new rules governing benefit sanctions; introduction of training vouchers.
Hartz II	January 2003	New benefits for business start-ups; reform of the legislation governing so-called 'mini–jobs' with limited social security contributions; preparations for the organisation of Job centres bringing together employment and social welfare services; first steps to reorganise the organisational structure of the public employment service.
Hartz III	January 2004	Continued restructuring of the public employment service to make it a more effective provider of employment services; simplification of active labour market policies.
Hartz IV	February 2005	Entitlement to the income-related unemployment insurance benefit (henceforth called UB I) was cut to a maximum of 12 months (reduced from 26 months) for those aged under 55 and to 18 months (reduced from 32 months) for those aged over 55. The income-related unemployment assistance benefit (UA) was abolished and merged with the means-tested social assistance benefit to create a new flat-rate benefit (UB II). The sanctions regime for UB II recipients was made stricter.

Source: adapted from OECD (2012c), Table 1.2; OECD (2009c), Box 10.2.

The Hartz reforms were grouped under four broad laws and implemented over the period 2002–5 (table 8). It should be pointed out that the Commission's work was eased by a reform adopted by the SPD–Green coalition in 2001 called 'Job-AQTIV'. This introduced quantitative job-profiling for the newly unemployed and sought to scale up more efficient ALMPs.[93] The Hartz proposals, particularly

---

93 OECD (2009c) notes that much of the Job-AQTIV reforms were inspired by the guidelines of both the EU Employment Strategy and the OECD's Jobs Strategy.

those under Hartz IV, were much contested, especially those which sought to cut the duration of UB I.[94] Hartz III and Hartz IV proposals were then embodied in the government's broader 'Agenda 2010' economic reform strategy unveiled in March 2003. Agenda 2010, however, also included proposals to reform EPL and collective bargaining. These were strongly resisted by the unions who, in the end, were prepared to strike a bargain with the Schröder government: when the government gave up the proposed reforms to EPL and collective bargaining, the unions ended their opposition to the cut in the duration of UB I.

Nevertheless, there was some backsliding on the Hartz IV reform. In 2007, it was agreed to extend the maximum duration of UB I for older workers: from 12 to 15 months for the unemployed aged 50–4, from 15 to 18 months for those aged 55–7 and from 18 to 24 months for those aged 58 and over. At the same time, however, the job-search requirements on the unemployed aged 58 and over were tightened in order to encourage them to search for work more actively. Prior to 2007, most of the unemployed aged 58 and over were effectively exempted from the job-search obligation, with the result that they could remain on benefits until they were eligible for a pension.

An unexpected bonus from the reforms was that the law required a systematic and rigorous *ex-post* evaluation of all the measures included under the laws. These evaluations were to be carried out at arm's length from the official agencies by research institutes and academics. This legislation, which is unique among EU members, has spawned a large number of evaluations highlighting which ALMPs and other measures were successful and which were not.

The many assessments of the impact of the Hartz reforms on the German labour market all agree that they were important in the creation of the 'job miracle', though they also highlight the role played by other factors.[95] At the same time, the studies concur that the reforms contributed to the growth of atypical forms of employment in Germany, and they, in turn, have added to growing earnings inequality and an increasing risk of poverty for certain groups, e. g. workers trapped in atypical jobs, single parents and the long-term unemployed.

---

94 Interestingly, there was much less opposition to the proposal to create UB II. OECD (2010a) points out that, while older workers were the main losers under this proposal because it reduced greatly the attractiveness of the UA benefit as a pathway to early retirement, up to one-third of the recipients of UB II received higher benefits after the reform.
95 See Rinne and Zimmermann (2013) and Eichhorst (2012) for discussions.

Minimum wage

The growing clamour in Germany about the dangers posed to social cohesion by rising earnings inequality and poverty risks among the working-age population has recently forced the hand of the coalition government to introduce a nation-wide statutory minimum wage. Up to that time, Germany was relatively unique among EU countries in not having a nationwide minimum wage. Instead, only a few specific industrial sectors had a minimum wage, which was set on the basis of collective bargaining in the sector.

As part of the bargaining, however, which led to the formation of the coalition government, the Social Democratic Party insisted on the establishment of a nationwide minimum wage of 8.50 euros per hour. This minimum wage is being implemented gradually over the period from the beginning of 2015 until the end of 2016. Set at this level, the minimum will be equivalent to about 50 per cent of the median hourly wage.

Simulations suggest that it will affect about 15 per cent of employees nation-wide, but a significantly higher percentage (23 per cent) in the so-called 'New Länder'. In addition to setting the level of the minimum wage, the coalition government has established a commission to review future levels.[96]

The introduction of a nationwide minimum wage is a radical reform for Germany with its long reliance on collective bargaining to set wages. It has been welcomed by OECD (2014) as a useful instrument to help tackle in-work poverty risks, though other commentators expressed concerns about the need to avoid excessive hikes in the level, as this would damage job prospects for low-wage workers.[97]

Reforms to encourage working longer

As noted above, population ageing is proceeding at a very rapid pace in Germany and there was fairly widespread agreement, dating back to the late 1990s, that action had to be taken to break the early retirement culture and offer incentives to older workers to work longer. A series of reforms to the first pillar of the pension system gradually cut replacement rates through changes to the indexation formula. The earliest age at which a pension could be drawn, was raised from 60 to 62 for women, though it was reduced from 63 to 62 for men. A bonus-malus system was introduced in the late 1990s to reward postponing retirement beyond

---

96 Unlike similar minimum wage commissions in other EU countries, e.g. France and the UK, the members of the German commission are to be nominated by the social partners alone.
97 See Zimmermann (2014).

65: the pension would be cut by 3.6 per cent if the individuals opted to retire aged 63–4; it would be 6 per cent higher for every year of working post-65. In 2006, the age threshold for an unemployed person to draw an early pension was increased from age 60 to 63, phased in up to 2010.

As we have seen, some of the Hartz reforms also raised the incentives for older workers to continue working or, if unemployed, to search for a new job more actively. In addition, the subsidised part-time work scheme for older workers (*Altersteilzeit*) was closed to new entrants from the beginning of 2010. Finally, in 2007, an earnings top-up had been introduced for the older unemployed who found a new job which paid less than their previous job.

In 2007, the statutory retirement age was raised from 65 to 67, with the increase phased in over the period until 2029. There has, however, been backsliding on this reform recently. The 2013 coalition agreement allowed workers with a contributions record of at least 45 years to retire on a full pension at age 63; this will rise gradually to 65, in line with the increase in the standard statutory age to 67. Pension top-ups will be paid to mothers whose children were born before 1992 and invalidity pensions will also be increased. The increased pension spending arising from the 2013 reforms will be financed by higher payroll taxes which, in turn, will widen the already high tax wedge on labour.

5.2.3 Conclusion

The period 2002–5 witnessed a major burst of reform activity on the German labour market following a prolonged period of rising unemployment and a growing consensus that something drastic had to be done to remedy the situation. This reform movement was led from the top by Chancellor Schröder, and his chosen instrument to force the reforms was the Hartz Commission, whose deliberations eventually resulted in the four broad Hartz laws which were introduced between 2003 and 2005. The laws were first implemented in a period of rising employment but they soon ran into a severe stress test with the advent of the Great Recession in 2008–9. The fact that the German economy and labour market rode out this major downturn so quickly and so well, compared with its major trading partners, is ample testimony to the fact that the Hartz reforms, in combination with other factors mentioned above, have greatly improved the resilience of the German labour market.

Thanks to the evaluation mandate which accompanied the Hartz legislation, we now know a great deal more about what worked well and what did not in the various reform measures, and why. The growing evaluation literature has already influenced the mix of spending on ALMPs in Germany and assisted other countries in their search for cost-effective labour market reforms.

Some of the Hartz reforms, together with other reforms to the pension system and the closure of existing early retirement pathways, have greatly raised the incentives for older German workers to work longer. The fact that older worker employment rates have risen significantly more in Germany since 2000 than in most other EU countries shows the power of such measures to affect people's behaviour.

At the same time, the reforms have also contributed to the growth of atypical employment and widening earnings inequality in Germany. Concerns about the negative side-effects of these developments on social cohesion and social mobility led the coalition government to introduce a nationwide minimum wage for the first time.

Looking to the future, population ageing will pose major challenges to Germany. OECD (2014g), Figure 3 projects that, unless Germany undertakes further structural reforms, the potential growth rate will drop to below 1 per cent per year over the next 30 years. Tackling this problem successfully will require another German miracle.

Table 9: Scoreboard for labour market outcomes and policies, Germany and EU, 1993–2013

	1993		2000		2007		2013*	
	DE	EU	**DE**	EU	**DE**	EU	**DE**	EU
1. Employment rate (% of the working-age population)	**65.7**	61.2	**66.2**	63.6	**70.1**	66.7	**75.0**	65.9
– male	**75.6**	71.8	**73.8**	72.9	**76.1**	74.2	**79.8**	71.6
– female	**55.5**	50.7	**58.6**	54.4	**64.0**	59.2	**70.1**	60.2
– youth (aged 15/16–24)	**52.7**	39.5	**47.2**	39.4	**45.9**	38.2	**46.8**	33.4
– older people (aged 55–9)	**50.3**	47.6	**56.7**	50.6	**66.7**	57.3	**75.9**	64.9
– older people (aged 60–4)	**17.6**	22.3	**20.0**	22.3	**32.9**	29.4	**49.9**	34.7
– older people (aged 65–9)		9.2	**5.1**	7.4	**7.1**	9.5	**12.6**	11.3
2. Unemployment rate (% of labour force)	**7.9**	10.8	**7.7**	8.9	**8.6**	7.1	**5.3**	10.7
– youth (aged 15/16–24)	**7.6**	21.0	**8.4**	17.4	**11.7**	15.5	**7.9**	23.3
3. Incidence of long-term unemployment (% of total unemployment) (a)	**40.3**	42.0	**51.5**	44.4	**56.6**	41.6	**44.7**	46.5
4. Part-time employment rate (b)	**12.8**	13.8	**17.6**	15.3	**22.0**	16.0	**22.4**	17.5
5. Temporary employment rate (c) (temporary employees as % of total employees)	**10.3**	10.5	**12.7**	13.1	**14.6**	14.8	**13.4**	14.0
– youth (aged 15/16–24 as % of total youth employees)	**36.9**	28.8	**52.4**	38.0	**57.4**	41.8	**52.9**	43.0
6. Low-pay incidence (d) (% of employees)	–	–	**15.8**	15.7	**18.2**	16.5	**18.4**	15.0

Table 9 (continued)

	1993		2000		2007		2013*	
	DE	EU	**DE**	EU	**DE**	EU	**DE**	EU
7. Protection of permanent workers against individual dismissal	**2.7**	2.6	**2.7**	2.5	**3.0**	2.4	**2.9**	2.2
– Protection of temporary workers	**3.3**	2.3	**2.0**	1.8	**1.0**	1.6	**1.1**	1.8
8. Public spending on labour market policies (% of GDP)	**3.9**	2.9	**3.1**	2.0	**2.0**	1.6	**1.7**	2.0
– Spending on active measures (e)	**1.4**	0.9	**1.2**	0.8	**0.7**	0.6	**0.7**	0.8
– Spending on passive measures (f)	**2.5**	2.1	**1.9**	1.1	**1.3**	0.9	**1.0**	1.2
9. Net benefit replacement rate (g) (averaged over four family types and two earnings levels)	–	–	**67**	65	**67**	61	**61**	54
– initial spell (h)	–	–	**70**	70	**71**	71	**71**	70
– after 2 years of unemployment	–	–	**66**	66	**75**	63	**58**	57

* 2013 or latest available year.
(a) Persons out of work for 12 months and over.
(b) Part-time employment refers to persons who usually work less than 30 hours per week in "their 'main job'".
(c) Temporary employees are wage and salary workers whose job has a pre-determined end date as opposed to permanent employees whose job is of unlimited duration. National definitions broadly conform to this generic definition, but may vary depending on national circumstances.
(d) Persons with a wage less than 2/3 of the median.
(e) 'Active' measures cover categories 1 to 7 of the OECD/Eurostat data base on public spending on labour market programmes.
(f) 'Passive' measures cover categories 8 and 9 of the OECD/Eurostat data base on public spending on labour market programmes.
(g) Data on net replacement rates for 2000 refer to 2001.
(h) Initial phase of unemployment but following any waiting period. For married couples, the percentage of AW relates to the previous earnings of the 'unemployed' spouse only; the second spouse is assumed to be 'inactive' with no earnings and no recent employment history. Where receipt of social assistance or other minimum-income benefits is subject to activity tests (such as active job-search or being 'available' for work), these requirements are assumed to be met. Children are aged four and six and neither childcare benefits nor childcare costs are considered. Unweighted averages, for previous full-time earnings levels of 67 % and 100 % of AW and out-of-work single and couple households with no children or with two children (children are assumed to be aged four and six and neither childcare benefits not childcare costs are considered). After tax and including unemployment and family benefits. Social assistance and other means-tested benefits are assumed to be available subject to relevant income conditions. Housing costs are assumed equal to 20 % of AW.
Sources: OECD Online Employment Database: www.oecd.org/employment/database; data on net replacement rates come from the OECD tax-benefit models (www.oecd.org/els/social/work-incentives).

6 Greece

6.1 Interview with Georgios Papandreou, 1 December 2014

'The more you create consensus, the more likely it is that your reforms will be long-lasting and thought-through.'

When you became Prime Minister in October 2009, you immediately had to embark on a number of reforms. With the wisdom of ample hindsight, could you please elaborate on these reforms? Where did you set your priorities? What do you consider a success and where do you see shortcomings?
Looking at the overall picture, I think we had two competing priorities during the last few years. One was the fiscal consolidation, but not just that but the whole view that austerity would be the solution. The other priority were the necessary structural reforms – in the labour market, the pension system, education and in health care, among other areas. These two priorities did not always match well, because sometimes when you carry out a reform you need to have more fiscal flexibility. Actually, Gerhard Schröder used to tell me all the time that he could not have carried out reform in Germany while at the same time complying with austerity measures, but we had the two at the same time. The pressure was more on austerity, because the requirement to cut the budget and to raise taxes was stronger. We therefore found ourselves in a very, very special situation. The second point was that we could not devalue our currency and the whole emphasis was on internal devaluation, which meant, in effect, that we had to push down wages and labour costs – but not only these, of course. I would say that the prices, the stronghold of certain oligopolies, for example, the administration and the bureaucracy, did not allow us to lower consumer prices as much as we would have wanted to, which resulted in more pressure on wages than on prices, which – in turn – created more of a recession and deeper problems. This is the general framework within which we were working.

I decided that we had to push through reforms as soon as possible, because the quicker we carried out the reforms the quicker we would have results – and the less need for cuts and painful burdens.

What were the main obstacles for the implementation of reforms?
We did not have a well-managed public sector and there were certain difficulties with our governance. I think this is one of the problems Greece shares with some of the periphery countries: historically, we came out quite recently from under dictatorships and authoritarian regimes and we had highly politicised institu-

tions that were often used for clientelistic purposes or for oppressing parts of our society. These institutions had not really changed at root, even though we did have a democracy. The bureaucracy, the judicial system, the tax system and the public sector had not fundamentally adapted to the new political circumstances over the years. We did not have a *glasnost* or a *perestroika*; we did not have the Copenhagen criteria to become part of the European Union, but basically we simply joined. Therefore, these weaknesses, I think, emerged during the crisis – even before, I would say, but particularly just after the 2008 crisis.

Greece was brought into the European Union in 1981 – as a full member. This was just six years after the dictatorship. The logic was that we needed to support democracy in Greece, but there was also this romantic view that Greece was the birthplace of democracy – and it was therefore felt important to let Greece in.

The terms on which Greece came in were not negotiated in depth. In this context it is worth remembering that the Copenhagen criteria had been created, because the majority of the countries that were coming in were former Communist countries, and their institutions had to go through a period of adjustment. This meant not just privatisation, but also carrying out reforms for good governance, and on their justice and parliamentary systems, human rights legislation and the role of the army, among other things. These were issues that were very important. We had nothing of the sort. Do not forget, we were on the other side of the Cold War, but we had been a dictatorship as well and not a democracy.

I think we also have to look at the political situation when we got into the European Union. We did not have strong incentives for reforms. There were major changes, of course, in Greece: we introduced elections at local and regional government level, which was new. Labour laws were brought in to protect the labour force and the health system was developed. I would say that a more robust welfare system was developed after we joined the European Union. This coincided with the period that our government – my father, Andreas Papandreou, was Head of PASOK (the Panhellenic Socialist Movement) then – pushed these things, too. I think both parties, PASOK und New Democracy, put the emphasis on really reforming the public sector in an efficient way, including the central governance and administrative structures.

We obviously face a number of challenges, like introducing transparency, good governance, fighting clientelism, bringing in more meritocracy in government, making government more accountable, more efficient, more flexible, more intune with the education system and the services, as well as making the whole welfare system more responsive to the needs of our society, of our growing economy and our citizens. These were basic issues, but they went much deeper than the sort of standard handbooks for economists put it when they talk about the need for a reform of the labour market and related structures.

That is part of it, but only a very small part compared to the impact that is needed to make comprehensive changes. I think we still have room for manoeuvre there. We have carried out quite a few reforms, but the dimension of the implementation has always been a problem.

What were the main challenges in the area of labour market and pension reforms?

That is a very important question. Let me just give you one point as to why the public sector, or public governance, became quite important – especially for labour and pensions, but other areas, too. First of all, with the liberalisation of politics in Greece, trading became stronger, particularly in the public sector. We had a very large number of small and medium-sized enterprises in Greece in the private sector – but they were all very small, with some 90 per cent of these businesses having approximately five workers. The structure of labour and industry in our country is very distinct.

The major trade unions were in the public sector, in the wider public sector, and they became much stronger, but not only that, they also developed very big privileges, as they became stronger. This was therefore one major reform we had to make: to equalise the public and private sectors. Doing this resulted in cutting lots of privileges of vested interests, privileges not only in terms of wages, but also in terms of certain types of benefits – for example, of course, pensions. So, these were the areas where we acted.

Another sphere where the public sector played an important role was education. First of all, there was a highly clientelistic form of employment in the public sector – initially even for permanent jobs, but then also for the so-called *stagiaires*, interns or trainees. The employment of *stagiaires* had become increasingly widespread, in order to circumvent the strict rules governing regular employment in the public sector, which were partly even enshrined in the Greek constitution.

The public sector became huge – we were crowded with *stagiaires*, who were somehow given the idea that maybe, later on, the law might change, and they could become a permanent part of the public sector. Thus, you had a massive public sector, with the whole idea of becoming a public-sector employee being attractive among the younger generation and, of course, families – because of the benefits. As a consequence, the entire education system was geared to people getting public-sector jobs. Education was not focused on the needs of the wider economy – of the private sector – and this led to structural unemployment, because students got degrees that had little to do with what the market or the different regions required. We had a very centralised educational system – very insular, with absolutely no proper links to the needs of the wider society and economy at all. It was obvious that we had to reform education.

We began the reform of tertiary education – that was a major reform. It was nothing that the Troika had asked for. This was of our own doing. We had a large majority in parliament. We were able to create a consensus. Slowly these institutions are starting to change with, of course, a lot of resistance internally in the education sector. Secondly, we tried to decentralise the training sector to make it useful for people to be employed in the private sector. Vouchers were introduced, to give the unemployed a choice of training centre, in contrast to the past, when the government was responsible for procurement: we would provide a great number of programmes to different private education institutions, which were not always accountable and which had also developed in a very clientelistic way. Naturally, we tried to break with that tradition and make the system more accountable and responsive to the needs of the unemployed.

One of the problems in this area was again, of course, that since everybody was looking for a public-sector job, this turned out to be the way we dealt with unemployment – and not through an active labour market policy, not through training and retraining, not through trying to find companies that had jobs to offer. We had a very weak training sector and also insufficient active labour market policies – another area in need of change. We started making these changes, for example, by publicising the services for the unemployed to give them better online information on the types of jobs that existed.

On pension reform, we moved very quickly – in about six months – using the momentum of the crisis to start with, which worked up to the point, when the situation became too painful for the citizens. In the initial stages, though, we were able to get a wider consensus. Our first major pensions reform was six months into 2010, when we harmonised the criteria for pensions and merged 60 to 70 pension funds: the system had been fragmented and inefficiently run. We also abolished perks and privileges in the pension system.

There was a huge lack of transparency in who had benefits and who had pensions. There were people who had died, who were still getting pensions – with their families drawing the money, even though they were not entitled to these pensions. There were a great number of benefits for the disabled, which were allocated in a clientelistic way to people who did not meet the criteria. Actually, we found quite a few people on such benefits who were not really disabled at all.

The general consensus now is that the pension and benefit systems are much more viable than in the past. We do have some problems because of the consistent recession and high unemployment – this has clearly taken its toll.

When you have 50 per cent youth unemployment, this obviously also hits your welfare system.

In formulating the content of your reforms, but also the implementation, did you draw explicitly on good practice from other countries? Did you look at analyses and recommendations from international organisations or other sources?
First of all, I asked both the IMF and the European Union to help us with expertise. I also reached out to other people around the world, particularly in the European Union. José Manuel Barroso finally set up a task force, which is now working in Greece under Horst Reichenbach – a German. He was leading the Task Force for Greece and in that capacity allocated some of the EU funding. I also asked him not just to do that, but to examine all the areas in our government structures, so that we could learn from examples of best of practice in the European Union.

We therefore looked at specific countries for certain areas of reform, for example, at Estonia for e-governance, because they are the best in that field in the European Union; at the Netherlands for the easy way they conduct business, and we asked ourselves how we could restructure our administration to make business simpler. What about central government? We do not have land rosters, so Germany is helping us with that – these are the types of things we did, but I think we can do more.

In addition, especially in dealing with public sector reform, we digested a lot of international expertise: the OECD conducted a study, as did experts from private companies. Thus, we had quite a few people looking at this area and we did reach out – both for design and implementation.

Did you have a stable coalition? Was there cohesion in the government? Did all this pressure from outside forge a very solid team or did you have internal difficulties to overcome as well?
I would say that, at first, there was a general consensus that we really had to push forward on reform. In the initial stages of the programme, there was much wider agreement, both inside the cabinet and in our society. I was elected on the slogan 'Either we change or we sink'. People realised that we were in a difficult situation, because of the pressures of the markets, the speed of the reforms and the depth of the cuts we had to make.

Even so, after almost two years in government, we still had, I would say, a pretty good consensus, but then we realised that we would not be able to access the markets in 2012 and that we needed a new programme. This was the so-called Second Economic Adjustment Programme and we were aware that it would lead to new problems. We tried to frontload all the difficult measures, such as the reforms and the cuts. Then, after a year-and-a-half, in mid-2011, the IMF and the Troika approached us with the words: 'Since you cannot access the markets we have to have another programme, and this will bring with it more cuts and further reforms.' At that stage, the consensus became more volatile and I then reached out to see if I could get a wider consensus. I had always tried that, from the very beginning, but I tried to push it even further by asking the opposition party to become part of the government. Initially they did not agree, but about four or five months later, when I called for a referendum, we ended up in a coalition government. In a way, I pushed them to come into the government. Basically, for the two years we were governing, it was just one party, because we had an absolute majority in parliament and a coalition would not really have been required, but internally our party became too divided about the fact that we alone had to carry the burden of all these changes and that we had to take the hit from all the sides. Thus, we established a coalition and with that we achieved a wider consensus from three parties. This kept the programme alive until we had elections in 2012 and we were able to restore stability.

When you started, you had a licence to operate a kind of mandate for change. Consensus in society and cohesion in government had been in place initially, but started to crumble when the call for the second programme came up. How did that affect the climate for reforms and what did you do to maintain consensus?
It was actually in June 2011 when I called on the opposition leader, Antonis Samaras, who later became Prime Minister, but we were not able to come to an agreement. I do not have to go into details. He was not really ready to cooperate. He just wanted to call elections, but I responded: 'That is not the issue; we need a wider consensus. Having new elections would simply polarise the situation and not help us in implementing the programme.' Then, of course, later on, when we did have the second programme, I called for a referendum, because I felt that this would be a way to get public support and circumvent the very, very strong resistance from the leaders of the opposition on both sides – on the Left and on the Right. As they were not cooperating on anything and basically undermining the implementation of the programme, they were not helping either in creating a consensus, but we needed a wider consensus.

Of course, during my entire political career – and even in the past as a minister of different departments – I tried to work with the social partners. I would bring them in to discuss these issues, in fact, one of my first meetings took place in early January 2010. I organised a big conference and invited some 500 people from all social partners, chambers of commerce, industry and universities – the wide civic society of Greece, if you like. In my address I said: 'We need a consensus when we make changes in our country, and it is going to be difficult if there is a crisis.' I continued in this way, ensuring that, when we did introduce labour reforms or changes in any areas of labour relations, we had the agreement of the social partners, the unions and the employers – and we generally did have their approval, at least up to a point, but then the Troika pushed through reforms which were no longer based on consultation and agreement. In other words, this sort of negotiation, with social partners, became less important and was basically abolished in Greece.

What also happened – with a lot of the business people – is that they would advise members of the Troika directly of their views and positions, influencing the agenda of the Troika, who then turned into a centre of power in policy implementation. This did not allow for much consultation and negotiation with the social partners and is, I think, one of the problems we had, and still have, to deal with.

Generally, we were pretty much able to have an internal consensus in Greece until the end of 2011, even on subjects like the labour market. Then things got more difficult. There was more of a sense of an imposition. For example, the social partners, both the employers' and the employees' unions, were not in favour of cutting the minimum wage too much, but the Troika had the state agree and lower the minimum wage arbitrarily. Now, whether that has helped or not is another question. In my view, it is a question of substance and not procedure.

While the second package of the Troika was certainly needed, just because we could not access markets, it also dampened the dynamics of carrying out structural reforms. There was much more emphasis on the fiscal area. I think people said that there was not the same will to carry out the reforms with regard to what we did during the second programme, and the political change in Greece. We have now reached a point where there are lots of reforms that are still not implemented. This is a problem between the Greek government and the Troika. Partly it is the responsibility of the government and partly the responsibility of the Troika itself, because they were simply pushing the fiscal aspect as a priority.

Proper communication is usually considered a key element for successful reforms. How did you seek to legitimise your reform endeavours? What did your communication strategy look like?
We aimed to spend more time on deliberation, wherever we could. Thus, first of all, we had two readings of the laws in the cabinet and two in parliament, which had not happened before. In addition, we introduced so-called 'Wiki-laws' – like

a sort of Wikipedia, we put laws on the internet to get public comments before they came to the cabinet for final decisions.

We tried to open up the cabinet meetings and have televised meetings on particular issues; we also asked some social partners and other important individuals to join the cabinet, to give support or to discuss certain policies. For our first cabinet meeting we brought in our Ombudsman to see what the Greek citizens' problems were. When we talked about migration and had to change the relevant legislation, we asked our Archbishop to join us, because he has supported the cause of migrants. In addition, we also held quite a few meetings with social partners, of course, not only I, but also the other ministers. These were the standard types of things we did.

Compensating those who lose out through structural reforms is typically regarded as a viable means to overcome resistance. Fully acknowledging the very specific situation in Greece with large shares of the population in this situation and virtually no room for manoeuvre financially, may I nevertheless ask if you have provided any sort of compensation?
Well – we tried. Our basic idea was that everybody would have to share the burden and we attempted to distribute the losses in a more equitable way. Thus, we targeted, let us say, in pensions, for example, or in public-sector wages, the higher pensions and higher wages. They paid a lot more percentagewise. In a sense, the cuts were progressive in nature. At the lower level, we tried to minimise the cuts, although contributions still had to be made, because of the amounts of fiscal adjustments we needed.

In the tax system we tried to target the higher income groups or the wealthier people. The problem there was that the lack of transparency in the whole economic and financial system in Greece, including in the tax system, did not make that easy. We therefore introduced, for example, tax on property, which had not existed before. That was a fair tax but a very heavy one. We also taxed luxury items, in order to try to get resources from those who were evading taxes. If you increase taxes across the board, and you still have large parts of the population, and particularly the upper middle and upper classes, finding ways to avoid taxes, then the tax burden falls disproportionately on the middle class and lower classes – and those who cannot avoid paying taxes, such as wage earners and employees, for example.

There were people who said: 'Well, okay, we don't like to pay for this; we don't like the fact that we have to pay higher taxes while our wages are cut. But, if it ends in a more efficient and just system, then it is worthwhile.' That was the main response of a large number of the members of Greek society, and, I would say, it still is, if people felt that this was just. Some people do, but some people do not.

However, there is a sense that some of the more powerful people in Greece are able to find ways around this and put pressure on the political system to avoid these tax laws. That was therefore something, which, naturally, I had to fight for. This leads us into politics now, of course – because these people had more control of media and the banks, for example, it was easy for them to make our measures more unpopular by using their influence. To me, this is a wider issue, as we have the phenomenon of high inequality and concentration of wealth around the world, which is undermining the ability of governments to create a wider consensus with our citizens. This has been very apparent in Greece.

Cohesion within government and a general societal consensus are important preconditions for successful reforms. A closely related question deals with striking the right balance between advancing reforms unilaterally and after negotiation. While the former might yield quicker results, the latter might prove to be more durable and sustainable. Where would you position yourself in this trade-off?

If we had had time, an approach with more consultation would have been preferable. Of course, some people say that a crisis is an opportunity. It is, and therefore there is also pressure, but it depends on how much pressure – you can have more pressure than you want. Again, the right balance has to be struck. Generally, it is my belief that the more you create consensus, the more likely it is that your reforms will be long-lasting and thought-through. You need, of course, to create a culture of deliberation, compromise, and consensus-building. That can sometimes take longer.

There are, however, certain situations, where I think you just need to take decisive action, for instance, when you know that there is some vested interest against the introduction of a reform which would be for the public good. For example, putting everything, including expenditure, online, was not popular with certain vested interests, both inside the public sector, but also outside, with some groups who had been profiting from the lack of transparency. I was determined that this was not an issue I was going to negotiate in any way. It was so clear that increased transparency through the web would be in the public interest.

There are some criteria, some very basic principles governments have to adhere to: if something relates to human rights, for example, government has to act without negotiating the basics – simply because human rights are so fundamental to our democratic systems.

In your opinion, what is a prerequisite to ensure the sustainability of reforms?

It has to be our democratic institutions: if they are well run, everything will, if not fall into place, have a natural, positive outcome. The structure of democratic institutions must therefore be strengthened, there must be more transparency, less bureaucracy, less clientelism, a fight against corruption – that is the basis and very important.

Let me give you pensions as an example. Since you had a clientelistic political system, allocation of pensions was based on this, too. This meant that those with greater power or clout, be it union members or politicians, would be able to procure benefits for certain people when others should have had priority – in a way which was neither equitable nor efficient. It all goes back again to the clientelistic system. The pension scheme was highly fragmented and extremely complex, with all kinds of different benefits for different types of people. It was basically a picture of the power structure in society and not much geared to the needs of the people in general. Maybe I am exaggerating a bit, but you could see how power relations were behind the distribution instead of the wider interests and needs of our society and our economy. That is, I think, more a question of democratic governance than of looking narrowly at the labour market or pensions system.

Could you give us an idea of where you think your leadership was key in the execution of your reform agenda?

The word 'leadership' has many connotations, of course. My view of leaders as politicians is that they have to be educators, who are themselves also welleducated and continuously learning. There has to be a sort of back and forth with public opinion, so that the kind of challenges we have can be tackled, consensus established and policies developed. Trying to inform and educate the public about the types of problems the country faced was key. A particular difficulty we now have is that the speed and the way the crisis has come upon us have not always given us time to deal with the situation as educators – it would have been better to act in a participatory and consensual approach. We clearly need to work together as a unit to slow down some of the negatives during a crisis.

In addition, I had to make very crucial decisions at times without being able to think of the ramifications for my own political career and popularity. I knew that I had to push through these reforms and changes, and that this would be highly unpopular – at least initially – if we succeeded, which we are, I hope, doing. In the end, people will accept some of the things that have been done and see them positively. Nevertheless, I had to make decisions, such as opening up to the opposition as much as possible, calling for a referendum, stepping down to form a coalition government, when I still had a majority in parliament. These were therefore decisions I had to make for the public good. I think that is what leaders need to do. Otherwise it is a game that is all about people looking out for their own narrow interests. But that is not why I am in politics.

I could have perhaps not stepped down in 2011 and kept the majority in my party – that would have been a possible, but short-lived, solution, I think. I might have been able to hold on to my position and maybe remain head of the party with a comparatively good percentage of seats, but I might not have been able to implement the reforms, and the whole reform programme would have fallen apart. I could have found scapegoats and blamed the opposition, but in the end, Greece would have most likely been in a much more difficult situation. It was not easy in any case, but stepping down to create a wider government enabled us to keep the programme aligned, maintain its support and continue with the necessary reforms – even if one might not agree on all the positions that the Troika had. At least we were able to continue this cooperation, which was crucial.

The situation of the European Union had an enormous impact on your reform agenda. Looking at its current state what are your ideas for restoring the EU's strengths?

I think we need to look at the structure of the European Union. There is a big discussion now about a need for some public investment, at the European level – the Juncker plan. Modernising Europe by creating an infrastructure that will be good for the single market, with communication, transportation, energy supply, training and innovation all being essential issues.

Aiming at a more integrated European labour market is also very important. I have always been in favour of this idea, an 'Erasmus scheme' for the unemployed. If we want to have more fiscal and economic coordination in the EU, then we also have to look at the labour market and the social benefits area, and consider what kind of things might be administered at the European level. If you give some benefits to the unemployed, protecting against unemployment might 'Europeanise', in a sense. The idea of giving vouchers to the unemployed seems quite sensible to me, under certain conditions, of course: it would have to be partly paid by national budgets and, to a larger extent, by European funds. Unemployed people could then go anywhere in Europe to train and retrain, or maybe take up an apprenticeship – perhaps as is done in Germany. Such initiatives could be very good.

Finally, here is an inevitable question I have to ask you: if you were still in office, which measures would you undertake today in order to reform Greece's labour market?

I would now focus more on the education and training area, as well as the wider benefit system for the unemployed. I would turn it into a more active labour market policy, where we ensure that we create a robust system of training – particularly linked to the comparative advantages that Greece has, i.e. in areas which would be highly competitive: tourism, shipping, fisheries, agriculture. We would, of course, also want to bring in high-tech, green and renewable energy. Moreover, in the construction industry, notably in the high-tech, new areas of the industry, we would want to be dealing with climate change issues and ensure quality in this area, too. Thus, creating high-quality products by educating and innovating, I think.

You need a more decentralised system of training and education linked more closely to the needs of the regions of Greece. We have very varied regions: we have highlands, mountains, plains – all very different. I would make that my key issue, because most of the other problems have been resolved, though there may, perhaps, be some room for improvement in the area of flexibility. I would want to take care that the young unemployed, or the unemployed in general, also feel a sense of security that there is a system which will help them not fall off the cliff – that they do not just have a few benefits for a number of months.

6.2 A note on Greek labour market performance over the past decade

6.2.1 The facts

Greek labour market performance since 2000 is a tale of two periods with radically different outcomes (see fig. 8). First, after Greece adopted the euro in 2001, it enjoyed a period of above-average employment growth and falling unemployment, which persisted until the Greek economy was hit by the hurricane winds of the Great Recession in 2008–9 and the bursting of a domestic bubble that had been fuelled by borrowing at record-low interest rates and large public sector deficits. Secondly, since 2010, when Greece was forced by pressure from the international financial markets and its EU partners to accept a bailout supervised by the Troika, output and employment has dropped like a stone, and unemployment has rocketed to record highs.[98] Several other small open EU economies

---

98 The Troika consisted of the European Commission, the IMF and the European Central Bank. Greece was forced to apply for a second bailout in 2012. It should be noted that the two bailouts

were forced to accept bailouts and Troika supervision in the wake of the euro-zone crisis, e. g. Ireland, Portugal and Cyprus. The drop in output and the pro-longed recession that followed the bailouts in Greece were, however, larger than in the other countries, reflecting the great loss in external competitiveness of the economy in the decade leading up to the crisis, the disastrous state of the Greek public finances and the extremely large fiscal consolidation which the authorities were obliged to make under the terms of the bailouts.[99]

Evolution of the employment and unemployment rates in Greece, 1970–2014

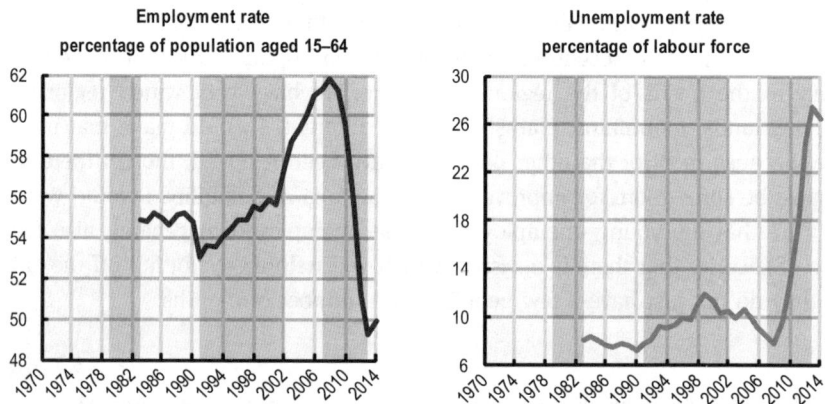

Note: Grey shaded areas refer to period of economic contraction (based on the output gap).
Source: OECD estimates based on the *OECD Labour Force Statistics, OECD Short-term Labour Market Statistics* and *OECD Economic Outlook Databases* (Cut-off date: 13 April 2015).

Figure 8: Labour market chart Greece

Even allowing for these unfavourable circumstances, the magnitude of the deterioration in Greek economic and labour market performance post-2008 is almost without precedent. The Greek harmonised unemployment rate, which stood at a decade low of 7.7 per cent in 2008, almost multiplied fourfold to reach 27.3 per cent in 2013 (see table 10). While 2014 saw some recovery in Greek output

---

mainly shifted its debts to new creditors while little was done to lower them relative to GDP. However, the interest rates which Greece pays on its debt were lowered drastically.
99 See OECD (2013c) for details. Between the end of 2007 and the end of 2013, GDP in Greece fell by 25 per cent, far exceeding the declines recorded in Portugal and Ireland. Indeed, the level of GDP only began to grow again in 2014.

and the beginnings of a drop in unemployment, the Greek unemployment rate was still 26.4 per cent in September 2014 (seasonally adjusted), the highest level in the EU and well over twice the EU28 average of 10.1 per cent. As a point of comparison, the seasonally adjusted unemployment rates in Cyprus, Ireland and Portugal in the same month were 15.1 per cent, 11.2 per cent and 13.6 per cent, respectively.

If we turn to the record on the employment front, the Greek employment rate rose by over 5 percentage points between 2000 and 2007, closing the gap on the EU average employment rate somewhat, from just over 6 to 4 percentage points. However, the crisis led to a huge drop in employment in Greece with the result that the employment rate fell to 50 per cent in 2013 and the gap with the EU average exploded to almost 16 percentage points in 2013.

OECD (2011d) highlighted the fact that, notwithstanding the apparent above-average labour market performance between 2000 and the onset of the Great Recession, there were persistent structural weaknesses, which the authorities failed to tackle. These included a high and relatively stable rate of structural unemployment, a large informal sector in a country with widespread tax evasion, and relatively low employment rates among certain labour force groups, notably women, older workers and youth. These structural weaknesses in the Greek labour market have been exacerbated by the crisis.

Relatively low youth employment rates and relatively high youth unemployment rates have been a long-standing problem in Greece, reflecting a very slow and ineffective school-to-work transition process and the growth of a dual labour market hindering the job prospects of youth, especially those with relatively poor skills.[100] Even allowing for this, the extent of the crisis is without precedent: the loss of youth jobs made the youth employment rate drop from 24 per cent in 2007 to 11.9 per cent in 2013, the lowest rate in the EU.

The female employment rate dropped by 8 percentage points between 2007 and 2013, bringing it back below its 2000 level, while the EU average rate dropped by only 1 percentage point over the same period. It should be added, however, that the male employment rate, which exceeded the EU average in 2007, dropped by over 17 points by 2013.

The employment rate among older workers, aged 55–9, rose from just over 48 per cent in 2000 to over 53 per cent in 2007, but was still below the EU average; since then, it has fallen back to below its 2000 level, while the EU average has continued to climb to over 62 per cent. For the age group 60–4, Greece had an

---

100 See OECD (2010e) for a detailed analysis of these structural weaknesses in the Greek youth labour market.

employment rate above the EU average between 2000 and 2007, but by 2013 it had dropped to almost 6 percentage points below the EU average. A similar pattern was recorded for the employment rate in the 65–9 age group.

Over the period since 2000, there has been a steep rise in the share of part-time work in Greece, from 5.5 per cent in 2000 to 10.3 per cent in 2013, but its share was still well below the EU average of 17.8 per cent. The share of temporary jobs has, however, dropped over the period, from 13.5 per cent of all employees in 2000 to 10.1 per cent in 2013.

A good indicator of the structural unemployment problem is the persistently high share of long-term unemployment, even during the period of relatively strong employment growth between 2000 and 2007. During that period, the proportion of long-term unemployment never dipped below 50 per cent and was consistently well above the EU average. Part of the reason for this lies in the fact that the Greek public employment service (OAED) was extremely ineffective in activating job seekers to find work and in developing and implementing cost-effective active labour market policies (ALMPs). A good illustration of the former weakness is the fact that, while a legal basis for imposing unemployment benefit sanctions in the case of non-compliance with job-search requirements has existed since 1985, no such sanctions had ever been applied in practice![101] As for public spending on ALMPs, Greece spent less than 0.2 per cent of GDP on such measures in 2007, one of the lowest spending efforts among OECD countries.

At the same time, the unemployment benefit regime has never been particularly generous in Greece by the standards of many other EU countries. The scoreboard shows that net benefit replacement rates in Greece were consistently well below the corresponding EU averages since 2000 and they have fallen significantly in the period since the crisis hit, especially for the long-term unemployed.

Not surprisingly, given the severity of the crisis and the huge jump in unemployment, the social consequences have been dramatic for the Greek population. Measures of relative poverty and inequality all point to a worsening situation, especially since 2010.[102] The Greek welfare state, prior to the crisis, had suffered from major structural weaknesses, which greatly hampered its ability to cushion large segments of the population from an increased risk of poverty. Social spending, excluding public spending on pensions and health, only amounted to 4.25 per cent of GDP in 2009; the sum was, moreover, very poorly targeted and the benefits administration was extremely inefficient. The steep rise in the number of jobless households, which was a

---

101 See OECD (2011d), p. 112.
102 See Koutsogeorgopoulou et al. (2014) and OECD (2013c), Chapter 2, for details.

result of the large-scale job losses, had a negative side-effect in terms of weakening the traditional family-sharing social safety net.

The adverse social consequences of the crisis are not just confined to losses in income and wealth. Other social indicators highlight how the Greek population has suffered in many different ways. Homelessness has increased and key indicators of health status point to a worsening situation. The large drop in employment means that the uninsured population has swelled. For example, OECD (2013c) notes that 10 per cent of the population was not eligible for health insurance in 2013, leaving them to depend on the emergency services of public hospitals for medical care at a time when these services were themselves under severe pressure.

Under these circumstances, it is hardly surprising that large segments of the Greek population blamed the Troika and the austerity programme for the adverse economic and social consequences of the crisis. The electorate treated the politicians in power as scapegoats and punished them by voting them out of office several times, culminating in the sweeping victory for the far-left Syriza party led by Alexis Tsipras in the January 2015 elections. This party's electoral platform called for an end to austerity, a major debt forgiveness programme and no further involvement of the Troika in monitoring the Greek bailout.

In short, Greece's labour market and social cohesion performance was profoundly marked by the hurricane that hit it in 2008–9. In 2009, the fiscal deficit ballooned to over 15 per cent of GDP and, in the following year, the ratio of public debt to GDP reached 140 per cent. Faced with this and with a significant erosion in Greece's international competitiveness,[103] the interest-rate premiums on Greek sovereign debt compared with German bunds exploded and the international financial markets refused to buy more Greek debt. This, in turn, forced the Greek authorities to seek external financial support from the Troika. Part of the price for this support was an ambitious programme of structural reforms to complement the major exercise of fiscal consolidation that was needed. These reforms touched upon large swathes of the Greek economy, including product markets, tax evasion and corruption, and public administration. At the same time, a significant part of these structural reforms dealt with labour market and pension issues, and major reforms have been made in these areas, to which we now turn.

---

103 OECD (2011d) shows that the growth of unit labour costs in Greece between 2000 and 2009 exceeded the EU average by 20 percentage points.

6.2.2 Major labour market and pension reforms since 2000

For many years prior to the crisis, international organisations such as the IMF, OECD and the European Commission had drawn attention to the structural weaknesses in the Greek labour market mentioned above and called for vigorous reforms to tackle them. These clarion calls for reform fell upon deaf ears, however, until the crisis in 2010 and the pressures from the international financial markets forced the hands of the Greek politicians.

Pensions

In 2010, Greece had the fourth largest share of public pension spending as a proportion of GDP in the EU27, behind Italy, France and Austria. Faced with rapid population ageing and strong incentives for early retirement, pension projections made by the EU Commission and the ILO – based on information applicable to the period before the first reform in 2008 – indicated an increase of almost 12 percentage points in the public pension-to-GDP ratio by 2050.[104]

The Greek public pension system had several structural shortcomings which contributed to this major financial sustainability challenge. First, it was an excessively complex system with multiple funds operating under different rules. Before the 2008 reform, there were 133 separate funds; the 2008 reform cut that number drastically to 13, but failed to harmonise the parameters for the different funds. Secondly, there were many pathways to early retirement before the statutory age of 65 and insufficient financial penalties for workers who opted for early retirement. For example, anyone who had contributed for 37 years could claim a full pension at age 58. Those who worked in a so-called 'strenuous occupation' could retire on a full pension at the age of 55, after 35 years of contributions. The list of these occupations was quite large and many workers were able to avail themselves of this early retirement option. The 2008 reform reduced the list of such occupations, but the change was only applied to new entrants into the labour force. Finally, the parameters for calculating pensions were very generous by international standards. The replacement rate was set at between 70 and 80 per cent of the average salary for the best five of the last ten years worked, and workers had to contribute only for 35 years to get a full pension at age 65.

But the timid reforms in 2008 did little to change this picture of a financially unsustainable pension system.[105] It was not until July 2010, under pressure from

---

104 See ILO (2008a), (2008b), (2008c) and European Commission (2009).
105 This conclusion was made by the Greek National Actuarial Authority (2010) and (2011).

the Troika, that the Greek authorities undertook a major reform of the system designed to ensure its long-term financial sustainability, to improve its equity and to encourage older workers to work longer. The main thrusts of the 2010 reform were fourfold:

- *Simplification.* The 13 pension funds were cut to six, and the benefit formulas and retirement ages under the different funds were equalised.[106]
- *Generosity.* The pension benefit formula in the contribution-based scheme was modified, in order to strengthen the link between contributions paid and the eventual pension received: the statutory accrual rate was cut to 0.8–1.5 per cent per year, depending on the number of years of service, compared with the 2–3 per cent rate, which had applied before 2010. Pensions were index-linked to both prices and wages. The period over which pension benefits were calculated was extended to the full working life, and 40 years of contributions were required for a full pension.
- *Safety net.* A means-tested basic pension was introduced for the uninsured or those whose contributions were insufficient.[107]
- *Retirement age.* The statutory retirement age was equalised for men and women at 65 and the phase-in was to be completed by end-2013. The minimum retirement age was raised to 60 and the list of strenuous occupations was revised to cover less than 10 per cent of the workforce. A penalty of 6 per cent per year was to be applied to anyone who had contributed for less than 40 years, but opted to take retirement between 60 and 65. A link was established to review and adjust both the minimum and the statutory retirement ages every three years, in line with increasing life expectancy; this link will come into play for the first time in 2021.

The 2010 reforms were supplemented by some additional reforms in 2012. The statutory retirement age for future cohorts was increased to 67. At the same time, the minimum age for access to the means-tested Pensioners Social Solidarity Benefit was also raised from 60 to 65. Supplementary pensions were reformed: the majority of such schemes would be merged into a single scheme and the resulting pensions would be computed in an actuarially neutral way based on workers' contributions and an adjustment mechanism explicitly de-

---

106 However, it should be noted that the reform left over 90 sectoral schemes operating under the six broad funds and these schemes continued to operate with different social security contributions.

107 A pilot minimum-income scheme was enacted in 2014. Plans to extend it nationwide, however, will depend on the results from the pilot scheme and whether there are sufficient public funds to support a national roll-out.

signed to guarantee the system's long-run financial viability. These reforms were accompanied by significant cuts in pensions, in some cases as large as 20 per cent.

The latest European Commission projections which incorporate these reforms show only a small increase in the pension spending-to-GDP ratio in Greece by 2060.[108] Thus, it seems likely that they will achieve their financial sustainability goal. It is, however, much too soon to assess whether these reforms will lead to a significant increase in older worker employment rates in Greece, once the Greek labour market begins to recover. Nonetheless, the experiences of other EU and OECD countries who have made similar radical reforms to their public pension systems suggest that this objective should eventually be achieved in Greece. To the extent that this employment goal is reached, the pension reforms should also contribute to greater equity of public pension spending in Greece.

Labour market reforms

The first programme for structural reforms agreed between the Troika and the Greek authorities included several measures which aimed to improve employment prospects:[109]

– *A shift in the locus of collective bargaining towards firm-level agreements.* Greece has a multi-layered bargaining system, but prior to the reform, intermediate-level bargaining (at sectoral and occupational levels) was predominant. Coverage of collective agreements was high despite low unionisation rates, reflecting the practice of administrative extension to all firms in the same sector or occupation. Firm-level agreements could only be signed by firms with 50 or more employees. In addition, the arbitration system played a major role in wage bargaining and gave extra bargaining power to the unions, who had the right of recourse to it, when the two parties disagreed. The 2010 reform introduced a new type of collective agreement, the special firm-level agreement (SFLCA) applying to all firms, which allowed firm-level wages to be less than the sectoral agreement – before the introduction of this reform, firm-level agreements could only top up wages negotiated at higher levels. Revisions were made to the arbitration system aiming to give equal access to it by both parties.

---

108 For details, see European Commission (2012).
109 This section draws heavily on OECD (2011d), Chapter 3.

- *Minimum wages.* Minimum wages bore heavily on the cost of hiring young workers in Greece, thereby contributing to high youth unemployment in Greece. The 2010 reform provided social security subsidies for first-time youth entrants: their gross wage was to be 84 per cent of the basic wage agreed at the national level. Employees' net earnings remained unchanged as their social insurance contributions were paid by OAED. Finally, one-year apprenticeship contracts were introduced for youth aged 15–18, paying 70 per cent of the minimum wage.
- *Employment protection legislation (EPL).* EPL for permanent workers was stricter than the EU average in 2000 and 2007 (see the scoreboard). Greece is one of the few EU countries which has differentiated EPL rules for white- and blue-collar workers. Protection for temporary workers was much higher than the EU average in both years. Unrestricted renewal of fixed-term contracts was permitted only if justified on objective grounds. Otherwise, a fixed-term contract had to be converted to a permanent one after three renewals or after a cumulative duration of 24 months. Very little use was made of temporary work agencies because the regulations governing them were very strict.
  The 2010 reforms made some significant changes. First, they cut the notice period for dismissals of white-collar workers significantly, e. g. for someone with 28 years or more of job tenure, the notice period was cut to six months from 24. Secondly, severance pay, once it exceeded two months' wages, could be paid in instalments. Thirdly, the firm-size thresholds governing collective dismissals were liberalised. Finally, the maximum duration of a fixed-term contract for workers hired through a temporary work agency was extended from 18 to 36 months and limits on the number of times a temporary work agency contract could be renewed were abolished.
- *More flexible working-time arrangements.* Overtime pay rates were cut; a short-time work scheme was introduced; and averaging of working time was facilitated.

The first wave of labour market reforms in 2010 was followed by a second wave in 2011, again at the behest of the Troika with the explicit aim of improving external competitiveness by reducing unit labour costs by 15 per cent between 2011 and 2014. There were four main thrusts to the second wave:

(i) *Further decentralisation of collective bargaining.* The practice of administrative extension of sectoral wage agreements was abolished. Firm-level agreements were further facilitated.
(ii) *Further easing of EPL for permanent workers.* The length of the notice period for dismissals and the amount of severance pay were cut further for white-

collar workers. The probationary period for new hires was raised from two months to one year.

(iii) *Cuts to the minimum wage.* It was cut by 32 per cent for young workers aged under 25 and by 22 per cent for those aged over 25. The responsibility for fixing the level of the minimum wage was taken over by the authorities; previously, it had been set by bargaining between the social partners.

(iv) *Greater flexibility of working time.* The legal working week of 40 hours was converted to a prescribed annual reckoning, enabling the pattern of the working week to fluctuate more widely, depending on the economic circumstances of firms.

These major labour market reforms have already had some effects. For example, there has been a significant drop in unit labour costs since 2011, helping to restore external competitiveness for Greek industry and services, e.g. tourism. It is, however, anyone's guess at this stage as to how much of this wage moderation is due to the reforms, as distinct from the impact of the sharp drop in employment and huge hike in unemployment since 2009.

The changes to EPL for both permanent and temporary workers have brought the OECD indicators for both types of contracts to below the corresponding EU averages, which should facilitate hiring, once labour demand recovers. The cuts to the minimum wage have led to it declining in both nominal terms and as a proportion of the median monthly earnings. Indeed, Eurostat (2015) highlights the fact that, among the 22 of the 28 EU member states that have statutory national minimum wages, Greece was the only one which recorded a drop in its monthly minimum wage between 1 January 2008 and 1 January 2015 – the decline was 14 per cent.

The Greek economy began to recover in 2014 and, with a lag, the output growth has led to some employment growth and a slight fall in unemployment. It is, of course, far too early to judge the extent to which this fragile recovery in the labour market can be attributed to the impact of these significant labour market reforms, and one also needs to take into account the significant product market reforms that have been introduced in Greece, under pressure from the Troika, at the same time.[110]

6.2.3 Conclusion

Greece suffered from several major labour market problems before the full-blown crisis erupted in 2008–9. The Greek authorities resisted making any reforms to tackle

---

110 See OECD (2011d) for a full description of these product market reforms.

these weaknesses in the decade up to the crisis, despite the urgent calls for such reforms from the international organisations. It was only when the international financial markets turned against Greece and effectively froze it out of borrowing abroad to
finance its exploding public sector deficit that Greece acted to implement an unprecedented series of structural reforms in the labour market and to the public pension
system – reforms which were dictated to the Greek authorities by the Troika.

There is no doubt, however, that the Greek population and economy have
suffered greatly since the crisis hit. GDP fell by over a quarter, unemployment
has soared to record highs and a wide array of social indicators testify to the
hardship that has afflicted significant segments of Greek society. At the time
of writing enormous uncertainty about the future direction of the Greek economy
exists and it is remains unclear if the Tsipras government is prepared to persist
with unpopular reforms. Hence, there is still a huge question mark over the sustainability of this major Greek reform episode.

Table 10: Scoreboard for labour market outcomes and policies, Greece and EU, 1993–2013

	1993		2000		2007		2013*	
	GR	EU	**GR**	EU	**GR**	EU	**GR**	EU
1. Employment rate (% of the working-age population)	**55.2**	61.2	**57.4**	63.6	**62.6**	66.7	**50.0**	65.9
– male	**74.2**	71.8	**73.6**	72.7	**76.6**	74.5	**59.5**	70.5
– female	**37.4**	50.7	**42.1**	54.3	**48.5**	59.2	**40.5**	58.2
– youth (aged 15/16–24)	**27.5**	39.5	**26.9**	39.2	**24.0**	39.1	**11.9**	32.1
– older people (aged 55–9)	**47.7**	47.6	**48.2**	50.4	**53.3**	57.5	**46.1**	62.2
– older people (aged 60–4)	**30.1**	22.2	**31.3**	22.1	**31.0**	29.1	**24.4**	30.1
– older people (aged 65–9)	–	9.1	–	7.3	**10.4**	8.5	**6.3**	10.5
2. Unemployment rate (% of la-bour force)	**9.0**	10.8	**11.2**	9.1	**8.4**	7.2	**27.5**	11.6
– youth (aged 15/16–24)	**28.8**	21.0	**29.2**	17.7	**22.7**	15.4	**58.3**	26.3
3. Incidence of long-term unem-ployment (% of total unemploy-ment) (a)	**50.9**	42.0	**54.7**	44.6	**49.7**	41.7	**67.1**	43.7
4. Part-time employment rate (b)	**7.1**	13.8	**5.5**	15.2	**7.7**	16.5	**10.3**	17.8
5. Temporary employment rate (c) (temporary employees as % of total employees)	**10.4**	10.3	**13.5**	13.0	**11.0**	15.4	**10.1**	14.4
– youth (aged 15/16–24 as % of total youth employees)	**23.9**	28.4	**29.5**	37.6	**26.5**	43.0	**26.4**	42.4
6. Low-pay incidence (d) (% of employees)	–	–	**20.0**	15.7	**17.6**	16.5	**12.5**	15.0

Table 10 (continued)

	1993		2000		2007		2013*	
	GR	EU	**GR**	EU	**GR**	EU	**GR**	EU
7. Protection of permanent work-ers against individual dismissal	**2.8**	2.6	**2.8**	2.5	**2.8**	2.4	**2.1**	2.2
– Protection of temporary workers	**4.8**	2.3	**4.8**	1.8	**2.8**	1.6	**2.3**	1.8
8. Public spending on labour mar-ket policies (% of GDP)	**0.6**	2.9	**0.6**	2.0	**0.5**	1.5	**0.9**	2.1
– Spending on active measures (e)	**0.2**	0.9	**0.2**	0.9	**0.2**	0.6	**0.2**	0.8
– Spending on passive measures (f)	**0.4**	2.1	**0.4**	1.1	**0.3**	0.8	**0.7**	1.3
9. Net benefit replacement rate (g) (averaged over four family types and two earnings levels)	–	–	**20**	65	**20**	61	**12**	54
– initial spell (h)	–	–	**43**	70	**46**	71	**37**	70
– after 2 years of unemployment	–	–	**21**	66	**22**	63	**9**	57

* 2013 or latest available year.
(a) Persons out of work for 12 months and over.
(b) Part-time employment refers to persons who usually work less than 30 hours per week in "their 'main job'".
(c) Temporary employees are wage and salary workers whose job has a pre-determined end date as opposed to permanent employees whose job is of unlimited duration. National definitions broadly conform to this generic definition, but may vary depending on national circumstances.
(d) Persons with a wage less than 2/3 of the median.
(e) 'Active' measures cover categories 1 to 7 of the OECD/Eurostat data base on public spending on labour market programmes.
(f) 'Passive' measures cover categories 8 and 9 of the OECD/Eurostat data base on public spend-ing on labour market programmes.
(g) Data on net replacement rates for 2000 refer to 2001.
(h) Initial phase of unemployment but following any waiting period. For married couples, the percent-age of AW relates to the previous earnings of the 'unemployed' spouse only; the second spouse is assumed to be 'inactive' with no earnings and no recent employment history. Where receipt of social assistance or other minimum-income benefits is subject to activity tests (such as active job-search or being 'available' for work), these requirements are assumed to be met. Children are aged four and six and neither childcare benefits nor childcare costs are considered. Unweighted averages, for previous full-time earnings levels of 67% and 100% of AW and out-of-work single and couple households with no children or with two children (children are assumed to be aged four and six and neither childcare benefits not childcare costs are considered). After tax and including unemployment and family ben-efits. Social assistance and other means-tested benefits are assumed to be available subject to rel-evant income conditions. Housing costs are assumed equal to 20% of AW.
Sources: OECD Online Employment Database: www.oecd.org/employment/database; data on net replacement rates come from the OECD tax-benefit models (www.oecd.org/els/social/workincentives).

7 Italy

7.1 Interview with Mario Monti, 28 March 2014

'Most politicians in most countries nowadays are exercising followership not leadership.'

In hindsight, how would you assess the reform package on the labour market and pensions that you introduced shortly after taking office in November 2011 as Prime Minister of Italy?
The pension reform that we introduced in December 2011 is generally considered a landmark achievement. It was a bold and widely unpopular reform which had two key objectives, both of them structural: to remove the substantial intergenerational inequity against future generations which characterized the previous system, and to make the system sustainable from the standpoint of public finance. The latter feature of the reform, addressing the main source of the deep concern of financial markets and international agencies as they were looking at Italy in the midst of the Eurozone crisis, had a powerful impact already in the short term. Together with the other measures adopted in the December 2011 package (introduction of a property tax and new instruments to fight tax evasion), the pension reform was the single most important factor that enabled Italy to recover – without any international assistance, unlike all other Southern European countries – from the financial and confidence crisis that had brought the spread between German and Italian government bonds from 150 to almost 600 basis points between June and November 2011.

In the spring of 2012, amongst other structural reforms, we introduced a reform of the labour market. It deed increase the flexibility of the market and rationalized somewhat the social protection for the unemployed. However, the overall perception, which to some extent I share, is that this reform, as finally adopted, fell short of my government's ambition and was less bold than the landmark pension reform introduced a few months earlier.

Rather than dwelling on the contents of these two reforms, widely reported by the international media and available on the Italian government's website, I would like to explore the possible reasons for this difference in outcome.

Here I should underline, first of all, that both reforms were put forward by the same member of the government, the Minister for Labour and Welfare Policies, prof. Elsa Fornero. In both cases, the measures were presented by her to the Council of Ministers in close consultation with me and, after thorough collegial discussion, were endorsed unanimously by the Council. We were fortunate to count on this independent academic personality, with a strong reputation for her competence on labour economics and, in particular, on welfare economics and pension systems, with extensive experience in policy advising in Italy and internationally, and widely respected by the different political parties.

Given the urgency of a deep structural reform of pensions, and the acute social sensitivity of both pensions and labour market issues, Elsa Fornero was not bound to enjoy great popularity. In fact, among all ministers she was the one who had to confront the toughest backlashes and attacks, although most competent and objective observers of Italian developments would widely agree that her pension reform was the single most decisive measure in avoiding Italy's financial collapse.

For readers of this publication I should clarify that I have not consulted Professor Fornero in drafting my answers, because I understood that what this research project was looking for were the views of the heads of governments on the overall strategy within which labour and welfare reforms were introduced, not the more sectoral, albeit certainly more competent, views of the ministers in charge. As a consequence, Elsa Fornero should of course not be held responsible for my broader assessments as presented here.

So, why has our pension reform generally been regarded as a landmark policy achievement, whereas the subsequent reform of labour markets was received in a more subdued way? Four main changes, in my view, had occurred in the short time span between the two reforms.

First, a decreased emergency. The reforms were undertaken in a different time context. At the end of 2011, the public opinion in Italy was in a state of shock. There was a predominant feeling of emergency, which had resulted in Prime Minister Silvio Berlusconi resigning and President of the Republic Giorgio Napolitano asking me to form a new government. The political parties were scared. They gave us the confidence vote with the largest majority since the beginning of the Italian Republic. In the spring of 2012, this sense of urgency had already partly vanished. Also, labour market reforms, because of their intrinsic nature, cannot have the same immediate influence on financial markets than is the case with pension reforms. Thus, reforming the labour market was perceived as having less urgency and was seen more as a measure to improve Italy's competitiveness in order to generate growth and employment. While a well performing labour market is extremely important, it is rather linked to the 'real' economy and not to the fiscal imbalances and financial tensions which, at the time, generated the sense of emergency in public opinion. When I took office, the situation in parliament was favourable. My government was composed of 'technocrats', a word often used but that I do not like. By the way. I had tried to have as ministers also a few politicians from the parties who had expressed support, personalities I trusted for their competence and integrity. However, the parties refused to do so, perhaps out of the concern that they would thus be further associated to a policy which, they knew, could hardly be popular. But, importantly, they were prepared to support the government programme with their votes in parliament. Which they did, with an unprecedented display of a much needed sense of national unity.

Secondly, the approaching elections. That wide and solid support, however, became gradually less strong almost by the month, not only due to the slowly receding financial emergency as a result of the drastic policy decisions and their impact on the markets; but also due to the obvious fact that the time to go before the next elections, to be held at the latest in Spring 2013, was becoming shorter and shorter. In the mindsets of political parties, the interests of their various constituencies inevitably were coming to the forefront, eroding the priority initially given to the general interest of the country.

Thirdly, a less powerful legislative track. The President of the Republic was so deeply aware of the emergency that had prompted him to give birth to our government, that he allowed us to widely avail ourselves, with his authorization as required by the Constitution in conditions of "necessity and urgency", of "decrees-law", the fastest and most powerful track for legislative measures to go into effect. So, the whole package of which the pension reform formed part (*Salva Italia*), was introduced through a decree-law. By contrast, when the turn came, a few months later, of the labour market reform, the government was not authorized to use a decree-law. The pertinent measures then had to be introduced through ordinary legislative procedure, with the effect of exposing the draft law for a much longer time, and without a comparable cogency, to the interventions of political parties in both houses of parliament.

Fourthly, more consultation with the social partners. Given the overwhelming urgency related to the financial crisis, we introduced the pension reform in December 2011 virtually without any consultation at all with the trade unions. Together with Minister Fornero, I invited the Secretaries General of the unions and, in less than two hours, we presented what we were going to decide in the Council of Ministers the following day. Inspite of the lack of a proper consultation, the climate in the country was such that there were virtually no reactions from labour movements, apart from a symbolic general strike of just two hours. Generally, the unions had the tradition of taking to the streets for much, much less radical reforms. However, at the time, the fear that the government, in case of default, would not have the money to pay salaries and pensions at the end of the month had generated profound concerns in the population. Italy had the deeply worrying example of Greece a few hundred miles away and, we were afraid, just a few months ahead of us in approaching the abyss. I do want to stress how mature and responsible was, at that juncture, the behavior of leaders of trade unions as well as of most political parties.

There was one transitory problem, however, which we did not assess as deeply as we should have done, the so-called *esodati* problem. The *esodati* is a group of workers typically around the age of 60 who had left their jobs by mutual agreement with their employers with the expectation to enter early retirement after temporarily being unemployed, living off benefits and severance payments. The pension reform, not foreseeing any transition period for the increase in the retirement age, caught them off guard. Retirement would be unattainable for a number of years while a return to previous employment or other jobs would be impossible or problematic. As Senator Pietro Ichino, another highly respected labour expert, put it, this problem could hardly have been avoided, since "the Monti government, as soon as it took office, had to do in two weeks what previous governments should have done over the previous two decades", to make the pension system sustainable. Initially, we estimated this group not to be larger than around 65,000 people while it turned out later they amounted to considerably higher numbers. With more time available to fine-tune the reform and with a more adequate data base, we could – and should – have reduced the size of this problem.

Unlike for the pension reform, when we came to reforming the labour market we did consult extensively with the social partners, i.e. trade unions and business organizations. Nevertheless, as I had never seen with favour the exhausting rounds of paralyzing consultations that had made Italian economic policies so inefficient and ineffective in the past, my government did not want to go as far as actually signing an agreement with the unions. What we did was rather to largely take into account the outcome of the consultations in drawing up the government's bill to be submitted to Parliament. I believe that the bill was actually quite good, with a level of ambition broadly in line with what had been done in the pension reform.

Shortly afterwards, however, the problems began. As mentioned above, we could not use the fast and comparatively safe track of a decree law. The parliamentary discussion took a long time and parties acted largely in the interest of their respective constituencies. In particular Pierluigi Bersani's *Partito Democratico (PD)*, the main party on the left, very close to the unions, was not ready to support our bill unless some of the features originally introduced to increase flexibility in the labour market were diluted or removed altogether. On that occasion, indeed, most of the difficulties were created by the *Partito Democratico*, whereas in the case of measures to enhance liberalization and competition the most significant resistances had come, curiously by European standards, from Silvio Berlusconi's *Popolo della Libertà (PdL)*, the main party on the right.

In hindsight, I would call our labour market reform a moderate success. It marked the beginning of a process. Yet, a lot remains to be done. The government of Prime Minister Matteo Renzi, who took over the control of *Partito Democratico*, set out to go further than we did, in the same direction. Being in control of the very party which had acted as a brake on this specific reform during my government, Mr Renzi is more likely to achieve the needed degree of reform of the labour market.

What exactly do you think the present Italian government needs to do in the near future?
There are several things. What Italy needs very urgently is a huge simplification of its labour law. Projects are there, notably thanks to Senator Ichino; it is the political will that must be generated. Italian labour law can hardly be translated into English because it is too byzantine. This gives no encouragement for investment. That is a clear sign we need a simplification. Also, we need greater trust in the quality of the relationship between companies and workers.

Could you give us an insight into the culture underlying the labour market in your home country and explain why, in general, it has proven so difficult to make changes to the labour market?
In Italy pragmatism is often not a highly regarded good. In our labour market there is much support and adherence to matters of principle, mainly by the unions and the judges dealing with labour law issues. Traditionally, the strong defence of the weak party in the labour contractual relationship, i.e. the worker, is allusive to Max Weber's ethics of intentions and ethics of responsibility. However, the tradition of the Italian left has in many cases given prominence only to the assertion of rights and to their enforcement. A comprehensive policy vision based on both rights and objective responsibilities, able to assess its effects on the labour market, has lacked. In sum, good intentions have not always resulted in good effects.

Two areas where this tendency has been seen very clearly for decades are the protection of workers and the protection of tenants. In both cases, in the 60s and 70s, there were strong provisions in our laws aimed at supporting the position of the weakest. However, that has often been counter-productive with respect to the logics of the market. In the case of the rental market for houses, for instance, the regulation has discouraged construction of new houses. It has become terribly difficult in certain places to find a home. As for the protection of the worker, the excessive rigidity of the so-called *Statuto dei lavoratori* of the late 60s and early 70s, has bounced back against workers themselves because while the theoretical protection was extremely high, the creation of jobs was extremely low. It is a trade-off between principle and reality.

Do not forget that Article 1 of our constitution stipulated, and still stipulates, *'L'Italia è una Repubblica democratica, fondata sul lavoro'*. 'Italy is a democratic republic based on labour.' This goes back to when the Constitution was drafted, in 1947, and to the influence that 'lavoro' had at the time. Unlike, for instance, post-war Germany, post-war Italy was for a long time dominated culturally by two influences: the Marxists and the Catholics, with always a very tiny Liberal component. In Italy, the *Soziale Marktwirtschaft*, the social market economy, was introduced many years later through the various European integration treaties – from the Treaty of Rome and its focus on markets and competition, to the Treaty of Maastricht asserting monetary stability and fiscal discipline, to the Treaty of Lisbon, which stipulates that the model of Europe is "a highly competitive, social market economy".

I would point out, however, that this culture has been undergoing some gradual changes in recent years. The unions, for example, have begun to alter their stance towards the markets. There have been piecemeal modifications to the Italian labour market. With the advent of the single market first, and of the single currency then, all domestic labour markets in Europe were forced to make adjustments due to the competition exercised through the single market in goods and services. In response, an indirect opening up and liberalisation took place. However, the EU does not have the power or the duty to harmonise labour market conditions and cannot dictate the competition principles in the labour market. In essence, the fundamentals shaping the labour market culture in Italy have not changed enough yet, in my view.

You highlighted your diverse experience with engaging with the unions in the pension and in the labour market reform. May we ask you to elaborate in general terms on how important you consider it to reach a consensus with the unions in Italy in order to carry out successful reforms?
It very much depends. If it is about changing labour contracts, I think it is important to come to an agreement – or at least an understanding – with the social partners. If it is more about the accompanying safety nets, provided largely by public finance, the consent of social partners may be less important. Ultimately, it depends on every country's tradition. I would also say that when a reform is made because of a macro-economic problem, such as taking away indexation, it could be very helpful that decisions are taken with a high degree of centralisation. However, if a reform is, for example, made to introduce a more disperse and decentralised correlation between productivity and wages, then a more decentralised decision-making process is preferable. However, I think Italy has always been one of the countries in Europe with excessive consultation processes and where the unions have been having, until recently, a somewhat unhealthy polit-

ical relevance. In 1970 a government (led by Prime Minister Mariano Rumor) even felt the duty to resign because the unions had declared a general strike. It is quite unorthodox, in my view, that the life of a government should not be decided in parliament, but rather suspended on a peculiar "vote of confidence", or "non-confidence", expressed by one group within the population, dependent workers and their organizations.

How important was proper government cohesion for carrying out your reforms, especially given the rather difficult parliamentary situation you just mentioned?
Very important indeed. I was lucky enough to have, through the entire 18 months of my government, a high degree of cabinet cohesion, which does not necessarily mean fully identical views on all topics. My government was "special" though: while normally governments are composed of a coalition of elected parties, my government was born out of emergency, with personalities whom I had a wide discretion to select and submit to the President of the Republic for nomination. In particular, it was essential for my government's effectiveness in tackling economic and financial emergencies that there should be total harmony between the Prime Minister and the Minister of Economy and Finance. This was achieved, for an initial period of seven months, as suggested by President Napolitano himself, by having me in charge of both responsibilities, with the invaluable help of Vittorio Grilli as Vice Minister. As the financial emergency began to recede, in July 2012, Professor Grilli took over the position of Minister of Economy and Finance and we continued to work very closely. As a matter of fact, some of the difficulties that had proven unsurmountable in 2011 for my predecessor, Prime Minister Berlusconi, were said to depend on a lack of understanding, and even of communication, between him and his Minister of Economy and Finance, Giulio Tremonti.

Do you consider it an advantage that you were not part of the political establishment when you became Prime Minister?
Yes, definitely. Italians were, like people in many other countries, rather fed up with traditional politicians. For several months my degree of popularity, according to the polls, was unexpectedly high. Then, of course, I knew that my job consisted, in a sense, in allowing that popularity to be eroded, through the adoption of measures that were needed for the country, although unpopular.

How did you explain these tough measures to the Italian public?
Our communication strategy regarding pension reform, designed in close cooperation between Minister Fornero and me, was to focus on its intergenerational

effects, i.e. putting an end to us Italians of today undermining the economic life of the Italians of tomorrow, our children and grand-children. In addition, on that reform, like on all others, I made a point of never saying to the public, or in parliament, that we had to accept these sacrifices because the EU wanted us to do so. I never mentioned any external pressure. This was important, especially given my previous service with the EU. In Italy, as in many other European countries, the EU has become more and more unpopular in recent years. If I ever had to mention that there was an EU constraint or recommendation, I said, 'Yes, the EU also asks for this measure, but we know that we need to do that first of all for our children.' Although people were aware, of course, of the pressure from the EU.

When I took office everybody was scared that Italy might default and, given the size of the country, bring down the Eurozone. My task, I must say, was not made emotionally any easier when I saw a cover of *Time* magazine (20 February 2012) with my photo and a question: 'Can This Man Save Europe?' Tough call. At any rate, everybody was scared. I was under considerable pressure from Brussels, Berlin, the IMF and the OECD. They all wanted Italy to succeed, yet they all felt pretty uncomfortable as markets were estimating at between 30 and 40 per cent the probability of Italian default, an event that might indeed have brought to the collapse of the whole Eurozone. So they were discretely asking me: "Are you sure that you do not want to apply for financial assistance, sign a memorandum of understanding and have the help of the Troika (Commission, ECB, IMF) in redressing your country?" With equal politeness, I firmly declined. I was convinced that we needed to come out of the difficulties with our own strengths. I am still convinced that this was the right choice. Some people say, 'Well, but, after all, if you had accepted international help, you would have tied the hands of your successors and of the succeeding parliament.' I am very happy that we were the only country in Southern Europe which did not seek or accept any money. I am also sure that, due to the psychology of Italians, it would have been more difficult to carry out the reforms if they had been seen as dictated by three gentlemen in black belonging to a Troika and sitting in Rome. And of course my successors, Prime Ministers Enrico Letta and then Matteo Renzi, would have had their voice all but silenced at the table of European leaders, had they been sitting there as leaders of an indebted country, which owed gratitude to the others for having rescued it.

How did you engage with those opposed to the reforms?
Initially, and for months, my government held the largest parliamentary majority of post-war Italy. There were opposition parties, but they were very weak. The problem emerged when Mr Berlusconi's *PdL*, although one of the three parties

supporting the government, started to loudly distance itself from reforms, even though it had systematically voted for them in parliament. Eventually, in December 2012, they withdrew their support on the whole issue of economic policy. Many observers believe that the *PdL* withdrew its support on 7 December 2012 because on the previous day the government had negotiated with the parties in parliament, including *PdL*, a package against corruption, including provisions for the expulsion from parliament of members definitively convicted for criminal offenses above certain thresholds. *PdL* was not happy about it, but as the elections were approaching fast, no party could really pronounce against measures designed to obtain a "clean Parliament", as they were called. Instead, according to those observers, Mr Berlusconi's party decided to convey their anger against the government by withdrawing their confidence on the (more decent) ground of economic policy.

Generally speaking, as an election date approaches, the quality of reforms tends to lower and the difficulties to increase. But there are exceptions. As for our plans to fight corruption and tax fraud, in particular when perpetrated by members of parliament, we deliberately waited until close to the elections. We knew that it would become practically impossible for those affected to oppose the bill shortly before an election. This strategy, I must say, proved successful. This teaches how the room of manoeuvre to make reforms can in fact be linked to forthcoming elections in two different, indeed opposite, ways.

Speaking of elections, can governments win a re-election after having put through tough measures? If yes, how?
This is a major discussion. I think what a country needs are politicians who are leaders. I am not speaking for myself; I was not a politician, and I have gone back to not being a politician. However, we need politicians who are leaders and not followers; namely who have a vision of what the country needs and wants to become. They need to project that vision to the public and get enough support to lead the country towards those objectives. Most politicians in most countries these days are exercising followership not leadership; they do what people want to see, they promise what people want to hear promised to them. Thus, if a country goes through difficult times and needs to do unpopular things, it may have recourse either to people who are not scared by elections because they are not politicians and couldn't care less about their popularity, or to politicians who are able to win consensus on tough measures because they have the ability to show that these measures will result in a brighter future for everybody.

When, how and to what extent did you provide compensation for those who lost out as a result of the reforms?
When structural reforms are introduced in times of normal economic and financial conditions, there may be a case for providing some compensation to certain categories of individuals or companies from which specific advantages are withdrawn. In our case, reforms occurred at a time of critical financial conditions generated largely by the assessment that Italy's public finances were not sustainable. Hence, there were no margins for compensations. The principle of justice in sharing the burden of the adjustment was, however, at the core of our strategy. This is why the package included measures which, as explained above, affected constituencies defended by the right as well as those defended by the left. This was a key feature of our programme, fully consistent with the grand coalition that was put together to give parliamentary approval to the whole package. In addition, efforts were made to reduce the burdens on lower income levels, in particular as regards the elimination of the indexation of pensions.

Did you look at other countries in the design of the labour market reform?
Yes, we drew on the model of *flexicurity*. I think there is a widespread belief in Europe that the Nordic countries, Denmark in particular, have a lot to say when it comes to labour market issues. Yet, one always needs to be aware of the differences between the social and political contexts of different countries.

In the end, drawing on the Danish model also served as a good argument in parliament. Most members of parliament believed that the time had come to increase flexibility in the Italian labour market, but they were eager not to put stability too much at risk.

To what extent did analyses and recommendations from international organisations influence your choices about the design, timing and sequencing of reforms?
There was indeed a consistent body of recommendations addressed to Italy by the EU, the IMF, the OECD, the ECB. They largely coincided with those formulated many times by the Bank of Italy and by many Italian economists, including myself, but some key recommendations had not been implemented for years, because of the unwillingness of the parties composing the governments, of the right and of the left in alternation, to bear the political costs of the recommended measures. Finally, under the emergency conditions, our non-political government had the determination to introduce many of those measures and was able to elicit from parties across the aisle the political support, although on occasions it was quite a reluctant support. Importantly, from a substantive and psychological point of view, all the measures that my government introduced were

adopted with the full ownership of the Italian government and parliament, not in execution of memoranda of understanding like those that the countries requesting support had to undertake with the Troika.

In some countries we have witnessed reforms made under the pressure of a crisis. As soon as the crisis is over, at least some elements of the reforms are reversed. How can reformers ensure their reform's sustainability over time?

I think the sustainability of a reform depends on the extent to which you are able to root it in the grounds of a specific country and on what its visible effects will be over a number of years. The first point is specifically relevant in Italy because the implementation process of reforms is quite complex, both legally and practically. Governments have often been rather short lived in Italy.

My government has worked quite a lot, not only to produce new measures but also to put them in place, and to effectively implement measures decided by the previous government. Naturally, there were limits to that. There were a few decisions that we clearly could not accept, like, for example, the transfer of some ministries from Rome to Monza, near Milan, that the previous government had decided in order to please the Northern League party, the junior partner in Prime Minister Berlusconi's government.

How important do you deem strong leadership to secure a successful reform process?

I believe this is a critical element. One thing is to have a public opinion shocked by a financial emergency, quite another thing is to lead the public opinion, and the parties linked to its various components, to accept that only through a set of specific, generally unpleasant, measures for each of them will the emergency be reined in and a process of "sustainable growth through reforms", rather than spurs of "ephemeral growth through deficits" be set in motion. May I add that, for a government where neither the prime minister nor any of the ministers belong to political parties, "strong" leadership cannot be derived from political power. It may come only from the credibility of the personalities involved and their capacity to persuade those with political power, and the public opinion behind them, that the proposed measures must be adopted.

I wish to add that the high authority enjoyed by The President of the Republic, Giorgio Napolitano, who was at the very origin of our government and supported our efforts although in full respect of the government's role and responsibilities, was a crucially important factor.

7.2 A note on Italian labour market performance over the past decade

7.2.1 The facts

Italy's labour market performance since the mid-1990s has been a tale of two periods, insofar as employment and unemployment are concerned: first, the period up to the Great Recession and, secondly, the subsequent period, since 2008. During the first period, Italy's overall labour market performance was relatively good, with the employment rate rising from 54.7 per cent in 2000 to 59.6 per cent in 2007. Thereafter, the employment rate dropped back to 57.5 per cent in 2013 (see fig. 9 and table 11). It has to be borne in mind, however, that, despite the rising employment rate during the run-up to the Great Recession, Italy's rate was always well below the corresponding EU average – indeed, the gap widened from 7 to over 8 percentage points between 2007 and 2013.

Evolution of the employment and unemployment rates in Italy, 1970–2014

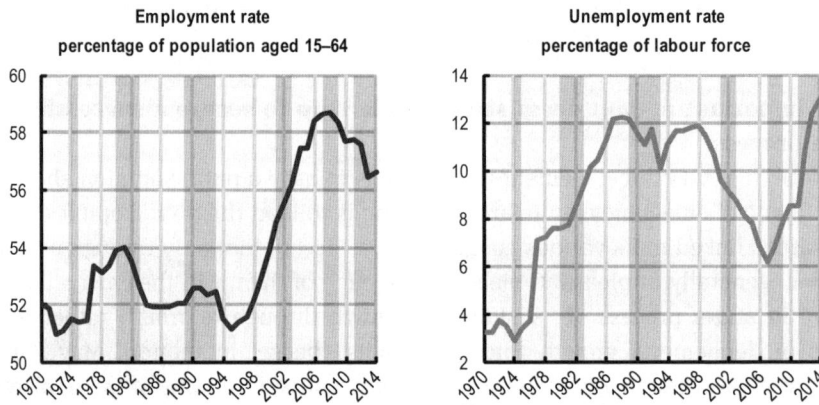

Note: Grey shaded areas refer to period of economic contraction (based on the output gap).
Source: OECD estimates based on the *OECD Labour Force Statistics, OECD Short-term Labour Market Statistics* and *OECD Economic Outlook Databases* (Cut-off date: 13 April 2015).

Figure 9: Labour market chart Italy

At the same time, it is important to see Italian labour market performance over this period against the backdrop of aggregate economic performance: the Italian economy was regarded as one of the 'sick men' of Europe. Real GDP hardly grew at all over the period 2000–7, and there has been no growth since the

Great Recession hit the economy. When this wretched growth record is combined with the employment growth record over the same period, it tells us that Italy's productivity performance over the past 15 years has been abysmal.

The corollary of the strong employment growth between 2000 and 2007 is that the Italian harmonised unemployment rate, which stood at 10.1 per cent in 2000, dropped steadily to a three-decade low of 6.1 per cent in 2007. After that, unemployment started to rise sharply, as the impact of the Great Recession and the subsequent prolonged downturn hit the Italian labour market very hard. At the time of writing, the latest harmonised data from Eurostat for September 2014 put the Italian unemployment rate at 12.6 per cent (seasonally adjusted), its highest level since the late 1980s and well above the EU28 average of 10.1 per cent.

This doubling of the unemployment rate since the Great Recession is a stark reminder of how poor the Italian economic and labour market performance has been in recent years. It reflects, among other factors, the continuing drop in export market shares, resulting from the loss of cost competitiveness since Italy joined the euro, compared to its major trading partners, especially Germany.[111] In addition, concerns in the international financial markets about the very large size of Italian public debt relative to GDP in the wake of the eurozone crisis, and the subsequent very sharp widening of the interest rate premiums for Italian sovereign debt over German bunds made fiscal consolidation an imperative in 2010 and subsequent years. This bout of fiscal austerity has added to the downward pressures on Italian output and employment levels over the past four years.

As noted above, Italy has had relatively low overall employment rates compared to other countries for many years. This is mainly because of comparatively low employment among certain demographic groups, notably women, youth and older workers (see Italy's scoreboard). While there has been some convergence towards the EU averages for the employment rates of women and older workers over the past decade, this is far from the case for youth employment. The youth employment rate in 2013 was over 15 percentage points below the EU average, and the gap had widened by almost five points compared with 2000. The counterpart of this is that the proportion of Italian youth who are neither in employment nor in education and training – the so-called 'NEETS' – has increased by

---

111 OECD (2015b) highlights that the response of wages to high and rising unemployment in Italy has been very sluggish, reflecting the fact that most collective bargaining settlements are struck for three-year periods and are applied uniformly over the country. While the social partners negotiated agreements in 2011 and 2012 which allowed for more local flexibility in wages and working conditions, these opt-out clauses have had little impact to date.

over 6 percentage points since 2008, to reach almost 23 per cent in 2013, the second-highest share in the OECD.[112]

The gap between the female employment rate in Italy and the EU average narrowed from over 14 points in 2000 to over 12 points in 2013. Below-average female labour force participation in Italy is strongly influenced by socio-cultural factors, often relating to caring responsibilities. Despite Italy having a low fertility rate and rising educational attainment of women – aspects which would be expected to push up female employment rates – women's employment in Italy is low; it is hampered by the relative lack of state childcare and care for the elderly. As for the labour market attachment of older workers, employment rates among the cohorts aged between 55 and 69 have risen steadily since 2000, especially since 2007, for those aged 55–9 and 60–4. As will be seen below, part of the explanation for this trend rise in older worker employment can be attributed to a series of major pension reforms over the past two decades.

In terms of the types of jobs which were created in Italy over the past 15 years, it is noticeable that there has been a sharp increase in the share of part-time work. The scoreboard shows that part-time work was less prevalent in Italy than the EU average in 2000. By 2013, however, it had progressed rapidly to exceed the EU average by 1 percentage point, reflecting the continuing increase in female employment.

One specific feature of the Italian labour market, which is often highlighted by commentators, is the high degree of duality, usually proxied by the gap in protection provided to permanent, compared to temporary, contracts. Workers with permanent contracts in firms with more than 15 employees – and they account for about 50 per cent of the total workforce – enjoy very strong employment protection; workers in small firms have less protection, while the rest of the workforce has almost no job security. A widely used proxy indicator for this duality is the share of temporary work in total wage and salary employment. The scoreboard shows that temporary work in Italy increased its share of wage and salary employment between 2000 and 2013 by just over 3 percentage points, bringing it close to the EU average. It should be noted, however, that there was no increase in the share of temporary work in Italy after 2007.

The fact that the share of temporary work in Italy is in line with the EU average, despite the concerns expressed about high duality, is partly a statistical illusion, as many de facto temporary workers in Italy are classified as being self-employed, and not as employees. This emphasises another specific feature of the Italian labour market, which is its relatively high share of self-employment. In

---

112 See OECD (2015b).

the mid-1990s, this accounted for about one in every three workers in Italy, compared with an EU average of just over one in six. While the proportion of self-employment in Italy has since then declined to 25 per cent of total employment in 2013, it was the highest share in the EU27 countries – the EU27 average in 2013 was 16.5 per cent. Part of this relatively high share of self-employment reflects a large underground economy and a form of so-called 'false self-employment', whereby both employers and employees circumvent taxes and labour regulations.[113] The tax wedge is relatively high in Italy, especially for low-wage workers. Social security contributions on employees are the second highest in the OECD, creating incentives to declare workers as self-employed when they are, to all intents and purposes, equivalent to employees.

The growth of these so-called 'non-standard forms of employment' (part-time, temporary, false self-employment) since the late 1990s owed much to a series of labour market reforms designed to encourage hiring under a wide variety of different, non-permanent contracts. Not surprisingly, given their over-representation among new hires, youth have been disproportionately affected by such contracts. Whereas in 2000, for example, 26 per cent of all youth employees were recruited on temporary contracts, by 2013 this share had doubled to almost 53 per cent, well above the EU average of 43 per cent and over twice the OECD average of 25 per cent. Thus, the expansion of employment from the late 1990s to 2007 was accompanied by a growing duality in the Italian labour market, which bore heavily on youth and women.

On the unemployment front, two specific patterns stand out for Italy: first, relatively high youth unemployment and, secondly, a persistently high incidence of long-term unemployment. The scoreboard shows that, while the youth unemployment rate dropped by almost one-third between 2000 and 2007, it has risen very rapidly since. In September 2014, the Italian youth unemployment rate stood at 42.9 per cent (seasonally adjusted), compared with an EU28 average of 21.6 per cent. This was the third-highest youth rate among the EU28 countries, after Greece and Spain.

The incidence of long-term unemployment in Italy consistently exceeded the EU average in the decade before the Great Recession, and this pattern has not varied in its aftermath. In 2013, long-term unemployment in Italy stood at almost 57 per cent, compared with the corresponding EU average of 46.5 per cent.

---

113 OECD (2015b), p. 28 quotes an estimate made by the Italian national statistical agency (ISTAT) that the number of workers in the underground economy is equivalent to 12 per cent of total employment.

These two specific features of Italian unemployment have to be viewed against the background that Italy has a relatively weak social safety net for many of the unemployed, especially new entrants and the long-term unemployed. One of the main components of such a social safety net in almost all OECD countries is the unemployment insurance (UI) system, but this is relatively underdeveloped in Italy and is far from universal, despite several extensions, which were added over the past decade. Instead, many workers in the industrial sector, especially those working in large firms, have been able to rely upon income support in the event of a cyclical downturn or a layoff in the form of short-term wage replacement benefits – provided through the Cassa Integrazione Guadagni (CIG).[114] The scoreboard shows that initial net benefit replacement rates are in line with EU averages for workers with full contribution records. The replacement rate, however, is zero for the long-term unemployed.

This patchy social safety net meant a high risk of poverty for non-eligible workers who were unemployed or who were forced to seek income support from the network of their family and friends; it also implied a very strong commitment to employment protection for those unionised workers lucky enough to benefit from the CIG. The lack of an adequate safety net for many of the unemployed also has to be seen in the context of an economy which devoted relatively few resources to active labour market policies (ALMPs) to help the unemployed find work. The scoreboard shows that public spending on ALMPs in Italy never exceeded the EU average over the period since 2007 despite the doubling of the unemployment rate over the same period.

The final statistical point to note about Italy's performance is the abysmal labour and total factor productivity record over the past two decades. This has been the main element behind the steady decline in Italian real GDP per capita relative to all other major EU and OECD countries. OECD (2013d) highlights the fact that the contribution of total factor productivity to per capita real GDP growth in Italy over the decade to 2011 was negative, at -1.25 percentage points per annum. Many critics cite this persistently weak productivity performance as the real Achilles heel of the Italian economy.

It has to be admitted that the causes of the disastrous productivity record in Italy remain a bit of a puzzle and they are the source of much debate in the literature. Many different hypotheses have been put forward to account for it, but it seems clear that no one factor on its own can provide the explanation. The con-

---

114 The CIG could offer a wage replacement benefit of up to 80 per cent and it could be claimed for far longer than the regular UI benefits which, in turn, offered a much lower benefit replacement rate – 30 per cent in the 1990s rising to 40 per cent in the early 2000s – with a maximum duration of only six months.

sensus view in the literature is, rather, that it represents the result of many different causes, which range far beyond the labour market and which interact with each other. OECD (2013d) lists eight often-cited hypotheses to account for the mystery of the productivity decline in Italy, at least three of which relate to the behaviour of the main labour market actors, as well as specific labour market institutions and policies.[115] It also highlights how these factors can potentially interact with product market regulations, a poorly performing education and training system, an ineffective public administration and a lack of respect for the rule of law to reduce growth potential.[116] In the next section, we will review selected labour market and pension reforms which have aimed to help combat these structural weaknesses.

7.2.2 Major labour market and pension reforms since 2000

Concerns about the need to boost employment rates among underrepresented labour force groups and to reduce the degree of duality in the labour market, along with worries about how to finance the welfare state in a sustainable manner with a rapidly ageing population, led to a series of reforms to labour market and pension systems since 2000, culminating in several major reforms over the past years, which are described below. These more recent reforms, however, grew out of a series of reforms to both pensions and labour markets in the 1990s, and we shall briefly describe them first, since they provide essential context to the more recent reforms.

Labour markets: the Treu and Biagi reforms

The first labour market reform was enacted in 1997; it is known as the Treu law after the then Minister of Labour and Social Protection, Tiziano Treu, who had previously been a professor of labour law before he was brought into the centre-left Dini government. The explicit aim of the legislation was to boost employment prospects for youth, and also for the South (Mezzogiorno). Its main provisions were as follows: it eased the regulations governing new apprenticeships

---

115 For a good review of the literature on these hypotheses, see OECD (2009b). See also Codogno (2009) for a more sceptical assessment of some of the possible explanations.

116 OECD (2015b) argues that the dismal productivity record is mainly due to a misallocation of resources: potentially more efficient firms cannot attract sufficient resources of labour and capital to enable them to grow rapidly, while inefficient firms are able to remain in the market and retain resources. See Andrews and Cingano (2014) for evidence in support of this hypothesis.

and on-the-job training contracts; it gave incentives for work-related training; it facilitated temporary work through temporary work agencies; it legalised worker-dispatching services for the first time and reduced the disincentives to the use of fixed-term contracts; and it created incentives to promote intra-regional labour mobility. The reform was partly motivated by Italy's wish to join EMU.[117]

The adoption and implementation of the Treu law was facilitated by three factors. First, the preparation of the law involved a long process of concertation, i.e. wide-ranging discussions and co-operation, between the government and the social partners. Secondly, side-payments were explicitly part of the bargain in order to entice the key actors to sign up to it, e.g. in the form of subsidies to the South and legislative concessions involving taxes and working time. Finally, there was a direct commitment made to the unions that the law would not touch the employment protection legislation (EPL) governing permanent workers. This was enshrined in Article 18 of the 1970 Workers' Statute which stipulated that employers in firms with more than 15 employees must rehire workers found by a labour court to have been dismissed without just cause and must reimburse them by giving them back-pay and social insurance contributions, as well as paying a large fine. Article 18 was regarded as sacrosanct by the unions and by a large part of the public. As we shall see, this 'totem-pole' status of Article 18 was to bedevil further attempts to reform Italian labour law until very recently.

In 2001, the centre-right Berlusconi government returned to the issue of labour law reform. Once again, this reform was motivated by concerns about slow growth and high unemployment and Italy's role as a member state of the eurozone. This reform, which was passed in 2002, is known as the Biagi law, after Professor Marco Biagi, a labour lawyer, who was asked by the then Labour and Social Welfare Minister Roberto Maroni to draw up proposals to push the Treu reforms further.

The draft legislation clearly sought to push on with the Treu attempts to make it easier for new entrants and other labour market outsiders to get into work. It included provisions to: permit private employment agencies to compete with the public services on a wide range of employment services; allow open-ended staff-supply contracts in certain circumstances; facilitate a wider range of apprenticeships; encourage firms to use part-time contracts; and provide

---

117 Another motivation for the reform was the need to respond to a European Court of Justice decision which had struck down Italy's restrictions on worker-dispatching services.

greater opportunities for, but also better regulation of, non-standard forms of work, such as on-call work, job-sharing and project-based work.[118]

Despite being in line with the Treu reforms and despite an initial attempt by the Berlusconi government to negotiate the passage of the Biagi proposals jointly with the social partners, there was strong opposition to them, led by the main left-wing union confederation (CGIL). Much of the opposition coalesced around what was presented by the unions and by many in the media as the draft reform's attempt to weaken Article 18. This gave rise to several nationwide strikes and culminated with the assassination of Professor Biagi in March 2002 by the Red Brigade.[119] In the face of these protests and divisions within the centre-right coalition, the government dropped the proposed modifications to Article 18 from the bill. This concession allowed the other two main union confederations (CISL and UIL) to enter negotiations and reach a compromise with the government and the main employers' confederation (Confindustria), but CGIL refused to sign up to the agreement.[120] Since some of the reforms depended on union acquiescence in order to achieve their aims, this resistance by the CGIL undermined part of the implementation of the Biagi reforms.

While it is difficult to quantify the precise contributions of these two reforms to the improved Italian labour market performance in the decade leading up to the Great Recession, most commentators agree that they did have a noticeable impact in spurring faster employment growth, especially, as noted above, among non-standard jobs, such as part-time and temporary work.[121] But they did little to diminish the strong duality in the labour market and may even have exacerbated it somewhat by not touching the most restrictive elements of EPL for permanent workers. This weakness, together with the poor productivity record, led international organisations such as the IMF, the OECD and the European Commission to issue repeated calls to the Italian government to engage in further structural reforms in the labour market, including some relaxation of the provisions of Article 18. These calls fell upon deaf ears until the technocratic government of Mario Monti took office in late 2011.

---

118 Such non-standard jobs are called in Italian *collaboratori coordinati e continuativi* or so-called 'co-co-co' jobs. See OECD (2014g), Box 4.3 for a discussion of these specific non-standard jobs.

119 Two other academics were assassinated previously by the Red Brigade for advocating reforms to Article 18: Enzo Tarantelli in 1985 and Massimo D'Antona in 1999.

120 See OECD (2009c) for a detailed discussion of the complex political-economy ramifications and specific contexts underlying both the Treu and Biagi reforms.

121 See Boeri and Garibaldi (2007), who call this the 'honeymoon effect' of the reforms.

Labour markets: the Fornero reforms

The Monti government arrived at a critical juncture for the Italian economy, when it was hit hard by the backwash from the Great Recession and the eurozone crisis. The international financial markets were spooked in the summer of 2011 by the large size of the Italian public debt and the lack of growth prospects. These concerns were reflected in the large interest-rate premiums on Italian sovereign bonds over their German and French counterparts. The markets and the European Commission pushed strongly for further fiscal consolidation measures, combined with a strong package of structural reforms to boost growth prospects. In these circumstances, it was inevitable that further reforms to the labour market would become a priority for the Monti government.

Monti entrusted the task of passing the reforms to Elsa Fornero, a professor of economics, and not a labour lawyer.[122] The Fornero reform broke with the Treu and Biagi reforms by seeking to take measures to rebalance EPL by modifying parts of Article 18, and by seeking to phase in a universal UI system so as to fill the holes in the social safety net identified above. In this way, it sought to establish an Italian version of a flexicurity system for the first time. It had an element of continuity with the past reforms, however, in that it also sought to modify the apprenticeship system to make it more attractive to firms and young workers. OECD (2013d), p. 25 characterised it as 'the first time that Italy has attempted to comprehensively tackle labour market weaknesses'.

The reform proposed policy measures in four main areas: (i) incentives to transform temporary to permanent contracts; (ii) a significant reduction in the number of non-standard contracts and reshaping of the incentives to offer fixed-term contracts; (iii) changes to the apprenticeship system; and (iv) rationalisation and expansion of the UI system to make it universal, to be phased in by 2017. In a radical break with past practice, and in line with a similar initiative in Germany as part of the Hartz reforms, it also mandated a programme of monitoring and evaluation of the reforms to discover what worked and what did not and why.[123]

Unlike the pension reform, which was pushed through with great speed and without concertation with the social partners (see below), it was agreed that the labour market reform would proceed more slowly through social dialogue and parliamentary debate. Once again, the proposals to modify Article 18 provoked a huge outcry from the unions, especially the CGIL, and from part of the

---

122 Professor Fornero is a leading Italian expert on pensions and welfare. See Fornero (2013) for a detailed and candid description of her attempts to reform pensions and the labour market.
123 Indeed, Fornero (2013) states that the Hartz reforms served as a benchmark for her reform proposals.

media; the discontent spread into the left-wing Democratic Party. The opposition was so strong, and the need for reform so urgent, that the government partly gave way to these pressures, making the eventual modifications to Article 18 more modest than originally proposed. They permitted judges to moderate the sanction against employers in a case of unfair dismissal rather than requiring them, as had been the case previously, to reinstate the worker. In these cases, the dismissed employee would be entitled to severance pay instead, ranging from 12 to 24 months of salary, depending on tenure. The grounds for reinstatement following unfair dismissal were restricted, too. The reform also introduced a compulsory pre-conciliation process in an attempt to reduce the recourse to long and costly court proceedings.

To help fund the expanded UI system and promote permanent contracts, the reform added a 1.4 percentage point surcharge on employers' social insurance contributions on fixed-term contracts. The surcharge is to be refunded if the temporary contract is converted to a permanent one. Nonetheless, this element of the reform package had the unfortunate side effect of increasing the already high total tax wedge on labour, hindering efforts to improve cost-competitiveness.

As a complement to the flexibility reform agenda, the Fornero reform also extended the social safety net significantly. It did this by gradually integrating the standard unemployment insurance regime and the CIG to create a new unemployment benefit, the 'Assicurazione Sociale per l'Impiego' (ASpI), with a completion date no later than 2017. At the same time, it expanded, in addition, benefit coverage to many temporary workers through a so-called 'mini-ASpI'. The Italian Social Security Institute (INPS) estimated that these reforms extended the coverage of potential beneficiaries by 1.5 million.[124] Cappellini et al. (2014) report evidence that the restrictions on 'co-co-co' jobs led to a decline in their usage by firms.

It is impossible to assess separately the potential effects of the Fornero reforms on labour market outcomes and on productivity growth, especially since they were followed rapidly by a further significant bout of reforms in late 2014 and early 2015 (cf. Italy's 'Jobs Act'). Nevertheless, it is interesting to note that the latest version of the well-known OECD indicators of the strictness of EPL, which incorporate several major elements of the Fornero reforms, shows only a moderate decline in the protection of permanent workers in Italy against individual and collective dismissals between 2008 and 2013.[125] The reforms restricted

---

124 See OECD (2015b), p. 67.
125 See OECD (2013f), Figure 2.10. However, it is acknowledged that several elements of the Fornero reforms dealing with enforcement issues, such as the introduction of a lighter and faster

the reinstatement rights of dismissed workers, and Bank of Italy research, quoted in OECD (2015), suggests that the frequency of reinstatement declined by around one-third, but the new law generated interpretation problems, which slowed the judicial process.

Labour markets: the Jobs Act

The latest episode of labour market reforms is the Jobs Act, which was designed by the left–right coalition government led by Matteo Renzi, endorsed by parliament at the end of 2014 and enacted into law in February 2015. Again, the Jobs Act was designed to convince Italy's eurozone partners and the international financial markets that Italy was serious about pursuing structural reforms with the twin aims of boosting growth potential and employment. To this end, the Renzi government launched a series of broad-based and ambitious reforms, aiming to exploit complementarities between reforms in labour and product markets, public administration and the judicial system. It also put much emphasis on rapid implementation of reforms, an area which many observers had criticised as the Achilles heel of previous reform efforts in Italy.[126]

In the field of labour market reforms, it began with a significant liberalisation of temporary contracts in May 2014. This permitted up to five renewals of a fixed-term contract within a three-year period, so long as less than 20 per cent of the firm's workforce were employed on such contracts. This was followed by the Jobs Act, which built upon the Fornero reforms and sought to extend them in several key directions. In this, the Renzi government was not hampered by the need to build consensus for the reforms through social dialogue, as it had a solid majority in parliament, which permitted it to dispose of what remained of Article 18.

It did so by restricting further the reinstatement rights of workers judged to have been unfairly dismissed: reinstatement is now limited to workers dismissed on discriminatory grounds; all others get severance pay instead. These changes apply only to new employment contracts; the rights of workers with existing permanent contracts are 'grandfathered'.[127] The Act also introduced a new dismissal route, whereby the employer can pay the worker compensation equal to one month's salary per year of service (with a minimum of two months' wages and

---

procedure for dispute resolution and legal tests designed to weed out cases of false self-employment, are not covered by the OECD indicators.

126 See O' Brien (2013) for evidence on this implementation deficit in Italy.

127 However, if a worker with an existing permanent contract changes employer, he or she can be transferred to a new contract, even if it is less generous. This reduces the incentive for them to switch employers.

a maximum of 18 months). A worker who accepts this compensation foregoes the right to appeal to the courts that the dismissal is unfair.[128] Both parties have an incentive to opt for this non-judicial route, since the compensation is exempt from social security contributions and taxes.

In addition, the Jobs Act introduced a major innovation into Italian labour law by creating a so-called 'single contract', with protection increasing in line with tenure. Under the reform, new employees hired on a fixed-term contract enjoy a basic level of protection until, after two years, they become entitled to a permanent contract. From then on, the level of severance pay rises with tenure up to a maximum of 24 months' wages.

With regard to the social safety-net improvements of the Fornero reforms, the Jobs Act extended coverage of the new unemployment legislation to benefit all dependent workers and it integrated the ASpI and mini-ASpI. Moreover, it made benefit receipt conditional on active job search or taking steps to improve employability, a regulation which was backed up by the threat of benefit sanctions. The implementation of this benefit conditionality, however, has still to be agreed between the new National Employment Agency and the regions.[129] A pilot programme of social assistance, the *Sostegno per l'inclusione attiva*, which is targeted at poor households, will be extended nationwide on a gradual basis. The Jobs Act also aims to boost spending on ALMPs and make them more effective.

Boosting labour demand by cutting the tax wedge

The Jobs Act reduces firing costs significantly. Economic theory suggests that this will increase both hiring and firing rates and result in more efficient labour re-allocation, thereby serving to boost productivity growth.[130] It will not, however, necessarily lower unemployment. In order to ensure that, the Renzi government took measures to boost labour demand by cutting the tax wedge, especially for low-wage workers – defined as those whose annual labour income is less than 26,000 euros. A lump-sum tax cut of 80 euros per month is paid on annual in-

---

128 This new non-court dismissal route is relatively similar to the *rupture conventionelle* in France.

129 Enforcing benefit conditionality in Italy will be no mean task. Conditionality was foreseen in a law passed in 2003, but has never been enforced in practice, because the various actors involved in the process could not agree on how to do it.

130 See Martin and Scarpetta (2012) for evidence that a virtuous circle exists between lowering the strength of employment protection, increasing labour reallocation and boosting productivity growth.

comes up to 24,000 euros, and is then phased out as incomes rise to the 26,000 limit. In addition to this in-work benefit, the government decided to exempt temporarily employers' social security contributions for new hires on permanent contracts during the period 2015–17; this payroll tax cut is targeted at low-paid workers earning less than 25,000 euros per year. The payroll cut is substantial, up to 8,000 euros per year. OECD (2015b) estimates that, when the in-work benefit is combined with this payroll tax cut, the tax wedge for a low-paid worker falls from 46 to 21 per cent. This is likely to lead to a significant increase in hiring; it will be an important test of the Jobs Act to see how many of the hires are made on the new open-ended contract. The Renzi government has pledged to make the tax cut permanent after 2017, if the fiscal situation permits this.

It is, of course, far too early to assess the effects of both the Fornero reforms and the Jobs Act on the labour market. There is also an unresolved issue of how fixed-term contracts will coexist with the new single contract: a new hire could find himself or herself on a temporary job for three years, followed by a new contract with minimal protection for another two years. Simulations reported in OECD (2015b) suggest, however, that the Renzi package of structural reforms, if they are implemented fully, could boost annual per capita GDP growth by 0.6 per cent over ten years. The Jobs Act and the cut in the labour tax wedge are simulated to account for about 40 per cent of this boost to per capita GDP, with a slightly larger proportion coming from the reforms to the product markets, indicating the potential complementarities between reforms in labour and product markets.

Pension reforms

The history of pension reforms in Italy is longer and more sustained than the history of labour market reforms. It begins in the early 1990s, when Italy had a PAYG pension system which was described by OECD (2009a), p. 106 as 'perhaps the most generous pension system in the developed world'. At that time, concerns about the future financial sustainability of the Italian welfare state, which was dominated by spending on public pensions, began to loom large, as did concerns about the need to rein in an excessive early retirement culture and raise the relatively low employment rates among older workers. This set in motion a series of pension reforms which have transformed the Italian pension system and gone much of the way towards achieving the desired objectives. The main features of the various reforms are set out in Box 7.

Box 7. The sequence of major pension reforms in Italy since the early 1990s
1992: The indexation of pensions in payment was shifted from wages to prices.
1995: The pension system was shifted from a defined-benefit (DB) system to one of defined contributions (DC), based on notional accounts, with a very slow phasing-in of the new system. Minimum eligibility requirements were tightened for both early retirement and old-age pensions. Provision was made for adjusting the conversion factors which linked pension benefits to life expectancy every ten years.
1997: The contribution requirements for early retirement by public sector workers were aligned with those of the private sector.
2004: Eligibility requirements were significantly tightened again for all three pension regimes (DB, DC and mixed). The retirement age was raised, to become effective by 2008.
2007: The rise in the retirement age under the 2004 reform was implemented faster than previously envisaged.
2010: The retirement age for women in the public sector was raised to align it with that of men. Entitlements to early retirement and old-age pensions were postponed. The statutory retirement age was linked to life expectancy through automatic and periodic revision.
2012: The DC regime was extended to all workers as of 2012. For women working in the private sector, the statutory retirement age was increased from 60 to 62 (63.5 for self-employed females) as of 2012, with plans for phasing in further increases to align them with that of all workers at the beginning of 2018, when they reach the age of 66 years and 7 months. Changes were made to the rules governing early retirement, to enable those under the statutory retirement age, up to a maximum of three years, to retire with a reduced pension, as long as they have contributed for over 20 years.
2013: The changes in the criteria for receipt of old-age and early retirement pensions, namely age and the number of contributory years, were indexed to life expectancy in the three preceding years.
Source: Adapted from OECD (2011e), Box 1.2 and OECD (2013d).

The key pension reform was made in 1995 – the so-called Dini reform – which shifted the Italian pension system from a DB system to a DC system based on notional accounts. This reform, as OECD (2009a) makes clear, was strongly resisted by the unions and sections of the public, especially as the initial reform proposals were made by the first Berlusconi government. The Berlusconi government, however, fell as a result of internal tensions within the coalition, and the passage of the final reforms took place under the technocratic government headed by Lamberto Dini.

While the Dini reform was a decisive step in reforming the pension system in Italy with the twin aims of ensuring financial sustainability and lengthening the average working life, it had some negative aspects. The main drawback was the very long transition period between the shift from the DB to the DC system. In addition, the specific features of the reform proposals significantly increased intergenerational inequities.[131] Finally, the link between pension benefits and life expectancy was not automatic; the first such adjustment was supposed to take place in 2005, but parliament did not pass the necessary enabling legislation.

Many of the subsequent pension reforms, summarised in Box 7, can be regarded as attempts to correct these two weaknesses of the Dini reforms; the most recent reform was introduced swiftly and without much consultation by Minister Fornero under the Monti government. Indeed, Fornero (2013) explicitly states that she was given 'the task of reshaping the Italian pension system in less than twenty days!' This meant that this reform was designed and implemented without social dialogue, unlike the Fornero reform of the labour market. The speed was necessitated by the need to demonstrate, both to the financial markets and to its EU partners, Italy's resolve to implement a significant pension reform. The upshot of all these reforms is, in sum, the following: the transition period has been considerably shortened, remaining incentives to early retirement have been reduced significantly and an automatic link has been established between the statutory retirement ages and life expectancy. Fornero (2013) claims that a significant achievement of her reforms is that they help re-establish generational fairness.

The reforms have produced concrete results. First, the latest EU Commission projections for public pension spending to 2060 show that the reforms, especially the ones in 2010 and 2012, have succeeded in stabilising the expenditure on pensions relative to GDP, albeit at the relatively high level of around 15 per cent in 2060.[132] At the same time, it is undeniable that the pension reforms have contributed to the significant increase in older worker employment rates in Italy, especially since 2007. It is highly likely that the Fornero reforms will serve to boost older worker employment rates in the future.

7.3.3 Conclusion

There is an important contrast between the labour market and pension reforms in Italy over the past two decades: it has proved easier to reform the pensions in a fairly radical manner by instituting a series of continuous reforms, following the systemic Dini reform of 1995. These reforms have produced concrete results, in terms of ensuring the financial sustainability of the Italian pension system, and they have improved incentives for people to work longer.

---

131 See OECD (2009a), p. 115 for some striking examples of such inequities.
132 For details, see European Commission (2012).

It has proved much harder to reform some aspects of labour legislation, notably the high degree of protection afforded to permanent workers through Article 18, and to put in place a modern social safety net, which provides sufficient security for workers against job loss, while at the same time helping them find a new job quickly. The most recent reforms, however, notably the Fornero reforms and the Jobs Act, have taken an axe to these obstacles and have put in place measures which, if fully implemented, will establish for the first time a new flexicurity model for Italy. This has the potential to increase the flexibility of the Italian labour market to respond to adverse shocks and to reduce significantly the duality in the labour market, thereby serving to boost medium-term productivity growth. Italy urgently needs such reforms to work their magic as the population is ageing rapidly.

It is noticeable that the major reform efforts of recent years have come about in response to strong external pressures on Italian policymakers. The international financial markets and Italy's eurozone partners have exerted irresistible pressure on Italy to enact meaningful structural reforms with the aim of boosting growth and employment prospects. It is very doubtful that, in the absence of external pressures of this type, Italian politicians would have undertaken such wide-ranging reforms. It now remains to be seen if implementation matches this frenetic reform activity and if the results live up to expectations.

Table 11: Scoreboard for labour market outcomes and policies, Italy and EU, 1993–2013

| | 1993 | | 2000 | | 2007 | | 2013* | |
	IT	EU	IT	EU	IT	EU	IT	EU
1. Employment rate (% of the working-age population)	53.4	61.2	54.7	63.6	59.6	66.7	57.5	65.9
– male	70.6	71.8	69.5	72.9	72.2	74.2	67.5	71.6
– female	36.3	50.7	40.0	54.4	47.1	59.2	47.7	60.2
– youth (aged 15/16–24)	30.0	39.5	27.8	39.4	24.7	38.2	18.0	33.4
– older people (aged 55–9)	40.8	47.6	36.9	50.6	46.1	57.3	58.7	64.9
– older people (aged 60–4)	19.5	22.2	18.4	22.1	19.4	29.1	25.9	30.1
– older people (aged 65–9)	6.8	9.2	6.3	7.4	7.3	9.5	8.1	11.3
2. Unemployment rate (% of labour force)	10.0	10.8	10.5	8.9	6.1	7.1	12.2	10.7
– youth (aged 15/16–24)	28.8	21.0	29.7	17.4	20.3	15.5	40.0	23.3
3. Incidence of long-term unemployment (% of total unemployment) (a)	57.7	42.0	61.3	44.4	47.3	41.6	56.9	46.5
4. Part-time employment rate (b)	10.0	13.8	12.2	15.3	15.2	16.0	18.5	17.5

Table 11 (continued)

| | 1993 | | 2000 | | 2007 | | 2013* | |
	IT	EU	IT	EU	IT	EU	IT	EU
5. Temporary employment rate (c) (temporary employees as % of total employees)	6.0	10.5	10.1	13.1	13.2	14.8	13.2	14.0
– youth (aged 15/16–24% as % of total youth employees)	14.7	28.8	26.2	38.0	42.3	41.8	52.5	43.0
6. Low-pay incidence (d) (% of employees)	–	–	9.5	15.7	9.7	16.5	9.5	15.0
7. Protection of permanent workers against individual dismissal	2.8	2.6	2.8	2.5	2.8	2.4	2.5	2.2
– Protection of temporary workers	4.8	2.3	3.3	1.8	2.0	1.6	2.0	1.8
8. Public spending on labour market policies (% of GDP)	1.5	2.9	1.3	2.0	1.2	1.5	1.9	2.1
– Spending on active measures (e)	0.3	0.9	0.7	0.9	0.5	0.6	0.5	0.5
– Spending on passive measures (f)	1.2	2.1	0.6	1.1	0.7	0.8	1.5	1.6
9. Net benefit replacement rate (g) (averaged over four family types and two earnings levels)	–	–	6	65	8	61	9	54
– initial spell (h)	–	–	56	70	66	71	71	70
– after 2 years of unemployment	–	–	0	66	0	63	0	57

* 2013 or latest available year.
(a) Persons out of work for 12 months and over.
(b) Part-time employment refers to persons who usually work less than 30 hours per week in "their 'main job'".
(c) Temporary employees are wage and salary workers whose job has a pre-determined end date as opposed to permanent employees whose job is of unlimited duration. National definitions broadly conform to this generic definition, but may vary depending on national circumstances.
(d) Persons with a wage less than 2/3 of the median.
(e) 'Active' measures cover categories 1 to 7 of the OECD/Eurostat data base on public spending on labour market programmes.
(f) 'Passive' measures cover categories 8 and 9 of the OECD/Eurostat data base on public spending on labour market programmes.
(g) Data on net replacement rates for 2000 refer to 2001.

(h) Initial phase of unemployment but following any waiting period. For married couples, the percentage of AW relates to the previous earnings of the 'unemployed' spouse only; the second spouse is assumed to be 'inactive' with no earnings and no recent employment history. Where receipt of social assistance or other minimum-income benefits is subject to activity tests (such as active job-search or being 'available' for work), these requirements are assumed to be met. Children are aged four and six and neither childcare benefits not childcare costs are considered. Unweighted averages, for previous full-time earnings levels of 67% and 100% of AW and out-of-work single and couple households with no children or with two children (children are assumed to be aged four and six and neither childcare benefits nor childcare costs are considered). After tax and including unemployment and family benefits. Social assistance and other means-tested benefits are assumed to be available subject to relevant income conditions. Housing costs are assumed equal to 20% of AW.

Sources: OECD Online Employment Database: www.oecd.org/employment/database; data on net replacement rates come from the OECD tax-benefit models (www.oecd.org/els/social/work-incentives).

8 The Netherlands

8.1 Interview with Jan Peter Balkenende, 5 July 2013

'Democracy is not only a matter of having the majority; it is also about listening to the minority.'

In 2002, your government embarked on a number of important labour market reforms. Could you give us a short overview of what you think were the most important reforms and tell us more about why you started the reform process?
When I took office in 2002, my government prompted reforms in four areas: first, in the labour market; secondly, in the health system; thirdly, in government finance; and, finally, we decided to introduce a stronger policy to promote innovation, in order to strengthen our economy. This is the context in which the labour market reforms must be seen.

Before 2002, governments of the Netherlands had been talking about the need to change the Dutch disability benefit system and curb early retirement, among other things. However, they did not manage to act on it. My government felt the need to introduce reforms, in order to make up for past shortcomings. We believed that the time had come to act and that we could not wait any longer. When we started, we wanted to do things differently and better. That was also the title of my book *Anders en Beter*.[133]

Even more important was the need to change the country's attitude towards social security. We believed that it was really important to redefine the whole concept using the motto: 'Do not think in terms of what people cannot do, but think in terms of what people can do, and try to do everything to support people to get back into the labour market.' Under the old system, all kinds of people with difficulties, be it health- or employment-related, were entitled to disability benefits. They did not have to work any more and were supported financially. After the reforms to the disability benefit system, which started in 2002, people were required to undergo new medical examinations, in order to establish if they could possibly re-enter the labour market. In fact, four considerations led to this reform: (i) it was obvious that so many people who had become dependent on disability benefits were not using their talents – and the country not tapping into existing human resources was clearly not a good thing; (ii) the fact that a

---

133 Jan Peter Balkenende, *Anders en Beter* (Uitgeverij Aspekt B.V., 2002).

great number of people depended on social security benefits obviously created a huge financial burden; (iii) naturally, we were also aware of adverse future demographic changes; (iv) lastly, we discussed the risk of skills shortage becoming a bigger danger for the Dutch economy than unemployment. For these reasons, we concluded that it was better to invest in the quality of people instead of just saying: 'You have your money and that is it.'

Then we found that we needed to curb incentives for early retirement. I remember the beginning of the 1980s very well: it was a time of youth unemployment, and in those days, the solution was to encourage people to retire earlier, in order to create jobs for the young. At the start of the decade, youth unemployment disappeared after two or three years, because the economy improved, but people considered retiring early under one of the new schemes as a right. This, on the other hand, was unsustainable, because of the potential costs caused by population ageing.

We started with the introduction of the reform package as early as 2002, during my first term in office. This term did not last very long, however, with the result that we had to implement the package during my second term, but all its elements had been on the agenda from the very beginning. The good thing about my second term was that we acted rather quickly, because we believed that, if we did not take the right steps at the start of the term, there would be a loss of momentum. The actual process of changing the legislation began in 2003.

In hindsight, to what extent, and in which way, do you consider this reform package a success? Where do you see shortcomings?
I would say that, in retrospect, we were successful in the area of disability benefits: the whole system was restructured, and we were also successful in changing early retirement and unemployment services. I think in these fields, you could say that the reform policies were successful.

As for the second part of your question, shortcomings, I think there is only one project we could not carry out, and that was the issue of employment protection legislation. It was not possible to introduce a significant reform in this field because of the unions and the political opposition.

As for the reforms of the disability benefit system, the literature tells us that these reforms were very successful in terms of curbing inflows to the benefit system and less successful in terms of increasing the outflow of people from benefits and into the labour market. Do you agree? If so, why was this the case?

I must say that I am more optimistic about the outflow. In order to establish the outflow you just have to consider the number of people dependent on disability benefits. 800,000 Dutch people drew disability benefits in 2002, and by 2009, the figure had dropped to 540,000: numbers had, therefore, gone down considerably. It was, however, not easy for the people involved, because they had to undergo a medical check-up and many were declared fit for work. This led to a change in people's attitude: eventually, we were able to get more people back to work and out of the disability benefit scheme.

After my government took office, local authorities generally began to be stricter about entitlements to benefit schemes, with a total of 30 per cent of the population leaving the benefit system. It was possible to encourage people to start working again. In short, I am a bit more optimistic, I must say, than the analyses you mention would suggest.

However, from an employer's perspective, things were slightly different. Although we were successful in bringing more people into the labour market, it was still difficult for some groups, such as middle-aged and older people, to find a job. This is, in fact, a more general problem in the Netherlands and it goes back to the 1980s, as I have already mentioned. At that time, it was customary to retire at an earlier age, in order to create room for younger people to find jobs, leading to the situation that employers did not really invest in people, because they thought: 'Well, they will work maybe for three or four years, so there is no point in investing in the skills of these people.' My government was convinced that we needed to change this mindset. The fact that older people have more difficulties finding a job is not necessarily because of the social security system: there is a much broader dimension to it, which is connected with the fact that about 20 years ago Dutch governments thought that people had to retire at an earlier age. Much of what we see today is an inheritance of the past.

You mentioned that after your government took office you sought to shift public opinion towards 'taking action'. How did you do that?
I would say that, first of all, it is important to formulate a clear reform agenda and then it is even more important to stick to it: staying the course is essential. Secondly, it is key to build a strong narrative. We based our argument on the need to safeguard public services for future generations. Time after time, we emphasised the threat of demographic change. We stressed that remaining on the same path would slowly erode our public services, that we needed to do things differently in the interest of our children and our children's children. The public has to feel a sense of urgency or there is no point even trying. I highlighted these

two elements in a speech I gave at the OECD in November 2010 on the general lessons for successful reforms.[134]

Let me list three lessons a reformer needs to learn in order to be successful: first, be persistent. As a politician, you do not make yourself popular by introducing reforms, at least not in the short term. You implement reforms because of your convictions, your moral compass. Secondly, be patient. You will not achieve reforms overnight, they are about falling down and getting up again. Proposals must be prepared carefully. Sometimes, reforms must be tried several times before they finally work. Thirdly, focus on results. In the end, politics is about showing that your policy has worked, and measuring the results is therefore important. In the Dutch case, external pressure, in the shape of an economic slowdown, helped to present the reform package as inevitable.

Did any international pressures play a role in your reform efforts?
In my view, there was no clear international pressure to embark on reforms, because the unemployment situation in the Netherlands was better than in other countries. In the 1990s, the then Prime Minister, my predecessor Wim Kok, was invited to the G8 to describe why the Dutch economy was performing better than other economies in Europe.

Some years later, however, in 2000 and 2002, we could see that things were going a bit wrong. This was connected with the wage development – with our competitive strength – and I was not very satisfied with the situation. We were losing our strength internationally, and therefore felt that we had to do things differently. There was a need for a more dynamic labour market, which forced us to introduce reforms, but it was a matter of our own conviction. We were, of course, talking about the European context, but there was, in fact, no external pressure.

How did you manage to establish a general consensus in your coalition governments in order to create proper government cohesion?
I must say that all parties in my different governments were convinced that we had to make changes. Let me start by saying something about my first government: it consisted of my own party, the Christian Democrats, the Christen-Democratisch Appèl (CDA); the List Pim Fortuyn (LPF), founded and led by Pim Fortuyn, the politician who, as you may remember, was assassinated in 2002; and the Liberal Party, the Volkspartij voor Vrijheid en Democratie (VVD). Pim Fortuyn

---

134 Jan Peter Balkenende, 'Fiscal consolidation and structural reforms – getting it right' (OECD, Paris, 26 November 2010).

believed that you always have to think about proper and more efficient policy-making: 'No money to the police or to education if they do not improve their results, their performance.' There was an enormous drive in that political group, among all three parties, to act in a more efficient way and to introduce reforms to that end. That particular coalition existed for 87 days, and then we had new elections. My second government consisted of the Christian Democrats, the Liberal Party and, as a new member, the Democraten 66 (D66), a more social liberal party. The D66 always supported reforms. In both terms of office, therefore, my governments were made up of very reform-oriented parties keen on more innovation, more efficiency, and eager to consolidate the budget. That was a consensus and it was not complicated. My third cabinet had the character of a caretaker government and continued the approach taken by my second cabinet; D66 was not part of that cabinet. My fourth cabinet consisted of my party, the CDA, the Labour Party, Partij van de Arbeid (PvdA), and a smaller Christian party, the ChristenUnie. My goal was to work on increased liberalisation of the labour market, but attempts to change the legislation relating to dismissal failed, because of opposition by the unions and the PvdA.

Naturally, in my party, there were sometimes critical remarks about the social character of this kind of policymaking, especially during my second cabinet, but we persevered nevertheless, and we had overall government agreement, with all the ministers very keen on change. In addition, we also enjoyed parliamentary support and, in the end, gained a majority, which was, of course, a great advantage.

I think my background was rather helpful, when it came to the rules of the political game. Most prime ministers had been a minister first, but I became prime minister 'out of nowhere'. I had never been a minister and had never held any official post in a government. My background was in academia – I was working with the think tank of my political party and was a professor at the Free University Amsterdam. I believe this was an advantage: I came to politics with very strong convictions about the long-term prospects for our society. What kept me busy, in fact, was not all the criticism I had to face, but the question of how we could make the Netherlands stronger and what was needed in the long run.

How about the cooperation between your reform-oriented government and the Dutch collective bargaining parties?

Collective bargaining parties play a huge role in Dutch society. In order to answer your question adequately, I would like to give you some background on our society and the characteristics of its economy. The Netherlands as a country runs on the so-called 'Polder Model', which goes all the way back to the Middle

Ages, when farmers had to work together to protect the dykes against floods. At that time, if you wanted to survive, keep your land and withstand the strength of the water, you had to work together – clearly an old idea. Nowadays, the Polder Model is built on the Dutch model of consensus-based economic and social policymaking. Interestingly, the Dutch East India Company, the first multinational corporation in the world, established in the 17th century, was also based on a model of cooperation, sharing risks and profits. Even in those days, ordinary people could buy shares in such a company: it was all about working together. In the 19th century, there were no class struggles in the Netherlands, and we had cooperation between employers and their employees. This cooperation must partly be considered against the background of the social teaching of the Roman Catholic Church and the views on society in Protestant-Christian circles. Both denominations emphasised the need for cooperation between employers and employees, thus improving the chances for the emancipation of workers and preventing a class struggle. In the Roman Catholic Church this approach was linked with 'subsidiarity', while Protestant attitudes were connected with 'sphere sovereignty', the conviction underlying both concepts being that 'it is better to work together'. After World War II people said: 'We must all strive to modernise our society to be able to build up our country together.' In the 1980s, however, we encountered huge difficulties, a wage–price spiral and high unemployment, which in turn gave rise to another form of cooperation, the Wassenaar Agreement between employers' organisations and labour unions to restrain wage growth in exchange for policies to fight unemployment and inflation. I hope this brief historical excursus has shed some light on the characteristics of Dutch society, giving the context for the answer to your question.

When we started our reform projects, we had the support of the employers, but the employees were critical, very critical. I remember when the leader of the biggest union in the Netherlands, the Federatie Nederlandse Vakbeweging (FNV), referred to my coalition government as a 'horror government'. We had demonstrations, the biggest one at the Museum Square in Amsterdam in the second half of 2004. I had to stay in hospital at that time and was confronted with huge criticism, not only from the collective bargaining parties, but also from the media.

If you want to change things in politics, you have to start with a very clear conviction and, when you have such a conviction, you must stand your ground firmly: there must be no doubt in your mind about what has to be done. You know, of course, that there will be criticism from the opposition in parliament to what you want to achieve. In addition, there will also be criticism from the population and, especially, from the unions. All of that had always been clear to me.

At the same time, as a government, we knew that if we wanted to introduce reforms, in the Dutch context, it was really important to get support from the unions. We held a great number of meetings and demonstrated our commitment by making it known that we were aware how important it was to get everyone's support for our policy, despite the criticism. Of course, we needed to compromise; in the area of disability benefits, for instance, we had to come up with proposals that would convince the unions to participate. Eventually, we succeeded, though: in those years we reached agreements with the unions four times. I think that was quite an achievement.

It is also a matter of trying to influence the public debate, to make people understand that the present system is unsustainable in the longer run. I remember a debate I had in parliament about early retirement. The heads of two unions were sitting there and watching us. There was also a chairman from the youth organisation of the Christian Labour Union, Christelijk Nationaal Vakverbond (CNV). He supported the Dutch government because, as a young man, he understood that if we did not change the early retirement schemes, the younger generation would have to pay the bill for it. This gave me the backing of the Christian Labour Union's youth organisation, which was an advantage, because I could constantly refer to the supporting voice of the younger people.

Influencing public opinion was less important for us, however, than getting the support of the unions. We knew that if we wanted to change laws and regulations, we had to have good cooperation with our labour unions – that was key. In the Dutch context, in the context of the Polder Model, to carry out labour market reforms successfully, an agreement with the unions was more important than an agreement with the political opposition.

Could you give us an example of a situation when you thought that the unions went too far and were no longer in line with your sense of direction – and when this made you decide against making a compromise?
Of course, you can never accomplish 100 per cent of your aims and your proposals. In government you will never satisfy everyone – that is impossible. There must always be room for compromise, for adjustments. That is, in fact, a key element of democracy. Democracy is not only a matter of having the majority; it is also about listening to the minority, and this is part of the whole political game. We have always shown great willingness to listen. If, for instance, we had said: 'We have the majority in parliament in the second and first chamber, so we can do whatever we want' – if that had been our approach, we might, I think, have achieved some results. It would, however, have led to enormous difficulties later on, because you also need union support in the planning of long-term strategies. I do not think it is very wise to focus on implementing reforms that are currently

on your agenda just because you have a majority, without taking account of all the other elements.

On the other hand, there must also be a moment when, after listening to the opposition, you have to proceed, because time is limited. You have to be determined to forge ahead, do things quickly and speed up matters against the background of criticism. You must not let the unions take you hostage; if they develop unacceptable positons – let us say because their plans are too expensive or too narrow in their focus – there can be a moment when you, as the head of government, say: 'Well, in that case this is it.'

Let me give you a very clear example of being faced with an attempt to stop or even withdraw some of my reforms that had nothing to do with the unions. When we were in talks to form a coalition with the Social Democrats, the PvdA, in 2007, the then leader of the Social Democrats, Wouter Bos, said: 'As far as the reforms your previous governments have put forward are concerned, I think we need to make some fundamental changes.' I replied: 'This is a red line for me. Of course, I know that we have another coalition government now. I understand that we must be willing to compromise. But one thing you cannot ask of me is that I stop my reforms or even go back to how things were before.' The clearest example was the system of public health and the premium system which was part of it. Bos wanted to have an income-related premium, but my second cabinet had opted for a flat-rate premium with financial compensation by the government for those who needed this support.

Could you give us more detail on the compromises you finally reached with the unions in order to secure your reform agenda?
It was, for example, impossible for us to reform the employment protection legislation. If we had gone too far over this issue, it could have jeopardised the results of all the other elements of our reform package, and that was the reason for the delay in bringing in this reform.

I was convinced that the changes to employment protection legislation were an essential part of our reform policy. However, some employers said: 'This is not the most important issue. We can live with the current situation in the Netherlands.' This lack of support was quite difficult for me, but then the employers' organisations continued: 'Let's try to calm down the situation, maybe it is better to wait a bit.' My government's response was: 'Let's complete the important and non-controversial parts of the reform package now, and let's take a bit more time to work on an employment protection legislation reform later.'

We also met with huge difficulties as far as the unions were concerned. I particularly remember one occasion, in 2007, when the leader of one of the unions said: 'I understand that some things are necessary in terms of labour market flexibility, but you cannot ask us to make any changes to the employment protection legislation. This must be a government's responsibility, and the Labour Party must be willing to show that they are able to implement them. We cannot do it.' Given this attitude, our plan was, first, to reach an agreement between the unions and the government – i.e. also with the Labour Party, as it was part of that government. The second step was that we, as the government, would take the necessary measures and put forward proposals to alter the Dutch employment protection legislation. The idea was that the social agreement would be about wage development, but also about investing in facilities to give younger people opportunities to get a better education. Separately, we would take action over the revision of employment protection legislation. That was the agreement. In a way, we had a kind of gentlemen's agreement that if we, as a government, including the Labour Party, would come up with a cohesive proposal, the unions would not oppose that reform plan.

What happened? We were able to reach a social agreement, and then suddenly the Labour Party and the unions started to criticise our approach, both starting to criticise Piet Hein Donner, the then Minister of Social Affairs and Employment from my party, on the matter of employment protection legislation. In fact, that was the end of it. If my government had spoken as one voice on this issue, I am sure that we would have been able to push it through. In any case, I have drawn one lesson from this episode: be absolutely explicit in your coalition agreement. I think that was the mistake we had made. The original arrangements had not been clear enough. Coalitions are a strange thing anyway. In my second and third terms, my government was continuously criticised by the Labour Party, and, after all those years, in my fourth term, we were, all of a sudden, forced to work together. Having said that, the cooperation with the Labour Party about how to tackle the financial crisis was good.

Earlier you mentioned the support of the Christian Labour Union's youth organisation in the debate on curbing early retirement. In general, is the voice of young people strong enough to play a role in the political debate or are politicians stuck with stakeholders representing the past?
In the Netherlands, the unions consider themselves to be the representatives of all workers. In fact, however, they represent the older generation. Membership among the younger generation is very low. Young people are not part of the traditional labour movement – they tend to say: 'The unions are not for me; I make up my mind by myself. I have my own convictions. I won't become a member.' They focus on what is happening at their company.

In a more general sense, what we call the 'ZZPers', *zelfstandige zonder personeel*, in the Netherlands, meaning self-employed professionals or freelancers, i.e. independent, non-affiliated workers, have increasingly gained more importance over recent years. These two developments, the increase in number of the ZZPers and the failure to represent the younger generation, make the unions vulnerable.

If the unions fail to attract young people in the long run, it may have serious consequences for the process of policymaking in the Netherlands, especially given that social dialogue plays such a decisive role in this country. Anyway, since the younger generations are less and less represented by the unions, it is up to the government to become increasingly aware of the younger generations' views and attitudes. Young people understand that it is necessary to have more flexibility in the labour market and will emigrate if the right solutions are not found, as we have seen in Spain. Young people are leaving the country, because they do not have opportunities – there is a lot of mobility among the young. It is therefore important to take the view of the younger generation into account in discussions about reform policy – it is not only a matter of talking with the unions. Let me give you the following example: when I chaired the International Advisory Board of Rotterdam a few weeks ago and in that capacity had various meetings with representatives of the companies based in Rotterdam and with city authorities, we were most impressed by the meetings with all kinds of young people involved in different bottom-up initiatives. You have to make the most of the great amount of creativity there is among young people.

In terms of communication, how did you sell the reforms to a wider public?
Conceptualising and carrying out reforms is about publicising why the reforms are necessary: be it for financial, demographic or any other reasons. However, hope must also be an aspect: make it clear that the changes you advocate will eventually lead to higher labour participation and will create more chances for people. It is always important to spell out that it is not only a matter of reducing services but also building up something new. If it only involves taking away services without giving hope, then I can imagine that people will lose trust – it is therefore important that your view of the future includes hope.

Generally, when we speak about communication, it is very difficult to explain the benefits of reforms at a micro-level. Four years after you have embarked on a reform package, or even sooner, there will be a general election. In the Netherlands, when you ask people if they are satisfied with their lives, about 85 per cent reply 'yes'. However, if you ask people whether they are satisfied with The Hague – with politics – everybody is very critical. This is a strange situation, because there must be a kind of link between decision-making in The Hague and your personal life, but people do not feel that way. When you present a cohesive, convincing analysis, people will admit: 'Yes, I understand that we have to do something, but not now and not for me.' That is the big problem.

Did you draw explicitly on good practice from other countries in designing the reforms?
We learnt a lot from Germany, from the reforms Gerhard Schröder had initiated. He showed the courage to implement reforms. That Germany's economy is currently doing so well is a consequence of those reforms. Sometimes, looking beyond your country's borders, in order to see what is happening elsewhere, can help.

As for increased flexibility in the labour market, we have had various role models in other parts of the world. In the Netherlands we believe that it is key to have a functioning national security system for the working population, but this security, such as employment protection, should not hamper flexibility on the labour market. Security for one part of the working population should not come at the expense of job prospects for another part. Take the US, where you have the 'hire and fire' policy. Of course, you can criticise the Americans, but on the other hand the reverse side of the coin is that, if you become unemployed, you will find another job much sooner.

What could other countries learn from the Dutch experiences?
Quite recently, I went to South Korea twice and was invited by the South Koreans to talk about the organisation of the Dutch economy, specifically about the Polder Model. When I was Prime Minister, I spoke with a representative from Mexico who invited me: 'Please, come to our country to talk about the way your pension system is organised.' These are areas where others can learn from us: cooperation, long-term orientation and the way of financing a pension system.

You were Prime Minister from 2002 to 2010, a period when Europe saw a number of important labour market reforms. Has there ever been informal coordination between different European governments?
There are, in fact, two dimensions. First, there is the official dimension of policy-making at the European level that is, to a large extent, about strengthening the competitiveness of European countries. The other dimension is rather informal and concerns talks between politicians from different European countries about what is happening at home. These informal discussions have, of course, no binding character, but there is a lot of exchange of views and advice. For example, when we started the whole discussion about raising the retirement age, we asked our European colleagues what their experiences had been, what role the unions had played and how they had tackled various specific issues. This

type of discussion is frequent, and it is important to learn from each other in this way. Of course, sometimes I could also use the good examples set by other countries during discussions with the opposition in our parliament.

What is your idea of leadership?
Leadership is about sound analysis of socio-economic developments, long-term thinking, generating new ideas, giving hope for the future, seeking cooperation with all stakeholders in the tradition of the Dutch Polder Model and listening to young people.

Which challenges do you consider most pressing for the European or the Dutch labour market in the near future?
First, I would say that we have to do more in the area of flexibility in the labour market in the longer run. There must be the right balance between employment protection on the one hand and, on the other hand, more investment in people, for instance, through life-long learning in between jobs, and more opportunities for people to get on the job market in the first place. I think the Netherlands must catch up in this respect.

Secondly, creating a better relationship between companies and the education sector is an important goal. Education should serve to tap into people's abilities – we need more creativity. I discovered that young people are much more motivated to finish their studies, if they get complementary training in companies – that way they will produce better results.

Thirdly, I would like to emphasise the importance of supporting an entrepreneurial spirit among people. There must be a willingness to be active, to use one's talents. People must know that they cannot simply rely on the welfare state, and government should start encouraging an entrepreneurial spirit in primary schools and continue to do so at universities.

Fourthly, I think we need a combination of entrepreneurship, innovation and sustainability. For example, I am happy that students in the Netherlands feel that sustainability should be part of every curriculum at university.

Fifthly, we need an atmosphere in which change and reform are part of the general political process. Of course, this is a general remark, but I am really convinced that it is important to continuously adjust the welfare state to new developments. In the Netherlands we are proud of the Polder Model and we should, in my view, stick to that model. That does not, however, mean that it cannot be open to review. We live in times of fundamental changes: disruptive change, robotics, big data, 3D-printing, the internet of things.

Sixthly, politicians must be aware of the international nature of many processes. Young people travel: businesses are active everywhere. Politicians must adopt an international mindset because people will wonder what the social security arrangements and labour market conditions are in other countries. This is connected with the business and investment climate in your country as well.

Finally, I think we should generate another type of public debate. This may mean more room for long-term thinking, the new economy and bottom-up initiatives. It may also mean more assessments of what the general public thinks about specific issues. Let us be more creative in this respect.

Can reforming governments win re-election?

Our reform agenda was crucial in the 2002 general election, mainly because of previous governments' inaction. Everybody felt that it was necessary to do things differently. That was also the reason I preferred a coalition with the Liberal Party. I had the impression that we would be able to implement more reforms with them. In addition, in the 2003 general election we campaigned on reforms. They were on the agenda in the run-up to the 2006 general election, too, but while in 2002 it was a matter of fighting for reforms, in 2006 it was more about defending what had already been done. At that time, we knew, of course, that we had asked a lot of the Dutch population. It is all about striking the right balance between taking painful, but right, steps and not losing people's approval. In the summer of 2006, after a long period of criticism by journalists, academics and the public, the mood started to change. People began to say: 'We have criticised that Balkenende II government, but we have to admit that the choices they made were necessary.' Then the criticism changed into a kind of admiration for what we had managed to do. That was the reason, in fact, why the Christian Democrats won the elections in 2006, after years of always coming second in the polls. Unfortunately, the Liberal Party did not have enough seats, which meant that we could not continue our coalition. In any case, in 2006 people could see the changes in the country's economic performance: they had made the link between economic performance and the reforms. We could also see that, indeed, the economy was improving. Our defeat in the 2010 general election is another story. That was connected with domestic political circumstances.

There is another point that I would like to underline: from time to time politicians feel that it is better to postpone decisions. I would advocate the contrary: very often it is better to act swiftly and put up with initial criticism. Let me give you the example of Turkey. I recently asked Ali Babacan, the Turkish Deputy Prime Minister: 'How come the Turkish economy has dealt so well with the 2008 crisis?' He replied: 'When the crisis struck, we took severe measures. We were criticised for that, but we said that it was necessary. That had, of course, a negative impact on our economy in the beginning, because we had to use up our savings, but at the same time, the markets trusted us.' In other words, the Turkish government was well compensated for the severe actions it opted to take. In 2002 and 2003, we often swam against the stream, but we did so, because we were convinced it was right. Later, we were rewarded by the return of people's trust. Waiting too long is never an option. One has to ask: 'What will the consequences of the delay be?' Eventually, people will realise that waiting and postponing comes at the expense of future options – that is the point. It is a matter of conviction and also a matter of showing courage. To politicians in office, I would recommend: 'Don't be too concerned about your own image or the next elections; worry about what is necessary today.' That is, in any case, what I learned when I was in office. In my second cabinet, we never spoke about the polls or the next elections; we spoke about what we needed to do.

8.2 A note on Dutch labour market performance over the past decade

8.2.1 The facts

The Dutch labour market has recorded relatively good performance over the past two decades, despite some setback in the aftermath of the Great Recession. The harmonised unemployment rate stood at 6.5 per cent in September 2014 (seasonally adjusted), the seventh-lowest rate in the EU28. This level was, however, more than twice the pre-crisis trough of 3.1 per cent in 2008. Since then, the Dutch economy has experienced a double-dip recession from which it is only now beginning to emerge. As the archetypical small open economy, not only was it hit hard by the steep drop in world trade in 2008–9, but it had also to cope with two large domestic shocks to aggregate demand. First, there was the bursting of the housing boom, which put severe pressure on the financial sector and on the household sector, as it had borrowed heavily on the basis of rising property values.[135] Secondly, the increase in public sector deficits and debt in line with the downturn led to a significant degree of fiscal consolidation in order to get the public finances in order. In these circumstances, it is hardly surprising that labour market performance deteriorated. Nevertheless, one could argue that it is

---

135 Teulings (2014) argues that the poor output and unemployment record of the Dutch economy relative to Germany over the period 2008–14 owes much to the bursting of the housing boom. The associated drop in consumption in line with the decline in housing wealth forced labour to shift from the non-traded to the traded sector. This led to a loss in industry-specific human capital contributing to the sharp hike in unemployment.

testimony to the resilience of the Dutch economy and its institutions that the deterioration in performance was so limited.

One indicator of this resilience can be seen in the fact that the overall employment rate was 76 per cent in 2013, virtually at its peak and over 10 percentage points higher than the EU average (see table 12). This was a huge improvement over the situation in the early 1980s when the Dutch unemployment rate peaked at over 14 per cent and the employment rate was as low as 50 per cent (see fig. 10). The dire labour market situation in the early 1980s gave rise to an unprecedented social pact between the social partners and the government – the Wassenaar Agreement – which helped lay the foundations for much stronger labour market performance over the following three decades.

Evolution of the employment and unemployment rates in the Netherlands, 1970–2014

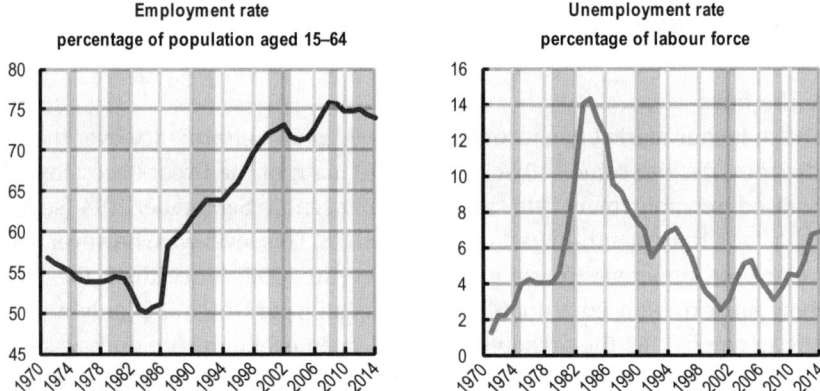

Note: Grey shaded areas refer to period of economic contraction (based on the output gap).
Source: OECD estimates based on the *OECD Labour Force Statistics, OECD Short-term Labour Market Statistics* and *OECD Economic Outlook Databases* (Cut-off date: 13 April 2015).

Figure 10: Labour market chart the Netherlands

In addition to the favourable role played by social dialogue in fostering support for the necessary structural transformations of the Dutch economy, the relatively strong growth and labour market performance owed much to the impact of globalisation on a small open economy such as the Netherlands. Large increases in trade openness, and in openness to foreign direct investment, contributed to fostering rapid change in the production structure of the Dutch economy and a well-educated workforce, together with a generous and wide-ranging social safety net, ensured that the labour market adapted to these structural changes relatively quickly and without excessive social costs.

A less desirable feature of the adaptation of the Dutch economy to these structural changes was, however, that part of it took the form of a growing early retirement phenomenon, closely connected with a large and continuous growth in the number of working-age individuals drawing disability benefits under the disability insurance law (the WAO).[136] At the beginning, disability benefits were mainly paid to older male, predominantly blue-collar, workers as a way of facilitating the shift from an industrial to a service-oriented economy. From the mid-1980s onwards there was, however, a notable shift towards younger workers going on disability benefits, most of whom were women.

The numbers of people of working age on disability benefits grew rapidly from 475,000 in 1976, approaching the one million mark in the early 1990s. As a result, the numbers of working-age individuals drawing disability benefits as a proportion of the labour force peaked at close to 12 per cent in the 1990s and public spending on disability benefits exceeded 4 per cent of GDP. This gave rise to serious concerns about the loss of labour supply represented by this phenomenon and its associated high fiscal burden, especially given the added problem of an ageing population.

Another feature of the Dutch labour market, which contributed to both early retirement and rather low labour mobility, is the fairly strict employment protection for permanent workers, especially against individual dismissals (see the scoreboard, which highlights the relatively strong protection provided to such workers, compared with their counterparts in other EU and OECD countries). The system benefits long-tenured workers, who can then combine generous severance pay with reasonably long-lasting and generous unemployment benefits, especially for those close to age 62. Employers who had to retrench their workforce often preferred to lay off older workers and pay the high dismissal costs as part of the bargain to preserve social peace with the unions.

At the same time, the degree of job protection afforded to temporary workers is relatively low in the Netherlands, ensuring that much hiring and firing by Dutch employers has a marked impact on this segment of the labour market. Indeed, it is notable that the share of temporary workers in total wage and salary employment in the Netherlands, which exceeded 20 per cent in 2013, is markedly higher than the EU average. The scoreboard also shows that the share of temporary work has risen significantly in the Netherlands over the period since 2000, whereas the EU average has been relatively stable over the same period. It is also

---

136 For a good discussion of this phenomenon, see De Jong (2007).

the case that youth account for a disproportionately high share among temporary workers in the Netherlands.

Indeed, the widespread prevalence of a disability and early retirement culture in the Netherlands, combined with relatively strict employment protection for long-tenured workers, has provoked many negative comments from international organisations such as the IMF, the OECD and the European Commission, and influential commentators have persistently called for reforms.[137] As will be seen below, these calls have been answered, at least in part.

On the other side of the ledger, one outcome of the relatively good labour market record of the Dutch economy over the past two to three decades, which is the envy of many of its EU partners, is its relatively high youth employment rate and relatively low youth unemployment rate. The youth employment rate in the Netherlands of over 62 per cent in 2013 was almost twice the EU average. Indeed, the Dutch rate was the highest in the EU in 2013 and the second highest in the OECD after Iceland.[138] While it has declined slightly since 2007, the drop has been much smaller than that recorded as the EU average.

As for youth unemployment, the picture is almost equally good. At a seasonally adjusted rate of 9.8 per cent in September 2014, the youth unemployment rate was the third lowest in the EU after Austria and Germany – the EU28 average was almost 22 per cent in the same month. The comparatively low youth unemployment rate reflects a relatively smooth and quick school-to-work transition for most Dutch youth which, in turn, rests upon a well-functioning vocational education and training/apprenticeship system, combined with strong age differentiation in minimum wages, which serves to align youth productivity with labour costs.[139]

Another dimension of Dutch labour market performance, which is better than the EU average, is the incidence of long-term unemployment. This has consistently been significantly below the EU average since 2000, even though the opposite had been the case during much of the 1990s.

While the Dutch employment performance has been very strong, it has to be noted that much of the growth has been in part-time jobs. Indeed, the Netherlands is the leader among EU and OECD countries in terms of part-time work:

---

137 For example, *The Economist* in a leader in a May 2002 issue entitled 'Going Dutch' referred to 'the much-abused and excessively generous disability system, which pays out to a ludicrous one in seven Dutch people of working age'. It laid much of the blame for a failure to reform the system at the door of the Dutch desire for consensus and social dialogue.
138 See OECD (2014g), Statistical Annex, Table B.
139 At age 15, a Dutch youth is paid 30 per cent of the adult minimum wage. This proportion rises year by year until at age 23 he or she is paid the full adult minimum wage.

in 2013, the rate of part-time employment was 38.7 per cent, compared with an EU average of 17.5 per cent. The next highest shares of part-time working in the EU are recorded in the UK and in Ireland, at around 24 per cent, far behind the Dutch level.

In addition, many part-timers in the Netherlands, especially women, work very short hours (fewer than 15 hours per week). As a result, labour utilisation is relatively low in the Netherlands. This can be seen immediately in the fact that the Dutch economy not only has the highest rate of part-time work in the EU, it also has the lowest amount of average annual hours worked per person employed.[140] In 2013, this stood at 1,380 hours per year in the Netherlands, compared with an OECD (weighted) average of 1,770 hours. The low rate of labour utilisation helps account for the fact that income inequality in the Netherlands widened over the past two decades, despite the strong growth in employment.[141]

With regard to the security dimensions of the Dutch flexicurity model, it is noteworthy that net benefit replacement rates are significantly more generous in the Netherlands than in many other EU countries. The scoreboard also highlights the fact that there has been no decline in benefit generosity in the Netherlands over the period since 2000 – indeed, there appears to have been a slight increase, which is in contrast to the trend for the EU average. In terms of another dimension of worker security, i.e. public spending on active labour market policies (ALMPs), the Netherlands has consistently outspent the EU average. It is, however, noticeable that the post-2008 period has not seen an increase in the ALMP spending effort, despite the sharp hike in unemployment, reflecting the overriding priority assigned to fiscal consolidation.

In sum, the main concerns in the Dutch labour market at the end of the 1990s focused on the need to curb early retirement and the explosive growth in the numbers receiving disability benefits. During the subsequent decade, this was joined by worries about (i) the need to raise the relatively low labour utilisation rate, caused by the large numbers of female workers working very short hours, (ii) the need to reform employment protection for permanent workers, in order to curb incentives for early retirement and foster greater labour market mobility, and (iii) the deterioration in labour market performance in the aftermath of the Great Recession, a period when fiscal consolidation pressures loomed large in the political scene.

---

140 See OECD (2012h), Statistical Annex, Table G.
141 For details, see OECD (2011a).

8.2.2 Major labour market and social policy reforms since 2000

Disability benefits

As noted above, the explosive growth in the numbers of recipients of disability benefits in the 1980s and early 1990s had already alarmed the public and the politicians, and a series of reforms to the WAO were introduced during the years after 1993. Chief among these were measures to make employers responsible for the first 12 months of sick pay (1996) and experience-rating of employers' premiums for disability benefit claims by their employees (1998).[142] These reforms had some initial success in curbing the inflow of new disability beneficiaries, but the relief did not last long, and by 2000 the numbers were heading rapidly towards the political 'milestone' of one million.

All sides – the public, politicians and the social partners – were in agreement that something drastic needed to be done, and this initiated an intensive sequence of reforms over the period 2002–6. This reform sequence was greatly facilitated by the establishment of an expert cross-party committee in the Dutch parliament (the Donner Committee) who was given the mandate to develop significant reforms to the disability insurance system.[143] The Donner reform proposals were passed to the leading tripartite body in the Netherlands, the Social and Economic Council (SER), in early 2001, and they published a report with a revised set of proposals at the beginning of 2002. These proposals ran into some opposition, notably from the social partners, and negotiations were then continued between the social partners in the context of the Labour Foundation, a specific institution in the Netherlands for the promotion of social dialogue.

This process of social dialogue eventually resulted in several major reforms which were phased in as follows:[144]

- *Gatekeeper protocol (2002)*. This specified the legal responsibilities of sick and disabled workers and their employers, respectively. It required both groups to agree a vocational rehabilitation plan after eight weeks of sickness absence.

---

142 The experience-rating was phased in over a five-year period. Koning (2009) finds that the introduction of experience-rating reduced the WAO inflow by 15 per cent between 2000 and 2002.

143 For a good discussion of the pivotal role played by the Donner committee in influencing the reform process, see OECD (2009c), Chapter 13. The Chair of the Committee was Piet Hein Donner, a Christian Democrat, who subsequently, from 2007 to 2010, became Minister for Social Affairs and Employment, in the fourth Balkenende government.

144 This description draws heavily on de Jong (2007) and OECD (2008d).

- *No-risk policy for hiring a disabled worker (2003).* The state agreed to pay sick pay for disabled workers, and firms which hired such workers were exempted from experience-rating.
- *Stricter eligibility criteria (2004).* The eligibility criteria for a WAO benefit were made stricter for new claimants.
- *Employer responsibility for sick pay was increased from one to two years (2004).* Under this new reform, employers could even be made to pay for a third year of sick pay, if they were judged not to have done enough to enable their sick workers to remain active in the labour market. This obligation on employers relating to sick pay is the most extreme in the OECD area in terms of the size of the sick pay burden falling on employers.[145]
- *Retesting the pool of disability benefit recipients (2004).* The new, stricter eligibility criteria were to be used to retest a large part of the existing pool of beneficiaries over the period 2004 to 2009. Originally, it was envisaged to retest all beneficiaries aged up to 55, but this generated significant political opposition and the age cut-off was subsequently lowered to 50, and then to 45, thereby exempting a significant part of the pre-2004 pool of beneficiaries from being reassessed and put at risk of losing their benefit or having it reduced.
- *Replacement of WAO by WIA (2006).* Under the WIA reform, two different benefit schemes were introduced: (i) a more generous scheme (IVA) for the fully disabled with no prospect of recovery and (ii) a less generous scheme (WGA) for the partially disabled and for the fully disabled who had some prospect of recovering their ability to work. The latter involved frequent retesting of beneficiaries and less generous benefits.

There have been several econometric studies on the effects of these reforms. They all concur in finding that they had a significant downward effect on inflows, which dropped from around 100,000 a year around 2000 to approximately 40,000 in 2010; this decline in the inflow led to a significant drop in the pool of beneficiaries of around 25 per cent over the period.[146]

---

145 While employers in most OECD countries provide some sick pay for their workers, the periods for which they are required to pay them vary greatly, with most countries imposing a duration of one to six months. The Netherlands require by far the longest period of any OECD country.

146 See, for example, van Sonsbeek and Gradus (2011) for an econometric analysis of the effects of the reforms using an administrative data set of disability benefit recipients over the period 1998–2010.

Despite this evident success, there was some rebound post-2008. This was perhaps inevitable following the steep rise in unemployment. Many of the older unemployed found their way into the category of disability benefit recipients, which partly explains the drop in the incidence of long-term unemployment between 2007 and 2013. The evidence also suggests little impact of the various reforms in terms of increasing outflow rates from the benefit category into work, with the sole exception of the policy of retesting of the pool of beneficiaries. Van Sonsbeek and Gradus (2011), however, show that the effect of the retesting of beneficiaries tended to decline over time. Finally, a worrying trend emerged of sharply rising inflows into the special disability scheme for youth aged 18 and over (Wajong). The caseload on this scheme doubled over the decade, finally exceeding 200,000, and this forced a reform in 2010, which tightened eligibility.

Nonetheless, it has proved extremely difficult to develop effective rehabilitation and activation services for the young and the partially disabled, especially after the responsibility for these services was decentralised and transferred to the municipalities, who often lacked the scale and expertise to deliver these services effectively and who faced conflicting financial incentives. As a result, further reforms were announced in 2012, in an attempt to improve the effectiveness of rehabilitation and activation services for these groups as well as for workers in sheltered workplaces.[147] There is no evidence yet as to the effectiveness of these most recent reforms.

Pension reform

The Dutch pension system rests on three pillars: (i) public pensions, (ii) occupational pensions tied to the employer, and (iii) private pensions. Much of the debate about pension reform over the period since 2000 has been dominated by the issue of raising the statutory retirement age in the public pension system. The statutory retirement age was raised from 60 to 65 in the mid-1990s, but ageing of the population and concerns about financial sustainability meant that the topic of raising the retirement age has not ended there. Just as in other EU countries, proposals were often floated after 2000 to raise the retirement age to 67 with a long phase-in period.

The unions, however, were strongly opposed to this proposal and for many years it remained blocked. It was not until 2012 that legislation was passed to raise the statutory retirement age to 67 by 2023. In 2014, it was proposed to short-

---

147 See OECD (2012d) for further details on the most recent reforms.

en the phase-in period and to link the retirement age to the rise in life expectancy.

The evidence suggests that the three-pillar design of the Dutch pension system, together with the recent increase in the retirement age, will ensure its financial sustainability into the foreseeable future. It is also very likely that these changes will increase the incentives for older workers to continue working.

Reforming employment protection

The relative lack of labour reallocation in the Dutch economy is partly connected to the comparative strictness of EPL for permanent workers, which has been noted above. In the Dutch system, employers can choose between two routes to lay off such workers: either a costly, but predictable, route of going to the courts or a potentially cheaper, but less predictable and slower, administrative route via the public employment service (UWV). The system is relatively generous by EU standards, and it is advantageous for long-tenured workers and serves to limit their mobility, since they cannot transfer their severance pay entitlements to a new employer. In addition, as noted above, it also served as an early retirement pathway for many older workers who can combine it with receipt of UI benefits for several years.

Recognising these concerns, several attempts were made to reform the system over the past decade, notably an attempt to cap severance pay at 75,000 euros. These efforts foundered on opposition from the unions and a failure to garner sufficient broad-based political support. Instead, in 2009 there was an adjustment of the general court guidelines governing severance pay, which led to a decline in such awards, especially for younger workers.

In view of the pressures of fiscal consolidation, however, the Dutch government finally managed in 2013 to negotiate an EPL reform with the social partners. Under this latest reform, the two dismissal routes will remain in place, though dismissal procedures for permanent contracts will be somewhat simplified: the court route will only be open for dismissals for 'personal reasons'; all other dismissals will be dealt with through the UWV route. The amount of severance pay will be linked to seniority rather than age. The maximum amount will be capped at 75,000 euros or one year's salary, whichever is higher. Workers aged over 50 will benefit from a more generous scheme until 2020. This new dismissal law will come into effect from July 2015.[148] It will, however, still leave the

---

148 See OECD (2014d) for details.

Netherlands with a relatively strict EPL system and may not significantly expand the career prospects for temporary workers.

Reforming unemployment benefits and the public employment service

The Netherlands has traditionally favoured a fairly generous safety net for the unemployed, combined with a strategy of activating job seekers to find work. This strategy worked well in the decade up to the Great Recession, when the Dutch unemployment rate was very stable around 3 per cent. The steep jump in unemployment post-2008, however, and the pressures of fiscal consolidation finally forced some cuts to the generosity of UI benefits. In 2013, it was agreed to cut the maximum duration of benefits from three to two years, to be phased in between 2016 and 2019.[149] At the same time, from July 2015, the period after which an unemployed person will have to accept all job offers will be cut from twelve to six months, and a wider definition will be introduced for the concept of 'suitable work'.

The Dutch public employment service (PES) was significantly decentralised in the 1990s, but its services were separate from the UI benefit agency. In 2002, however, a first attempt was made to integrate the employment and benefit agencies by creating two new agencies: (i) a self-governing agency (UWV) to administer benefits and offer employment services to the unemployed after six months of unemployment; and (ii) Centres for Work and Income (CWI) to process new benefit claims and offer employment services for claimants with unemployment periods of less than six months. Furthermore, reintegration services were transferred to the municipalities who were expected to arrange contracts with private providers.

In 2009, after the Great Recession hit, it was decided to merge the CWI and UWV into an integrated PES, offering both benefit and employment services to UI clients through a network of over 120 offices. In a further dramatic shock to the system, the new centre-right government in 2010 announced drastic budget cuts, of the order of 50 per cent for the PES, as its contribution to the fiscal consolidation effort. The PES, in turn, sought to respond to this severe budget cut by greatly expanding its use of online services for UI claimants and by cutting back extensively on face-to-face meetings with clients and more costly case management, with the sole exception of the most hard-to-place clients. The result is that, within the past few years, the Dutch PES has gone the furthest in the EU in the direction of reliance on online services for clients. Today, over 90 per cent of UI

---

149 The social partners can, however, agree on additional insurance if they wish.

clients interact with the PES online. There is little evidence of whether this radical shift in its delivery provision has made the Dutch PES more effective in terms of matching job seekers to available jobs, but client satisfaction with the new arrangements has declined, as many UI clients regret the fact that they are unable to get personalised services and advice from specialised case managers. Hence, there may well be a trade-off between reducing the costs of delivery of integrated benefit and employment services through greater reliance on ICT and fostering a speedy return to work for UI benefit claimants.

Increasing work effort, especially among female part-timers

Almost two-thirds of female workers hold part-time jobs, contributing greatly to the low rate of labour utilisation. Among the factors which, to some extent, cause the very high share of female part-time employment are insufficient provision of childcare services, high marginal effective tax rates for second earners and cultural preferences in favour of part-time work.

Spending on childcare was expanded significantly in recent years to reach 1.7 per cent of GDP.[150] In 2009, an income-dependent combination tax credit (IACK) was introduced to encourage second earners to increase their working hours; a new income-dependent tax credit (IAK) was introduced to encourage inactive people of working age to enter the workforce; and the tax credit for workers with non-working partners was gradually phased out. Most recently, since 2013, the maximum amount of the IAK was raised from 1,611 to 1,732 euros, in an effort to encourage low-income earners to work and increase their working hours.

Some of the reforms designed to lower marginal effective tax rates on second earners are being phased in very slowly over the period up to 2025 and provision of childcare services still lags behind those of the best-performing countries in the EU. When this is combined with the revealed preference of many Dutch households for the second earner to have a part-time job, it has proved very hard to encourage most Dutch part-timers to make greater efforts to work.

8.2.3 Conclusion

In sum, the Netherlands succeeded in making major reforms to the disability benefit system over a sustained period by relying upon the social dialogue

---

150 However, the recent coalition agreement to cut public spending on childcare by 2015, as part of the cuts in public spending, is likely to hinder the efforts to increase female work effort.

and consensus system which was attacked by *The Economist* in its leading article in 2002. These reforms have significantly weakened the early retirement culture in the Netherlands and contributed to a major increase in older worker employment rates. Nonetheless, although they represented a real success, they did not completely solve all the problems and there was a further weakening in labour market performance following the Great Recession. Clearly, strong pressures for fiscal consolidation were needed to generate the political will to embark on additional reforms, especially to the Wajong system. Similarly, the logjam blocking reform of the employment protection system through social dialogue was only broken recently under the double demand that the competitiveness of Dutch industry be improved and fiscal consolidation achieved. Even allowing for this reform, employment protection remains relatively strict for permanent contracts and it seems likely that further reforms will be required in order to boost career prospects for temporary, mainly young, workers. This will pose quite a challenge for the 'Polder Model'.

Table 12: Scoreboard for labour market outcomes and policies, the Netherlands and EU, 1993–2013

	1993		2000		2007		2013*	
	NL	EU	**NL**	EU	**NL**	EU	**NL**	EU
1. Employment rate (% of the working-age population)	**63.8**	61.2	**72.7**	63.6	**75.4**	66.7	**76.0**	65.9
– male	**75.2**	71.8	**82.0**	72.9	**82.6**	74.2	**81.1**	71.6
– female	**52.0**	50.7	**63.0**	54.4	**68.1**	59.2	**70.8**	60.2
– youth (aged 15/16–24)	**55.5**	39.5	**66.5**	39.4	**65.5**	38.2	**62.3**	33.4
– older people (aged 55–9)	**41.7**	47.6	**53.5**	50.6	**65.5**	57.3	**71.9**	64.9
– older people (aged 60–4)	**14.1**	22.3	**18.8**	22.3	**29.6**	29.4	**47.4**	34.7
– older people (aged 65–9)	–	9.1	**6.0**	7.4	**9.8**	9.5	**13.1**	11.3
2. Unemployment rate (% of labour force)	**6.1**	10.8	**3.0**	8.9	**3.6**	7.1	**6.7**	10.7
– youth (aged 15/16–24)	**9.7**	21.0	**6.1**	17.4	**7.0**	15.5	**11.0**	23.3
3. Incidence of long-term unemployment (% of total unemployment) (a)	**52.4**	42.0	**26.5**	44.4	**39.4**	41.6	**35.9**	46.5
4. Part-time employment rate (b)	**27.9**	13.8	**32.1**	15.3	**35.9**	16.0	**38.7**	17.5
5. Temporary employment rate (c) (temporary employees as % of total employees)	**10.0**	10.5	**14.0**	13.1	**18.1**	14.8	**20.6**	14.0
– youth (aged 15/16–24 as % of total youth employees)	**23.2**	28.8	**35.4**	38.0	**45.1**	41.8	**53.1**	43.0

Table 12 (continued)

	1993		2000		2007		2013*	
	NL	EU	**NL**	EU	**NL**	EU	**NL**	EU
6. Low-pay incidence (d) (% of employees)	–	–	**12.7**	15.7	**13.8**	16.5	–	15.0
7. Protection of permanent workers against individual dismissal	**3.1**	2.6	**3.1**	2.5	**2.9**	2.4	**2.8**	2.2
– Protection of temporary workers	**1.4**	2.3	**0.9**	1.8	**0.9**	1.6	**0.9**	1.8
8. Public spending on labour market policies (% of GDP)	**4.2**	2.9	**3.2**	2.0	**2.5**	1.6	**2.9**	2.0
– Spending on active measures (e)	**1.4**	0.9	**1.5**	0.8	**1.1**	0.6	**1.0**	0.8
– Spending on passive measures (f)	**2.8**	2.1	**1.8**	1.1	**1.4**	0.9	**1.9**	1.2
9. Net benefit replacement rate (g) (averaged over four family types and two earnings levels)	–	–	**70**	65	**73**	61	**71**	54
– initial spell (h)	–	–	**74**	70	**80**	71	**79**	70
– after 2 years of unemployment	–	–	**74**	66	**76**	63	**75**	57

* 2013 or latest available year.
(a) Persons out of work for 12 months and over.
(b) Part-time employment refers to persons who usually work less than 30 hours per week in "their 'main job'".
(c) Temporary employees are wage and salary workers whose job has a pre-determined end date as opposed to permanent employees whose job is of unlimited duration. National definitions broadly conform to this generic definition, but may vary depending on national circumstances.
(d) Persons with a wage less than 2/3 of the median.
(e) 'Active' measures cover categories 1 to 7 of the OECD/Eurostat data base on public spending on labour market programmes.
(f) 'Passive' measures cover categories 8 and 9 of the OECD/Eurostat data base on public spending on labour market programmes.
(g) Data on net replacement rates for 2000 refer to 2001.
(h) Initial phase of unemployment but following any waiting period. For married couples, the percentage of AW relates to the previous earnings of the 'unemployed' spouse only; the second spouse is assumed to be 'inactive' with no earnings and no recent employment history. Where receipt of social assistance or other minimum-income benefits is subject to activity tests (such as active job-search or being 'available' for work), these requirements are assumed to be met. Children are aged four and six and neither childcare benefits nor childcare costs are considered. Unweighted averages, for previous full-time earnings levels of 67 % and 100 % of AW and out-of-work single and couple households with no children or with two children (children are assumed to be aged four and six and neither childcare benefits nor childcare costs are considered). After tax and including unemployment and family benefits. Social assistance and other means-tested benefits are assumed to be available subject to relevant income conditions. Housing costs are assumed equal to 20 % of AW.

Sources: OECD Online Employment Database: www.oecd.org/employment/database; data on net replacement rates come from the OECD tax-benefit models (www.oecd.org/els/social/work-incentives).

9 Poland

9.1 Interview with Jerzy Buzek, 10 May 2015

'Structural reforms should not be prepared, enacted or implemented with partici-pation restricted only to the government and the coalition parties. Successful im-plementation requires ensuring widespread participation of various groups of stakeholders, even the opposition parties, but most of all of the legitimate represen-tation of the social partners.'

It has been 18 years since the government you led embarked on a number of important labour market and pension reforms. Could you please elabo-rate on these reforms? In hindsight, where do you see strengths which are, at the same time, perhaps also weaknesses in the changes that were intro-duced?
The government I led implemented four major reform projects, two of which had a significant long-term impact on the labour market. I am referring to the revolu-tionary changes in the pension system and the education system reforms. It was our deliberate aim to improve labour market dynamics by changing these sys-tems, at a time when many did not even recognise the close interrelations.

The idea behind the first of the two reforms, the changes to the pension sys-tem, was to switch from the traditional pay-as-you-go arrangement, based on a defined benefit, to the multi-pillar arrangement with two components: notional defined contribution (NDC) and funded defined contribution (FDC), the objective being to replace the totally unrealistic promise of a future pension level with a realistic one relying on contribution-generated income.

At the same time, the reform introduced mechanisms increasing the real value of the future pension by means of a few drivers. First, by reducing the bur-den on labour (the social insurance contribution in Poland rose sharply from 12.5 per cent to 45 per cent over the period covering the 1980s and 1990s). Secondly, by encouraging people to stay in work longer in schemes where the pension de-pends on the sum of the contributions paid and on the retirement age. Thirdly, by introducing the obligatory second social insurance pillar with an incentive to pay contributions, which, by public demand, were invested through open pen-sion funds (OPF) on the Warsaw Stock Exchange. That meant introducing an in-direct way of transferring resources from privatisation of state-owned enterprises into the Polish economy, thus strengthening it. Fourthly and lastly, the system's aim was to reduce generous early retirement privileges through a new, medically based definition of difficult conditions of work, which would give an option for earlier retirement.

Today we can see the positive developments we were expecting. In the late 1990s, Poland faced the challenge of very low employment figures, especially among those in age group 50 and over, and for women. When we look at the dynamics of the changes in this area, we can see a considerable improvement – a trend that is likely to continue. According to the OECD, Poland will be one of only four countries in the EU in which pensions-related public spending will decrease in relation to the GDP, enabling future growth and job creation. Economic growth and creation of new, stable jobs were also the result of investments made by the OPFs through the Warsaw Stock Exchange, which was an extremely important aspect of the reform. Moreover, the process of OPF investments contributed to the Warsaw Stock Exchange becoming the most important stock market in the region.

Important changes have been introduced in the recent years, which did not seem so urgent when I was the Prime Minister. At the time, we witnessed the generation of baby boomers born in the 1970s and 1980s enter the labour market, and there was no large-scale emigration, as experienced in the past decade. We expected the demographic trends in Poland to look different from the way they do today. Thus, from 2013, the retirement age in Poland started to rise to 67, from 60 for women and from 65 for men.

Obviously, as is the case with any reform, certain interest groups started exerting pressure on the government not to complete some of the changes and even to withdraw others. Several years after my government's term in office, this pressure resulted in the reinstatement of the previous schemes for members of the uniformed forces and for the miners. Two years ago, facing budgetary deficit, the government decided to withdraw part of the money saved in the open pension funds arbitrarily and at the same time OPF contributions were considerably reduced, to the extent that they are now voluntary. All these decisions certainly weakened reforms significantly and thus lessened their positive impact.

Politicians lack motivation and often fear completing reforms. Sometimes they even want to undo them. It is noteworthy that, despite this, nobody has managed to derail completely the train of changes that were started when I was Prime Minister. The main reason for this is that the fundamental solutions had won broad public support at the outset.

Were you able to start your changes in a climate of reform? If not, what did you do to generate such a climate?
Changes were announced in the pre-election manifestos of both political partners that would form the government, and they constituted the basis of the co-

alition agreement. The sentiment around the reform mainly stemmed from the citizens' dissatisfaction with the existing social protection systems. Society expected that, after the implementation of the economic reforms of the early 1990s, changes would be introduced in this area. Also, opinion leaders and experts, in particular within the Solidarność Trade Union, displayed a political and intellectual readiness for the changes. It should be emphasised that studies on these changes had been carried out for a few years, even during our predecessor's term of office.

One can say that the reforms were inspired by public expectations, but those expectations were broadly evoked through deliberate efforts made by political and social leaders. Luckily, we did not pursue them amidst political scandals or external pressures. We enjoyed expert support from international institutions – the World Bank, in particular. However, it was my government that finally expressed the need for the reforms. As I have mentioned before, we paid a lot of attention to strengthening economic growth and public expenditure consolidation. This, however, related to long-term results more than to an annual budget.

I am certain that we made the most of those windows of opportunity. The far more restrained willingness of consecutive governments to introduce changes on a similar scale, as well as their attempts to revoke some of the reforms, seem to prove the point.

To what extent could you rely on, or were you able to establish, a general consensus and cohesion in your government?
Ensuring endorsement for changes by one's allies is extremely important. This was particularly true when the coalition government was formed by two entities: AWS (Akcja Wyborcza Solidarność, the Solidarity Electoral Action) and UW (Unia Wolności, the Freedom Union), and the AWS was itself a coalition of four parties! However, reaching a consensus was not very difficult, as both coalition members had openly informed the public about their intentions to introduce the reforms that were implemented later.

Of course, the dialogue with political allies and their involvement in implementing and explaining the reforms was indispensable. One has to bear in mind that the Solidarity Trade Union formed the political background for AWS. Therefore, winning the support of trade unions was a prerequisite to the implementation of the reforms. We succeeded in attaining this goal within the framework of the Tripartite Commission dialogue, bringing together representatives of government, employers and trade unions.

In your reform efforts, how did you engage with the relevant stakeholders and the general public?

It should be emphasised that the reforms and their objectives were first announced in the election manifestos. Of course, such declarations are not enough by their very nature. They never contain any details of the suggested solutions. I do not intend to pretend that similar changes, especially with respect to social insurance and health care, had not been developed by our predecessors, which facilitated our endeavour.

No change is easy to introduce, and the process requires a continuous dialogue with citizens and stakeholders. The context of Poland's accession to the European Union, with negotiations starting in 1998, was a meaningful factor in convincing the public of the need for introducing systemic changes. All four reforms had a great impact on economic growth and creating jobs, increasing the efficiency of social services, preparing young generations for competition on the global labour market, improving local self-government administration and efficient use of structural funds. Let me also underline that the government coalition consisted of the only political forces which strongly supported Poland's EU and NATO membership since the early 1990s, and this was a significant factor in that context.

Each of the four reforms introduced by my government – to the pension system, health care, education and local self-government – was of a different nature and required its own specific kind of communication.

I shall start with the reform of the pension system. On the one hand, explaining its rules was very difficult because of the complicated nature of the subject matter. On the other hand, it was, paradoxically, easier because of the very clear public expectations of what the changes would bring, and the fact that they corresponded with our proposals. At the time, the system lacked the financial means to pay both disability benefits and pensions, and people were aware of that fact.

Members of parliament and the social partners – trade unions and employers – were provided with detailed information about the work in progress. The dialogue was not limited to consultations with the Tripartite Commission. Information and awareness-raising activities were also directly offered in work places. Winning the general endorsement of two major trade unions was unprecedented.

In the case of the issue that might have generated protests, namely the impact of the changes on the situation of those who had already retired, we stressed very clearly that the reform would not have any adverse effect on their situation and that it would, in fact, not apply to them at all. Finally, the reform introducing a mechanism giving individuals a choice, which was built into the proposals, was of significant importance. Everyone between the ages of 30 and 50, that is a sizable portion of the public, could decide whether they wanted to leave their pension contribution in the first pillar (under the 'pay-as-you-go', notional defined contribution system) or whether they wanted to divide it between the first and second pillars (the pension funds). A majority of the public supported the recommendation that the level of contributions paid and the amount received should be linked. As for the rest of the population, those older than 50 remained in the first pillar and those under 30 had to participate in the newly introduced second and the now reformed first pillar.

Regarding health care reform, it was necessary to gain support, or at least acceptance, from numerous stakeholders in the system and we obviously had to inform the public about the practical dimensions. That was an extremely difficult task. I believe that we succeeded in achieving it, as shown by the fact that the share of those not satisfied with the system dropped from 70 per cent in 1999 to 47 per cent in 2002.

It was even harder to win support for the education reform. Any changes in this area will always go against the grain of teachers' habits, and sometimes also against their interests. In addition, parents may not be in favour of the changes for fear that their children would not be able to cope. Therefore, it was of fundamental importance to ensure direct communication with these two groups on the reform process, which was based on introducing a new level of education – lower secondary school (ISCED 2). This move meant increasing the mandatory general education from eight years of primary school to nine years: six years of primary school and three years of lower secondary school.

It was essential to make sure that everyone knew what was awaiting them in the near future and what decisions they would have to make to adapt. It seems that we were successful in doing just that, even if the introduction of the lower secondary level has stirred rather ambivalent reactions for many years and continues to be criticised even nowadays, especially as regards the discipline-related issues. It is mainly because of the fact that an important premise of the reform, which in the end was not fulfilled, was that the lower secondary schools should have been physically placed with high schools and not with primary schools, as is the case today.

Despite of that, we can say that this reform has brought positive results. These are apparent in the constant and rapid increase in the PISA test scores achieved by Polish students. The increase between the 2000 and 2003 results can be clearly attributed to the impact of the reform. The effects of the change are permanent. Since 2003, Poland has advanced in the competence rankings of lower secondary education by ten positions in mathematical skills (to take fourth place among OECD countries), and by the same number in natural sciences. In reading and comprehension skills we now hold third position.

Education in Poland is the only component of the innovation index that is assessed positively and it constitutes our main potential area in developing a knowledge-based economy. Undeniably, the introduction of obligatory lower secondary education has contributed to greater equality in educational opportunities, particularly for students in rural regions and small municipalities. Furthermore, this equality of opportunities was at least partly responsible for the significant increase of the share of young people with university education reaching the Europe 2020 goal long before the deadline. Most importantly, the quality of education is of immense importance to the labour market. The Polish educational system enjoys a positive international reputation: indeed, it is highly regarded abroad and much less appreciated in our own country.

Finally, the local self-government reform created 16 regions and established a new district level in addition to communes and municipalities, which were introduced in 1990. The reform was in principle supported by the public because it held high expectations regarding the prospect of having more say in their neighbourhoods. Aside from defining the competences and financing of each level of local government, we had put a tremendous amount of effort into consulting the communities on where borders of individual regions and districts should run. The link between this reform and excellent efficient use of EU-funds today seems to be quite obvious. Available data show that entrepreneurs and businesses are satisfied with their cooperation with local authorities. Moreover, the districts today, when financed properly, can play a crucial role in fostering growth and job creation in small municipalities, as well as driving the innovative, knowledge-based economy of the future.

How did you approach those most directly affected by reform and potential opponents such as the leading opposition parties? Did you provide compensation for those who lost out as a result of the reform?
I will go back to what I was saying earlier. In the case of the reforms implemented by my government, especially the pension reform, the opposition parties, back when they were in power, had already worked on developing similar changes. Additionally, we also secured trade union support before the introduction of the new solutions.

We fundamentally reformed the old first pillar of the system, introducing the principle of defined contributions, which was absolutely crucial for the success of the new system. The abolition of unjustified pension privileges, like early retirement, was also of great importance. We adopted a precise calendar for implementing all those elements of the reform. The mechanisms introduced through laws by my government as part of the reform were used by my successors to carry on with these changes in 2008. On the other hand, the principle of defined contributions, which was also implemented at the time, in fact made early retirement tantamount to a substantial decrease in the amount of pension received. As a result, the 2008 changes did not lead to any loss of public support for the government, which had decided to take that step. This was presumably because of the extensive social dialogue on the pension issues, which followed the pattern introduced by my government. Another change, introduced only in 2013, about which I have already talked, was raising the retirement age to 67, and this was in line with our intentions.

A significant element that reduced potential criticism was that there could be no change in the pension system for farmers. At the time, the farmers were not subject to the regular national income tax regime and, whatever their pension contributions generated, covered only 5 per cent of the benefits.

As far as the compensation mechanisms are concerned, our reform included bridging pensions, which were finally also implemented. The bridging pensions were intended for those who might have lost the right to early retirement through the reform, but who had worked in conditions which could, according to current medical advice, justify earlier withdrawal from the labour market.

Did you draw explicitly on good practice from other countries in either designing your reforms or seeking to sell them to voters?
We made use of experiences gained by many developed countries. For instance, the combined experience of Sweden and Chile was of paramount significance for our pension reform. Polish experts were well acquainted with the solutions introduced in those two countries and thus were able to design a system that capitalised on their advantages while avoiding the pitfalls. It was very important for us to provide leading Polish opinion makers with a chance to become familiar with both these solutions in practice.

In the case of the health care reform, we relied to a large degree on the German experience in health insurance funds. As far as education is concerned, we based the reform on the fact that lower secondary schools are the standard solution in a majority of OECD countries. The key issue for us was to prepare the young generation better for the competition in the global labour market. Extending the period of mandatory general education by one year was part of that aim. For the local self-government reform, the palette of foreign know-how was very rich and it would be difficult to tell you exactly whose experience we relied on the most.

When implementing the changes, especially those of the pension system, we made use of expert support from international institutions. The World Bank reports in particular triggered substantial discussions on the design of pension systems in Central and Eastern Europe that would be able to withstand the consequences of expected population ageing, mainly through reducing implicit pension liabilities and through diversification of future sources of pension income. This change was timely, also because of the fact – mentioned earlier – that we could use the privatisation proceeds to support the reform effort and lower the transition costs to the new system, as well as to strengthen the economy.

I am certain that all the changes that we proposed were evidence based.

Would you agree that reformers should aim at striking a balance between unilateral and joint actions in carrying out structural reforms?
It is obvious that structural reforms should not be prepared, enacted or implemented with participation restricted only to the government and the coalition parties. The significance of structural reforms, especially in areas as sensitive to the public as the labour market or social security, requires special treatment. Even if parliamentary mathematics guarantees that their drafts may be forced through the voting process without problems, I have no doubt that in the case of structural reforms such a forceful approach is wrong. In my view, because of the long-term consequences for the population, their preparation, enactment and implementation requires ensuring widespread participation of various groups of stakeholders, even the opposition parties, but most of all the legitimate representation of the social partners.

Structural reforms should be carried out as a joint action. However, this requires a high level of competence both on the side of the government and public administration initiating these reforms, as well as on the side of other participants in the reform process. Aside from a solid analysis of the problems that the reforms are aimed at, I consider it of utmost importance to enable all the stakeholders engaged in the reform process to learn and understand their respective interests and expectations regarding the reform.

Any reform is a complex game of many, frequently opposing, interests. If the government accepts the burden of their implementation and adopts the role of the process coordinator, then it should strive to develop solutions guaranteeing the minimum accepted level of problem-solving efficiency, which a majority of the reform stakeholders find acceptable. It is obvious that not everyone's expectations can be met. It is therefore up to the government to prepare and agree with all the interested strategic or operational partners on the mechanisms of solving conflicts and disputes during the process of preparing and implementing the reforms.

That is why, based on the positive experience of cooperation within the Tripartite Commission, my government took the decision to put in place its legal framework by introducing legislation on the Tripartite Commission for Socio-Economic Issues. Until then, its work had been regulated by a government decree. With the new law, we furnished the Tripartite Commission with binding rights, which obliged the government and the public administration to consult it on all draft laws, including the draft budget, as well as demands that the Tripartite Commission agrees on salary increases for public administration, minimum wage levels, as well as pension increases.

The fact that it was possible to prepare and implement these reforms is to be credited, to a large extent, to the moment in time when the decisions were made. In the first half of our term in office, my government enjoyed a high level of public support. We had the public mandate to carry out fundamental changes, bringing to life what we had promised in the electoral campaign.

There was an undeniable challenge of ensuring coordination in preparing the four reform packages. But the reforms had to be implemented together, in parallel. The local governments, which had only just been established, took ownership and responsibility for most health care institutions, as well as for schools and their financing. The pension system reform led to the creation of the largest IT-driven public services management system in Europe at the time, which could also be used in the health care system. All the elements of change were interconnected.

How can reformers ensure the sustainability of the changes they introduced once labour market performance improves?
There were some principal reasons why Poland weathered the global crisis of 2008 so well. The low exchange rate of the Polish currency, which facilitated exports, and the EU structural funds that flowed to Poland and kept investments going at the time of crisis, are both often mentioned. Some of the reasons relate to the social welfare system. Namely, the lowering of the disability pension contribution and its burden on employment cost, which was possible because of the changes implemented by my government. Reduction of early retirement helped to sustain the level of pension expenditure. Continued OPF investments on the stock exchange strengthened Poland's economy and, according to some studies, contributed to the creation of some half million jobs since they were established.

The importance of the changes introduced is much greater in terms of strengthening Poland's resilience to the threats that it is facing today and in the near future. Protection against increases in unjustified social spending, increased employment, as well as the revenue base linked with it, have significant impact on the competitiveness of our economy. This can be clearly seen in the forecasts published by such international institutions as the World Bank, IMF, OECD and the European Commission.

The coalition partners in the government that I led lost the elections which followed the reforms. One may always point to other reasons, but it was largely because of the scale of the changes introduced by us. By their very nature, changes always stir a sense of anxiety among voters – whether this is justified or not. It takes time to get used to operating under new circumstances, which is a risk one has to take into account.

One can, equally, lose an election without having introduced any urgent reforms, and one can, of course, also win an election having carried out difficult reforms. In our case the most significant threat to reforms came from the strongest opposition party, which was highly populist and which came into power after our term in office.

As a result of decisions our successors took, the pension reform was weakened. The education reform was stopped, preventing, for example, the much-needed changes to the modern, skills-oriented curriculum at the high-school level – quite different from the focus of the lower secondary level – and also preventing the introduction of a new type of vocational schools, as well as satisfying populist demands by eliminating mathematics from the final high-school examinations. All of this hampered the adaptation of the education system to the demands of a modern, highly skilled global labour market. Even the health care reform was reversed, leaving a very inefficient system that is far from what we had envisaged. The process of ensuring the stable financing of local government was not carried forward, which had most dire consequences at the district level.

Speaking more generally, however, a politician's role is not to stay in power for power's sake only, but to use it in order to implement solutions that are of benefit to constituents beyond a single term of office. This is in fact what we managed to do in our term in office. If I had to make a decision on implementing these reforms once more, I would do it again, but I would probably put even more emphasis on communicating the significance of the changes.

How important do you consider strong leadership for a successful reform process?

Leadership is fundamentally important to the successful implementation of reforms, and this is not only my experience. However, the key point is that this leadership must be modern in character, based on team building, dialogue and communication, and not on imposing one's own opinion.

The work of the government, and of the politicians more broadly, needs to be carried out in the most transparent way. This should be reflected in the existing legal framework, obliging all levels and branches of government to act in a straightforward and unambiguous manner. For example, it should not be allowed to conceal part of the public deficits, which is still the case in many countries of the European Union.

There is one method that would increase the readiness of politicians to go ahead with necessary changes in social policy, especially regarding pension systems. An effect of the crisis is that today we pay a lot of attention to the question of public debt. The issue is well known and public opinion understands its significance. However, national accounts do not include hidden debt, i. e. the debt which results from today's liabilities of the social welfare system and from the future demographic situation. If the constituents become aware of the magnitude of this debt, they will also realise that the retirement promises of today are not realistic and that changes are necessary. Inclusion of the hidden public debt in national calculations would make it easier for politicians to make hard, but essential, decisions. Our awareness of the debt's size was also one of the most important reasons behind carrying out the Polish reforms 18 years ago.

It cannot be denied that we did not manage to avoid all mistakes, and the reforms, despite being founded on successful models introduced in other countries, had a number of weaknesses. Structural reforms cannot be fully completed within a single term of office. They had to be complemented, followed through according to the timetable adopted at the outset and modified to respond to the changing nature of the challenges the country continues to face. That is what we counted on and what had, in fact, been the political reality of a total of eight governments in Poland during the 1990s. The worst path with regard to long-term structural reforms is one where there is a lack of continuity, capitulation to simple populism and withdrawal from difficult changes. Reforms that are not followed through, or worse, which are shattered or reversed, will never yield results that had initially been expected. This is the lesson from Poland's experiences of the past decade and a half: the citizens' trust in any government and in the state more generally is undermined. As we see from numerous examples today, this path usually also leads to us living at the expense of future generations. People – citizens and voters – have a natural tendency to concern themselves primarily with short- and medium-term issues. Politicians must think and act with the longer term in mind. That is the essence of leadership.

9.2 A note on Polish labour market performance over the past decade

9.2.1 The facts

Polish labour market performance has exhibited a roller-coaster ride since the fall of the Iron Curtain in 1989 heralded the beginning of a long and slow process of transition to a market economy. During the 1990s and into the early 2000s, performance was poor, with large-scale labour shedding and significant restructuring of the economy leading to falling employment and high unemployment rates. Once GDP growth resumed in the mid-1990s, however, and especially after Poland joined the EU in 2004, the Polish economy has performed extremely well and this improved economic performance has been reflected in both increasing employment rates and falling unemployment (see fig. 11).

Evolution of the employment and unemployment rates in Poland, 1970–2014

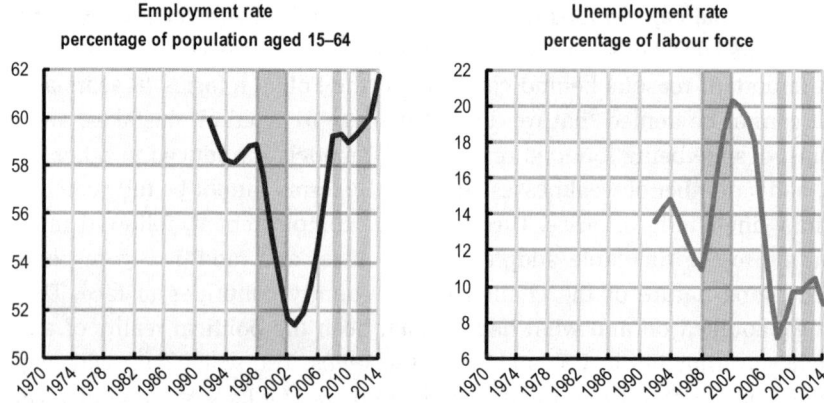

Note: Grey shaded areas refer to period of economic contraction (based on the output gap).

Source: OECD estimates based on the *OECD Labour Force Statistics, OECD Short-term Labour Market Statistics* and *OECD Economic Outlook Databases* (Cut-off date: 13 April 2015).

Figure 11: Labour market chart Poland

Polish membership of the EU sparked off an inward foreign direct investment (FDI) boom as firms in the US and in other EU countries were attracted by the relatively low labour costs in Poland, compared with their competitors and the rather large domestic market. In addition, Poland benefited greatly from EU transfers: after joining the Union, it became the largest recipient of EU cohesion funds, with these transfers exceeding 3 per cent of GDP annually in recent years. The upshot was a marked convergence in living standards between Poland and the EU average, a degree of catch-up which exceeded that recorded by Poland's neighbours in the Visegrad Group.[151]

---

151 The Visegrad Group is an alliance of four Central European countries – the Czech Republic, Hungary, Poland and Slovakia – which was established for the purposes of fostering cooperation between them and furthering their European integration.

This process of convergence was not derailed by the Great Recession, either. Indeed, it is noticeable that Poland rode out that crisis extremely well: it was the only major EU economy which did not experience falling output in 2008–9. It owed this good outcome to a combination of luck, sound macroeconomic policies, a sharp depreciation of the zloty, relatively little exposure to international trade and a solid domestic financial sector.[152] All in all, Poland's growth performance has been very impressive since it joined the EU and this has boosted labour market performance over the same period.

The prolonged period of economic transition, which lasted until the early 2000s, saw a significant drop in the overall employment rate as unemployment rose to a peak of 20 per cent in 2002–3 and there was a steep fall in labour force participation, as people resorted to early retirement on a major scale which facilitated large-scale restructuring of the economy and minimised social tensions. The employment rate fell to 56.4 per cent in 2000, over seven points below the EU average (see table 13). The employment rate has, however, risen significantly since then: it reached 61 per cent in 2012, but despite this improvement, the Polish employment rate still lags almost 5 percentage points behind the EU average.

The below-average employment rate reflects relatively low employment rates among youth, older workers and women. In 2013, the youth employment rate in Poland was only 24.2 per cent, compared with an EU average of over 33 per cent, and it has recorded no increase during the period since 2000. Indeed, unlike the overall employment rate, the youth rate has fallen slightly since the Great Recession. Part of the explanation for the poor youth employment performance lies in a strong rise in educational enrolment rates over the period, along with the fact that a relatively small proportion of Polish youths combine work and study.

Older worker employment rates, as can be seen from the scoreboard, are below the EU average in each of the five-year age groups from 55 to 70. As noted above, the labour force participation rates among older workers were cut sharply in the 1990s, brought about by a range of early retirement pathways which led to a steep fall in the average effective age of retirement for Polish workers. Poland, like most other EU and OECD countries, however, recorded an increase in employment among older workers over the period since 2000, with especially large gains since 2007 for those aged 55–9. As will be seen below, part of this increase reflects major reforms to the pension system to encourage longer

---

152 See OECD (2012e) for a discussion of how the Polish economy fared during the Great Recession and its immediate aftermath. The Economist (2014) also provides a good discussion of this episode.

working lives and a systematic dismantling of some of the major early retirement pathways.

The female employment rate also increased over the same period, from 50.1 per cent in 2000 to 54.2 per cent in 2013, but it still remains significantly below the EU average because of a combination of policies and social norms. For example, there is joint taxation of household income in Poland, which tends to discourage the employment of second earners. Childcare facilities and pre-primary education are relatively underdeveloped, as are long-term care facilities for the elderly. Thus, the burden of caring responsibilities falls heavily on Polish women.

In addition, part-time employment, which makes it possible – for women in particular – to combine working with household tasks, is relatively underdeveloped in Poland: it accounted for only 7.7 per cent of total employment in 2013, less than half the EU average of 17.5 per cent. It is also notable that the part-time employment rate fell in Poland since 2000, whereas it rose in most other EU and OECD countries over the same period.

Another feature which sets the Polish labour market apart from many of its neighbours is the high degree of segmentation between permanent and temporary contracts. The share of temporary employment as a percentage of dependent employment in Poland in 2013 was the second highest in the OECD at 26.9 per cent, behind Chile. This share was over 12 percentage points higher than the EU average and more than double the OECD average. Youth are disproportionately represented among temporary workers in Poland: in 2013 almost 69 per cent of young employees were on temporary contracts compared with an EU average of 43 per cent.

Part of this high share of temporary jobs in Poland may reflect a relatively lax employment protection regime for such contracts. In addition, Polish employers can hire workers under a specific contract which is lightly regulated under civil-law provisions rather than the Labour Code. Such contracts are less costly for employers, and they can be more rewarding for employees in the short term, as only very low social security contributions have to be paid, resulting in proportionately low social security coverage – hence, the pejorative Polish expression 'rubbish contracts'.[153] Such contracts accounted for about 7 per cent of dependent employment in 2012.[154] The evidence suggests that temporary contracts serve less as a pathway into permanent jobs in Poland, especially for youth, than they do in many other EU countries. Instead, they serve mainly as a screening device for employers.

---

153 See Baranowska et al. (2011).
154 See OECD (2014e), pp. 64–6.

Yet another specific feature of the Polish labour market is a relatively high share of informal employment. While estimates of the size of this phenomenon are necessarily very approximate, Andrews et al. (2011) review various proxy measures and conclude that informal employment and under-declaration of labour income is a significant problem in Poland. They link this to the complexity of the existing tax system, tax and social security advantages given to the self-employed and a certain lack of trust on the part of citizens in the rule of law in Poland.

The unemployment rate is the traditional indicator of disequilibrium in the labour market. Judged on this measure, Polish labour market performance was very poor in the 15 years following the transition, but improved significantly in the decade since accession to the EU. The rate remained in double-digits throughout the 1990s and then jumped to a peak of around 20 per cent in 2002–3, following the economic slowdown at the beginning of the 2000s. As the economy recovered sharply from this slowdown and grew strongly in the years immediately after Poland joined the EU, however, the harmonised unemployment rate dropped significantly to a post-transition low of 7 per cent in 2008. Subsequently, it rose again steadily to a peak of 10.6 per cent in the second quarter of 2013, before dropping back slowly to 8.7 per cent in September 2014 (seasonally adjusted), significantly below the EU28 average of 10.1 per cent.

One notable feature of Polish unemployment are the regional divisions. Unemployment rates are much higher in the poorer regions to the East of Poland compared with those in the West. There is also very little internal labour mobility between the regions so that the East–West unemployment gap has been very persistent over time.

The youth unemployment rate, which had exceeded 35 per cent in 2000, before dropping back to 21.7 per cent in 2007, increased after the Great Recession to exceed 27 per cent in mid-2013, before beginning a slow decline. By September 2014, it dropped to 22.6 per cent, relatively close to the EU28 average rate of 21.6 per cent (both rates seasonally adjusted).

The proportion of long-term unemployment (as a share of total unemployment) has tended to be below the EU average in recent years. In 2013, it was 36.5 per cent, very close to the OECD average of 35.3 per cent but 10 percentage points less than the EU average.

In terms of the public expenditure on labour market policies, Poland spends relatively little compared with other EU and OECD countries. In 2012, its total expenditure was only 0.7 per cent of GDP, compared with averages of 1.4 and 2 per cent for the OECD and EU, respectively.

The unemployment insurance (UI) system is relatively ungenerous in Poland, compared with that in many other EU or OECD countries. The benefit is flat-rate, with a maximum duration of six months, though it is somewhat higher for the older unemployed and those living in high-unemployment regions – their UI benefits are extended to 12 months. The eligibility conditions for UI in Poland are relatively strict.[155] The upshot is that the net (after-tax) benefit replacement rates are below average in Poland for many of the unemployed, though there are some exceptions, e.g. the low-wage unemployed who qualify for family and housing benefits and the older unemployed.

The public employment service (PES) is extremely decentralised in Poland, but it is generally regarded as low quality and has few contacts with local employers and shows no effective activation of job seekers.[156] Given the relatively low UI benefits and the very strict eligibility conditions, the lack of productive activation may not harm work incentives as much in Poland as it does in other OECD countries which have more generous UI systems.

A final distinguishing feature of Poland, which heralds serious current and future challenges to its economic and labour market performance, is its extremely low fertility rate: in 2011, it was the third lowest recorded among the OECD countries, just ahead of Korea and Hungary, and far below the population replacement rate of 2.1. Thus, the Polish population and workforce is ageing rapidly and the demographic situation is not helped by the fact that Poland remains a net emigration country. One striking illustration of the immediate challenge which population ageing poses for Poland is that the number of young Poles aged 19–24 is projected to drop by a staggering 27 per cent between 2012 and 2020.[157] EU Commission projections suggest that Poland could well record the second-largest rise in the old-age dependency rate in the EU28 between 2010 and 2060, after Romania.

In sum, Poland faces a major demographic challenge over the coming decades, if it is to sustain its growth rate and continue to converge toward the living standards of its EU and OECD partners. To meet this challenge, it will have to raise its overall employment rate significantly; much of its labour market and social policy reforms over the past two decades, especially those concerning its pension system and early retirement pathways, have in part been motivated by this goal. It must be conceded, however, that better labour market performance in Poland will not be achieved by labour market and social policy reforms alone. The European Commission, the IMF and OECD have all drawn attention to

---

155 For details, see Venn (2012). In 2012, only 20 per cent of the registered unemployed were eligible for UI benefits.
156 See Kaluzna (2009) for a critique of the Polish PES.
157 See The Economist (2014), pp. 14 – 15.

the fact that product market competition and innovation have to be boosted and corruption has to be fought, if Poland is to continue its catch-up process.

9.2.2 Major social and labour market policy reforms since 2000

Even though the main focus of this note is on major reforms since 2000, it is important not to neglect the landmark reform of the Polish pension system which came into effect in 1999 (see Box 8). This set the stage for a subsequent series of reforms, aimed at increasing the length of the average working life: these reforms are still ongoing. The 1999 reform, which was itself partly inspired by pension reforms in other OECD countries, has in turn had an influence on the continuing pension reform debates in many other OECD countries.

The 1999 pension reform

Post-communist Poland inherited a pay-as-you-go (PAYG), defined-benefit (DB) system that was not financially sustainable in the context of the transition to a market economy and the looming demographic challenge of an ageing population. Part of this problem arose from the widespread extension of early retirement rights to large sections of the workforce in the 1980s and much of the 1990s. In the late 1990s, pension spending amounted to more than 15 per cent of GDP, up from 8.6 per cent in 1990.

Box 8. The 1999 pension reform
The pension system was separated from the rest of the Polish social insurance system. The main feature of the pension reform was that it replaced a single-pillar PAYG system with a three-pillar system as follows:
A substantial PAYG pillar based on notional defined contributions (NDCs) retaining 12.2 per cent of gross wages. The first-pillar benefits depended on lifetime contributions, the indexation rules and age at retirement. A minimum pension was guaranteed to all with 25 years of contributions.
A second, mandatory, pillar, funded by a contribution of 7.3 per cent of gross wages, was to be managed by private pension funds, which were subject to rules on portfolio diversification. Participation in this pillar was mandatory for those born in 1969 or later; those born prior to 1948 had to retire under the first pillar. Those born between 1948 and 1969 could opt to join the second pillar or to stay in the first. Benefits under the second pillar depended on contributions, age at retirement and the net rate of return on the fund's investments.
The third pillar was a voluntary one, consisting of company pension schemes and other private savings instruments.
This three-pillar model was advocated by the World Bank and other international organisations advising the Polish authorities and it drew on elements of both the Swedish and Chilean pension systems.
For further details, see Chlon-Dominczak (2004), Góra (2001) and OECD (2009c), Chapter 6.

The debate on the reform lasted three years, from 1996 to 1999, and it was rather unique among the major pension reforms in OECD countries, in that it was supported by both left- and right-wing governments. Another unique feature of this reform, which distinguishes it from attempts at major pension reforms in other large EU member countries, such as France and Italy, is that it enjoyed wide support among the general public, who had come to the view the old DB system as both unfair – there was an extremely weak link between contributions paid and pension benefits – and financially unsustainable.[158]

The reform had three main objectives. First, it should increase work incentives by creating a clear and stable link between contributions and benefits and thereby raise the average effective retirement age. Secondly, it should put the pension system on an actuarially sound footing for the future, especially with an eye to an ageing population. Finally, it sought to ensure that pension liabilities would be fully funded.

But even with the backing of strong public support, introduction of the reform was not all plain sailing.[159] Several groups with vested interests, notably the unions and the farming lobby, had a major impact on the debate and the final shape of the reform. The unions were keen to prevent a rise in the statutory retirement age and to protect the early retirement rights of their members, which had been expanded greatly in the 1980s and 1990s.

The agrarian lobby wished to protect their special social security regime – the KRUS – which covered health care, disability, pensions and other social benefits for the farming community. While it was nominally a social insurance system separate from the general Polish social security system (ZUS), the KRUS was in reality a non-means-tested social welfare programme for farmers and their families. The average KRUS contribution paid by farmers was only about one-sixth of the average contribution to the ZUS: OECD (2009c), Chapter 7 pointed out that over 90 per cent of KRUS spending on benefits was financed by transfers from the public budget. The KRUS prevented much-needed restructuring in the agricultural sector, by enabling small, inefficient farms to be retained.

The upshot of this intensive lobbying was that both the cuts on early retirement rights for specific occupations and the reform of the KRUS were set aside in the final reform. With regard to the former, the reform created a so-called 'bridge pensions' system under which the existing early retirement rights of workers

---

158 The unprecedented degree of public support for the reform is well documented in OECD (2009c), Chapter 6.

159 Another specific feature of the Polish situation at the time – which favoured the reform – is that Poland was able to use the large privatisation revenues to offset part of the transitional cost in moving to the new pension system.

were 'grandfathered' for specific age cohorts. Although the KRUS was left untouched by the 1999 reform, both issues continued to dominate the debate about further pension reforms in Poland to the present day.

The failed reform of the KRUS, 2003–5

A major attempt was made to reform the KRUS in 2003–5, under the so-called 'Hausner Plan'.[160] The main impetus for the reform effort was the perceived need to achieve fiscal consolidation by reining in public social spending. This put the spotlight on the KRUS, whose subsidy from the public purse amounted to 2 per cent of GDP in 2002–3.

As had been the case in 1999, however, the farming lobby fiercely resisted any reform of the KRUS. OECD (2009c) pointed out that for most Polish farms, KRUS benefits accounted for a larger share of income than farming activities and so it was inevitable that the farm sector would fight tooth and nail to protect their rents. The large size of the agricultural sector in Poland was also mirrored in its political weight in parliament (the Sejm): since 1989, no Polish government has been able to muster a majority in parliament without the support of at least one of the major farming parties.

The Hausner Plan sought to curb spending on the KRUS through several methods: (i) restricting access to benefits by requiring the richest farmers to join the ZUS and changing the definition of 'farmer' in a more restrictive way; (ii) raising contributions, especially from richer farmers; (iii) establishing a closer link between pension benefits and contributions; and (iv) changing the indexation formula for non-pension benefits.[161]

In contrast to the situation at the time of the 1999 reform, however, there was much less public support for the Hausner Plan. The left-wing government which sponsored it went out of office in early 2004 and the subsequent Belka government was not at all strong politically and rapidly lost any enthusiasm it might have had for reforming the KRUS. At the same time, economic growth recovered and the state of the public finances improved, weakening the case for fiscal consolidation – which was the lynchpin for the KRUS reform – fatally.

The upshot was that the vested interests derailed the Hausner Plan and since then there has been no serious attempt to reform the KRUS, but greater success

---

160 This was named after the then Minister for Economy, Labour and Social Policy, Jerzy Hausner, who was the key architect of the proposed reform of the KRUS.
161 For more details on the Hausner plan proposals, see OECD (2009c), Box 7.1.

was achieved on the other unresolved issue from the 1999 reform, the large and generous pathways to early retirement.

Closing off early retirement pathways

The easy granting of early retirement rights through special occupational schemes and disability pensions in the 1980s and 1990s was highlighted above as one key factor behind the relatively low employment rates in Poland in the early 2000s. Hence, one priority of the reforms was to close off these routes to early retirement.

This began with a series of reforms tightening eligibility for disability pensions, better health checks of applicants and making benefits temporary rather than permanent. The result was a significant fall in inflows to the disability pension rolls and a decline of 10 per cent in the number of disabled pensioners between 2010 and 2011 – though the pool of recipients remained relatively high at 5–6 per cent of the working-age population over the period 2007–11.[162]

In 2008, access to the so-called 'bridging pensions early retirement scheme' was tightened significantly. The reform excluded many occupations, which had previously been classified as 'difficult' or 'hazardous' from eligibility for an early retirement pension. One measure of the success of this reform is that, while over one million workers were eligible for early retirement under this provision before 2008, the reform cut this to around 250,000. These reforms, combined with the effects of the 1999 reform, have raised incentives to work longer in Poland and thereby contributed to the significant increase in employment rates among older workers aged 55–9, as highlighted above. Nevertheless, other routes into early retirement still exist in Poland for specific occupations, e.g. farmers (through the KRUS), miners and members of the uniformed services.[163]

In 2012, the statutory retirement age was raised from 65 to 67 for men by 2020 and for women from 60 to 67 by 2040. These changes should also help boost employment rates for older workers in the future.

Finally, it is important to note that part of the landmark 1999 pension reform was reversed in 2014 in relation to the second pillar. The ostensible reason for this reform was the need for fiscal consolidation, in order to prevent the public

---

162 These data come from the OECD database on recipiency rates for inactive benefits paid to the working-age population.

163 As one illustration of this, OECD (2014e), p. 89 points out that 12 per cent of men who retired in 2011 were miners and their average effective retirement age was 47.9 years, whereas the statutory retirement age for Polish men was 65.

debt/GDP ratio from breaking the 60 per cent limit set by the Polish constitution. Under the reform, a significant part of the net assets in private pension funds in the second pillar were transferred to the first pillar under the ZUS. Public securities – which accounted for the vast bulk of the assets transferred – were cancelled. Workers were given the choice of continuing to invest a small part of their pension contributions (up to 15 per cent) in private funds. Tax incentives for individuals to invest in the third pillar were increased.[164]

This reform traded off a reduction in the debt/GDP ratio against a possible future drop in pension replacement rates which were already relatively low in Poland. OECD (2014e) suggests that the reform will lead to small falls in the structural public sector deficit and the debt/GDP ratio. Its impact on incentives to work longer is difficult to predict at this stage, though, if it does result in a drop in future replacement rates, because it gives greater weight to the first pillar, this could lead Polish workers to extend their working lives, in order to maintain their income in retirement.

Cuts in the tax wedge on labour; investments in childcare and pre-schooling
In an attempt to boost employment rates, several reforms were introduced over the period 2007–9 with the aim of 'making work pay'. These reforms included
–   the introduction of a child tax credit (2007);
–   cuts in social security contributions (2007–8);
–   simplification of, and cuts to, personal income taxes (2009).

These reforms should help boost female employment, as should recent reforms to spur investment in childcare and pre-schooling in Poland. In 2011, pre-schooling became compulsory from the age of five. In 2013, the government cut the costs of accessing childcare, and it announced that every four-year-old would have the right to participate in pre-primary education from September 2015 and every three-year-old from 2017.

At the same time, in an effort to boost the very low birth rate, the length of paid maternity leave has, however, been increased several times since 2006, including most recently in 2013 to an OECD record high of 52 weeks. In addition, the parental leave period of three years is the longest among OECD countries. Thus, the potential conflict between boosting the female employment rate and raising the fertility rate has probably been widened in recent years by reforms.

---

164 See OECD (2014e), Box 1 for a fuller description of this recent reform.

Employment protection legislation (EPL)

Regulations governing temporary contracts were relaxed between 2001 and 2003, in an effort to boost labour market flexibility. This was one factor behind the very rapid growth in temporary employment in Poland in the period prior to the Great Recession. Subsequently, these regulations were tightened in an attempt to minimise dismissals when the financial crisis hit the labour market, but the increased strictness of temporary work regulation since 2007 has led to only a slight drop in the incidence of temporary working in Poland. At the same time, regulations protecting permanent workers against individual and collective dismissals in Poland have been unchanged over the same period and are in line with the OECD average degree of strictness.[165]

This gap in the strictness of EPL between permanent and temporary contracts in Poland is certainly one factor behind the large degree of segmentation in the Polish labour market and it hinders the school-to-work transition for young workers. For this reason, OECD (2014e) recommended to Polish policymakers that they should raise the costs to employers of dismissing temporary workers while lowering the costs of dismissing permanent workers in a cost-neutral shift in the composition of EPL.

9.2.3 Conclusion

The Polish economy has made great strides over the past 15 years, improving its performance to the extent of convergence towards living standards in the other EU and OECD countries. Policies to boost employment have played an important role in this through significant reforms to pension and early retirement systems, which have helped to raise the average effective age of retirement significantly. Nonetheless, the overall employment rate, and the employment rates for certain key groups, such as for older workers, women and youth, remain relatively low, by comparison with EU and OECD averages.

Poland's fertility rate is one of the lowest in the OECD and the population and workforce are ageing rapidly. Hence, it is imperative for Poland to push ahead with further structural reforms in labour, social and product market policies, to give a boost to employment and productivity growth in the future.

---

165 For details, see OECD (2013f), Chapter 2.

Table 13: Scoreboard for labour market outcomes and policies, Poland and EU, 1993–2013

	1993 PL	1993 EU	2000 PL	2000 EU	2007 PL	2007 EU	2013* PL	2013* EU
1. Employment rate (% of the working-age population)	**60.4**	61.2	**56.4**	63.6	**58.0**	66.7	**61.0**	65.9
– male	**69.1**	71.8	**63.0**	72.9	**64.8**	74.2	**67.8**	71.6
– female	**54.3**	50.7	**50.1**	54.4	**51.3**	59.2	**54.2**	60.2
– youth (aged 15/16–24)	**29.5**	39.5	**24.5**	39.4	**25.8**	38.2	**24.2**	33.4
– older people (aged 55–9)	**43.2**	47.6	**37.0**	50.6	**36.8**	57.3	**55.3**	64.9
– older people (aged 60–4)	**26.8**	22.3	**20.4**	22.3	**18.4**	29.4	**24.0**	34.7
– older people (aged 65–9)	**n/a**	9.2	**10.8**	7.4	**8.5**	9.5	**9.4**	11.3
2. Unemployment rate (% of labour force)	**14.0**	10.8	**16.1**	8.9	**9.6**	7.1	**10.3**	10.7
– youth (aged 15/16–24)	**12.6**	21.0	**35.2**	17.4	**21.7**	15.5	**27.3**	23.3
3. Incidence of long-term unemployment (% of total unemployment) (a)	**43.5**	42.0	**37.9**	44.4	**45.9**	41.6	**36.5**	46.5
4. Part-time employment rate (b)	**11.9**	13.8	**12.8**	15.3	**10.1**	16.0	**7.7**	17.5
5. Temporary employment rate (c) temporary employees as % of total employees)	**n/a**	10.5	**11.7**	13.1	**28.2**	14.8	**26.9**	14.0
– youth (aged 15/16–24 as % of total youth employees)	**n/a**	28.8	**35.5**	38.0	**65.7**	41.8	**68.6**	43.0
6. Low-pay incidence (d) (% of employees)	**n/a**	n.a.	**n.a.**	15.7	**21.8**	16.5	**20.7**	15.0
7. Protection of permanent workers against individual dismissal	**2.2**	2.6	**2.2**	2.5	**2.2**	2.4	**2.2**	2.2
– Protection of temporary workers	**0.8**	2.3	**0.8**	1.8	**1.8**	1.8	**1.8**	1.8
8. Public spending on labour market policies (% of GDP)	**2.3**	2.9	**1.1**	2.0	**1.0**	1.6	**0.7**	2.0
– Spending on active measures (e)	**0.5**	0.9	**0.3**	0.8	**0.5**	0.6	**0.4**	0.8
– Spending on passive measures (f)	**1.8**	2.1	**0.8**	1.1	**0.5**	0.9	**0.3**	1.2
9. Net benefit replacement rate (g) (averaged over four family types and two earnings levels)	**n/a**	n.a.	**59**	65	**53**	61	**53**	54
– initial spell (h)	**n/a**	n.a.	**63**	70	**62**	71	**66**	70
– after 2 years of unemployment	**n/a**	n.a.	**57**	66	**51**	63	**51**	57

* 2013 or latest available year which is 2011 for low-pay incidence and 2012 for the spending data on labour market policies.
(a) Persons out of work for 12 months and over.

(b) Part-time employment refers to persons who usually work less than 30 hours per week in "their 'main job'".

(c) Temporary employees are wage and salary workers whose job has a pre-determined end date as opposed to permanent employees whose job is of unlimited duration. National definitions broadly conform to this generic definition, but may vary depending on national circumstances.

(d) Persons with a wage less than 2/3 of the median.

(e) 'Active' measures cover categories 1 to 7 of the OECD/Eurostat data base on public spending on labour market programmes.

(f) 'Passive' measures cover categories 8 and 9 of the OECD/Eurostat data base on public spending on labour market programmes.

(g) Data on net replacement rates for 2000 refer to 2001.

(h) Initial period of unemployment, but following any waiting period. Calculations consider cash incomes (excluding, for instance, employer contributions to health- or pension-schemes for workers and in-kind transfers for the unemployed), as well as income taxes and mandatory social security contributions paid by employees. In addition to unemployment benefits, it is assumed that social assistance and housing-related benefits are available as income top-ups for low-income families. Family benefits are included. Severance payments are excluded. Net replacement rates (NRRs) are evaluated for a prime-age worker (aged 40) with a long and uninterrupted employment record. The NRRs reported are averages over four different stylised family types (single and one-earner couple, with and without children) and two earnings (67% and 100% of average full-time wages). Any income taxes payable on unemployment benefits are determined in relation to annualised benefit values. For married couples, the percentage of the AW relates to the previous earnings of the unemployed spouse only; the second spouse is assumed to be inactive with no earnings and no recent work history in a one-earner couple. Children are aged four and six and neither childcare benefits nor childcare costs are included.

Sources: OECD Online Employment Database: www.oecd.org/employment/database; data on net replacement rates come from the OECD tax-benefit models (www.oecd.org/els/social/work-incentives).

10 Slovakia

10.1 Interview with Iveta Radičová, 13 July 2013

'The winner of an election is always the biggest minority in society.'

Would you describe how the Slovak Republic, from a broader point of view, developed from 1989 towards a modern, market-based economy?
In 1989, when the Iron Curtain fell, there was no general agreement of the direction the Slovak Republic should take, let alone a consensus about the need to transform into a liberal economy and democracy. Half of the population wanted socialism re-established – but with a human face – rather than introducing a liberal democracy. 23 years later, half of the population still expects 'socialism with a human face'. Nothing has changed. This half of the population consists of several subgroups. First there are those who are nostalgic for the communist regime. This group is very strong and corruption is a huge problem among them. Secondly, there are those who lost their privileges and are now out of the game. Thirdly, there are those who try to survive but, for different reasons, are not able to grasp the opportunities the new system offers, because of their age, their education or because they failed to seize opportunities in the first place. They are out of the labour market and totally dissatisfied. This is why there is no 'societal agreement' in Slovakia similar to Rousseau's *contrat social.* What kind of state do the Slovaks wish for? Strong or weak? Do they expect more or less intervention by the government? Do they want a strong welfare state or the opposite? With the constant change of government, oscillating between centre right and centre left, the answer to the crucial question 'liberal democracy or social democracy?' is constantly changing, too. There is no, or very little, continuity.

Democracies with a longer history can resort to stable pillars or institutions. In new democracies, the democratic institutions – and it does not matter if they are liberal or social – are not stable, as they are still developing. That is why there is so little trust in the legal system in Slovakia, and – as a consequence – in the state as a whole. This is a specific feature of countries in transition, in comparison with countries that also undergo changes in terms of their societal or political fabric, but where the core institutions are clearly defined, functioning, independent and stable. These institutions guarantee the rule of law and they are responsible for the public services: I am talking about the courts of justice, for example the constitutional court and the office of public prosecutor, but also about the labour market and the social insurance agencies – in other words, institutions ordinary people consider to be 'the state', because they determine their everyday life. In our country, the majority of people still perceive these institutions as totally negative, as consisting of 'those who are against us, against the citizens'.

It has been a couple of years since the government you led embarked on a programme of important reforms. In hindsight, to what extent do you think these reforms were a success? Were there any which revealed shortcomings?

The 2011 Labour Code reform, for instance, was a success. Among other things, we aimed at equalising employment protection for permanent and temporary workers – that is, for insiders and outsiders. In 2012, however, the new, left-wing government under Robert Fico reversed the reforms we had put in place. The Fico government made, in my view, two or three really positive changes, such as improvements in the employer–employee relationship, but they also made some terrible changes, resulting in higher labour costs because of rising social security contributions and severance payments. In addition, the Fico government chose, once again, to protect insiders. My government managed to lower unemployment through the reforms we introduced, but now unemployment is back at a higher level.

The major driver for improved employment performance in Slovakia in the last decade was neither any of the Labour Code reforms of 2001, 2003 or 2011, nor the 2004–5 pension reform, nor the various social security reform measures, but the tax reform of 2004, which immediately attracted foreign investments, thus creating 150,000 new jobs in companies such as Volkswagen, KIA, Peugeot and various US companies. Tax reform was implemented alongside a banking sector reform. In 1999, Slovakia was in default. This is the reason, by the way, why I have great understanding of countries in default – because we have been down this road. In 1999, following a period of wild, unregulated privatisation, 1,500 Slovak companies went bankrupt and, as a result, Slovakia witnessed a total collapse of the whole banking sector. We lowered the tax level for entrepreneurs, thus pushing for an economic recovery. The entire restructuring of the banking sector cost 12 per cent of GDP, which our citizens paid for through their taxes. It was very expensive, but there was no alternative, because otherwise society as a whole would have collapsed – it was the hardest situation imaginable.

For Slovakia, as a transition country, reforming the labour market meant first of all enforcing the rule of law, creating conditions for entrepreneurship, creating space for innovations and fighting corruption – that is to say, changing the environment to make good labour market performance possible. This is why, for us, another crucial reform was the reform of the justice system, and we started that immediately after my government took office. In the first three months, we introduced 12 new laws in this area. We became the only country in the world to introduce a Public Procurement Act in 2005, securing public procurement for supply contracts, such as construction and service contracts, for example. This was a remarkable achievement and it helped fight corruption. When I was in the Czech Republic six months ago, I saw that they tried to introduce this type of legislation, but so many institutions opposed it. Can you imagine? Public procurement is made completely transparent in this way and, as a consequence, within the first year, the government earned hundreds of millions of euros that would otherwise have been lost to corruption. Hundreds of millions! This was therefore clearly a crucial reform for us and we now have concrete proof of the advantages of the measures we have taken, together with a 100-point programme about how to reform the entrepreneurial environment, which we called the 'Singapore Programme', because Singapore ranks first by any measure of good national entrepreneurship. My government was able to complete the first 25 steps, and these reforms were essential for me.

To repeat, the Labour Code can make a difference of about plus/minus 0.3 per cent as far as unemployment is concerned, not more. The Slovak Labour Code regulates the relations between employer and employee, and can improve employment figures marginally. However, it cannot help increase productivity; it cannot help with innovations; it cannot increase investments; it cannot help create new jobs. To achieve this, there have to be good macroeconomic conditions and a favourable environment. On the other hand, if there is a rigid Labour Code, high taxation and no rule of law, then unemployment increases immediately. The specific combination of the different factors is crucial.

What were the shortcomings in retrospective?
There were some shortcomings in the implementation of the pension reforms in 2004 and 2005. The reforms were prepared with the help and support of advisors of the World Bank, the International Monetary Fund (IMF) and other organisations. I have written about this in several publications. In 2005, a second, defined-contribution pillar was introduced to the Slovak pension system on the recommendations of the IMF without, and this is crucial, allowing for a transition period between the old and the new system. This created great financial problems for the old, mandatory, publicly managed, defined-benefit security system that was financed on a pay-as-you-go basis. It turned out to be a terrible error. As Minister of Labour, Social Affairs and Family I tried to change things immediately in 2005. That such a mistake had been made by this incredibly renowned institution – it seemed unthinkable: simply a dreadful mistake.

The biggest problem was that all the good aspects of the reform, like the measures we introduced to react to the ageing of the population and the combination of different financial sources to fund the pension system, were rejected by the population because there was no transition period and because of the ensuing financial problems. It was only one mistake, but it was such an important mistake that it provoked hostility against the entire reform concept. People started asking publicly whether it would not be better to have a completely different kind of reform. We made some corrections to the package immediately, but it was very expensive.

As a result, we have since then been involved in a continuing, stupid discussion on whether the pensions under the new, combined system will be higher than those under the old pay-as-you-go system – and this is absolutely not the case. People think that politicians from both sides are lying: both sides are debating with arguments which are 'non-arguments'. A two- or three-pillar system does not offer higher pensions – it only spreads the risks, nothing else. It does not solve the problem of an ageing population – it just balances the pressure of an ageing population a bit, between the public and private spheres. That is all – it was a mistake from the beginning.

Let me take this opportunity to tell you more about the role of international institutions. My government managed the second-highest consolidation of sovereign deficit in Europe at the time (Estonia was highest), from 7.7 to 4.8 per cent within one year. Can you imagine? And then I read in an IMF document that our course of action had been a mistake and that we should have proceeded with the consolidation more slowly. There was a similar reaction to the way we introduced the pension reform – 'oh, sorry', they seemed to say, 'a 9 per cent contribution to the defined-contribution pillar in the second year was perhaps a mistake: it's too high.' 'Come on!' was my response: 'You cannot carry out experiments on us as if we were animals.' The question why we were listening to these people and why we acted on their recommendations remains justified and my answer is: 'We were not listening.' There was an open fight over pension reform between the Ministry of Finance and the Ministry of Social Affairs. Eventually, the decision was taken by the then Minister of Social Affairs, Ľudovít Kaník, and that was a mistake. Yet, the starting point of the fight was the concept prepared by the IMF. The concept of the Minister of Finance had always been based on a 4 to 6 per cent contribution to the second pillar of the pension system – four to six; and then, 'oops!' there was an increase to 9 per cent. Very expensive! The IMF now thinks that the 2003 pension reform was in principle well designed, and in line with their recommendations. As we speak, this pension system is about to be changed again radically, according to a completely new design. And again, the IMF thinks that this is fine. How is that possible? I am sorry, but I do not understand that. There are two different designs on the table, and both are okay for them? Come on!

You know I am very critical of the European institutions and I have every right to be, because I paid the highest price of all prime ministers to keep the eurozone and the EU alive: I lost my position in government – I sacrificed it. My stance towards the EU is therefore clear. I have a right to be very critical, and I am. Slovakia had a huge sovereign deficit. I know that the only way to clear a deficit is through national reforms. Without the introduction of reforms, neither the EU nor any other international organisation can help – nobody can. Deficits are created at home, and so is productivity. The only thing we need in order to implement reforms are comparisons between different countries and models, sharing good practice with each other – and also bad practice – to avoid repeating the same mistakes.

Were there examples of good or bad practice, internationally, that you took into account when you proposed your reforms?
There are: when we prepared the 2011 Labour Code reform, we studied the Danish, the Swedish and the British models. It was a first step, and we copied some of the measures from the Danish.

Judging from the experience you had with the IMF, do you think that one of the conditions for successful reforms is to introduce them less radically?
Not necessarily – it depends – often the contrary is true: if reforms are not introduced immediately and radically, they never will be. You have to take a decision and then act on it. Otherwise you will only see something that is, more or less, far from the original concept. Yet, you always have to be open to the need for corrections, because – for one thing – it is not possible to measure the effects of synergy before reform processes have actually started. If you launch three or four reforms at the same time, you cannot know how they interact and you cannot know, plan, measure, analyse all the effects that reforms have on society. There must, therefore, be an opportunity to make corrections. That is why it is always necessary to explain reforms, and to allow question marks to remain alongside certain measures, where appropriate, ensuring that they can be modified at a later point in time. You could say: 'If we have a better environment for entrepreneurs, then we will be able to change this and that in the Labour Code. If not, we have to be more flexible.' Reality keeps changing, and so do successful reform designs. They constantly need to be adapted to a changing reality. The role of international organisations, and the impact of international pressure, should not be underestimated in the sense that they can give good arguments for the direction to take. In general, I would however say that the size and the depth of reforms, and whether there should be a more prudent or more radical approach, depend more on the historical and the present national context than

on external, international influences. In addition, when there is a window of opportunity for structural reforms, one should not hesitate to seize it. It is always better to opt for action in these cases, risking the need for later corrections than to wait until one has the final answer, because there is never a final answer – there is always a need for corrections. Most importantly, as a politician you have to make your electorate aware from the very beginning that there is a need for corrections.

Going back to the moment when you came into power, did you have a mandate for reform?
We campaigned for a socio-economic strategy that would be more liberal, and my party, the Slovak Democratic and Christian Union (SDKÚ-DS), got enough seats in parliament to form a coalition, but there was no clear majority at that time for reforms. In a more general sense, the winner of an election is always the biggest minority in society, and power is based only on the legislative majority in parliament. In Slovakia, from 1989 onwards, a minority of the population supported the country's transition to a democratic social market economy. How do you promote development and reforms as a policy-maker under such conditions? These conditions were the reason why the first Dzurinda reform government, in power from 1998 to 2002, had to be a left–right government based on strong compromises, but even so, unemployment results were not good: they peaked at about 20 per cent on average in Slovakia at that time. The country had been governed by two different right-wing governments; the Dzurinda governments from 2002 to 2006, and my government from 2010 to 2012. Both saw early elections, my government after two years and the second Dzurinda government after three years. However, we managed to implement far-reaching reforms. I do not know if I would go so far as to say that my government lost power because of the reforms we introduced, but I am very near to saying it. I just have to remind myself of the social stratification and the lack of trust among the population in Slovakia. Moreover, do not forget that 85 per cent of the Slovak population had a monthly income lower than 400 euros before taxation – terrible. One of the main reasons why it is so difficult to keep the majority in parliament after introducing reforms is that the results of the reforms only become visible much later. In particular, the reforms aimed at creating an environment favourable to good labour-market performance were very unpopular among some of the politicians in our country. For my government, implementing these reforms was not easy, but I am sure that there was no alternative. I am certain that the major factor for success, and by 'success' I understand guaranteeing people's quality of life and human dignity, is trust – trust in institutions and also in productivity and the economy. Without that no Labour Code can solve any problem.

Anyway, it is a big challenge to keep social peace, to make reforms and to maintain power, all at the same time. Unfortunately, we had to dissolve the government and call early elections.

Sometimes it can be very unpopular to implement what you think is a good decision. Let me give you an example: when the Dzurinda government introduced some major reforms to the social security system in 2003–4, a serious and widespread Roma protest followed. It was so severe that we had to use the army to keep order. As a politician you are always caught between two stools. You need to have support, must be popular and have people's votes, but you often have to implement measures that are very unpopular. It is all about striking a balance: if, for instance, a reform is very costly, you have to compensate some of the groups that are negatively affected by the measure. Otherwise, you will lose the support of the opposition parties immediately and have no chance to implement the 'good reforms'. In the end, you may be rewarded: I remember when I prepared a reform to family benefits and the care of children in 2004, everyone was against it. Now, ten years later, it is one of the policies the government shows off to the world as a good solution – it is, in fact, perfect and working very effectively. In the beginning, however, I kept asking myself over and over again: 'Is what I am doing really okay, against everybody? Is it really okay? Wouldn't it be better to stop it?' In the end, knowledge and solid analyses helped me develop firm convictions about what was right. I was strengthened by my belief that with the reform we would really be able to help children in need. The benefits to larger families were reduced and the money was put into a newly established scheme for childcare. In addition, we cancelled benefits for families whose children were not at school. It was a fair approach to the specific problems the Roma posed. We created the so-called *osobitný príjemca*, a special institution or person who receives all the social benefits for a specific family. We stopped giving the money to the parents but covered the cost of food, clothes and other essentials directly. You can imagine the parents' reaction, but it is really working. Within a year, school attendance by Roma children increased by 40 per cent – forty!

Was it easy to reach a consensus in your government for the reform programme, given that it was made up of the SDKÚ-DS, the liberal centre-right Sloboda a Solidarita (SaS), the Christian Democratic Kresťanskodemokratické hnutie (KDH), and the inter-ethnic centre-right Most-Híd or did that pose a big problem?
It did pose a big problem – always. Just a little footnote: I had a discussion once with Angela Merkel, and I asked her: 'What is easier, a coalition with left-wing parties or with parties from the same political spectrum?' She replied that a coalition from the same spectrum was worse. This is because each political party –

and that is my interpretation, not Angela's – tries to have its own profile. The life of a political party lasts four years, from election to election. If parties want to keep the voters' support, they have to be recognisable and have their own programme with specific features; and it is more complicated to have these at the same end of the spectrum than at opposite ends. Parties on the same spectrum have to agree on some fundamentals, they must have something in common, for the cohesion; but they also need to have something which enables citizens to distinguish between them – in Slovakia it was the Christian Democrats, the Slovak Democratic Christians and the Liberals. This is why some issues spark much fiercer fights between, let us say, two centre-right parties than they would between a right-wing and a left-wing party.

I remember very well the impassioned discussions I had with my coalition partners concerning the Labour Code. There was one party who had very tough views: no minimum wage, no minimum rights for employees, thus a free reign for entrepreneurs – really extreme. On the other hand, the Christian Democrats' main proposals were that women and families should be taken care of. In the end, we reached a compromise. This was fine, because it was a good compromise resulting from intense dialogue. However, each party, that is each part of the coalition, suddenly believed that they had lost something. In politics, it is important that you feel you are a winner, at least a little bit, and not only that you lost something. That is why we agreed that each coalition party had to define their priorities, and that we would support this one priority. It was the only way to keep cohesion in the government without appearing 'authoritarian'.

Which role did the European dimension play in your reform programme?
My answer to this question is twofold. The position of the EU was not the same before and during the Euro crisis. Before the crisis, the EU confined itself to issuing recommendations to my country. We discussed these recommendations. At the time, the EU was open and flexible, so when my government, or the Fico government, initiated the Labour Code reforms, the EU's evaluations used to be positive. The reforms took place within the scope of the EU's requirements, but there was no specific EU requirement of what the Labour Code should look like – none at all. Within the existing framework of requirements, every country could choose specific issues for itself: some countries opted, for example, for a minimum wage, some opted against. It depended very much on each country's specific circumstances. Yet, in order to avoid the loss of thousands of jobs in Slovakia, in my capacity as Minister of Labour, Social Affairs and Family from 2005 to 2006, I used the power of veto at the European level from time to time. During the Euro crisis, however, when Slovakia was among the countries

with a very high sovereign deficit, we were under the control of the EU regarding the preparation of a national reform programme. If my country's sovereign debt had been higher, we would have lost some of our sovereignty over the budget. In other words, there were totally different situations before the crisis and during the crisis.

How did you explain, or 'sell', the reforms to (a) stakeholders, (b) the general public and (c) target groups? That is, how did you communicate the case for reforms?
As a first step you have to understand the atmosphere, the mood within the society you wish to reform. What are people thinking? How do they see reality? What is going wrong from their point of view? If, as a result of your enquiries, you understand what the actual problems are – and all of us know that there are problems with unemployment and with wages that are too low at present – you are able to interpret the situation and talk about the population's thoughts, feelings and living conditions openly and publicly. You are then required to take action and offer solutions to the problems identified. In this way, we started to speak out on corruption at a certain point. We declared that corruption was the major barrier to a better social fabric, to society's trust in public institutions, to a better atmosphere in society. Then we launched a programme to fight corruption. But before doing that, and I cannot emphasise this enough, we had to identify and agree on what was the major problem for society. If your perception is incongruent with what society feels, people will ask: 'Why are you taking these steps? What are you doing? With whom are you fighting?'

How would you describe your engagement with the trade unions in carrying out the reforms?
The Labour Code, for example, is something that people perceive as a politicians' game, as a sort of 'theatre'. The Slovak Labour Code is indeed an ideological and political instrument – part of the dramatic performance and under its spell, so to speak, as well as a symbol of the fight between entrepreneurs/employers and the trade unions/employees. From 2001 onwards, successive governments have made changes and carried out reversals to the Labour Code. Left-oriented governments, because of their official agreement with trade unions, usually change the Labour Code according to the requests of trade unions when they are in office. My government had no agreement with the trade unions, none at all. Our intention was never to play on either side but to increase wages and to increase the number of jobs. These were the only two criteria in our heads.

Yet, there is no doubt that the Labour Code is absolutely necessary. As human beings, we do not always behave ethically and morally, which is why we need regulations. This is terrible, but that is the way it is. Let me tell you a story, because it is so sensitive that I am not able to say it in any other way. Once, a young girl at a summer university asked me: 'What has changed over the last hundred years?' You can imagine what went through my head. World War I, World War II, an economic crisis, then a second and a third economic crisis, two totalitarian regimes, Fascism, Communism, poverty, high unemployment, concentration of the wealth in the hands of 1 per cent of the population. What are you going to say to this girl? I replied as follows: 'Nobody in history has had such freedom as we have now. Nobody in history has had such political and civic rights as we have now.' We therefore have to educate the people to be responsible: the Labour Code will then be of less and less importance, because individuals will be able to negotiate their rights. That was my answer. If there is ideological and political pressure, based on a polarised plurality system, we need regulations to protect the people and employees. In countries with a moderate type of pluralism, based on dialogue, however, regulation is fine, but the contracts are based on gentlemen's agreements – that is how it works.

If you were re-elected Prime Minister of Slovakia in the near future, which reforms would be on top of your agenda?
There are more important reforms than that to the Labour Code to improve labour-market performance. One of the very important reforms in the social sphere in Slovakia, in my opinion, was the regulation of employment services. If I were re-elected, I would continue with this reform, which I started in my time as Minister for Labour, Social Affairs and Family. When I was Prime Minister, my government tried to bring forward the reform and create a so-called 'inclusive market'. I was working as an expert for the EU Commission on the new concept of an inclusive market. It is supposed to be an alternative to the private market – for those who are long-term unemployed and have no chance of ever being involved in the regular labour market again – never ever. The idea was, therefore, to create a specific new market. We started, as a first step, with an intermediate market, and the second step would have been the inclusive market. I had already assigned a team to work on it in my government. However, we did not have the time to bring it through parliament and implement it. Anyway, this was 'my' reform to the labour market with which I would like to continue. Secondly, if I were re-elected, I would continue with the reform of the justice system: it is absolutely necessary to implement further steps in the anti-corruption programme – rigorously, radically, quickly – and to continue work on the Open Procurement Act, with all its statutory instruments, because this is the only way to give citizens control over the authorities and to ensure they can negotiate with them.

If you look back at your time in government, is there anything you would like to have done differently?
Yes, one thing: I would have approached my negotiations with the doctors in the autumn and winter of 2011 differently. Slovak doctors went on strike in the second half of 2011, because they wanted higher wages. This created a time of terrible pressure during which we had to resort to *núdzový*, i.e. staff emergency cover. The hospitals were closed, doctors stopped treating patients – it was a terrible situation. I kept it going for five months, and then I gave in to their demands. In hindsight, this was a dreadful mistake. I agreed to increase their wages, although I did not accept their maximum claims. I did it, because I did not have the strength to continue with empty hospitals, without doctors. But I should not have done it: it would have been better to reject the demands for any wage increases. In the end, the wages were increased in the midst of the crisis! If you give in to the doctors' claims, you have to give in to teachers' claims and so on. Eventually, we also increased the wages for teachers during the crisis.

10.2 A note on Slovakian labour market performance over the past decade

10.2.1 The facts
Slovakia's unemployment performance has been rather disappointing over the period 2000–13 compared with other European countries, especially with its neighbours in the Visegrad Group.[166] In September 2014, its harmonised unemployment rate was 13 per cent (seasonally adjusted), the sixth highest in the EU28 and the highest among the Visegrad Group: it was between five and six percentage points higher than the harmonised rates in Hungary and Poland, and well over twice the rate in the neighbouring Czech Republic. While Poland had the highest unemployment rate in the Visegrad Group over the period 1995–2006, since then this unenviable position has been held by Slovakia. Nonetheless, the current unemployment rate is still well below the peak of 19.5 per cent, which was recorded in 2001 (see fig. 12).

The Great Recession hit the Slovakian labour market hard, after a steep fall in unemployment from its 2001 peak to a low of 9.6 per cent in 2008. Between 2008 and 2010, the unemployment rate jumped by five percentage points. Even though the economy rebounded rather quickly, it has taken a long time for the economic

---

166 For details on the Visegrad Group, see fn. 151 in the Polish country note.

Evolution of the employment and unemployment rates in the Slovak Republic, 1970–2014

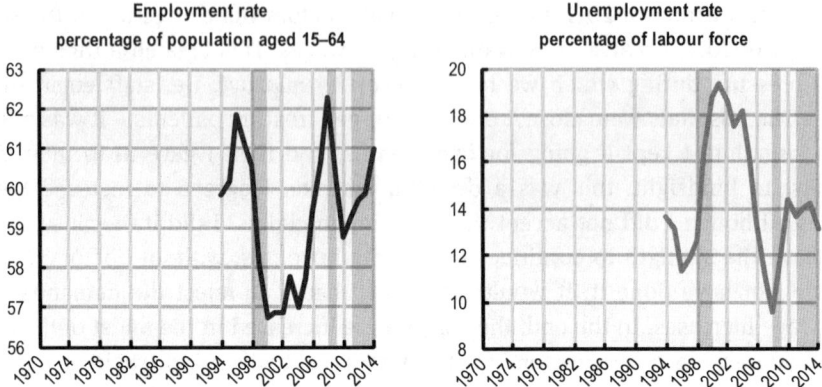

Note: Grey shaded areas refer to period of economic contraction (based on the output gap).

Source: OECD estimates based on the *OECD Labour Force Statistics, OECD Short-term Labour Market Statistics* and *OECD Economic Outlook Databases* (Cut-off date: 13 April 2015).

Figure 12: Labour market chart Slovakia

upswing to reverse the rising trend in unemployment, and progress has been slow in unwinding the large unemployment legacy of the crisis.

Its employment performance over the past decade is more positive than that of its Visegrad counterparts. Only the Czech Republic had a higher employment rate in 2013; the Slovak employment rate of 60.2 percent was equal to that in Poland and almost 1.5 percentage points higher than the Hungarian rate. In addition, the Slovak Republic recorded the second largest increase, after Poland, in the overall employment rate among the Visegrad countries between 2000 and 2013. If, however, Slovakia's employment record is compared with that of the EU28 average, there has been little convergence since 2000 (see table 14).

There are some distinctive features in the Slovakian labour market performance which need to be highlighted. First, Slovakia has consistently recorded relatively high youth unemployment: its youth unemployment rate was 28.5 per cent in September 2014, compared with an EU28 average of 21.6 per cent (both rates seasonally adjusted). Youth unemployment is significantly higher in Slovakia than in the other Visegrad countries: the next highest youth unemployment rate in September 2014 was in Poland, where it stood at 22.6 per cent.

Secondly, Slovakia has consistently recorded a very high incidence of long-term unemployment as a share of total unemployment. While Slovakia had the same incidence of long-term unemployment as the EU average in 1993, by 2000 the incidence was 10 percentage points above the EU average, and by 2007, this gap widened to almost 30 percentage points. Even in 2013, when long-term unemployment had dropped back a little in Slovakia, it still exceeded the EU average by 20 percentage points.

Thirdly, unemployment, and the incidence of long-term unemployment, is extraordinarily high among the minority Roma population who, in turn, are predominantly located in the high-unemployment regions in Slovakia.[167]

Fourthly, on the employment front, relatively low rates compared with the EU averages are recorded among youth and older workers. In 1993, the scoreboard shows that the youth employment rate was 5 percentage points below the EU average; by 2000 this gap had doubled, and it increased still further to 13 percentage points in 2013. Among older workers, the scoreboard highlights the opposite pattern for those aged 55–9: whereas their employment rate in 2000 was 16 percentage points below the EU average, by 2013 this gap virtually disappeared. For the age group 60–4, there was also significant convergence towards the EU average after 2000. Nonetheless, for this age group, the employment rate in 2013 was still 14 percentage points below the EU average. For the age group 65–9, the employment rate in Slovakia is only 3 per cent and the gap with the EU average has widened from 5 to 8 percentage points.

Fifthly, part-time work is little developed in Slovakia: it accounted for just over 4 per cent of total employment in 2013, compared with an EU average of 17.5 per cent, and the share has hardly risen since 1993.[168] The same holds for temporary work which, at 7 per cent of all employees in 2013, was only half the EU average of 14 per cent, though its share has risen since 1993.[169] The very low part-time employment rate in Slovakia is linked to the below-average share of female employment, especially among mothers with young children, reflecting, among other fac-

---

167 Jurajda and Mathernova (2004) highlight that the Roma accounted for less than 10 per cent of the Slovak population, but accounted for half of the long-term unemployed in 2003. OECD (2012f), p. 76 quotes a UNDP estimate that the Roma unemployment rate exceeded 70 per cent in 2010.
168 The very low share of part-time work is common to the other Visegrad countries. OECD (2014g) Table H shows that part-time work accounted for 4–5 per cent of employment in the Czech Republic and Hungary, and under 8 per cent in Poland in 2013.
169 The low proportion of temporary work is again shared with two of the other Visegrad countries, the Czech Republic and Hungary. The exception is Poland, which – according to OECD (2014g), Table I – had the second highest share of temporary work in 2013 among OECD countries at 26.9 per cent.

tors, difficulties associated with access to quality childcare at affordable prices and strong fiscal disincentives to work for second earners in a household.

Sixthly, self-employment has increased significantly in Slovakia since the end of the 1990s, especially after 2004: between 2004 and 2013, the share of self-employment as a proportion of total employment doubled to reach the EU average.[170]

Finally, while the onset of the Great Recession in 2007–8 hit the Slovak economy particularly hard because of its high reliance on exports and foreign direct investment, it recovered a bit faster than many of its trading partners, reflecting the close ties with Germany, a relatively rapid adjustment by its industrial sector and specific counter-cyclical policies adopted by the Slovak government. The adoption of the euro in 2009 also helped the recovery.

On the labour market front, the impact of the sharp downturn on employment was cushioned by the introduction of a short-time work scheme combined with a system of working-time individual accounts, the so-called *Flexikonto*.[171] As the scoreboard shows, there was, however, no expansion of the public spending effort on active labour market policies (ALMPs), in contrast to the situation in most other EU countries. Indeed, the high rates of youth and long-term unemployment in Slovakia are linked with the lack of a real activation strategy on the part of the public employment service (PES) (cf. OECD (2012f)). This is highlighted by the abnormally high caseworker/client workloads facing the PES staff, the relatively low public spending effort on active labour market policies (0.2 per cent of GDP in 2013, compared with an EU average of 0.8 per cent) and poor targeting of labour market policies to the most at-risk unemployed.[172]

10.2.2 Major labour market and social policy reforms since 2000

In any discussion of reforms in Slovakia since 2000, due account must be taken of the starting point. Slovakia was, and still is, in a transition from a centrally planned economy to a fully fledged market economy. During this process it joined the EU in 2004 and adopted the euro at the beginning of 2009. The transition process has demanded many structural reforms to enable the Slovak economy to adapt to

---

170 See OECD (2010c), Box 1.2 for a discussion of the growth of self-employment in Slovakia and the possible determinants of this increase.

171 The *Flexikonto* was introduced in 2009. It allows employees to work reduced hours on full basic pay, with the unworked hours recorded in individual employee working-time accounts. When product demand recovers, the workers are required to compensate for those hours by working unpaid overtime.

172 See OECD (2012f), Chapter 2, for an extensive discussion of the weaknesses of activation measures in Slovakia.

the requirements of a market economy and a democratic society, and the process is far from over. The OECD and other international organisations have highlighted the need for wide-ranging tax reform, tackling corruption and establishing the rule of law, and reforming the public sector.[173] Reforms to labour and product markets and to social policies, some of which are discussed below, are probably of second-order importance to these fundamental reforms, although they are important complements.

In this section, we highlight the fact that there was a very vigorous period of reforms to labour market and social policies – including pensions – which were undertaken between 2003 and 2005, and which affected some of the key core facts noted above. It is also the case that some of these reforms had their origins in reforms undertaken between 1998 and 2002, following the financial crisis in 1997–8 and the fall of the Mečiar government. The government in power between 1998 and 2002 was a broad coalition led by Prime Minister Mikuláš Dzurinda. Following elections in 2002, Dzurinda was again appointed Prime Minister, but he now headed a centre-right coalition government which was committed to rapid structural reforms of the Labour Code, the social benefit system and the pension system. The second Dzurinda government lost office in 2006 and, since then, there have been several changes of government, oscillating between the centre-right and the left, which have introduced additional reforms in these areas, including partial reversals of previous reforms. We now review each of these reforms in turn.

The Labour Code
Jurajda and Mathernova (2004) highlight the fact that the first Dzurinda government adopted a reform of the Labour Code in July 2001, under pressure from the left-wing parties in the coalition and the unions, which reduced labour market flexibility and increased the bargaining power of the unions. Among other changes, the 2001 reform set maximum weekly working hours at 40, set a three-year limit for fixed-term contracts, forced firms to get union approval before dismissing workers and changing workplace practices, and allowed for the automatic abolition of workers' councils in firms where trade unions operated. On the other hand, the first Dzurinda government was able to abolish some early retirement programmes in 2000, reform social assistance benefits in 2001 and modify some of the provisions of the 2001 Labour Code, before they came into force in early

---

173 See OECD (2012f), Chapter 1, which highlights the fact that the cost of tax collection in Slovakia in 2007 was the highest in the OECD.

2002.[174] Thus, the direction of structural reforms in the labour market and social policy fields under the first Dzurinda government inevitably reflected the need to trade off the different political preferences of the coalition partners, their respective bargaining powers and the main interest groups in society.

Employers were particularly unhappy with the 2001 changes to the Labour Code which, they argued, hampered the ability of the Slovak labour market to respond quickly to shifts in product demand. Indeed, the OECD's well-known indicator of the strictness of employment protection legislation (EPL) shows that Slovakia had a degree of protection for permanent workers equal to the EU average in 2000, whereas the degree of protection afforded to temporary workers was below the EU average (see scoreboard). Thus, employers seized the opportunity of the change of government in 2002 to lobby hard for a further reform of the Labour Code designed to give them greater freedom to hire and fire workers, to set working-time arrangements and to weaken the bargaining power of unions. In addition, Jurajda and Mathernova (2004) highlight the fact that public opinion on the 2001 reform had turned against the left-wing parties and the unions by adopting the view that it was too rigid and gave too much to the unions. It is probably no coincidence that this shift in public opinion came about at the moment when Slovakian unemployment peaked at over 19 per cent and public opinion polls showed that unemployment was the number one problem for Slovakian voters.

The 2003 reform to the Labour Code cut the costs of firing workers by reducing severance pay for workers with tenures of over five years, cut the statutory notice period for dismissals, effectively allowed for indefinite extensions of fixed-term contracts,[175] increased regular weekly working hours to 48, averaged over a year, and it permitted a significant hike of the maximum annual overtime hours to 400 (150 at the discretion of the employer and an additional 250, if agreed with the worker). The 2003 reform also weakened the bargaining power of unions by eliminating their veto over organisational changes at the workplace or the firing of workers; instead, they now had to be merely notified of such changes. The reform also put workers' councils and trade unions on an equal footing, except that the former were not allowed to engage in collective bargaining, whereas the latter were.

---

174 Specifically, the amendments extended the amount of overtime hours and allowed for flexible shift work.

175 As the scoreboard shows, this particular reform had a major impact on the OECD's EPL indicator for temporary workers which dropped to one of the lowest values for any OECD country, far below the EU average of 1.6 in 2007.

The Dzurinda government, however, lost the general election in 2006 and was succeeded by a left-wing government led by Robert Fico, which had been actively supported by the unions. The Fico government reversed part of the 2003 reforms to the Labour Code in 2007. In particular, it went back to the pre-2003 regulation that the maximum duration of a fixed-term contract be limited to three years, and it increased the strictness of EPL for temporary workers significantly.[176]

A further bout of reforms to the Labour Code was introduced in 2011 under the Radičová government. These reforms cut notice periods and severance pay significantly for dismissals of permanent workers and removed the obligation on employers to negotiate with the public authorities in the case of collective dismissals. The 2011 reforms, however, did not reverse the increased protection offered to temporary workers following the 2007 reform.[177] When the Radičová government was replaced by another left-wing Fico government, they promptly reversed some of the 2011 reforms to the Labour Code, notably reintroducing severance pay, although at a reduced level, and tied it more closely to job tenure.

The end result, as noted in the scoreboard, is that EPL for permanent workers in Slovakia is below the EU average now, whereas prior to the reforms it had been equal to the average. EPL for temporary workers, on the other hand, has increased significantly since the reforms – to equal the EU average. Legislation and collective agreements, however, are not the only aspects of the Labour Code which matter for hiring and firing decisions. Another important dimension, which is excluded from the OECD indicators, is the enforcement of the regulations through the courts. There is some evidence here that the legal process in Slovakia is a barrier for employers. OECD statistics, taken from a large sample of countries, show that the average time it takes for a court to reach a decision in a dismissal case is longest in Slovakia (almost three years).[178]

Thus, reforms to employment protection and working-time arrangements in Slovakia have see-sawed somewhat with the shifting political balance between left- and right-wing governments. As a consequence, the potentially beneficial effects of reforms on employment may have been offset by a lack of confidence on the part of employers that the reforms would continue under a new government.

---

176 The impact of the reform on protection for temporary workers can be seen in the OECD indicator which tripled from 0.6 to 1.8, a level at which it has remained since then and which is equal to the EU average in 2013.

177 OECD estimates of the strictness of EPL for permanent workers in Slovakia show that the impact of the 2011 reform cut the index from 2.2 in 2011 to 1.8 in 2012 which is a large change and which brought it well below the EU average. For details, see OECD (2013f), Chapter 2.

178 See OECD (2013f), Figure 2.13.

Reforms to the social welfare system

The second Dzurinda government introduced major reforms to the social safety net system in 2004, with the explicit objective of 'making work pay' by improving work incentives, especially for the low-skilled, and by activating the unemployed to find work. Prior to these reforms, the structure of social benefits and the links to family size created very significant so-called 'unemployment traps' in Slovakia.[179] At the same time, the fairly generous benefit replacement rates and levels of public social spending led to relatively low levels of income inequality (as proxied by the Gini coefficient) in Slovakia.[180]

The 2004 reform introduced a basic social assistance benefit whose level depended on the number of people in the household. It also introduced a so-called 'activation benefit': anyone in receipt of this benefit had to search for work actively or participate in ALMPs; a long-term unemployed person who found a job could retain the activation benefit for six months. The 'making work pay' principle was reinforced by introducing more gradual tapers for the withdrawal of social benefits, if the recipient found a job. This was also backed up by several related reforms designed to improve the activation of the unemployed, e.g. they were required to register more frequently with the PES; individual action plans were drawn up, especially for the long-term unemployed; a self-employment benefit was introduced; and private employment agencies were licensed for the first time.

Work incentives were also increased for the unemployed receiving unemployment insurance (UI) benefits: the maximum duration of these benefits was cut from nine to six months and the benefit replacement rate (i.e. the ratio between the benefit and earnings in the last job) was cut from 55 to 50 per cent. The significant effect of the latter changes, in terms of the decline in the net (post-tax) benefit replacement rate at the beginning of an unemployment spell and after two years in unemployment, can be seen clearly in the scoreboard comparison of the very large declines in Slovakia between 2000 and 2007. Indeed, it could be argued that the steep cuts in benefit generosity over the past decade have made it unnecessary for Slovakia to invest heavily in ALMPs. The low benefit replacement rates on their own provide strong work incentives for the unemployed to find work.

Finally, in 2009, as part of a package of measures designed to stimulate employment, the Fico government introduced an explicit in-work benefit – the so-

---

179 The unemployment trap occurs when the percentage of gross earnings, which is taken by higher income and payroll taxes, and the loss of unemployment and related social benefits, when an unemployed person finds work, is very large, i.e. of the order of 50 per cent or more. Indeed, in some cases, the loss can approach 100 per cent.

180 OECD (2011a) shows that in 2008, Slovakia had one of the lowest levels of income inequality in the EU or the OECD countries.

called 'employee bonus': this earnings top-up was paid to workers on regular contracts earning close to the minimum wage. The level of the benefit was not, however, high enough to have a significant effect on employment, especially once account was taken of the regular hikes in the minimum wage.

Pension reforms

A rapidly ageing population put severe financial pressures on public pension
spending in Slovakia and that, combined with a relatively low effective retirement
age,[181] prompted the second Dzurinda government to introduce major reforms to
the pension system in 2004 and 2005. When it began its economic transition in
1993, Slovakia had a public PAYG pension system. Given the relatively low overall
employment rate and a rapidly ageing population, this system was clearly not financially sustainable over the long term – a point highlighted by the European
Commission in its projections of public pension spending in Slovakia to the
year 2060.[182] At the same time, concerns about the relatively low employment
rates among older workers created a situation in which it was possible to envisage
further steps to curb the early retirement culture in Slovakia.

The first stage of the reforms was made in 2004 and it involved significant
changes to the parameters of the PAYG system:
-   the overall contribution rate to pension insurance was increased from 28 to
    28.75 percent, with employers paying 21.75 per cent and employees 7 per cent;
-   the upper ceiling of the base of pension contributions and entitlements was
    set at three times the average wage;
-   pension benefits were based on a points system which provided pensioners
    with 1.25 per cent of the average lifetime wage for every year of service;
-   pension payments were indexed 50 per cent to wages and 50 per cent to pri-
    ces;
-   the statutory retirement ages for men and women were both raised: to 62 from
    60 (for men) and from 53 to 57 (for women, depending on the number of chil-
    dren). These increases were phased in; the new limit was reached for men in
    2006 and for women with four or more children in 2015.

These reforms reduced significantly the redistributive element that was inherent in
the old PAYG system and shifted it substantially towards a system based on the

---

[181] OECD estimates put the average effective retirement age for men at 59.8 years in 2003 and
56.1 years for women. For details on how these OECD estimates are computed, see fn. 28 in the
Austrian country note.
[182] For details, see European Commission (2012).

insurance principle. Indeed, OECD (2010c) claimed that the reform created 'one of the tightest links of pensions to earnings among OECD countries'.[183]

These parametric changes to the public pension pillar, however, were – on their own – insufficient to achieve financial sustainability for the pension system. Thus, the Dzurinda government followed them up with a further set of reforms in early 2005, which introduced a second, defined-contribution (DC), pillar to the system. Under this reform, 18 per cent of the overall contribution rate of 28.75 per cent devoted to pensions was split equally between the two pillars. The defined-benefit (DB) entitlements were to be derived from the pension points as before, with years of payment only to the DB system regarded as generating full years of contributions, while years of contributions under the mixed system would generate only half years of contributions. While existing workers were allowed an 18-month transition period from 1 January 2005 to opt either to stay in the DB system or switch to the mixed system, participation in the latter was mandatory for all new labour force entrants after December 2004. The mixed system proved to be rather attractive: by December 2007, over 1.5 million people out of the total of 2.6 million enrolled in the pension system were participating in the mixed system.

Despite this apparent success of the mixed system, the rules governing participation in the DC pillar were modified temporarily in 2008 and 2009 under the first Fico government. These reforms allowed those who found the switch to the mixed system financially disadvantageous to revert to full coverage under the DB pillar and vice versa. Relatively few workers switched, though it was mainly people over the age of 45 who opted to return to the DB pillar; since the simultaneous increase in the minimum contribution period to 15 years meant few of them could expect to draw a DC pension, this was not an unexpected outcome. One reason for this temporary change in the rules was to provide some short-term relief to the fiscal deficit in the first pillar through increased pension contributions.

After the Radičová government left office in 2012, having lost an early election, the second Fico government introduced more far-reaching changes to the mixed pension system. The sustainability of the PAYG pillar was improved through the increase in the retirement age: it was decided to link it to life expectancy, and the indexation formula for pensions was modified. But the size of the DC pillar was reduced significantly and new labour force entrants had to opt in to participate in the DC pillar within the first six months of their first wage contract. The drop in the contribution rate to the second pillar from 9 to 4 per cent will be reversed in 2017, when it will increase by 0.25 per cent every year to reach the new target level of 6 per cent in 2024.

---

183 See OECD (2010c), Box 1.4, p. 35.

The latest European Commission projections suggest that, while these changes helped reduce the size of the financial sustainability challenge facing the Slovakian pension system, they did not resolve it. While OECD estimates of the average effective age of retirement for Slovakia show an increase since the reforms for both men and women, they still remain well below the corresponding OECD averages: between 2004 and 2011, they rose in Slovakia from 59.7 to 60.4 years for men and from 56 to 57.7 years for women.

Did these reforms have an impact on labour market performance? It is hard to conclude that the reforms to the Labour Code in 2003 and 2007 had a major impact on hiring and firing patterns. The reforms in 2011 reduced dismissal costs significantly for permanent workers, but they were partly reversed in 2012. While it is far too early to assess the impact of these latest reforms, their see-saw nature suggests that they are unlikely to have a major impact on job creation, especially for young workers. It does seem probable, however, that part of the steep rise in employment rates among workers aged 55–64 over the past decade can be attributed to the pension reforms and the reforms to the social safety net designed to make work pay.

10.2.3 Conclusion

Slovakia witnessed a major burst of labour market, social and pension policy reforms in a short window between 2003 and 2005, which coincided with the coming to power of the second Dzurinda government. This government had a popular mandate for these reforms, which coincided with a peak in the unemployment rate and concerns about the financial sustainability of the pension system. Implementation of these reforms was facilitated by an FDI-driven boom in export-oriented manufacturing which helped to spur employment growth and reduce unemployment. Some of these reforms, notably those to the Labour Code in 2003, were reversed by the subsequent left-wing Fico government. The return of a centre-right government in 2010 led by Ms Radičová, however, produced another significant reform to the Labour Code, especially in terms of lowering the dismissal costs for permanent workers, but the second Fico government reversed them partially, as it had done before, in 2007. This see-saw process of reforms to the Labour Code has undoubtedly weakened the effect of the reforms on hiring and firing, since employers had little confidence in the longevity of any particular reform. Reforms to the pension system have helped ensure the financial sustainability of the public pillar and boosted older worker employment rates, but these moves have gone hand-in-hand with steps to weaken the second pillar. Thus, it is difficult to assess now whether the recent reforms in total have significantly improved the sustainability of the pension system in Slovakia or not. Given the rapid ageing of its population, answering this question is an urgent priority.

Table 14: Scoreboard for labour market outcomes and policies, Slovak Republic and EU, 1993–2013

	1993 SK	1993 EU	2000 SK	2000 EU	2007 SK	2007 EU	2013* SK	2013* EU
1. Employment rate (% of the working-age population)	60.1	61.2	56.9	63.6	60.9	66.7	60.2	65.9
– male	67.6	71.8	62.4	72.9	68.6	74.2	66.7	71.6
– female	52.7	50.7	51.5	54.4	53.2	59.2	53.6	60.2
– youth (aged 15/16–24)	34.4	39.5	29.0	39.2	27.6	39.1	20.4	33.4
– older people (aged 55–9)	36.2	47.6	34.3	50.4	50.3	57.5	64.2	64.9
– older people (aged 60–4)	6.7	22.2	6.1	22.1	15.4	29.1	20.7	34.7
– older people (aged 65–9)	2.7	9.1	2.0	7.3	2.3	8.5	3.1	11.3
2. Unemployment rate (% of labour force)	13.7	10.8	18.8	8.9	11.0	7.1	14.2	10.7
– youth (aged 15/16–24)	27.3	21.0	37.0	17.4	20.1	15.5	33.6	23.3
3. Incidence of long-term unemployment (% of total unemployment) (a)	42.6	42.0	54.6	44.4	70.8	41.6	66.6	46.5
4. Part-time employment rate (b)	2.7	13.8	1.9	15.3	2.4	16.0	4.3	17.5
5. Temporary employment rate (c) (temporary employees as % of total employees)	2.9	10.5	4.8	13.1	5.1	14.8	7.0	14.0
– youth (aged 15/16–24 as % of total youth employees)	4.4	28.8	10.5	38.0	13.7	41.8	21.3	43.0
6. Low-pay incidence (d) (% of employees)	–	–	17.0	15.7	18.0	16.5	19.0	15.0
7. Protection of permanent workers against individual dismissal	2.5	2.6	2.5	2.5	2.2	2.4	1.8	2.2
– Protection of temporary workers	1.4	2.3	1.4	1.8	0.6	1.6	1.8	1.8
8. Public spending on labour market policies (% of GDP)	–	2.9	1.2	2.0	0.6	1.6	0.6	2.0
– Spending on active measures (e)	–	0.9	0.3	0.8	0.2	0.6	0.2	0.8
– Spending on passive measures (f)	–	2.1	0.8	1.1	0.4	0.9	0.4	1.2
9. Net benefit replacement rate (g) (averaged over four family types and two earnings levels)	–	–	92	57	35	52	37	51
– initial spell (h)	–	–	80	70	63	71	66	70
– after 2 years of unemployment	–	–	92	66	35	63	35	57

* 2013 or latest available year.
(a) Persons out of work for 12 months and over.

(b) Part-time employment refers to persons who usually work less than 30 hours per week in "their 'main job'".

(c) Temporary employees are wage and salary workers whose job has a pre-determined end date as opposed to permanent employees whose job is of unlimited duration. National definitions broadly conform to this generic definition, but may vary depending on national circumstances.

(d) Persons with a wage less than 2/3 of the median.

(e) 'Active' measures cover categories 1 to 7 of the OECD/Eurostat data base on public spending on labour market programmes.

(f) 'Passive' measures cover categories 8 and 9 of the OECD/Eurostat data base on public spending on labour market programmes.

(g) Data on net replacement rates for 2000 refer to 2001.

(h) Initial phase of unemployment but following any waiting period. For married couples, the percentage of AW relates to the previous earnings of the 'unemployed' spouse only; the second spouse is assumed to be 'inactive' with no earnings and no recent employment history. Where receipt of social assistance or other minimum-income benefits is subject to activity tests (such as active job-search or being 'available' for work), these requirements are assumed to be met. Children are aged four and six and neither childcare benefits nor childcare costs are considered. Unweighted averages, for previous full-time earnings levels of 67% and 100% of AW and out-of-work single and couple households with no children or with two children (children are assumed to be aged four and six and neither childcare benefits not childcare costs are considered). After tax and including unemployment and family benefits. Social assistance and other means-tested benefits are assumed to be available subject to relevant income conditions. Housing costs are assumed equal to 20% of AW.

Sources: OECD Online Employment Database: www.oecd.org/employment/database; data on net replacement rates come from the OECD tax-benefit models (www.oecd.org/els/social/work-incentives).

11 Spain

11.1 Interview with José Luis Rodríguez Zapatero, 17 September 2013

'In Spain there is no agreement when it comes to diagnosing why we have so much unemployment in periods of crisis and why we create so much employment in periods of prosperity.'

Looking back at the time when you were Prime Minister, what were the major challenges your government had to face with regard to the Spanish labour market?
While in government, I experienced some unique cycles: first, a period with very strong employment growth. That lasted until 2008 and was followed by a period which saw a steep drop in employment. In the first period, my government achieved the lowest rate of unemployment ever in the history of Spain – 8 per cent. I still remember the day we celebrated: 8 per cent unemployment in Spain felt like full employment. It was full employment. Then, from 2008 to 2011, the unemployment figure went up from 8 to 22 per cent. Hence, we saw two incredible developments within three years.

When I took office in 2004, the problem was not how to create more jobs, but that the jobs created were rather precarious, more specifically, that there was an excessive share of temporary jobs. At the time, this form of employment accounted for 32 per cent of all jobs. As a result, we implemented a number of labour market reforms to promote and incentivise permanent hiring, and we were able to reduce temporary employment to 25 per cent. One incentive consisted in tax reduction for business leaders, when they hired young people on a permanent basis. Along with that, we also implemented reforms that restricted employers resorting to temporary hiring. You have to remember that Spain, because of its industrial structure and the two very powerful sectors of tourism and construction, generally has a higher rate of temporary employment than other countries – that is inevitable and it is intrinsic to our economic system.

When the economic crisis hit in 2008–9, the labour market's reaction was one of an overall adjustment in employment, not in wages. Let me give you an interesting figure in this respect: in 2008 and 2009, Germany and Spain lost a similar number of working hours relative to their economies, yet in Spain unemployment was double that in Germany. Economic scholarship has placed the emphasis on labour institutions in Spain as the main cause for this difference. Essentially, two features of the Spanish labour market are considered responsible for this: first, a very rigid collective bargaining system; secondly, strict employment protection legislation. During the crisis, my government implemented reforms to change both of these, i.e. to make collective bargaining more flexible and to reduce severance pay.

I believe, however, that there is a more important problem. The Spanish economy has enormous capacity for wrecking employment during crises, regardless of the labour institutions or the type and extent of regulation. The companies that decided to make salary adjustments during the crisis, through an agreement with workers, did so regardless of labour market regulation. In other words, labour market regulation is not, or was not, an obstacle. The point we are talking about now is crucial: where were most adjustments made in order for wages to be proportionate to productivity? The answer is that it was in large companies, for example carmakers. Spanish automobile factories are more productive than the European average and have always negotiated in a way that linked productivity with wages. Spanish companies with more than 250 workers are more productive than the European average, which raises the question of what the problem is with our industrial structure. It is that we have a very high number of small and medium-sized companies. For historic reasons, we do not have enough capital to have a corporate base of medium-sized and large companies, and there has been a lot of atomisation of companies, with the result that, as soon as a crisis arrives, the slightest breeze carries them away. Therefore, the major problem is not connected to labour market institutions, it is about companies disappearing.

A good example is the construction industry. In Spain, 70 per cent of the employment lost – 70 per cent – had depended directly or indirectly on housing construction. The Spanish economy is excessively dependent on the construction sector. Imagine that in Spain the ratio of new houses built runs parallel to the number of jobs created. That is the point. All three economic crises since democracy began in Spain were preceded by expansion, a real estate boom: there had always been a lot of employment in that area, and when the crisis hit, it dropped. The problem is, as I said, that the construction companies simply disappear: small construction companies, real estate companies – they disappear in a couple of months! It is not a question of flexibility, the fact is that there is nothing left 'to make flexible'. They disappear. The problem is therefore that Spain, because of its geographic, demographic and climatic conditions, has a construction sector that, as soon as the economy looks up, starts growing – with a boom! This is because almost everybody wants to have a place in Spain. Many Europeans buy apartments here – some 150,000 per year. The trouble is that Spanish families know that investment in housing has, until now, been more profitable than bonds and equities. It is not going to be that way anymore, and this is a brutal change. The problem of unemployment in Spain cannot be understood without an analysis of the phenomenon of construction over the last 30 years.

Finally, I believe that the Spanish corporate culture, with its high share of temporary work, poses another problem. Employers are aware that there will be a lot of mobility among their workers and will thus not pursue policies to retain them, for example through training. The workers, who are aware that they will probably be with their company only for a short time, also do not feel tied to it. That is clear and a big challenge for us. Economists are recommending the introduction of single, open-ended contracts, but no government has dared to do this, because there is no certainty that it will bring the desired results. For example, Spain has – and this was one of the basic issues during the crisis – a low rate of part-time hiring. If the European average is 20 per cent, Spain is at roughly 10 per cent. Governments have been trying to carry out reforms to facilitate part-time employment, but have met with strong union resistance. Why? The unions argue that there are many companies that use part-time hiring to camouflage what should be permanent, full-time work.

Let me add one more challenge. Before the crisis hit, we were creating employment at a rate of 400,000 to 500,000 jobs per year. In fact, in the 2008 election campaign, both my party, the Partido Socialista Obrero Español (PSOE), and the conservative Partido Popular (PP) were campaigning on the promise of full employment. We were almost at full employment, but our problem was finding a way to stop all the immigrants who were coming to Spain to work. They came to work and they found work. In one decade, Spain took in four million immigrant workers. Our active population has increased like no other country's. The number of individuals employed has not decreased. Everyone wanted to come to Spain, and we were Europe's port and Europe's defence barrier that prevented immigrants moving from Spain to France or Germany. We took in people from North Africa and Latin America – there were many immigrants, a very small percentage of whom have left. They are here, taking care of themselves, and by the way, they are the ones who adapt best to crises.

After 2008, were there also external pressures that played a role in your plans to reform the labour market?
Generally, I have to say that the most active and most concerted push my government got to reform the Spanish labour market during the crisis came from the Central European Bank. More specifically, when the markets put pressure on our treasury to solve the country's sovereign debt problems, I made a great effort to have meetings with all big private investment funds in the world – at one meeting the funds represented were worth almost twice Spain's GDP.

What were the main concerns about Spain? Two questions arose most frequently. First, rather than talking about labour relations or labour institutions, the private investment funds asked about the unions in Spain, whether they were radical or willing to enter into alliances. They asked me that directly, though confidentially. The markets, i.e. the investors, were very worried about the Spanish unions, and it was my job to encourage the funds to invest and keep their Spanish debt holdings. The second question they asked me related to the sustainability of the Spanish pension system, which is naturally very closely related to the labour market, because all European countries, but especially Spain, have a high life expectancy. Spain has a life expectancy of 83 years, which is, by the way, the highest in Europe.

Institutions such as the IMF, the EU Commission and the OECD have always pushed for, indeed called for – to use the word 'pressured' might be a bit excessive, because international organisations are always respectful towards governments – labour market reforms; namely, as we have already discussed, for reforms of the collective bargaining system and of employment protection legislation. I remember, for example, a long conversation with Olivier Blanchard, Chief Economist at the IMF and one of the greatest authorities in the field I have ever known, in which we discussed the topic of the labour market reforms that would be necessary in Spain. As I said to Mr Blanchard, I believe that some key features of our labour institutions have not helped to soften the drop in employment in a crisis situation, but the economic aspects of our industrial structure and the role that construction has played are, in my opinion, more relevant. We must bear in mind that Spain is a country that has for a long time borne the brunt of the remnants of an economic model which originated in autarchy, with its many captive markets. Opening up the Spanish market to competition has proved to be a big endeavour.

At present, there is much debate in Spain about 'mini jobs'. In contrast, for example to Germany, where this model works very well, mini jobs are viewed negatively in Spain. In my opinion, the concept of flexicurity, which has been developed in the Nordic countries, especially in Denmark, and which works very well there, is the path that Spain with its particularities should actually follow. But, of course, in Spain we still do not have the levels of social security that exist in the countries where flexicurity has taken hold. The fact that Spain is only on the bottom rungs of the welfare security ladder explains a little the societal difficulty in adopting the flexicurity model in our country. I believe that this is the underlying problem. The crisis has hit Spain at a moment of great labour market performance. Now, after the crisis, which has been detrimental for Spain, a great number of issues are being reconsidered. In order to increase flexibility, not in the labour institutions – I believe there is enough flexibility there – but in the labour market and in the corporate culture, which form the basis of this country, we need to strengthen the other side of the coin, by establishing better security in terms of welfare benefits. If we do not manage to create the right balance, we will see the informal employment increase in the future.

Were there other countries, apart from Denmark, where you looked for good practice for your reforms?
Yes, indeed: we primarily drew our inspiration from three countries, namely Denmark, Germany and Austria. When I was in office, we employed specialists in the labour ministry who were tasked, as government advisers, to look beyond our country's border. Germany was our role model because of its dual system; Denmark, as I said, for the concept of flexicurity; Austria for the individual saving accounts which had taken the place of severance pay – which is, by the way, pretty original. The advantage of the Austrian approach is that it was acceptable to the unions: it had a better reception than any of the mini-job experiments one could think of, at least with the Spanish unions. We also pondered the Austrian model. The problem is that, in general, the particularities of such very strong countries, which should be looked at as individual, separate cases, because of their unique history, industrial structure and culture, make it extremely difficult to transfer specific models.

At the moment, European countries have very contradictory feelings. In the South, Europe's periphery looks to Central and Eastern Europe with distrust rather than admiration. Southern countries think that Central European countries are too hard on them, while Central European countries believe that they do things very well. Oddly, even though Central European countries look at us with some scepticism, most of their population would like to live in the South. I therefore think that we should reinforce the social ties throughout the political European community: it would be good to establish some type of social and political 'Erasmus exchange programme' for politicians, business people and similar groups, enabling them to learn from each other's experiences and best practice in policy making. I participated in an ambitious US State Department programme which could serve as a model. Young political leaders from around the world are invited for one or two months, so that they can learn how the political and business systems work in the US – I think European countries should have such an exchange programme, too, to help everyone familiarise themselves with arrangements in other countries. We should put that in motion.

To what extent do you see the role of the trade unions and the culture around the trade unions in Spain as a strength or a weakness of the Spanish labour market?

On a scale from one to ten, from conservative to very open, I would rate the Spanish unions somewhere in the middle. We must not forget that the unions in Spain have signed many corporate dialogue agreements, that they are very pro-European and have excellent relationships with their fellow EU unions, especially with German unions. For them, Germany, and in particular the German metal workers' union, is an important reference point. The German dual-apprenticeship model is without a doubt great, but one has to take into account that the German training institutions have existed for decades. In Spain, people historically looked down on vocational training and criticised it; it held no prestige. In fact, our educational pyramid is very distinct: the percentage of university graduates is clearly above the European average in Spain, but as a consequence the proportion of vocational training degrees is below the European average.

To what extent did you seek to reach a consensus with the trade unions in pursuing your reforms?
There is no doubt that social reforms based on agreements with the unions are much more effective, plus, in the long run, more sustainable. For example, in my time in office, in 2011, I implemented a pension reform that, with the consent of the unions, increased the retirement age to 67 years. This had a lot of support and, as a result, today no one argues anymore that the retirement age needs to be raised and that the pension system will not be sustainable. The present government wants to carry the reform further and is currently seeking the cooperation of the unions. Every country does some things well and some things not so well. In Spain, we have always known how to implement timely pension reforms. We also carried out one big reform in 1986. To this day, our pension system works well. Successive Spanish governments, however, have not excelled in reforming the labour market.

In answer to your question: labour market reforms based on social agreements are doubtless much more powerful, more useful and more effective. Labour market reforms made without such agreements can work – more or less well. It is clear, however, that if a reform meets open, determined, firm and unified opposition from the unions, the government's actions lose their legitimacy. Resistance by the unions substantially reduces the political power of reform processes, at least in Spain. The unions may not be important actors at the opinion-making stage, but they are important actors when it comes to invalidating reforms they do not like – that is the reality.

Could you count on a general consensus within the government and the coalition to put through your reform agenda?

As for my government, I would essentially say yes. Of course, in parliament it was different: because of the lack of a majority I was dependent on a number of deputies from other parties to support my party's bills. Let us say that, when I was Prime Minister, there was always the possibility of reaching a majority in parliament in favour of reforms. Problems generally occur when there is a crisis, as the opposition is not very keen to support the government which has to deal with it, because they do not want to engage in such a painful and nasty task. As for my situation, I never experienced any major opposition or restraint from parliament as a whole nor internally, from my own party, over my attempts to carry out reforms. My experience has always been that when a head of government wants to do something, he does it: he has enough authority and power to do so.

What did you do to convince the general public of the need for reforms before the two elections your party won in 2004 and 2008?

It is key that there is first a very intense public debate on a central topic such as reforming the labour market and the labour market institutions. The problem is that in Spain there is no agreement when it comes to diagnosing why we have so much unemployment in periods of crisis and why we create so much employment in periods of prosperity. There is no internal consensus on these questions. Some people point to our industrial structure, others refer to the size of Spanish businesses, yet others to labour market regulation. That is why, in my view, we would need a debate, a round-table discussion, which could perhaps be led by a foundation, for example, a European institution. Political parties, business people, unions and specialists might take a month to discuss the background and a variety of explanations. Of course, once a crisis has occurred it is too late: political urgency prevents policymakers from entering into a phase of sound and calm reflection. I believe that expectations are now a little more realistic, so this could be the right moment to consider these issues, but this can, naturally, not be done in a day: if you look at our reforms of the pension system, you will see that we debated this over and over again before we took action.

Could you please tell us about your communications strategy to sell the reforms?

When it comes to communication, what I would call 'bargaining agents' become essential. As a government you can strain to explain what is good about a reform to those affected – the workers, but it is the unions who shape opinions eventually. For you as a government it is crucial to seek alliances with the unions to be able to explain and sell a reform well. This is decisive, really decisive. The problem in terms of communication is that in times of crisis the word 'reform' always sounds bad. Reforms are supposed to take things away from people, such as benefits, rights, regular salary rises. In times of severe crisis, the meaning of reform is equivalent to 'making cuts'. I believe, however, that the successful implementation of reforms is in essence dependent on the content of the reform: if a reform is solid and credible, it is easier for a government to communicate its effects. When governments claim that their communication strategies do not work, it normally means that they do not have anything to communicate or that what they do wish to communicate does not work.

How did you interact with the biggest opponents of your reform agenda?
Such an interaction needs to be very close and very discreet. An important part of what needs to be done to put reforms through can only be done out of the media spotlight and away from microphones and cameras. The 2011 pension reform took about 15 private sessions of around three or four hours of negotiations each time, and it needed a lot of personal trust; moreover, the government has to be very transparent relating to the information on the policies under discussion. Whenever I conduct political negotiations, the method is the same: trust, transparency and discretion. This is the method that has worked for us – it worked for me with the unions in many political matters.

At the end of January 2011 your government managed to reach an important compromise after long negotiations with the unions on reforming the Spanish pension system. Many commentators regarded this as a vital domestic success for your government. Why did this success story not continue throughout 2011?
It should be borne in mind that the 2008–9 crisis did not provoke a drop in Spanish GDP greater than the European average. We actually remained above the European average, though a higher unemployment rate was indeed triggered, which is something that has happened in all crises in Spain. We did not have to inject money into the financial system. In 2009, we almost completely preserved the AAA rating of two big rating agencies. In the spring of 2010, the Spanish economy started to recover. Spain had a risk premium of 70 and 80 base points. There was no reason for me to worry – the question was rather: 'When will the crisis finally be over?'

At that point, however, the crisis in Greece occurred, and this changed everything. Why? Because the international financial markets started to examine Spain very closely. We had to change our approach. We intensified our reform policies. From May 2010 onwards, I took some unpopular steps, I reduced, for instance, the wages of government officials by 5 per cent, which had never been done before in Spain, and I froze pensions. I took some measures that are quite unlikely to increase the popularity of a head of government. We acted on so many fronts: labour market reform, pension reform, reform of the financial system, fiscal consolidation, adoption of the EU services directive to increase competition, other supply-side policies and many more. As a result, things went well for us and we had the support of the European Central Bank.

But in July and August 2011, another disaster set in. The second bailout of Greece took place and, like the first, it was born late, with difficulty and with defects. In July 2011, when private sector participation in the aid package to Greece had been approved after the summit meeting in Dublin, our risk premium exploded. So after three or four quarters of growth in Spain – four quarters and a stabilised employment situation – everything crashed again: boom! An example of the famous double-dip recession which economists explain so brilliantly.

Given this mutual dependency or interconnectedness between European countries, do you think that every country should carry out the necessary reforms itself or should there be a coordinated effort? Which would be the shortest route to success?

Personally, I think that as far as labour market reforms are concerned, Europe is the solution. Please allow me to make a very brief declaration of principles. First, the euro is an irreversible project, I have no doubt about that. It is more a political than an economic project and is therefore irreversible. Secondly, the euro was born with serious design flaws. The common currency treated different countries in a similar way. And that triggered serious asymmetries. Thirdly, the euro and the eurozone countries have to fulfil two conditions, namely responsibility and solidarity – responsibility taken on by each of the countries and solidarity among the group. As progress is made in terms of increased economic unity and increased fiscal unity, progress will also be made in terms of successful reforms. There will be Eurobonds, in about ten years. Then countries in need of reform will implement reforms, and they will do so with more conviction, and in a more solid way. I am not saying simultaneously. That is why I deliberately said, 'in ten years' there will be Eurobonds.

Of course, people often ask: 'Would you, as head of government, have been willing to give more power to Brussels?' I think most heads of government would be willing to do so. The eurozone is undoubtedly under Germany's leadership. This is a fact, okay; we accept that, but if that leadership wants to build a zone, an irreversible, competitive economic union – the way we tried to do it with the Lisbon Treaty – it is not a question of asking how much aid or loans we are going to give. The decisive question is what kind of economic union we want, what its ultimate design will be. Some steps towards the final design have been taken because of the crisis, there have been a lot of reforms, but everything still has a provisional look about it.

What do you think needs to be done to make the European labour markets fit for the 21st century?
One of the basic problems is that individual countries carry out labour legislation; this does not, and will not, come from the European community. I think, however, that we should start to discuss a European minimum wage. Moreover, we should consider having a European retirement age. These structural factors affect the competitiveness of an economy, and in the long run Europe's economies will only be competitive as one, unified economy. This means, of course, that we will have to overcome some very big national obstacles.

In addition, there is one thing that is very evident: we need European societies, European citizens, i.e. we need more elements than a common currency to identify with – elements that determine an individual's trajectory of life, such as certain civic and legal rights, same retirement conditions and similar matters. This is, I think, a big challenge; it is the project Germany has to take on. When the money is placed in your hands, it is cold, and it is just cash. A common currency is a great achievement, let us not belittle this: a common currency is very important, but it is not enough to create a European identity.

If these are your recommendations for a future European labour market, may we ask if there is anything you would like to have done differently in hindsight?
Making a retrospective judgement is a very difficult task, but there is one thing that is clear to me: when the crisis started in 2008, we had a public surplus and the debt had been reduced to 36 per cent of the GDP. We therefore had a broad margin for implementing fiscal stimuli. Yet, if I had to start over today, or if I could, I think I would run smaller public deficits. I think it was a mistake to reach a double-figure deficit in 2009 of 11 per cent, 11.2 per cent and so on. I would definitely not do it again, also because now my experience tells me that not even supply-side reforms guarantee more growth, nor do Keynesian policies guarantee that you will alleviate a recession. It depends on the circumstances and on each case.

Do you think that reform governments can win re-elections?
Not if there is a major crisis and not if it is a big economic crisis. No one has won an election in such circumstances. I think that a crisis of the type Spain and other European countries had to face in recent years, bringing with it such extensive reform attempts, will cause two or three governments to step down. Citizens vote for changing governments to see if conditions will change, too.

11.2 A note on Spanish labour market performance over the past decade

11.2.1 The facts

During the past decade, Spain's situation changed dramatically from being one of the strongest labour market performers in the EU and the OECD to becoming one of the worst. The Great Recession in 2008 and the subsequent banking and sovereign debt crisis marked the major turning point for the Spanish economy and labour market.

From the mid-1990s until the onset of the crisis in 2008, Spain enjoyed relatively rapid employment growth which was associated with large increases in female employment and great numbers of incoming foreign workers.[184] Following Spain's adoption of the euro in 1999 and the very steep drop in real interest rates, employment growth was fuelled by a major property bubble. Between 2000 and 2008, Spain converged quickly with the EU average on the employment-rate front. In 2000, the gap between the overall employment rate in Spain and the corresponding EU average was almost 6 percentage points; by 2007, the gap was eliminated and the Spanish rate slightly higher, even, than the EU average (see table 15). By 2013, however, the large and continuing drop in employment had widened the gap again to almost 10 percentage points. On the other hand, it should be noted that the long double-dip recession came to an end in Spain in the second half of 2013, as exports served to boost domestic demand, followed by a gradual pick-up in consumption. Since then, GDP growth has been positive and this has spilled over into the labour market. OECD (2014a) notes that employment grew strongly in 2014 for the first time in six years, and this led to a drop in unemployment.

In the mid-1990s, the Spanish harmonised unemployment rate had peaked at around 24 per cent, before it began a steady decline for over a decade which brought it to a level of 8.3 per cent in 2007 (see fig. 13).[185] The severity of the double-dip recession, however, led to a massive hike in unemployment, which saw the rate exceed its previous peak in 2013, when it reached 26.1 per cent, the second-highest rate in the EU, after Greece. Since then, there has

---

184 Over the decade which preceded the Great Recession, net inward migration to Spain exceeded 500,000 people per year, accounting for about 90 per cent of the total population increase over the period. After the crisis, net inward migration turned negative.

185 It is worth noting that in that year, for the first time since comparable labour force survey data became available for both countries, the Spanish unemployment rate dropped slightly below the French rate.

been a slow decline in unemployment, with the recovery gathering steam. At the time of writing, the seasonally adjusted unemployment rate in Spain in September 2014 was 24 per cent, still the second-highest rate in the EU.

**Evolution of the employment and unemployment rates in Spain,
1970–2014**

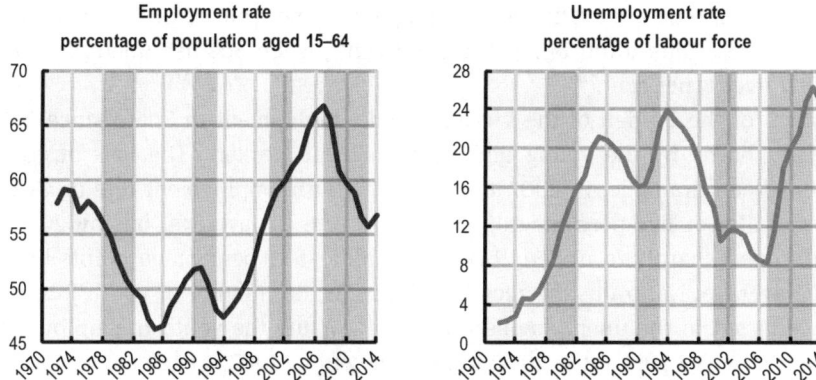

Note: Grey shaded areas refer to period of economic contraction (based on the output gap).

Source: OECD estimates based on the *OECD Labour Force Statistics, OECD Short-term Labour Market Statistics* and *OECD Economic Outlook Databases* (Cut-off date: 13 April 2015).

Figure 13: Labour market chart Spain

The huge hike in unemployment after 2007 has had an inevitable impact on long-term unemployment. While the incidence of long-term unemployment more than halved between 2000 and 2007, bringing it to 20.4 per cent, over 20 percentage points below the EU average, it exploded to almost 50 per cent in 2013, exceeding the EU average. Long-term unemployment on this scale involves serious hardship for the individuals concerned and their families; it also has a serious negative impact on productivity through loss of skills and of motivation.

The steep jump in unemployment has contributed to a large rise in inequality in Spain between 2007 and 2012. Indeed, OECD (2014f) highlights the fact that income inequality in Spain, as proxied by the well-known Gini coefficient, rose to the highest level in the EU over this period. This leap in inequality occurred despite the fact that the tax/transfer system in Spain is relatively effective in terms of redistribution.

The scoreboard shows a mixed picture in relation to help available for Spain's unemployed, subsidising their income and assisting them with finding new jobs. With regard to the net benefit replacement rate, the Spanish system is more generous than the EU average for the initial spell and after a two-year period of unemployment. It is also noteworthy that the Spanish replacement rates dropped very little in the period after 2008. As for public spending on active labour market policies (ALMPs), Spain has consistently spent in line with the EU average on such policies. The large hike in unemployment post-2008 has not, however, coincided with a ramp-up of spending on ALMPs: in 2012 (the latest year for which data are available), Spain spent 0.6 per cent of GDP on such policies, even less than it did in 2007 (0.8 per cent), when Spanish unemployment was just over 8 per cent.[186]

Much of the burden of the big hike in unemployment in Spain since 2007 has been borne by the young and by immigrant workers. The loss of youth jobs has been dramatic: in 2007, the Spanish youth employment rate of 43 per cent was almost five percentage points above the EU average, but by 2013, it had dropped sharply to under 19 per cent, almost 15 percentage points below the EU average. Naturally, the recent collapse in the number of youth jobs has been reflected in the unemployment numbers. While the youth unemployment rate fell from 25.3 per cent in 2000 to 18.1 per cent in 2007, it tripled over the following six years to reach 55.5 per cent in 2013. It is also remarkable, and a worrying indicator, that the recent improvement in the Spanish labour market has had almost no impact to date in lowering the extraordinarily high Spanish youth unemployment: the seasonally adjusted rate in September 2014 was 53.7 per cent, the highest rate in the EU.[187]

A distinctive characteristic of the Spanish labour market, which is closely linked to the high youth unemployment rate, is its marked duality. This is best reflected by the very large proportion of temporary jobs in the economy. The

---

186 Activating unemployed benefit recipients in Spain is made more difficult, because the responsibility for delivering re-employment services and ALMPs rests with the public employment service (PES), which is controlled by the regions, while the unemployment benefit system is the central government's responsibility. One negative side effect of this division of responsibilities is that it has proved very hard to monitor job-search activity by the unemployed in Spain and there is great reluctance to use the threat of benefit sanctions to ensure that the unemployed are actively seeking work or taking steps to improve their employability. In addition, OECD (2014f), Table 5 highlights the fact that the average client caseload per PES staff member is relatively high in Spain, when compared with the norm in many other EU countries.

187 It should be noted, however, that this figure does not mean that over one in every two Spanish youth is unemployed, since a large proportion of young people are staying on in education and training. Nonetheless, Spain has one of the highest shares in the EU28 of youth aged 16–24 who are neither in employment nor in education and training – the so-called 'NEETs'. In 2011, 20 per cent of Spanish youth were in the NEET group.

high share of temporary workers is connected, among other factors, with the relatively strict employment protection legislation (EPL) for permanent contracts. In 2000, almost one in every three jobs was a temporary job – almost 69 per cent of these jobs were held by youth (see the scoreboard). Despite reforms in the mid-1990s and in 2006, which aimed to reduce this duality, the proportion of temporary workers was still almost 32 per cent in 2007, compared with an EU average of 15.4 per cent. The period since then, however, has witnessed a significant drop in the share of temporary jobs: in 2013, they accounted for only 23.1 per cent of total wage and salaried employment, the lowest share recorded over the past two decades.[188] Even with this sharp drop in the share of temporary jobs, it is important to note that they continue to be a vital source of jobs for youth: in 2013, almost two-thirds of such jobs were held by young people. While the drop in the share of temporary workers owes much to the prolonged recession, it also reflects recent changes to EPL, as will be shown.

While Spain continues to be a country with a heavy reliance on temporary jobs, this is not the case for part-time jobs, a trait which sets Spain apart from many other EU countries. Even though the period since 2000 has witnessed a rise in the share of part-time jobs, a trend which was not interrupted by the crisis, the share of 14.7 per cent of employment in 2013 was below the EU average of 17.5 per cent. The trend rise in part-time working is associated with the strong rise in female employment in Spain since 2000, and the fact that female employment declined much less than male employment over the period 2008–13 accounts for the rising share of part-time jobs, despite the steep drop in the overall employment rate.[189]

Another distinguishing feature of the Spanish labour market is the high degree of nominal wage rigidity with respect to the business cycle. For example, OECD (2012g) highlights the fact that collectively bargained wages rose strongly during the period from 2007 to 2011, when unemployment was rising rapidly to over 20 per cent. It is only more recently that nominal wage behaviour has moderated significantly and Spanish unit labour costs have begun to decline significantly in comparison to its major trading partners. This improvement in cost-competitiveness has been a key factor behind the improvement in export performance which, in turn, has helped drive the recovery. As a result, the cur-

---

188 See OECD (2014g), Chapter 4.

189 The fact that female employment held up much better than male employment post-2008 reflects the bursting of the property bubble and the subsequent huge drop in employment in the construction sector. The latter employed predominantly males, typically either low-skilled natives or immigrants.

rent-account balance shifted massively from a deficit of 10 per cent of GDP in 2007 to a surplus of almost 1 per cent in 2013.

Most of the large falls in employment in the first few years after the onset of the Great Recession were concentrated among temporary workers, and it is only more recently that permanent workers in Spain have begun to experience major layoffs. The high degree of nominal wage inertia in Spain is related both to the collective bargaining structure and to the high proportion of temporary jobs; temporary workers have relatively weak bargaining power compared to the so-called 'insiders' in the Spanish workforce, the workers with permanent contracts.[190]

In sum, Spanish labour market performance has undergone a 'boom-and-bust' cycle over the period since the mid-1990s, with the Great Recession and the subsequent sovereign debt crisis marking a watershed. Youth, temporary workers and immigrants have borne the brunt of the hike in unemployment since 2007. Specific features of the Spanish economy, such as its strong duality, the high cyclical elasticity of employment and unemployment, and the high degree of nominal wage inertia have all been linked to key determinants, such as the strict EPL for permanent workers and the structure of collective bargaining.[191] As we shall see in the next section, much of the reform efforts in the Spanish labour market since the mid-1990s has concentrated on tackling these specific features.

11.2.2 Major labour market and collective bargaining policy reforms since 2000

Very strict EPL for permanent workers compared to the EU average in the early 1990s (see the scoreboard), which is reflected in high severance pay, led to a relatively rigid dual labour market in Spain. This, in turn, had negative effects on hiring, employment and productivity and generated efforts to reduce the strictness of EPL, starting in the mid-1990s and continuing to the present day. Some of these reforms were part of a package that sought to deal with collective bargaining issues, as well. The latter will be dealt with separately, though it is

---

190 See OECD (2014a), Figure 7 and OECD (2014g): they highlight the fact that, unlike the typical short-run reaction in most countries to a decline in labour demand, which leads first to a drop in average hours worked before significant layoffs occur, average hours worked increased in Spain during the double-dip recession, as the vast bulk of layoffs was concentrated on temporary workers.

191 See Costain, Jimeno and Thomas (2010).

important to note that some of the EPL reforms reflected implicit or explicit trade-offs with reforms to the collective bargaining system.

EPL reforms

The growth of temporary jobs surged after a reform in 1984, which allowed firms to use temporary contracts for jobs which were not temporary in nature. The same reform allowed for very low severance pay when temporary workers were dismissed. The rapid surge in temporary jobs in the following decade then generated pressures to curb them. As a result, reforms were introduced in both 1994 and 1997, with the twin aims of restricting the recourse to temporary contracts and reducing mandatory dismissal costs for permanent workers. These reforms were introduced by minority governments: the 1994 reform by the Socialists led by Felipe González, and the 1997 reform by the centre-right People's Party led by José-María Aznar. The reforms were motivated by the high unemployment rate in the mid-1990s and the perceived need to make the Spanish labour market more flexible as part of the convergence process for European Monetary Union (EMU). It is worth noting that the 1994 reform was introduced despite objections by the social partners, especially the unions. The 1997 reform, on the other hand, was negotiated by the social partners, with the government acting as a facilitator.[192]

Prior to the reforms, severance pay for permanent workers who were dismissed for reasons which the courts determined to be 'unjustified' was extremely generous: up to 45 days' wages per year of service, up to a maximum of 42 months. Severance pay was much lower in the case of dismissals which were held by the courts to be 'justified', but the courts almost always ruled in favour of the worker, often after long and costly legal procedures. For these reasons, firms usually opted to pay the 45 days' wages upfront (the so-called *despido exprés*), rather than fighting the case through the courts.

Under the 1994 reform, dismissal procedures for both individual and collective cases were to be made simpler and more coherent for employers, but severance pay for permanent workers was not cut. The 1997 reform went further by creating a new contract for permanent workers – the so-called 'star contract' (PEP contract) – targeted at those groups of workers most at risk of unemployment. This new contract provided for significantly lower dismissal costs for un-

---

192 Toharia and Malo (2000) point out that the social partners had learned their lesson from the 1994 episode and were keen to avoid further unilateral reforms in this area by the government. See also OECD (2009c), Chapter 14 for a thorough discussion of the political economy behind the reforms of EPL and collective bargaining in 1994 and 1997.

justified dismissals: 33 days' wages per year of service, up to a maximum of 24 months. The new contract was to be trialled for four years and reviewed in 2001. At the same time, in order to encourage the use of the new contracts and reduce recruitment on a temporary basis, the government introduced a two-year rebate on employer social insurance contributions on the new contracts.

Evaluations of the effects of the 1994 and 1997 reforms showed that they had some impact in terms of increasing the rate of permanent contracts among new hires, but that the effect was only short-lived and that it was closely tied to the temporary social insurance rebates.[193] When the 2001 review of the star contract was undertaken, the Aznar government initially hoped to align the severance pay for unjustified dismissals under permanent contracts with the lower costs linked to the star contracts, but the unions were not willing to accept this and the government backed down. In the end, the key outcome of the 2001 reforms was the extension of the PEP contract.

The Socialist Government led by Mr Zapatero returned to the task of reforming EPL in 2006. It opened up the possibility of converting temporary contracts to PEP contracts for workers aged 31–45 who had been hired before the end of 2007, and introduced social insurance tax rebates for employers who converted temporary contracts to PEP contracts of more than three years' duration before the end of 2006. At the same time, legislation was introduced for automatic conversion of workers' temporary contracts to permanent contracts, if they had been with the same employer and in the same job for two years within a period of 30 months. These reforms, unlike those in the 1990s, were followed by a significant drop in the proportion of temporary workers: by 2009, it had decreased to 25.4 per cent, compared with 31.7 per cent in 2007. It is, however, very difficult to separate the effects of the 2006 reforms from the effects of the Great Recession and sovereign debt crisis, which led to a large fall in employment concentrated almost entirely on temporary workers during the years before 2011.

The most recent reforms to EPL in 2010, 2012 and 2014 were designed and implemented under very different circumstances to those which prevailed when the earlier reforms were made. The latest reforms were introduced in the context of the Eurozone crisis which hit the Spanish economy, and the economies of several other 'peripheral' countries, such as Greece, Portugal, Ireland and Italy, particularly hard. Several of these countries had to accept international bailouts to recapitalise their banking sectors and help them cope with an unsustainable build-up of sovereign debt. Spain came under severe pressure from the

---

193 See Bentolila, Dolado and Jimeno (2008).

international financial markets at the beginning of 2010, and in line with the advice from international organisations such as the European Commission, the IMF and the OECD, it was deemed necessary to reform EPL further, in order to cut labour market duality as part of a large package of structural reforms aimed at convincing the international financial markets that Spain would be able to put 'its house in order' and would not need a Troika bailout.

The 2010 reform of EPL had four major components: (i) it made it easier for firms to have dismissals accepted as justified by the courts; (ii) it made it easier for firms to apply the lower severance pay requirements of the PEP contract to a wider range of dismissed workers on permanent contracts; (iii) it proposed the introduction of a capital-funded component to severance pay similar to the Austrian individual savings account reform of 2003 (for details, see pp. 49–51 of the Austrian country note); (iv) it made the use of temporary contracts more restrictive and slightly more costly.[194] Nonetheless, while applauding this reform, OECD (2010d), p. 103 concluded that 'severance pay may still be excessively large. It may therefore be desirable to reduce severance pay for new permanent contracts further.' It recommended a switch towards a single permanent contract for new hires, with an initially low severance payment that would rise gradually with job tenure.

Despite the seemingly radical nature of the 2010 reforms, there was no change in the proportion of temporary workers as part of the Spanish workforce.[195] The pressures of the international financial markets on Spanish interest rate premiums over German bunds continued unabated. The desire of the international financial markets and Spain's EU partners to see more tangible progress on both fiscal consolidation and structural reforms led the new centre-right Rajoy government to introduce a further EPL reform in early 2012. This reform was part of a Memorandum of Understanding agreed between Spain and the European authorities in the context of Spain's request for European financial aid to enable it to recapitalise its financial sector.

---

194 Establishing the capital fund quickly ran into difficulty. Funding it would have required either an increase in employer payroll taxes, which was ruled out because of the need to restore cost-competitiveness of Spanish industry, or an injection of public funds, which was also ruled out because of the pressures for fiscal consolidation. For these reasons, the innovative idea of transforming part of the severance pay system into an individual savings account like the Austrian example was not implemented. Severance pay for temporary workers was raised from 8 to 12 days per year of service, to come into effect by 2015.

195 Bentolila, Dolado and Jimeno (2012) argue that the 2010 reforms were ineffective, because they followed the traditional piecemeal approach and failed to tackle the root cause of the duality, namely the excessive dismissal costs for permanent workers.

The 2012 reform pushed on beyond the 2010 reform relating to EPL by cutting severance pay significantly. Under the new law, if a dismissal of a permanent worker is deemed unjustified, the maximum severance pay is cut to 33 days' wages per year of service up to a maximum of 24 months, compared with a maximum of 45 days, and 42 months, respectively, under the old system. This cut applies to all new hires and to future years of service on existing permanent contracts. A justified dismissal now gives entitlement to a severance pay of only 20 days' wages per year of service up to 12 months' wages, and the new law has changed the definition of a justified dismissal to include more dismissals under this heading in the future. Finally, it is now easier for firms to justify dismissals for economic reasons.

As for collective dismissals, the reform abolished the requirement for administrative authorisation for such dismissals, while maintaining the requirement on firms to undertake negotiations in good faith with unions and workers before any layoffs can take place. The reformed law also specifies more precisely the objective reasons which allow employers to engage in collective dismissals.[196]

A new full-time, permanent contract (*Contrato de apoyo a emprendedores*) was created for small firms (i.e. those with fewer than 50 workers) that permits an extended trial period of one year for firms that had not made use of either collective or unfair dismissal procedures in the six months before the starting date of the new contract. The contract was supported by hiring subsidies. Small firms loom very large in the Spanish economy: in 2014, only 0.8 per cent of firms had more than 50 employees.

The 2012 reform of EPL marks a decisive break with previous reforms in that it cut severance pay entitlements significantly for permanent contracts across the board and sought to make it easier for firms to lay off permanent workers. This is reflected in the drop in the OECD indicator of the strictness of EPL for permanent contracts between 2010 and 2013. It must be noted, however, that this change in EPL still left permanent contracts well protected in Spain compared with the EU or OECD averages, especially in terms of the generosity of severance pay.

In a further attempt to reduce labour market duality, the Rajoy Government introduced, in March 2014, a temporary and conditional cut in employer payroll taxes for new permanent contracts to 100 euros per month. This cut applied to posts created between 25 February and the end of 2014, and is valid for two years from the start of the contract. After the two-year period, very small firms

---

196 In August 2013, the Spanish parliament made further changes to the law, in order to clarify the situation governing collective dismissals. It set limits to the power of the courts to nullify the collective dismissals procedure.

(with fewer than ten workers) are entitled to a permanent cut of 50 per cent in their employer payroll taxes. The reduction is dependent on the firm not having dismissed workers in the previous six months and the contract leading to a net increase in the number of employees in the firm. OECD (2014 f), however, pointed out that the flat rate is an expensive option for the public purse and instead argued the case for a permanent reduction in employer payroll taxes targeted at low-paid workers, as this would lead to the biggest employment gain per euro spent.

Reforms to the collective bargaining system

The high degree of nominal wage inertia in Spain has been linked to the structure of collective bargaining in Spain, the widespread practice of indexation of wages and the administrative extension of wage agreements. Collective bargaining mainly takes place at the sectoral or provincial levels, and collective agreements have legal status affecting all workers and firms in the relevant areas. Thus, the Spanish system tends to lie midway between centralisation and decentralisation. This intermediate collective bargaining system, combined with the practice of administrative extension, leaves Spain with a system which many theoretical and empirical studies suggest is detrimental for labour market performance, as it leaves little scope for firms, especially SMEs, to adjust their wages and working conditions to their productivity levels or to accommodate negative demand shocks.[197]

The first tentative steps to reforming the collective bargaining system began with the 1993 reform. The then government proposed a process of decentralisation and strengthening the role of collective bargaining in labour relations. It proposed to allow lower-level collective agreements to include better (or worse) conditions than those agreed at a higher level – until then lower-level bargaining could only improve on what had been negotiated at higher levels. The unions were hostile to this reform and when the Aznar government embarked on a further round of reform in 1997, the unions were able to persuade it to return to the pre-1994 arrangements concerning lower-level agreements.[198]

No further serious effort was made to reform collective bargaining until 2010. The 2010 reform made it easier for firms and workers to opt out *ex post* from collective agreements; the opt-out no longer required union consent, if the workers in

---

197 Calmfors and Driffill (1988) is the classic reference to the theoretical literature. See Bassanini and Duval (2006) for an empirical cross-country study which highlights the negative effects of intermediate bargaining levels on employment and unemployment.
198 However, as OECD (2009c) notes, it was not only the unions which resisted the changes to the collective bargaining system. Employer negotiators at the provincial and sectoral levels also resisted fiercely the transfer of bargaining authority to other levels.

the firm agreed to it; and the opt-out clauses could now cover more than just wages, e. g. they could include working time or other elements of the firm's internal work organisation.

This initial reform was rather timid, reflecting the close links between the socialist government of Mr Zapatero and the unions. As had been the case with the EPL reform, however, the international financial markets and Spain's EU partners demanded further reforms to the collective bargaining system. The centre-right Rajoy government obliged them by introducing a significant reform in February 2012.

The 2012 reform aimed to improve competitiveness by aligning labour costs more closely to productivity, and by allowing employers greater recourse to varying working conditions in response to adverse demand shocks, to facilitate employment retention and reduce dismissals. It sought to achieve this aim by granting great freedom to firms to strike firm-level collective agreements by eliminating the restrictions that sectoral-level bargaining had previously been able to impose on firm-level agreements. It made opt-outs from collective agreements easier for firms in cases where employers and workers had failed to agree – the new law imposed binding arbitration in this situation. Finally, it limited to one year the maximum period during which the terms of a collective agreement would remain binding beyond the period struck in the original agreement.

Effects of the 2012 reforms

It takes time for major labour market reforms, such as those introduced in 2010 and 2012, to have significant impact on employment, wages and productivity. It could well be argued that insufficient time has elapsed since these reforms were implemented to enable sound quantification of their effects. In addition, the reforms were implemented during a period of major macroeconomic disruption in the Spanish economy, rendering it even more difficult to quantify separately the impact of the labour market reforms from other determinants of employment and wages.

Notwithstanding these difficulties, OECD (2013h) made an initial rigorous evaluation of the effects of the reforms to EPL and collective bargaining, which were implemented in 2012. It did so by using state-of-the-art econometric methods to quantify the joint effect of the reforms to EPL and to collective bargaining, which had occurred in early 2012.[199] Because the estimation method rests for its validity on ex-

---

199 The estimation method used was a regression discontinuity model. The estimated equations all included controls for the business cycle and other relevant determinants. For more details, see OECD (2013h), Box 1.

ploiting the effects of a time discontinuity, the results might reflect not only the impact of the 2012 reforms to EPL and collective bargaining, but also other structural reforms to labour and product markets which occurred at about the same time.

The results of the evaluation suggested that the reforms increased hiring, especially on permanent contracts: the estimates suggested that the reforms increased hiring by 25,000 new permanent contracts per month, with the impact concentrated in small and medium-sized firms (with fewer than 100 employees). The reform also served to limit the average duration of periods of unemployment by speeding up the transition to a permanent contract among the unemployed who had previously held a temporary job. Finally, OECD (2013h) reports the results of simulation exercises based on the experiences of a large sample of OECD countries over a lengthy period, which indicates that the 2012 reforms could potentially increase long-run productivity growth in the Spanish business sector by 0.25 of a percentage point per year.

OECD (2013h) is careful to stress that the estimated impact is preliminary, and much more time is needed to assess the long-term effects of such reforms. Despite the reduction in EPL for permanent contracts, Spanish firms are still wedded to the use of temporary contracts. In addition, while the 2012 reform allowed firms much greater scope to opt out from sectoral agreements, OECD (2014f) notes that relatively few firms have made use of the flexibility to come to firm-level agreements.

In sum, it is too early to declare a victory on the 2012 reforms to EPL and collective bargaining. The initial evaluation of the reforms undertaken by OECD suggests, however, that they have had a favourable impact on hiring rates and on the transition from temporary to permanent contracts. At the same time, OECD (2013h) and OECD (2015a) call for further reforms, especially to EPL, in order to reduce the duality further.

11.2.3 Conclusion

The Spanish economy has been on a roller-coaster ride since the late 1990s. The period up to the Great Recession saw above-average growth rates, leading to dynamic employment growth and unemployment falling to a record low. Since then, Spain has experienced a double-dip recession, which was accompanied by an unprecedented drop in employment and increase in unemployment to a record high of over 26 per cent. Since late 2013, the Spanish economy has begun to recover, and this has been reflected in employment growth and a slow drop in unemployment. Part of the labour market improvement can be plausibly attributed to the significant reforms to EPL and collective bargaining, which were introduced in early 2012. These reforms were introduced after strong pressure on Spain from the international financial markets and its EU partners. Without these external pressures for reform, it is very doubtful that Spanish policymakers would have agreed to such significant reforms or implemented them so quickly.

The current economic recovery is fragile, however, and Spain faces a long difficult path ahead as it seeks to boost employment rates and make significant inroads into its huge unemployment problem, especially the very large numbers of long-term unemployed. In addition, it faces a major medium-term challenge of boosting its poor productivity performance. In order to deal with these problems, more structural reforms to labour and product markets will be required, as will policies to upgrade the skills and competences of the Spanish workforce.

Table 15: Scoreboard for labour market outcomes and policies, Spain and EU, 1993–2013

| | 1993 | | 2000 | | 2007 | | 2013* | |
	ES	EU	**ES**	EU	**ES**	EU	**ES**	EU
1. Employment rate (% of the working-age population)	**48.5**	61.2	**57.8**	63.6	**67.1**	66.7	**56.0**	65.9
– male	**65.0**	71.8	**73.3**	72.9	**78.0**	74.2	**60.6**	71.6
– female	**31.9**	50.7	**42.2**	54.4	**55.8**	59.2	**51.7**	60.2
– youth (aged 15/16–24)	**29.5**	39.5	**36.3**	39.4	**43.0**	38.2	**18.6**	33.4
– older people (aged 55–9)	**41.7**	47.6	**46.3**	50.6	**55.1**	57.3	**54.3**	64.9
– older people (aged 60–4)	**27.4**	22.3	**27.0**	22.3	**33.0**	29.4	**30.7**	34.7
– older people (aged 65–9)	–	9.2	**3.8**	7.4	**5.3**	9.5	**4.6**	11.3
2. Unemployment rate (% of labour force)	**22.4**	10.8	**13.9**	8.9	**8.3**	7.1	**26.1**	10.7
– youth (aged 15/16–24)	**41.0**	21.0	**25.3**	17.4	**18.1**	15.5	**55.5**	23.3
3. Incidence of long-term unemployment (% of total unemployment) (a)	**52.7**	42.0	**42.4**	44.4	**20.4**	41.6	**49.7**	46.5
4. Part-time employment rate (b)	**6.0**	13.8	**7.7**	15.3	**10.7**	16.0	**14.7**	17.5
5. Temporary employment rate (c) (temporary employees as % of total employees)	**32.2**	10.5	**32.1**	13.1	**31.7**	14.8	**23.1**	14.0
– youth (aged 15/16–24 as % of total youth employees)	**73.9**	28.8	**68.6**	38.0	**62.8**	41.8	**64.7**	43.0
6. Low-pay incidence (d) (% of employees)	–	–	**16.3**	15.7	**16.0**	16.5	**15.3**	15.0
7. Protection of permanent workers against individual dismissal	**3.5**	2.6	**2.4**	2.5	**2.4**	2.4	**2.1**	2.2
– Protection of temporary workers	**3.8**	2.3	**3.3**	1.8	**3.0**	1.6	**2.6**	1.8

Table 15 (continued)

	1993		2000		2007		2013*	
	ES	EU	**ES**	EU	**ES**	EU	**ES**	EU
8. Public spending on labour market								
policies (% of GDP)	**4.0**	2.9	**2.1**	2.0	**2.2**	1.6	**3.6**	2.0
– Spending on active measures (e)	**0.5**	0.9	**0.8**	0.8	**0.8**	0.6	**0.6**	0.8
– Spending on passive measures (f)	**3.5**	2.1	**1.3**	1.1	**1.4**	0.9	**3.0**	1.2
9. Net benefit replacement rate (g)								
(averaged over four family types and								
two earnings levels)	–	–	**49**	65	**48**	61	**46**	54
– initial spell (h)	–	–	**73**	70	**73**	71	**69**	70
– after 2 years of unemployment	–	–	**65**	66	**65**	63	**63**	57

* 2013 or latest available year.
(a) Persons out of work for 12 months and over.
(b) Part-time employment refers to persons who usually work less than 30 hours per week in "their 'main job'".
(c) Temporary employees are wage and salary workers whose job has a pre-determined end date as opposed to permanent employees whose job is of unlimited duration. National definitions broadly conform to this generic definition, but may vary depending on national circumstances.
(d) Persons with a wage less than 2/3 of the median.
(e) 'Active' measures cover categories 1 to 7 of the OECD/Eurostat data base on public spending on labour market programmes.
(f) 'Passive' measures cover categories 8 and 9 of the OECD/Eurostat data base on public spending on labour market programmes.
(g) Data on net replacement rates for 2000 refer to 2001.
(h) Initial phase of unemployment but following any waiting period. For married couples, the percentage of AW relates to the previous earnings of the 'unemployed' spouse only; the second spouse is assumed to be 'inactive' with no earnings and no recent employment history. Where receipt of social assistance or other minimum-income benefits is subject to activity tests (such as active job-search or being 'available' for work), these requirements are assumed to be met. Children are aged four and six and neither childcare benefits nor childcare costs are considered. Unweighted averages, for previous full-time earnings levels of 67% and 100% of AW and out-of-work single and couple households with no children or with two children (children are assumed to be aged four and six and neither childcare benefits nor childcare costs are considered). After tax and including unemployment and family benefits. Social assistance and other means-tested benefits are assumed to be available subject to relevant income conditions. Housing costs are assumed equal to 20% of AW.
Sources: OECD Online Employment Database: www.oecd.org/employment/database; data on net replacement rates come from the OECD tax-benefit models (www.oecd.org/els/social/workincentives).

12 United Kingdom

12.1 Interview with Tony Blair, 7 January 2015

'The Left and Right can argue about what the solution is, but not about the reality of the challenge.'

Could you elaborate on the general approach and on the contents of the reforms you implemented during your time as Prime Minister? In hindsight, which of these reforms would you consider a success and what would you have done differently?

The approach that we took was very much to keep in place the principal reforms that Mrs Thatcher had made, which were really to grant a legal framework within which trade unions operated: it recognised that unions had to operate according to certain legal principles that introduced provisions, for example, for ballots before strikes and for the election of union leaders by their membership.

In other words, we kept those basic Thatcherite provisions. Our policy innovation was to supplement them with individual rights: we introduced the first ever minimum wage in the UK. We introduced equal rights for part-time workers, for example, maternity leave, and we actually gave people the right to join a trade union, but it was very much based on the individual rights of workers, and rights for unions were always balanced by responsibilities. That was one part of our labour market reforms, and I would say those worked pretty well on the whole. The minimum wage that was quite fiercely opposed by the Conservatives at the time is now part of the accepted consensus.

Secondly, we introduced a whole series of what I would call 'welfare-to-work' measures. These were the new deals for specific groups, such as the young employed, the long-term unemployed and lone parents. Those measures were, I think, more mixed in their impact. What they did do was to create a sense in which people no longer felt that it was either right or possible to remain on benefits all their life, as it were, without really bothering to engage with the world of work. People understood that with the right to welfare came a responsibility to seek work. That was a programme that, in principle, worked quite well. I believe that once you look at it in detail, however, you will find that there are some people who are very hard to reach and some cases that are very hard to deal with. A lot of these people will come back into the labour market, but – without the right skills and education – they fall back out of the labour market again quite quickly. I would therefore say that the results of that initiative were mixed.

Then we had reforms around pensions, disability benefit, incapacity benefit, indeed, the whole range of the benefit system – also for excluded families. This meant that we also looked very carefully at how to deal with those people who are what we call 'socially excluded'. To put it differently: most socially excluded people are unemployed, but not all unemployed people are socially excluded – they are a kind of separate category.

On the socially excluded families, and social exclusion, I think we got to the right answer towards the end of my time, but that programme was not really pursued after I left. In my view, to deal with the really hard-to-reach families, and there may be no more than 100,000 or 150,000 of them in the whole country, a completely different type of framework is required. You need early and tough intervention. You need a 'tough-love approach' to that. The pilots were very successful, but they were always controversial, because they involved saying to families, even if they were committing no offence: 'We are going to put you under a strong set of constraints.' Now, I personally feel that this is a huge issue for all modern, developed societies. I was convinced that our approach was the right one, but – as I say – it came towards the very end of my time and we were not really able to implement it.

Also towards the end of my time as Prime Minister, two sets of reform proposals were presented with a longer-term perspective. The first were the so-called 'Turner Proposals', named after the Chairman of the Pensions Commission, Lord Adair Turner. They are now basically implemented. I think they were pretty successful and formed a long-term basis for the UK pension system. The second one was the so-called 'Freud Report on the future of welfare to work' a review led by David Freud on the future of labour market policy, on which I was, frankly, very keen. My successor was not so keen, but the present Conservative Government is implementing many of those proposals. It is probably too early to say, but I think they are important.

In summary: this is the range of the different policy initiatives that we had.

Labour came into power in 1997. In what sense was there a climate for reform at that time? Did you deliberately work to create such a climate during your campaign?
The reason why New Labour, as we called it, was a strong political concept and a successful one, was because it was obvious to people that the world had changed, that you could not have the policies of the 1970s back and that you had to have flexibility in your labour market. On the other hand, you also had to have certain guaranteed basic rights for people. This sort of approach, which is very much a centre ground political approach, did have real traction among the public. In the hundred years of our history, Labour had never won

two full terms before; and my government won three, basically – in my view – because this was our position.

We worked closely with business. The Low Pay Commission, established under my government in 1997, involved businesses as well as unions, and it was that advisory body which recommended the introduction of the minimum wage. We kept this labour market flexibility and in some ways enhanced it. Today the need for structural reform in welfare systems and labour markets is absolutely obvious and I would maintain that this is, fundamentally, still correct.

In addition, you have to create a sense of challenge in order to get people's attention on the need for reform. One really important thing to consider in the planning of reforms nowadays is – and I study this a lot myself – that you have got to give people an awareness, especially in the European context, of the way the world is changing. You cannot simply look at your country in isolation from either the rest of Europe or the rest of the world – clearly this is also an essential matter people must know. In this sense, countries are like companies or communities: if the world around you is changing fast, you have to change, too.

I argued for these reforms from a centre-left perspective: my reasoning for the reforms was not really left/right at all. My reasoning was very simple: the world had changed. Thus, to take the example of pensions, you could not ignore the fact that the demography of Europe had been transformed in the previous 30 years. The reality is that if you do not change, you are increasingly going to have systems that are unsustainable, which means that the working population of the future cannot afford to maintain them. It is not a question of whether you think change is a good idea or a bad idea. It does not really matter – the Left and the Right can argue about what the solution is – but what you definitely cannot argue about is the reality of the challenge. As a politician you need to create awareness of that sense of inescapability.

One thing we made very clear before we came to power was that we were going to govern as a centre ground party. In the end, however, it does not help you when you start to make the reforms, because when you talk about reform, if you do it in general terms, everyone is in favour. It is when you become specific that the problem starts.

When creating your reform agenda, did you take experiences of other countries into account? Did you consider instances of good practice from other countries or were you entirely focused on the UK?
I always thought it was important to check out what other countries were doing. We looked, for example, at some that shared the reforms: Germany, for instance, and I think we looked at some of the Dutch reforms, too. Regarding schools, we

looked at Sweden, Finland and the US, among others, but I also, strangely enough, looked at countries such as Singapore.

In today's world, people are changing jobs constantly, new companies are springing up, small businesses really matter in employment terms and big businesses of 20 years ago are not necessarily the big businesses in 20 years' time. Under these circumstances, I feel that it is essential to recognise that flexibility around the labour market becomes absolutely fundamental. There can be no real economic progress without adapting to changed conditions.

When a new government takes over, there are almost always certain groups who hope that the reforms of the preceding government will be rolled back. How did you deal with this threat to the sustainability of reforms?
First of all, and quite simply, I made it very clear I just was not going to do it, and this was therefore an issue of the leadership of the party for me. Technically, we reduced the power of the trade unions within the Labour Party. In addition, we built a consensus among the public, but there was always huge pressure to go back. Whenever we did 'welfare to work', pension reform or benefit reform, it was always painful.

One of the things about making reforms – I learnt this over time – is that the rhythm of reform runs something like this: when you first propose a change, people tell you it is terrible; when you are doing it, it is hell; but after you have done it, you wish you had done more of it. Over time, I have learnt that this is the normal rhythm and, as a result, we were probably more radical towards the end than at the beginning.

How did you handle the opposition the New Deal was facing?
The problem with reform is this: the people who are directly affected by a reform do not like it. The broad public might agree with it, but the broad public is silent. The broad public is not out on the street. Members of the broad public are not chaining themselves to the railings – people who do are the people who are affected. In other words, the New Deal reforms and the disability reforms were very unpopular, but they were necessary. What is important is not to get distracted or dismayed by the noise. I actually learnt over time that if there is no noise then there is probably no reform. I remember, when we carried out our first pension reform, I felt that it was quite radical at the time, and then, after a couple of years, I noticed that no one was protesting and came to the conclusion that we had not really done much, which was the right conclusion, as I realised when I went back and reanalysed it. So, I just think that is the way it is.

Apart from the influence of affected groups the ease or difficulty of implementing reforms also hinges upon backing within the ruling party. What would you say about the general consensus in the Labour Party to continue the reform path?

There was never a consensus, really, but, there was always a very vigorous debate. I think for any centre-left party that is trying to reform, systems at the centre-left field, like welfare and public services, play an important role. It is always really tough. The unions are a very, very difficult factor. That is the truth of it. The unions tend to defend their interests extremely strongly. Many people in progressive politics consider the unions a political movement, but they are, of course, also an interest group. Distinguishing between those two things is terribly hard sometimes.

What you can do, though, is to create stakeholders even within the sector that is going to be subject to change. I found in the education and health reforms that I carried out, which were not at all easy and opposed by many, we could always create some sections, even if they were a minority, who were prepared to come out and say: 'No, actually this is a good idea; this is the way of the future.'

A very interesting notion – can you tell us more about these stakeholders who are more open-minded or even supportive of reforms?

You have got to have agents of change. Since the change is usually hotly contested, it is far better to have the voice of someone working within the system than a politician.

In the case of the New Deal reforms, for example, those stakeholders were certain people who would say: 'Well, look, I know people don't like the fact that the New Deal is obligatory, but on the other hand I have been long-term unemployed; they are not giving me a chance.' So, it would be people within those systems who would be saying: 'Yes, we should be doing this.'

In addition, there are some trade unions on the more moderate side, who would say: 'Look, what we have got to do as trade unions is adapt to the new world; it is right that we do. This is better for the long-term interest of our members.'

Actually, there were one or two trade unions that came out actively and supported the New Deal; for example, the Usdaw, which is the shop workers' union. It is a moderate private sector union that came out and supported the reforms. In the public sector, however, I frankly always found it really hard. If it had not been for the changes introduced during the Thatcher period, which reduced the power of the trade unions, it would have been even tougher.

An important question in this respect is obviously how to deal with the potential opponents. Did you have to pay a high price to get everybody on board? Did you have to compensate those who were considered losers in a reform?

Yes, sometimes. Sometimes, if you are reforming incapacity or disability benefit, for example, you might have to say: 'I am going to reform it for future claimants. But I cannot touch past or existing claimants.'

It helped a lot that we were able to say: 'Look, there are positive things happening as well with what you regard as negative.' One of the toughest things about reform today is when you are working in an era of shrinking budgets and when your reforms just consist in taking away rights. On the other hand, it is in some ways harder to reform when times are good; whereas in bad times, you can force people to a choice. One of the problems I have continually had with the reforms I was undertaking was people saying to me: 'Why are we doing all of this, politically?'

Would you say that to be successful in carrying out reforms you have to be very clear from day one?

Yes. There is also something that I say to a lot of the prime ministers who are reforming in Europe now. There is something I learnt to be very important. When I say it, it seems absolutely obvious, but it is nonetheless crucial: it is essential to get the right analysis leading to the right policy prescription, because otherwise you could end up having 'a sort of general idea of reform', leaving the details more or less to the system to work out. You just say something along the lines of: 'OK, well, this seems like a good reform, let's go with it.' In fact, what you realise after a time is that the detail really matters. As I say, I know that is obvious, but you can make quite small, apparently quite technical, changes that have a revolutionary impact.

At the beginning we did not really have such an analysis, just a vague idea of reform and knew our basic political position. We constructed our political compass, but we did not have a detailed map.

How long did it take to get that analysis?

It took most of my first term, actually. One of the things I constantly say to people in power now: 'Do learn from that, because you need to put the right systems of quality advice in place' – which, by the way, can be advice from outside the traditional system, as well as from inside – 'but put that in place right away, pay real attention to the structure you have around you as leader that allows you to get a proper grip on what reforms are necessary'.

I constructed a wholly different system in my second term. I constructed a new policy unit, I brought in people from outside to help with policy, I had a strategic policy unit that was looking at the medium- and longer-term questions. Then I had a delivery unit, which focused on performance-managing the priorities of the government in a private-sector oriented way.

These new bodies were internal and at the centre. After a time, the departments replicated this system to a degree. I think one of the biggest mistakes you can make, as an incoming leader, is to think: 'If you have got the general idea, then the rest will follow.' The rest does not follow unless you make it follow.

12.2 A note on United Kingdom labour market performance over the past decade

12.2.1 The facts

UK labour market performance was relatively good in international comparison over the 15 years leading up to the financial crisis in 2007–8, which hit the UK economy hard. Between 1993 and 2007, the total employment rate rose by almost 5 percentage points; the harmonised unemployment rate almost halved over the same period from 10.3 per cent to 5.3 per cent (see fig. 14). Nonetheless, while the financial crisis and the subsequent recession caused the UK economy great damage, the impact of the slowdown on the labour market was much less severe than many commentators had predicted, when the crisis first hit.

The initial drop in employment post-crisis was relatively modest: other EU countries, such as Denmark and Spain, which have recorded similar GDP losses as the UK since 2008, experienced larger percentage falls in employment. The UK economy has recovered strongly since the end of 2012: GDP growth in 2014, at 2.6 per cent, was the strongest performance among the G7 countries in that year. Real GDP has exceeded the pre-crisis peak. Macroeconomic policies have played a key role in supporting the recovery, as have structural reforms to labour and product markets. Indeed, the OECD credits these policies with 'sustaining one of the most flexible economies in the OECD'.[200] This recovery in output has been accompanied by a strong labour market performance, compared with past recession episodes in the UK. The overall employment rate in 2013 was almost back to its pre-crisis peak of 74 per cent, and more recent data show that it has since surpassed this level (see table 16). The counterpart of this more resilient employment performance since 2008 has been a drop in productivity, which

---

200 See OECD (2015c), p. 14.

Evolution of the employment and unemployment rates in the United Kingdom, 1970–2014

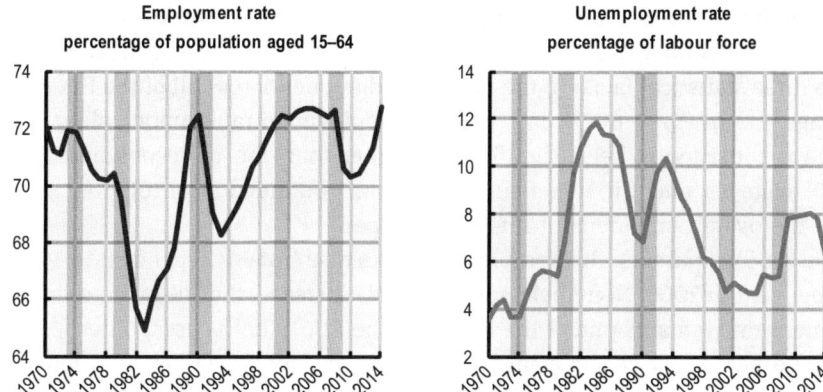

Note: Grey shaded areas refer to period of economic contraction (based on the output gap).

Source: OECD estimates based on the *OECD Labour Force Statistics, OECD Short-term Labour Market Statistics* and *OECD Economic Outlook Databases* (Cut-off date: 13 April 2015).

Figure 14: Labour market chart United Kingdom

contrasts strongly with the pattern seen in previous downturns in the UK economy. This so-called 'productivity puzzle' has sparked a lively debate in the UK as to its causes and consequences.[201]

Part of the explanation for the more resilient employment performance since 2007 is related to the increased flexibility of the UK labour market which, in turn, owes much to a series of continued labour market reforms stretching back to the mid-1980s. One manifestation of this is the fact that real wages fell significantly during the downturn, encouraging firms to limit layoffs, especially of skilled workers. At the same time, the threat of higher unemployment has also persuaded workers and unions to shift their bargaining positions so that they have been more ready to trade off lower real wages in exchange for a promise of job security. Indeed, it is only recently that the tightening labour market has seen real wages begin to increase again in the UK, reversing a long trend of weak, or negative, real wage growth. Adjustments in working hours over the period 2008–12 also helped to cushion the impact of falling labour demand on employment.

---

201 See Hughes and Saheleen (2012) and OECD (2015c) for comprehensive summaries of this debate.

In terms of specific labour force groups, there have been notable increases in the employment rates of older workers and lone (i.e. single) parents. The increase in older worker employment predates the crisis, as can be seen from the scoreboard. It is worth noting, however, that older worker employment rates have been on a rising trend since the mid-1990s and the scoreboard highlights three statistical facts: (i) the rising trend applies across all of the three five-year age groups (55–9, 60–4, 64–9); (ii) UK employment rates among older workers have consistently been significantly higher than the corresponding EU or OECD averages and (iii) the rising trend has continued post-2007, at a time when the overall employment rate has dropped.

As for lone parents, their employment rate rose from 44.6 per cent in 1997 to 56.7 per cent in 2009. Nonetheless, despite this increase, the UK lone-parent employment rate remains one of the lowest in the EU. In both cases, older workers and lone parents, it seems clear that changes to labour market, pensions (for older workers) and tax-benefit policies were important drivers of these increasing employment rates.

Another distinctive feature of the UK employment record since the early 1990s, setting it apart from many other EU countries, has been a relatively high share of part-time work, compared to international statistics. The scoreboard shows that in 2013 one in every four jobs in the UK was part-time, 7 percentage points above the EU average, and the share of part-time jobs has increased since 2007. Many of the part-time jobs created were in self-employment. However, the period since 2013 has witnessed significant growth in full-time jobs, whose number now exceeds the pre-crisis level. At the same time, the crisis has also seen some small increase in temporary work but, at 6.2 per cent in 2013, it was still less than half the EU average at that time.

With respect to the harmonised unemployment rate, while it rose from 5.3 per cent in 2007 to a peak of 8 per cent in 2011, it has since declined steadily to 5.9 per cent in September 2014 (seasonally adjusted), the fifth-lowest rate in the EU28 in that month. This latter rate is equivalent to 1.92 million persons unemployed. Yet, when the crisis hit the UK economy, many commentators predicted that UK unemployment would soar to well over the 3 million mark, based on the output–unemployment ratio observed over previous cyclical downturns in the UK. Fig. 14 illustrates this nicely: it highlights the fact that the UK harmonised unemployment rate has been on a downward trend since the recession of the early 1990s and, while it has risen since 2007, current levels are converging towards the pre-crisis trough of just under 5 per cent which was recorded in 2004–5.

As for the generosity of the benefit system in the UK, the scoreboard shows that the net benefit replacement rate is below the EU average at the beginning of an unemployment spell. For longer spells of unemployment, however, the replacement rate in 2013 was above the EU average, reversing the trend since 2000. In terms of public spending on active labour market policies, the UK has consistently devoted fewer resources to such policies than the EU average: in 2013, it spent only 0.2 per cent of GDP on ALMPs compared with an EU average of 0.8 per cent.

While overall labour market resilience in the UK is impressive and, as will be argued below, can in part be attributed to the cumulative impact of a sequence of labour market and tax-benefit reforms stretching back to the mid-1980s, there are nonetheless some worrying black spots. First, in the 1980s and early 1990s, long-term unemployment was a particular concern for UK policymakers. In 1993, it accounted for almost 43 per cent of total unemployment, just below the EU average of 46 per cent. Following a series of reforms designed to activate recipients of unemployment benefit and prevent them from drifting into long-term unemployment, the incidence of long-term unemployment fell very sharply in the UK, so that by 2007 it was down to 23.7 per cent, almost half its level at the beginning of the 1990s and 18 percentage points below the EU average. The incidence of long-term unemployment, however, has increased sharply in the UK since the onset of the recession, to exceed 36 per cent in 2013, raising concerns that the loss of motivation and skills implied by such large numbers of long-term unemployed would have a negative impact on future growth prospects.

A second worrying feature of UK unemployment has been a persistently high youth unemployment rate, though there has been a noticeable decline in the rate since the end of 2013. The youth rate in September 2014 (seasonally adjusted) was 16.7 per cent, 5 percentage points below the EU28 average, though still over 2 percentage points above its 2007 level. It is noticeable, however, that the rise in the UK youth unemployment rate predates the crisis. The reasons for the rise in youth unemployment prior to 2007, a period when it was declining in most other EU and OECD countries, are not well understood. Various culprits have been suggested, e. g. the national minimum wage (NMW), which came into force in 1998, or the EU enlargements in the early 2000s, which brought into the UK large inflows of labour migrants, especially from Eastern Europe, who may have competed directly with young people for entry-level jobs.[202] In any event, with current levels of youth unemployment still exceeding 700,000, concerns

---

202 See OECD (2008c) for a review of this literature. It is fair to say, however, that there is no concensus as to which are the main culprits for the pre-2007 rise in youth unemployment.

about the costs associated with a 'lost generation' loom large in the public debate.[203]

Third, while the UK employment and labour force participation rates are above the EU and OECD averages, there is still a large proportion of the working-age population relying upon inactive benefits for financial support. This is particularly the case with benefits for lone parents, and especially the disabled of working age. The share of the working-age population in receipt of disability benefit in the UK rose sharply during the 1980s and 1990s. It subsequently stabilised and has dropped slightly since the mid-2000s, partly in response to policy reforms designed to get more people off such benefits and into work and to prevent people with health problems, but who have some work capacity, from getting on to disability benefit in the first place. However, the large numbers still relying upon this benefit pose a major challenge. OECD (2014h) shows that, at the end of 2012, the incidence of disability benefit receipt among the UK working-age population was 6.8 per cent (equivalent to over 2.5 million people), the ninth-highest rate among the 28 OECD countries for which comparable data were available.[204]

There has been more success in reducing the benefit recipiency rate among lone parents. While the recipiency rate rose through the 1980s and the early 1990s, it peaked in the late 1990s and, as noted above, the period since then has coincided with a rising employment rate among lone parents.

Finally, there has been a long-standing concern in the UK about a growing polarisation between so-called 'work-rich' households and 'work-poor' households, where no adult is in work or where those who are in work are only in part-time jobs. At the same time, the incidence of low-paid work in the UK remains well above the EU average, at over 20 per cent, so that there is a significant concern about the phenomenon of the 'working poor', linked to insufficient financial incentives for low-paid workers to find work or increase their work effort.

---

203 See Bell and Blanchflower (2011) for evidence that high youth unemployment in the UK generates long-lasting scars.

204 These data come from the new OECD benefit recipiency database. While every effort has been made to correct for double-counting of receipt of cash transfers in the database, it is still possible that some remains, which may exaggerate slightly the magnitude of the phenomenon. For example, the OECD data for the UK include recipients of 'Carer's Allowance' and 'Income Support for Carers', who should probably be excluded: together these groups amount to about 400,000 people and, if they were excluded, this would lower the disability benefit recipiency rate in recent years by just over 1 percentage point. Nonetheless, there is no doubt that the incidence of disability benefit recipiency among the working-age population is very high in the UK in international comparison and it has not declined significantly in recent years.

The latter two features of UK labour market performance over the past two decades, together with the relatively high and growing share of part-time work, have contributed to the trend rise in earnings and income inequality in the UK.[205] These employment and inequality outcomes have been linked in the UK to specific features of the design and implementation of the tax and welfare benefit systems and to perceived weaknesses in the activation of working-age benefit recipients to help them find work. As we shall see below, the main motivations for a continual series of labour market and tax-benefit reforms in the UK, covering almost three decades, have been to remedy these weaknesses.

12.2.2 Main labour market and tax-benefit reforms since 1997

When discussing reforms in the UK in the labour market and tax/benefit areas, it is important to bear in mind that there are large elements of continuity and of change which characterise the stance of both Conservative and Labour Governments in these policy-domains. Both shared a common concern to promote a 'welfare-to-work' approach by effectively activating benefit recipients to find paid work, beginning with recipients of unemployment benefit and then extending the approach gradually to lone parents and to the disabled of working age. They also shared an objective of 'making work pay', i.e. that any benefit recipient who found a job should gain financially from this choice and not be better off relying on welfare benefits. At the same time, there were some significant differences in the political choices made to tackle these concerns – witness the plethora of 'New Deals' under New Labour and, more recently, the Coalition Government's two flagship initiatives, the 'Work Programme' and 'Universal Credit'.

The element of continuity must be remembered when assessing the various reforms since 1997. When New Labour came to power under Tony Blair in 1997, they did not begin with a clean sheet on their welfare-to-work agenda. Instead, they built upon a series of earlier reforms, which began in the mid-1980s under the Conservatives led by Margaret Thatcher. For this reason, we begin with a brief summary of the main relevant events.

Main activation reforms introduced by the Conservative Governments prior to New Labour

Fig. 14 shows that the UK unemployment rate peaked in the mid-1980s, at a time when the incidence of long-term unemployment was rising rapidly. Concerns

---

205 See OECD (2011a) for details.

about the labour market and fiscal implications of high and persistent unemployment led the Thatcher Government to embark on a decade-long sequence of reforms to the unemployment benefit system.

The main features of the reforms introduced by the Conservative Governments and their timing are as follows:[206]

- 1986: 'Restart' introduced mandatory job-related interviews every six months for the unemployed; benefit agency staff numbers were increased to monitor job search more intensively; the maximum length of a benefit sanction was increased from 6 to 13 weeks. In subsequent years, much testing was undertaken with different types and schedules of job-related interviews, and the most successful variants were then rolled out nationwide.
- 1989: 'Actively seeking work' became a requirement for benefit eligibility.[207] The benefit administration and the job placement agency were amalgamated over a period of several years into a one-stop shop – Job Centres.
- 1991: Participation in a one-week job-search course was made obligatory for those who had been unemployed for over two years.
- Early 1990s: The introduction of the 'stricter benefit regime' led to a doubling of benefit sanctions.
- 1996: Jobseeker's Allowance (JSA) replaced unemployment benefits. It was a flat-rate benefit with a duration of six months. Those on JSA were required to visit a Job Centre once a fortnight and, after three months of unemployment, to search for an alternative occupation.

Thus, over a ten-year period monitoring of the job-search activity of unemployment benefit recipients was tightened progressively and more re-employment services were made available to support them, backed up by the threat of a stronger benefit sanctions regime. As the Labour market chart UK shows, this period coincided with a very significant drop in unemployment, which was attributed, in part, to these reforms.[208] Hence, it is not surprising that New Labour chose to

---

206 This description draws heavily upon OECD (2003), Table 4.3 and van Reenen (2004).

207 This was a key principle in what became known as the 'Rights and Responsibilities' agenda; later it became known as 'Mutual Obligations'.

208 For example, evaluations have shown that Restart raised significantly the outflow rate from unemployment benefits to work – see van Reenen (2004) for a review of this evidence. It is noteworthy that Restart and the subsequent modifications to it have served as a model for similar interventions in other EU countries.

maintain this position on reform, while adding some specific innovations of their own.[209]

The New Deals

When the Blair government took office in 1997, it immediately decided to assign high importance to reinforcing activation through a series of so-called 'New Deals'. The basic principle behind the New Deals was that the unemployed were to be guaranteed intensive re-employment services after a specific duration of unemployment had elapsed and, at that point, all JSA claimants had to be placed in a job or participate in a full-time employment activity; failure to respect the requirements resulted in a benefit sanction. Jobcentre Plus (JCP) was assigned a key role for delivering re-employment services and the task of Personal Advisers (PAs) in counselling their clients and monitoring their job-search activity was reinforced. At the same time as the New Deals were introduced, another innovation was launched in several high-unemployment areas, the designation of so-called 'Employment Zones'. In these areas, re-employment services were delivered by private sector organisations on the basis of payment-for-results contracts.

The first of the New Deals was launched in 1998 and targeted at young people. This was then swiftly followed by very similar, as it were 'cloned', initiatives. The following were among the various New Deals:[210]

- New Deal for Young People (NDYP): This was targeted at young people aged 18–24 receiving JSA after an unemployment spell of six months. Participation began with an intensive period of job-search counselling with a PA that could last for four months – the so-called 'Gateway' period. If a job was not found within the Gateway period, then claimants were presented with several options in which they had to participate full-time for up to six months. The options consisted of subsidised employment in the private sector, temporary public sector jobs or full-time education and training.
- New Deal 25 Plus (ND25): This programme was mandatory for JSA claimants aged 25–49 who had been claiming benefit for 18 of the past 21 months. It

---

209 It should be noted that the UK Treasury, when Gordon Brown (who succeeded Tony Blair as Prime Minister in 2008), was Chancellor, took the lead in designing many of New Labour's labour market and welfare reforms. The Department of Work and Pensions, which was created in 2001, played a secondary role, being mainly charged with policy implementation.
210 This description draws heavily on Finn and Schulte (2008), Figure 8. Note that there was also a voluntary New Deal for the non-working partners of benefit recipients, which has been omitted from the above list because of its small size.

consisted of an initial Gateway period, followed by an 'Intensive Activity Period' lasting between 13 and 26 weeks, which could involve work experience or job placements, work-focused training and assistance with motivation and soft skills.

– New Deal for Lone Parents (NDLPs): Unlike NDYP and ND25, this was a voluntary programme. It involved work-focused interviews with a PA and assistance with training and childcare together with a time-limited payment, if a job was found. Assistance for this group was also heavily conditioned by policies which involved major changes to the tax and benefit systems (see below).

– New Deal 50 Plus (ND50): This, too, was a voluntary programme, targeted at JSA claimants aged 50 and over. Like NDLPs, it relied upon work-related interviews with a PA to coax the participants into actively looking for work.

– New Deal for Disabled People (NDDP) and Pathways to Work: Participation in the NDDP programme was voluntary. It was gradually, beginning in 2003, replaced by Pathways to Work, which was developed as a new response to the perceived failure of NDDP to activate many of the target population. Pathways combined activation through work-focused interviews and the development of an action plan with a PA for those disabled people who had some work capacity; the PA would refer clients to a range of options designed to help them find work.

It is clear from the above description that the intensity of activation varied significantly across the different New Deals. Activation was most strict for the NDYP and ND25 target groups, followed by that for lone parents, and it was most relaxed for the NDDP group, notwithstanding the gradual nationwide roll-out of the Pathways programme after 2003.

Several evaluations of the impact of the various New Deals were undertaken.[211] They show that the NDYP did have a significant positive impact on the exit rate for the young unemployed into jobs, but the main impact occurred during the Gateway period. Among the subsequent options, only the wage subsidy yielded positive outcomes. A fairly similar picture emerged from the evaluations of ND25. Here, though, the evaluations also suggested that the Employment Zone providers were able to achieve slightly better employment outcomes than JCP for the same target group. As noted above, lone-parent employment rates rose significantly during the period of the New Deals and the evaluation evidence sug-

---

211 See Finn and Schulte (2008) and Brewer (2008) for reviews of the relevant evaluations.

gests that a combination of NDLP and various tax and benefit policies accounted for a significant part of the increase.

However, the evaluations also highlighted two worrying features of the New Labour reforms. First, there was a significant group of repeat entrants to the programmes. Secondly, while the 'work-first' approach behind the New Deals undoubtedly helped many benefit claimants find work, it tended to trap some into low-paid jobs with few career prospects. This was, at least in part, an outcome of New Labour's stance towards 'making work pay'. We now turn to this.

Making work pay (MWP) policies

New Labour came into office with the objective of ensuring that any benefit claimant, irrespective of his or her personal and family situation, who found a job would be financially better off in work than relying upon state benefits. Given the design of the UK's benefit system,[212] this is very difficult to achieve and can be in conflict with other policy objectives, such as reducing child poverty.

The first MWP policy introduced by New Labour was the nationwide minimum wage in 1998. This included a sub-minimum rate for youth aged 18–21. Over time, there has been a small rise in the value of the minimum wage relative to the average or median wage, but the UK rate remains relatively low in international comparison.[213] Its aim has been to serve as a low-wage floor in the UK labour market and it appears to have achieved this. Indeed, it is noticeable that the Coalition Government, which took office in 2010, has maintained this flagship New Labour policy.

New Labour introduced two major changes to the tax and benefit system to help meet the MWP objective. First, in late 1999, they replaced Family Credit with the Working Families Tax Credit (WFTC), with the explicit aim of raising work incentives, especially for low-wage parents. Secondly, they introduced, in early 2003, the Child Tax Credit (CTC) and the Working Tax Credit (WTC); the rationale

---

212 Benefits are flat-rate and means-tested, with a variety of top-ups through cash payments or tax credits. There are earnings disregards and tapers, by which benefits are withdrawn, as income from work increases.

213 In 2010, the UK minimum wage was 47 per cent of median monthly earnings which put the UK in sixteenth position among the 22 EU Member States which had a statutory minimum wage, in terms of this indicator. See Eurostat (2015) for details.

for this latter change was less one of MWP, but to put a greater emphasis on the need to cut child poverty.[214]

WFTC was a refundable tax credit, i.e. it was payable even if it exceeded the family's tax liability. Entitlement to it depended on at least one adult in the family working for 16 or more hours per week. There was a basic credit for each family, with additions for each child. The credit was withdrawn once earnings exceeded the disregard, and once the withdrawal rate (including income tax and employee social insurance) was 69 per cent. WFTC was much more generous than Family Credit, and in that way it cut the marginal effective tax rates for those who would have been eligible for Family Credit, while at the same time increasing the numbers who faced a marginal effective tax rate in excess of 60 per cent. In addition, it was assessed on the joint income of a couple, implying that, as more families with children became eligible for it, work incentives for many potential second earners in couples (mostly women) were reduced.

CTC, which was introduced in 2003, was the largest change in support for children in the UK, since child benefit was first introduced in 1977. It merged several parts of the tax and benefit system that had previously supported families with children. Eligibility for the CTC, however, was not made contingent on work or active job-search. WTC extended an in-work benefit to adults without children for the first time.

New Labour also sought to make childcare provision more flexible and more affordable for working parents. It did this by expanding provision of childcare and by introducing a childcare tax credit. In this way, it provided a strong work incentive for many lone parents and, as noted above, this, together with the activation reforms, accounted for part of the strong rise in lone-parent employment rates over the period.[215] For couples with children, however, these tax and benefit changes tended to cut work incentives for many second earners.

The Freud report
By 2006, it appeared that the early successes of the key NDs were on the wane, and there was general agreement that the 'softly-softly' approach to disability benefit recipients was not working. In response to these concerns, Labour commissioned a series of reviews of its activation and welfare-to-work approaches,

---

214 In 1999, Tony Blair promised to eradicate child poverty 'within a generation'. This goal was then transformed into a target to halve the number of poor children from 3.4 million to 1.7 million in 2010. However, New Labour failed to meet this ambitious objective and it was later dropped before the 2010 election.
215 See Blundell et al. (2014) for a review of the evidence.

the most notable of which was undertaken by David Freud in 2007.[216] Freud proposed a major restructuring of the NDs and the benefit system. He called for job-search requirements and monitoring to be extended to lone parents (once the age of the youngest child was seven, as opposed to 16) and many disability benefit claimants. While he proposed not to shift the responsibility for activation of the short-term JSA claimants from JCP, he made the radical proposal that the long-term unemployed should be supported by private employment service providers operating under performance-based, long-term contracts, with larger outcome payments for sustainable employment results. This proposal drew upon the past experience with Employment Zones, but went much further in terms of scope and ambition.[217]

The Labour Government accepted some of the Freud proposals. These were encapsulated in the so-called Flexible New Deal that started to replace the NDs and the Employment Zones in 2009. In 2008, job-search requirements were extended to lone parents, initially to those whose youngest child was aged over 12, but by 2010 this age limit was dropped to seven. In addition, in 2008, Invalidity Benefit was replaced by the Employment and Support Allowance (ESA) for new and repeat claimants for disability benefits. During an initial 13-week assessment period, new ESA claimants were paid JSA and had to undergo both a work-capability assessment (WCA) (undertaken by a private contractor) and a work-focused interview. Those who were assessed as having some capacity for work were required to complete an Action Plan with a PA and to attend additional work-related interviews with more monitoring. Those who were assessed as having a significant disability were essentially exempted from activity requirements and received a benefit greater than JSA.

Faced with rising unemployment post-2008, however, and amid concerns voiced within its ranks about increased privatisation in the employment services market, Labour did not adopt the most radical of Freud's proposals. Freud had to wait until the Labour Government was defeated at the election in 2010 and replaced by the Coalition Government led by David Cameron.

---

216 Other reviews were conducted by Sandy Leitch and Paul Gregg.
217 Freud's proposals were also inspired, in part, by the Australian model of sub-contracting re-employment services to a network of private, for-profit and non-profit, providers who were paid by results. See OECD (2014a), Chapter 4, for details.

The Coalition's flagships: the Work Programme and Universal Credit

Prior to the election, the Conservatives had criticised Labour's strategy, highlighting the relative failures of the New Deals, especially NDDP/Pathways, and the weakening of work incentives for second earners through the myriad of tax and benefit changes. They embraced fully the radical proposal in the Freud Report and made it the centrepiece of their first flagship programme, the Work Programme.[218]

The Work Programme replaced around 20 previous welfare-to-work programmes. It involves private employment service providers or consortia who operate on a regional basis, with at least two prime contractors operating in each of the 18 regions in Great Britain. Prime contractors also rely upon a wide range of sub-contractors to deliver activation and reintegration services for jobseekers. The contractors are funded on the basis of pay-for-sustained job outcomes: they get an initial fixed fee for each client, a job-outcome fee and an additional fee for a longer-term sustained job. Fees are larger for more at-risk clients in an attempt to reduce the well-known 'cream skimming' effect. The providers enrol the young and long-term unemployed while a smaller JCP helps the short-term unemployed. The private providers were offered five-year contracts in order to entice a sufficient number to enter the market. Under these contracts, private providers are allowed a great deal of freedom to decide on personalised services to help their clients find work.[219] At the same time, DWP tries to spur competition between the prime contractors within each region by market-share shifts, transferring 5 per cent of client inflows, from the worst to the best performing provider, when the performance gap is significant.[220]

The second Coalition flagship – Universal Credit (UC) – is even more radical in its ambition.[221] It aims to unify all of the main means-tested benefits (with the exception of the Council Tax Benefit) into a single working-age benefit with a

---

218 Indeed, the Conservatives produced a political coup by recruiting David Freud to their cause from Labour. They made him a Peer subsequently and put him in charge of reform of the benefit system.

219 This so-called 'black-box' approach to service delivery is a significant difference between the Work Programme and its Australian counterpart, Job Services Australia, where the providers have to meet clearly specified quality targets in terms of the services delivered to their clients.

220 These market-share shifts are small and may do little to boost average provider performance. However, in March 2014, DWP terminated for the first time a contract because of poor performance by the prime contractor.

221 It is noteworthy that the main architect of Universal Credit is the current Secretary of State for Work and Pensions in the Coalition Government, Iain Duncan Smith, not the Treasury, which took a leading role under the Labour Government. He developed the blueprint for Universal Credit while in opposition.

generous earnings disregard and a single withdrawal rate (65 per cent) of the benefit unit's income in excess of the disregard. UC also involves major changes in benefit conditionality. Support for childcare through the benefit system will be made available for parents regardless of the number of hours they work – under the old system, they had to work at least 16 hours per week to qualify for support. The aim is to improve work incentives for most families compared with the current system. Universal Credit began a slow-rollout on a pilot basis in 2013 and is planned to be fully operational in 2018.

Universal Credit aims for a considerable simplification of the tax/benefit system. Simulations suggest that it will increase work incentives for many, but not all, families. Households in the bottom half of the earnings distribution should, on average, be better off, while those in the upper half may marginally lose out.[222]

Both flagship programmes, especially Universal Credit, are too recent to permit any *ex-post* evaluations of their effectiveness. The evidence so far with regard to the Work Programme suggests that some of the teething problems which dogged its introduction have been overcome and that provider performance has improved. The evidence also suggests, however, that current funding levels are too low, especially for the most at-risk groups. Attempts to activate more of the disabled into work have been particularly fraught with difficulties, with the key gatekeeping role of the WCA coming in for much public criticism. OECD (2014h) highlights the fact that the Work Programme providers do not find it easy to identify and provide effective support to clients with health-related problems, especially those with mental health conditions.

Universal Credit is also facing serious implementation problems, notably whether the information systems needed to produce real-time information on income will deliver effectively and on time. In addition, there is a major question mark as to whether the Treasury will provide the extra funding necessary to ensure that there are relatively few losers compared to the number of winners.

At the same time, the UK economy is now recovering and unemployment is falling, which makes the macroeconomic environment more favourable. It is also noticeable that the proportion of workless households between April and June 2013 was 17.1 per cent (3.5 million), the lowest rate recorded since comparable data on this phenomenon were first collected in the UK in 1996. This may be a good omen for further successes of the two flagship programmes, especially if teething problems with implementation and programme design can be overcome.

---

222 See OECD (2014h), Chapter 2 for a discussion of Universal Credit and its likely impact.

12.2.3 Conclusion

It should be clear from the above that there has been much continuity in labour market reforms in the UK irrespective of whether Labour, the Conservatives or the Coalition have been in power. All parties have been committed to intensifying activation of unemployment benefit claimants and, more recently, lone parents with young children. It has been much more difficult to apply activation strategies to many disability benefit claimants or to design and implement effective work-related approaches for this heterogeneous target group, many of whom suffer from mental ill-health. It remains to be seen whether the Work Programme will do better with this group than Labour's New Deal/Pathways to Work initiative.

It has proved very difficult to increase work incentives for many low-paid workers, especially for potential second earners in couples with children, because of the inherent complexity of the UK's tax/benefit system. The Coalition Government has tried to introduce a radical reform in this area with Universal Credit, but it represents quite a gamble and only time will tell if it pays off or not.

In the meantime, the UK economy faces a significant medium-term challenge regarding the underlying poor productivity performance, which is in need of improvement. Some of the labour market and tax/benefit reforms have probably contributed to this weak productivity performance by encouraging benefit recipients to take low-wage, part-time jobs with relatively poor career prospects. It will be important in the future for activation strategies in the UK to pay more attention to the need to upgrade skills of benefit recipients, in order to ensure that they can access jobs with career prospects.

Table 16: Scoreboard for labour market outcomes and policies, United Kingdom and EU, 1993–2013

	1993		2000		2007		2013*	
	UK	EU	**UK**	EU	**UK**	EU	**UK**	EU
1. Employment rate (% of the working-age population)	**69.4**	61.2	**73.4**	63.6	**74.0**	66.7	**73.8**	65.9
– male	**76.2**	71.8	**80.5**	72.9	**80.6**	74.2	**79.2**	71.6
– female	**62.7**	50.7	**66.5**	54.4	**67.5**	59.2	**68.5**	60.2
– youth (aged 15/16–24)	**58.8**	39.5	**61.5**	39.4	**56.5**	38.2	**48.8**	33.4
– older people (aged 55–9)	**58.7**	47.6	**63.2**	50.6	**68.9**	57.3	**72.5**	64.9
– older people (aged 60–4)	**33.9**	22.3	**36.1**	22.3	**44.6**	29.4	**46.1**	34.7
– older people (aged 65–9)	**9.8**	9.2	**11.2**	7.4	**15.2**	9.5	**20.4**	11.3
2. Unemployment rate (% of labour force)	**10.3**	10.8	**5.5**	8.9	**5.3**	7.1	**7.5**	10.7
– youth (aged 15/16–24)	**17.3**	21.0	**11.7**	17.4	**14.2**	15.5	**20.9**	23.3

Table 16 (continued)

	1993		2000		2007		2013*	
	UK	EU	**UK**	EU	**UK**	EU	**UK**	EU
3. Incidence of long-term unemployment (% of total unemployment) (a)	**42.5**	42.0	**28.0**	44.4	**23.7**	41.6	**36.3**	46.5
4. Part-time employment rate (b)	**22.1**	13.8	**23.0**	15.3	**22.9**	16.0	**24.5**	17.5
5. Temporary employment rate (c) (temporary employees as % of total employees)	**5.9**	10.5	**6.8**	13.1	**5.9**	14.8	**6.2**	14.0
– youth (aged 15/16-24 as % of total youth employees)	**9.9**	28.8	**13.2**	38.0	**13.3**	41.8	**14.7**	43.0
6. Low-pay incidence (d) (% of employees)	–	–	**20.4**	15.7	**20.5**	16.5	**20.6**	15.0
7. Protection of permanent workers against individual dismissal	**1.0**	2.6	**1.2**	2.5	**1.2**	2.4	**1.0**	2.2
– Protection of temporary workers	**0.3**	2.3	**0.3**	1.8	**0.4**	1.6	**0.4**	1.8
8. Public spending on labour market policies (% of GDP)	**1.5**	2.9	–	2.0	**0.5**	1.5	**0.5**	2.1
– Spending on active measures (e)	**0.4**	0.9	–	0.9	**0.3**	0.6	**0.2**	0.8
– Spending on passive measures (f)	**1.1**	2.1	**0.3**	1.1	**0.2**	0.8	**0.3**	1.3
9. Net benefit replacement rate (g) (averaged over four family types and two earnings levels)	–	–	**60**	65	**61**	61	**61**	54
– initial spell (h)	–	–	**60**	70	**61**	71	**61**	70
– after 2 years of unemployment	–	–	**60**	66	**61**	63	**61**	57

* 2013 or latest year available (2011 for data for public spending on labour market policies).
(a) Persons out of work for 12 months and over.
(b) Part-time employment refers to persons who usually work less than 30 hours per week in "their 'main job'".
(c) Temporary employees are wage and salary workers whose job has a pre-determined end date as opposed to permanent employees whose job is of unlimited duration. National definitions broadly conform to this generic definition, but may vary depending on national circumstances.
(d) Persons with a wage less than 2/3 of the median.
(e) 'Active' measures cover categories 1 to 7 of the OECD/Eurostat data base on public spending on labour market programmes.
(f) 'Passive' measures cover categories 8 and 9 of the OECD/Eurostat data base on public spending on labour market programmes.
(g) Data on net replacement rates for 2000 refer to 2001.

(h) Initial phase of unemployment but following any waiting period. For married couples, the percentage of AW relates to the previous earnings of the 'unemployed' spouse only; the second spouse is assumed to be 'inactive' with no earnings and no recent employment history. Where receipt of social assistance or other minimum-income benefits is subject to activity tests (such as active job-search or being 'available' for work), these requirements are assumed to be met. Children are aged four and six and neither childcare benefits nor childcare costs are considered. Unweighted averages, for previous full-time earnings levels of 67% and 100% of AW and out-of-work single and couple households with no children or with two children (children are assumed to be aged four and six and neither childcare benefits not childcare costs are considered). After tax and including unemployment and family benefits. Social assistance and other means-tested benefits are assumed to be available subject to relevant income conditions. Housing costs are assumed equal to 20% of AW.

Sources: OECD Online Employment Database: www.oecd.org/employment/database; data on net replacement rates come from the OECD tax-benefit models (www.oecd.org/els/social/work-incentives).

Chapter 3
Conclusion

In recent years, students of economics and political economy have produced a considerable body of theoretically and empirically informed literature concerned with establishing factors that make for successful labour market and social policy reforms in Europe and beyond. By providing the views of former European heads of government, all of whom bore ultimate responsibility for designing and implementing major labour market and social policy reforms, this book adds a high-level practitioner perspective to this body of literature.

Indeed, the semi-structured interviews with Wolfgang Schüssel (Austria), Anders Fogh Rasmussen (Denmark), Andrus Ansip (Estonia), François Fillon (France), Gerhard Schröder (Germany), Georgios Papandreou (Greece), Mario Monti (Italy), Jan Peter Balkenende (The Netherlands), Jerzy Buzek (Poland), Iveta Radičová (Slovakia), José Luis Rodríguez Zapatero (Spain) and Tony Blair (United Kingdom) offer intimate accounts of these 12 former heads of government on how they set out to reform labour market and social policies and what lessons they draw from their experiences. To put the interviews into context, the main part of this book gives background information of labour market developments in each country for the period from 1993 to 2014, as well as descriptions of the most important labour market and social policy reforms implemented since 2000.

The interviewees have different political backgrounds, led countries from different regions of the European Union and operated in different labour market models. Moreover, the constitutional positions of some of these heads of government differ significantly: while the French prime minister's power, for instance, is counterbalanced, and ultimately – in many policy domains – severely limited, by the President of the French Republic, the Italian prime minister who gave us an interview, Mario Monti, led a technocratic cabinet, having been invited by the Italian President to form a government; in other words, Mario Monti did not win an election to gain legitimacy.

Despite these differences among the interviewees, a set of common lessons can be drawn about how to design, implement and communicate LMBP reforms in a successful manner, as well as about how to overcome some policy makers' resistance towards embarking on programmes of structural reforms. Indeed, by adding the perspective of 12 high-level reform practitioners who were at the helm of their respective governments during times when some of the most significant LMBP reforms in recent European history were implemented, various factors that make for successful, or unsuccessful, LMBP reforms can be identified.

The Conclusion seeks to highlight the opportunities, challenges and problems in the policy area of labour market reforms and to establish under what conditions labour market reforms can be successfully advocated, adopted and implemented. Moreover, it aims to discover whether, and to what extent, practitioners' perspectives confirm or invalidate the empirical literature on the political economy of reform, as laid out in the Introduction. Accordingly, in providing an evaluation and assessment of the interviews, the Conclusion will follow the structure of the LISC model presented in the Introduction, which is based on the existing empirical evidence on the criteria for the success of labour market reforms:

– Legitimacy
– Implementation
– Stakeholders
– Communication

1 Legitimacy through domestic climate, external pressures and sound evidence

The vast majority of former heads of government interviewed for this book were elected on the promise of reforms, and they all agreed that an electoral mandate constitutes a key indicator of public approval of reform endeavours and hence a cornerstone for building legitimacy for LMBP reforms. As former Danish Prime Minister Anders Fogh Rasmussen puts it: 'All political processes start with seeking support from the electorate, the public. If you cannot get sufficient support from the public, or at least from your own electorate, it is difficult to get other political parties on board for your purposes. You therefore need to make a convincing case in public before you can reach an agreement in parliament.' **(p. 61)**.

In discussing the need for legitimacy, many interviewees noted that the government had to have credibility and that there had to be a sense of trust between the public and the reform stakeholders. The former Slovak head of government, Iveta Radičová, says: 'I am certain that the major factor for success, and under "success" I understand guaranteeing people's quality of life and human dignity, is trust – trust in institutions and also in productivity and the economy. Without that no Labour Code can solve any problem.' **(p. 260)** Former Austrian Chancellor Wolfgang Schüssel notes the importance of keeping undertakings given to allies: 'Concerning pension reform in general, it would have been preferable to calculate pensions on the basis of full lifetime salary contributions, instead of counting only the ten years of highest contributions or the ten years immediately preceding retirement. Nevertheless, I stuck to the compromise formula, although

I could have been more ambitious, which would have been better for Austria, but politically it was important to have most of the social partners on board.' **(p. 37)**

However, they also confirm the vital importance of the right domestic climate, external pressures, and sound evidence in bolstering the legitimacy of LMBP reforms.

1.1 Fiscal consolidation arguments are key to creating a domestic climate conducive to advocating and implementing LMBP reforms

Most interviewees offered fiscal consolidation as the primary justification for promoting the legitimacy of designing and implementing LMBP reforms. Wolfgang Schüssel, for example, states: 'Before 2000, Austria's budgetary performance was very poor and if the budget had not been reformed and stabilised, also by means of our reforms, we would now find ourselves in the same position as the so-called "crisis countries".' **(p. 34)**

Similarly, Gerhard Schröder declares: 'Another purpose of the reforms was to save money – which they did – and those savings could be invested in research and development, and also in education [...] These two goals, keeping the welfare state affordable and freeing up resources to invest in the future, were the motivation for Agenda 2010.' **(p. 127).**[223] In general, the interviews suggest that, particularly in the cases of Germany and the Netherlands, the implications of ongoing demographic change were at the heart of desires to consolidate budgets.

Among interviewees, Gerhard Schröder most forcefully declared that labour market performance served as a powerful justification for introducing LMBP reforms: '... what really prompted the Agenda was that unemployment was rising. It was approaching the five million mark, and we simply had to act – it would have been irresponsible not to.' **(p. 135)**

---

223 While the Agenda 2010 may have helped to consolidate the state budget over the longer term, it has to be noted that Germany failed to meet the Maastricht criteria for the public deficit from 2002 to 2005, consecutively.

1.2 External pressures play a key role in legitimising reforms all over Europe

Not surprisingly, the former heads of government from Southern Europe, in particular, stress the global economic crisis that started in 2008 as a catalyst for introducing LMBP reforms. José Luis Rodríguez Zapatero, for example, acknowledges that the international financial markets put strong pressure on Spain to reform: 'When the markets put pressure on our treasury to solve the country's sovereign debt problems, I made a great effort to have meetings with all big private investment funds in the world – at one meeting the funds represented were worth almost twice Spain's GDP [... They] asked about the unions in Spain, whether they were radical or willing to enter into alliances [...] The second question they asked me related to the sustainability of the Spanish pension system.' **(p. 280/281)** He also argues that the euro crisis put Spain into the firing-line and that Spain would not have reformed to the extent it did without this external pressure. A similar line of reasoning is pursued by Mario Monti: 'The President of the Republic was so deeply aware of the emergency that had prompted him to give birth to our government, that he allowed us to widely avail ourselves, with his authorization as required by the constitution in conditions of "necessity and urgency", of "decrees-law", the fastest and most powerful track for legislative measures to go into effect. So, the whole package of which the pension reform formed part (*Salva Italia*), was introduced through a decree-law.' **(p. 177)** Georgios Papandreou generally shares the view that a crisis can be a reform catalyst, but also warns that 'using the momentum of the crisis [...] worked up to the point, when the situation became too painful for the citizens'. **(p. 155)**

While certainly a temptation, the Italian Prime Minister refrained from using the external pressure for shifting the blame: 'On [pension] reform, like on all other reforms, I made the point of never saying to the public, or in parliament, that we had to accept these sacrifices because the EU wanted them. I never mentioned any external pressure. [...] I said: "Yes, the EU also asks for this measure, but we know that we need to do that first of all for our children".' **(p. 182)** Andrus Ansip has a similar view, when asked about the influence of the EU: 'All in all, the strongest argument we used when we made the case for change was that reforms were clearly in the interest of the Estonian economy and people.' **(p. 83)**

Greece stands out as an example where too much external pressure turned the reform climate from positive to negative very quickly. Georgios Papandreou states that 'after almost two years in government, we still had, I would say, a pretty good consensus, but then we realised that we would not be able to access the markets in 2012 and that we needed a new programme. This was the so-called Second Economic Adjustment Programme and we were aware that it would lead to new problems. We tried to frontload all the difficult measures, such as the reforms and the cuts. Then, after a year-and-a-half, in mid-2011, the IMF and the Troika approached us with the words: "Since you cannot access the markets we have to have another programme, and this will bring with it more cuts and further reforms." At that stage, the consensus became more volatile.' **(p. 156/157)**

However, the global economic crisis also prompted non-Southern EU member states to launch ambitious LMBP reforms. Anders Fogh Rasmussen notes: 'When we implemented the 2006 pension reform, we made every effort to get the broadest political support possible to ensure that the reform would not be reversed after the next election, in case we lost. In fact, in this particular case, the implementation of the pension reform was accelerated after a few years. The crisis helped at that time. So this example substantiates the well-known expression "Every crisis is an opportunity in disguise". We seized that opportunity.' **(p. 63)** Despite having headed the government of one of the most influential member states within the EU, the former French Prime Minister François Fillon admits without hesitation that 'what [...] moved us in 2010 to carry out new reforms and to increase the retirement age to 62 [...] was, again, the national deficit, of course, but it was mostly the pressure of the international markets: the risk of being downgraded by rating agencies. In addition, the European Union played an important role. In other words, the 2010 pension reform was primarily done to show the outside world that France was carrying out reforms. One year later, in 2011, the European sovereign debt crisis and the attacks on the European currency kicked in. In 2011, rating agencies exerted very strong pressure on France, and we were downgraded for the first time. We reacted, among other things, by taking a whole series of measures to reduce the deficit, some of which were tax increases, but also by accelerating the phasing in of the new retirement age.' **(p. 108)**

Significantly, when looking at reforms that were introduced before the 2008 financial crisis, concerns about being competitive in the face of increasingly integrated world markets were being mentioned much more frequently as drivers for reform than has been the case since 2008. As Gerhard Schröder, for example, explains in relation to the LMBP reforms he introduced starting in 2003: 'What did play an important role, however, was the fear of losing our ability to compete, which would have meant higher unemployment. We knew how dependent Germany is on exports and that inability to compete would have had serious consequences for Germany's business, which in turn would have affected employment.' **(p. 129/130)**

It is important to note that the former heads of government interviewed perceive international organisations as sources for comparative data and good practice and see their role as directing rather than triggering reforms. Anders Fogh Rasmussen, for example, suggests that in Denmark reports by international organisations have an impact within the political establishment, but do not serve as strong instruments to shape the debate among the general public: 'Within the political establishment, if I may use that expression, analyses and recommendations by international organisations are, of course, read, and they have an impact – they really do. On the other hand, when I go to my electorate, having the support of an OECD report is not, with the greatest respect, the strongest argument. When I talk to political colleagues, however, or when I speak with unions or representatives of what I call "the political and economic establishment", then such reports – whether from the OECD, the EU or any other international player – do of course have an impact, but they are not strong tools in shaping the debate with the general public. That is a hard fact.' **(p. 64)**

Two political leaders found referring to the Nordic countries especially helpful in conveying the positive aspects of their reform efforts. Thus, Andrus Ansip argues: '[W]e took account of the experiences other countries had had, especially the Nordic countries. Referring to the Nordic countrîes may have helped with the public perception of the reform.' **(p. 83)** While it seems hardly surprising that Estonia would look to Northern peers for inspiration for labour market and social policy reforms, it is interesting to note that also Italy took Denmark as a role model for its reform efforts. As Mario Monti points out: '[D]rawing on the Danish model also served as a good argument in parliament. Most members of parliament believed that the time had come to increase flexibility in the Italian labour market, but they were eager not to put stability too much at risk.' **(p. 184)**

Some former heads of government have even been critical of the very idea that international organisations may act as facilitators of LMBP reforms, rather suggesting the opposite. Thus, Iveta Radičová argues that during her term in office Slovakia received 'bad' advice from the IMF and the World Bank on the pace with which Slovakia should consolidate its budget: 'My government managed the second-highest consolidation of sovereign deficit in Europe at the time (Estonia was highest), from 7.7 to 4.8 per cent within one year. Can you imagine? And then I read in an IMF document that our course of action had been a mistake and that we should have proceeded with the consolidation more slowly. There was a similar reaction to the way we introduced the pension reform – "oh, sorry", they seemed to say, "a 9 per cent contribution to the defined-contribution pillar in the second year was perhaps a mistake: it's too high." "Come on!" was my response: "You cannot carry out experiments on us as if we were animals."' **(p. 258)** Thus, Radičová had to learn the hard way that, even when using external advice, national political leaders ultimately need to make their own assessment of the current situation and take their own decisions because they will be held responsible by the public for any of the reform outcomes. Indeed, she is very explicit when she says: 'I know that the only way to clear a deficit is through national reforms. Without the introduction of reforms, neither the EU nor any other international organisation can help – nobody can. Deficits are created at home, and so is productivity.' **(p. 259)** Furthermore she argues that '[t]he role of international organisations, and the impact of international pressure, should not be underestimated in the sense that they can give good arguments for the direction to take.' **(p. 259)**

While former heads of government may differ in their views on the utility of the role international organisations can play in facilitating LMBP reforms, they agree on the importance of looking beyond a country's borders to establish what good practice might look like. Radičová, for example, believes: 'The only thing we need in order to implement reforms are comparisons between different countries and models, sharing good practice with each other – and also bad practice – to avoid repeating the same mistakes.' **(p. 259)** Some heads of government even travelled to other countries with journalists (Wolfgang Schüssel) or union leaders (François Fillon) to facilitate learning through taking over good practice elsewhere.

1.3 Sound evidence is at the heart of any compelling justification of LMBP reforms

Interviewees underlined the value of externally produced evidence as a compelling justification of LMBP reforms. Iveta Radičová, for example, believes that, in relation to an unpopular reform to family benefits and childcare in 2004, in her words: 'In the end, knowledge and solid analyses helped me develop firm convictions about what was right.' **(p. 261)** Focusing more on the validation of reforms, Jan Peter Balkenende says: '[...] politics is about showing that your policy has worked, and measuring the results is therefore important.' **(p. 207)**

Some former heads of government interviewed highlight the importance of advice from independent bodies or commissions, when looking for unity over the questions of whether and how to do reforms. Zapatero sees the problem as follows: '[t]here is no agreement when it comes to diagnosing why we have so much unemployment in periods of crisis and why we create so much employment in periods of prosperity. There is no internal consensus on these questions.'

(p. 284) He calls for a round-table discussion to cure what he considers a disease.

Rasmussen's government, on the other hand, set up a 'welfare commission', whose sound arguments produced agreement between the government, the opposition and the wider public: '[...] we established a welfare commission consisting of independent members – that is people who did not have any connections to the government, but "free spirits", in particular from academia. That commission delivered a report in December 2005 with a number of very controversial suggestions. [...] The commission was harshly criticised at first, but over time it created some kind of platform for debate and provided room for manoeuver for my government.' **(p. 59)** Referring explicitly to his government's reform on the increase of the retirement age, Rasmussen notes: 'There was also a point when I thought about making substantial compromises on the content in order to get the support of the opposition parties. Eventually, the welfare commission was useful: backed up by their work, we approached the opposition and, because of the commission's sound arguments, we were able to reach a broad political agreement.' **(p. 63)**

Like Rasmussen, Tony Blair, too, alludes to the longer-term effects of commissions. Indeed, despite Blair wishing to implement some more radical labour market and social policy reforms, neither his party nor his successor in office, Gordon Brown, were willing to do so. It therefore fell to the coalition government led by David Cameron to implement these reforms, claiming that the reforms entailed an element of continuity with the reforms implemented under the previous conservative governments of the late 1980s and 1990s, although they were actually informed by commissions set up by the Blair government. Pointing to the proposals of the Turner Commission on Pension Reform Tony Blair states: 'I think they were pretty successful and formed a long-term basis for the UK pension system.' The other welfare proposals were wrapped up in the so-called Freud Report on the future of the welfare to work, on which Tony Blair, was, in his own words 'frankly, very keen'. He acknowledges: 'My successor was not so keen' but appreciates, that 'the present Conservative Government is now implementing many of those proposals.' **(all Blair quotes above p. 303)** The episode underlines that even if creating a commission is sometimes regarded as a government attempt to dilute responsibility and to avoid concrete reforms in the short term, it nevertheless helps to ignite and to broaden reform debates and it frequently sets the reform path for the longer term.

Some former heads of government also referred to commissions as 'depoliticisers' where especially longer-term issues can be analysed and sufficiently prepared in order to make them ready to enter the political debate. In this respect, for example, François Fillon explains that '[i]n 2000, the then government established a forum to which all relevant stakeholders were summoned to discuss the country's future pension reforms. The *Conseil d'orientation des retraites* allows us, every year, to take a clear and independent view on the current pension arrangements. This mechanism is very important in France, because there is a total lack of faith in political debates. [...] The *Conseil d'orientation des retraites* is made up of totally independent people: there are trade union representatives on it, as well as managers of pension funds, which makes it a forum that is respected by everyone. Nobody contests the annual reports made by the *Conseil*. It is an extremely helpful instrument to establish a broad consensus.' **(p. 103).** A major challenge, however, exists in translating results achieved by a commission into actual policymaking.

José Zapatero comes up with an interesting idea to institutionalise mutual learning: 'I think it would be good to establish some type of social and political "Erasmus exchange programme" for politicians, business people and similar groups, enabling them to learn from each other's experiences and best practice in policymaking. I participated in an ambitious US State Department programme, which could serve as a model. Young political leaders from around the world are invited for one or two months so that they can learn how the political and business systems work in the US – I think European countries should have such an exchange programme, too, to help everyone familiarise themselves with arrangements in other countries.' **(p. 282)**

Box 9. Creating legitimacy for LMBP reforms and implementing them poses a particular challenge in some of the newer EU member states

In the eyes of some former heads of government interviewed for this book, creating legitimacy for LMBP reforms appears to pose an even greater challenge in some of the newer EU member states than it does in the older member states. Iveta Radičová makes this point particularly forcefully when she explains: 'Democracies with a longer history can resort to stable pillars or institutions. In new democracies, the democratic institutions – and it does not matter if they are liberal or social – are not stable, as they are still developing. That is why there is so little trust in the legal system in Slovakia, and – as a consequence – in the state as a whole. This is a specific feature of countries in transition, in comparison with countries that also undergo changes in terms of their social fabric, but where the core institutions are clearly defined, functioning, independent and stable. I am talking about the courts of justice, for example the constitutional court and the office of public prosecutor, but also about the labour market and the social insurance agencies – in other words, institutions ordinary people consider to be "the state" because they determine their everyday life. In our country, the majority of people still perceive these institutions as totally negative, as consisting of "those who are against us, against the citizens".' **(p. 255/256)**

However, Radičová also stresses that implementing LMBP reforms in some of the newer EU member states is not only a particularly big challenge, because of a general lack of public trust in what state institutions do, but because of the need to reform other policy domains first, before meaningful LMBP reforms can be introduced. Referring to the case of Slovakia during her time as head of government, she explains: 'For Slovakia, as a transition country, reforming the labour market meant first of all enforcing the rule of law, creating conditions for entrepreneurship, creating space for innovations and fighting corruption – that is to say, changing the environment to make good labour market performance possible. This is why, for us, another crucial reform was the reform of the justice system. [...] the Labour Code can make a difference of about plus/minus 0.3 per cent as far as unemployment is concerned, nothing more. The Slovak Labour Code regulates the relations between employer and employee, and can improve employment figures marginally. However, it cannot help increase productivity; it cannot help with innovations; it cannot help increase investments; it cannot help create new jobs. To achieve this, there have to be good macroeconomic conditions and a favourable environment. On the other hand, if there is a rigid Labour Code, high taxation and no rule of law, then unemployment increases immediately. The specific combination of the different factors is crucial.' **(p. 256 and 257)**

2 Factors for successful implementation

The interviews with former heads of government confirm that there is no single right strategy for the successful implementation of public policy reforms. Rather, factors beyond the control of the stakeholders involved in reform implementation often play a decisive role. The success or failure of LMBP reforms, for example, seems often to be shaped by the existence or absence of a so-called 'reform ripeness'. Thus, individual LMBP reforms can be more easily pursued when they are part of a larger economic policy change, making them blend in with, rather than contradict, the grain of economic policy.

At the same time, successful reforms often benefit from preceding, smaller, piece-meal reforms or reform attempts. While some former heads of government seem less keen on highlighting this element of path dependency in implementing reforms and, instead, underline the novelty of their reform approaches, many of the country notes published in this book clearly highlight the importance of path dependency in implementing LMBP reforms. Indeed, Tony Blair explicitly acknowledges an element of continuity with the reforms implemented under the preceding Conservative Governments of the 1980s and 90s: 'The approach that we took was very much to keep in place the principal reforms that Mrs Thatcher had made, which were really to grant a legal framework within which trade unions operated: it recognised that unions had to operate according to certain legal principles that introduced provisions, for example, for ballots before strikes and for the election of union leaders by their membership.' **(p. 302)** For Wolfgang Schüssel, previous unsuccessful reform attempts paved the way for the implementation of his severance payment reform: 'In the 1997 to 2000 coalition, Chancellor Viktor Klima (SPÖ) was very much in favour of such a system. However, he was blocked by the unions and parts of his own party, and the business leaders were not very supportive either. The real debate started after 2000. The first step was a proposal for legislation by the ÖVP. This was rejected by other parties with the claim: "It is not enough, it is not fair enough." Then the social partners, especially the trade unions, stepped in, consenting to some aspects with proposals for changes. In 2002, we reached a compromise.' **(p. 37)**

2.1 Acknowledging path-dependency and creating the right eco-system is crucial for successful reforms

While few of the former heads of government explicitly elaborate on it, it becomes apparent from many interviews that a good idea for reform is not sufficient to achieve successful implementation. A sophisticated reform plan is necessary not just to envision the big picture, but also to get the details right. According to Tony Blair, 'it is essential to get the right analysis leading to the right policy prescription'. **(p. 307)** In addition, he counsels: 'You need to put the right systems of quality advice in place – which, by the way, can be advice from outside the traditional system as well as from inside – but put that in place right away, pay real attention to the structure you have around you as leader that allows you to get a proper grip on what reforms are necessary.' **(p. 307)** At the beginning of his second term, Blair set up two new policy units which included experts from outside the political system. One was the strategic policy unit looking at medium- and longer-term issues. The other was the delivery unit focusing on performance managing the government's priorities.

Failed reform attempts often demonstrate the importance of having a sound reform plan in place from the start. Explaining why his government failed on delivering the promise made in the 2007 election campaign to introduce a single employment contract, François Fillon rather openly admits that the reform was badly prepared: 'In a way, I also think we did not work hard enough to conceptualise the reform before we tried to launch it. We knew that we wanted a single contract – but the issue is not knowing *that* you want a single contract, it is knowing *what* you want to put into the single contract.' **(p. 100)**

Comprehensive reforms in specific areas tend to be more easily achieved if they are preceded by smaller reforms with similar goals paving the way for more substantial activities in the same areas. So it might be fair to speak about path dependency also from this angle. Examples include a lightweight reform on activation ('Job-AQTIV-Gesetz') before the Hartz reforms in Germany, labour market reforms of the early 1990s in Austria before the severance pay reform or Denmark's labour market reforms in the mid-1990s that provided the foundation for the subsequent reforms of Anders Fogh Rasmussen. Mario Monti states it explicitly: 'I think the sustainability of a reform depends on the extent to which you are able to root it in the grounds of a specific country and on what its visible effects will be over a number of years. [...] My government has worked quite a lot, not only to produce new measures, but also to put them in place, and to effectively implement measures decided by the previous government. Naturally, there were limits to that. There were a few decisions that we clearly could not accept [...].' **(p. 185)**

Georgios Papandreou points to the difficulties arising from a lack of institutional and administrative ability that is necessary to implement reforms: 'We did not have a well-managed public sector and there were certain difficulties with our governance. I think this is one of the problems Greece shares with some of the periphery countries: historically, we came out quite recently from under dictatorships and authoritarian regimes and we had highly politicised institutions that were often used for clientelistic purposes or for oppressing parts of our society. [...] The bureaucracy, the judicial system, the tax system and the public sector had not fundamentally adapted to the new political circumstances over the years. We did not have a *glasnost* or a *perestroika*; we did not have the Copenhagen criteria to become part of the European Union.' **(p. 153)**

2.2 Governments must start implementing LMBP reforms immediately upon election

Most heads of government point to the fact that the earlier governments embark on reforms during a term in office the more likely it is that they can harvest the fruits of their labour and create political capital with the electorate based on reform successes. Indeed, out of the 12 interviews only Gerhard Schröder waited for his second term in office to launch reforms. **(p. 128)**. However, it was not planned that way from the very beginning. Still profiting from the New Economy boom at the turn of the millennium, he announced the 'politics of the calm hand'. Only when the world economy came to a grinding halt in late 2001 did he realise that he had to take a more active stance.

The former Austrian Chancellor Wolfgang Schüssel states: 'The more you can agree on from the outset, the better things work out in the years thereafter; and the faster you start the reforms – at the very beginning of a legislative period – the easier it is. If half of the period is gone, negotiations become very difficult, because the next election overshadows everything.' **(p. 39)** Iveta Radičová suggests: '[i]f, reforms are not introduced immediately and radically, they never will be. You have to take a decision and then act on it. Otherwise you will only see something that is, more or less, far from the original concept.' **(p. 259)** Jan Peter Balkenende criticises a tendency of procrastination when it comes to implementing difficult reforms: '[f]rom time to time politicians feel that it is better to postpone some decisions. I would advocate the contrary; very often it is better to act swiftly and to put up with initial criticism **(p. 216)** [...] Waiting too long is never an option. One has to ask: "What will the consequences of the delay be?" Eventually, people will realise that waiting and postponing comes at the expense of future options – that is the point.' **(p. 217)** Reflecting on his government's failure to successfully introduce a single employment contract reform, François Fillon alludes to the problem of waiting 'for the right time': 'You have to understand that in 2008 we were getting to grips with the financial crisis, and we felt that this was not really the right time to introduce important social reforms. [...] We should have introduced this reform later, say in 2010 or 2011, but by then we were approaching the presidential election.' **(p. 100)**. However, politicians always find themselves in the trade-off between doing what is best for the country and taking care of their own prospects, and, as always in cases of high uncertainty, there may be a considerable advantage in waiting.

Finally, Anders Fogh Rasmussen puts it: 'One could actually say that when you want to implement reforms, the first step is to profit from the momentum created during an election campaign and following an election victory. It is, I think, a general experience that immediately after an election you have some opportunities. My advice would always be to grasp them.' **(p. 59)**

Asked about other reasons for implementing the reforms as quickly as possible, many former heads of government also mentioned the time it takes until a reform makes the first positive inroads, which means that reforms implemented at a relatively late stage of a government's term in office often come at the price of electoral defeat. As Gerhard Schröder explains: 'There's another reason why policymakers often fail to seek reform, and that is the gap between the time when a reform is initiated, with negative effects on certain groups, and its desired effect. Two, three, and sometimes even five years may pass before a reform shows a positive impact. This delay can spell defeat for democratically elected politicians. Believe me, I know what I am talking about. That is why – you see this in the current government – many people say: "Let's not rock the boat, things are running smoothly, we're in good shape. Let's rather do a pension reform because its negative consequences won't show up for another ten or fifteen years."' **(p. 131/132)**

While Mario Monti agrees with the view that governments should deal with important reform endeavours immediately after coming into power, he also has some qualifications: 'Generally speaking, as an election date approaches, the quality of reforms tends to go down and the difficulties tend to increase. But there are exceptions. As for our plans to fight corruption and tax fraud, in particular when perpetrated by members of parliament, we deliberately waited until close to the elections. We knew that it would become practically impossible for those affected to oppose the bill shortly before an election. [...] This teaches how the room of manoeuvre to make reforms can in fact be linked to forthcoming elections in two different, indeed opposite, ways.' **(p. 183)**

The former heads of government interviewed for the book failed to agree on the most opportune time for launching a reform package. Gerhard Schröder maintains that an 'economic upswing, when the economy is healthy and stable' **(p. 133)** constitutes the ideal time for tackling reforms, although his own government felt compelled to do the opposite: 'Normally, or rather ideally, significant reforms should be tackled during an economic upswing, when the economy is healthy and stable. That makes it much easier. We pushed the Agenda through at a time of crisis, and under such circumstances reforms can make the crisis worse.' **(p. 133)** Rasmussen points out that, in contrast, the crisis in 2008 and 2009 created the right conditions for the Danish government to embark on reforms: 'Actually, it is not easy to introduce reforms when the economy is flourishing, when you are in an economic upturn; you do not have a "burning platform" then and this makes it more difficult to move forward on reforms.' **(p. 58)**

Politicians involved in coalitions agreed on the need to be precise and clear about the aims and content of an envisaged reform package when negotiating potential co-operation, in order to prevent disputes or conflicts at a later stage. As Wolfgang Schüssel, for example, points out: 'In Austria we have a tradition of long and painstaking negotiations for a coalition treaty [...] Some of my "friendly" opponents and fellow negotiators complained about me, saying: "He is so precise, he negotiates everything in detail."' **(p. 39)** Tony Blair supports this view and stresses the need not to just start with a general reform idea, but to know about the necessary ingredients beforehand as well, 'because otherwise you could end up having "a sort of general idea of reform", leaving the details more or less to the system to work out. You just say something along the lines of: "OK, well, this seems like a good reform, let's go with it." In fact, what you realise after a time is that the detail really matters.' **(p. 307)**

2.3 Government cohesion is vital but can be brought about by different leadership approaches

All interviewees emphasise the paramount importance of governments speaking with one voice during the course of implementing LMBP reforms. In particular, they point to the value of government cohesion to prevent the opposition from exploiting frictions. For example, Jerzy Buzek states that 'Ensuring endorsement for changes by one's allies is extremely important. [...] However, reaching a consensus was not very difficult, as both coalition members had openly informed the public about their intentions to introduce the necessary reforms.' **(p. 233)** Gerhard Schröder talks about the difficulties his government faced in gaining public approval for Agenda 2010 because they had not obviously been at one: 'The criticism from our own people obviously made it easier for the opposition to discredit our reforms than if we had presented a united front.' **(p. 130)** Similarly, Jan Peter Balkenende notes with regard to the issue of reforming employment protection legislation: 'If my government had spoken as of one voice on this issue, I am sure that we would have been able to push it through. In any case, I have drawn one lesson from this episode: be absolutely explicit in your coalition agreement. I think that was the mistake we had made. The agreement was not clear enough.' **(p. 212)** Andrus Ansip corroborates this view: 'Good leadership is about winning consent for sure. It has been a rule in all my cabinets to take decisions unanimously. Sometimes it took dozens of meetings to get somewhere; sometimes it took a change in the coalition. **(p. 83)** [...] As for the policies we introduced, the trust in the government of Estonia and the outcome of the elections speak for themselves.' **(p. 84)**

Mario Monti's answer to the question about government cohesion is simply 'very important indeed.' **(p. 181)** He goes on emphasising the importance of having a common understanding with key actors: '[...] it was essential for my government's effectiveness in tackling economic and financial emergencies that there should be total harmony between the Prime Minister and the Minister of Economy and Finance.' **(p. 181)** Again, Italy was a special case at that time, because – after the fall of Silvio Berlusconi – Mario Monti presided over a technocratic government, which had never gone through a national election. There had been no campaign and no manifesto that had asked for support on LMBP reforms: 'My government was born out of an emergency, with personalities whom I had a wide discretion to select and submit to the President of the Republic for nomination.' **(p. 181)** However, it was not too dissimilar to the Lamberto Dini government of the mid-1990s, which was also technocratic in nature and which had managed to introduce major systemic pension reforms.

The interview with François Fillon underlines the difficulty of implementing major LMBP reforms in semi-presidential systems, where the Prime Minister and the President often compete over thought leadership in the political debate. Thus, Fillon elaborates on the way in which disagreement between his government and the Élysée posed a constant challenge to his ability to implement reforms: 'Between 2007 and 2012, when I was Prime Minister, the difficulties came from President Sarkozy, who, after having announced that there were going to be some profound changes, in reality did not support any substantial change. In my view, there are two reasons for this. The main reason was, I think, that he was really afraid strong opposition forces would develop in French society. He was frightened of all sorts of public protest. The second reason was that he was a man who always wanted to do everything himself, on his own. He would, for example, speak directly to the trade unions, bypassing the Prime Minister and the government. I think that this was a very bad course of action, because when the President of the Republic holds direct talks with trade unions, there is no exit route – no way to escalate. Once the talks have taken place, you are stuck with the result! Whereas if a minister conducts the talks, he or she can be overruled by the Prime Minister, and if it is the Prime Minster, he can be overruled by the President. President Sarkozy, however, did not understand that.' **(p. 106)** Fillon blames Nicolas Sarkozy in even stronger terms for the failure of one of his government's main reform endeavours when he says: 'I think in 2010 we should have decided on a legal retirement age of 65 instead of 62 only – that is for sure. I do not think there would have been a single additional demonstrator on the streets. President Sarkozy, however, was not tough enough, despite what you might have heard. A lot of people think of him as very hard, but I believe that he was quite consensual, and he was worried about his re-election. The problem is that Sarkozy, in his role as President, was inexperienced in dealing with the trade unions. He held discussions with the union leaders in the way one would do with political partners – he believed that he could "score points" against them. As a lawyer, he thought that he would be able to persuade them by force of character, but experience shows that syndicalism just does not work like that. It is not about personalities, but it is essential to consider serious sociological factors. In the end we did not raise the retirement age to 65, which I regret now.' **(p. 101/102)**

Anders Fogh Rasmussen also points to the particular challenges that maintaining government cohesion over reform implementation which leadership of a coalition government can pose: '[... t]his cohesion proved crucial [...] the opposition would not have hesitated to exploit these frictions within the coalition. You have to demonstrate unity within the government, show clear leadership and set the course. That is a prerequisite, I think, for carrying through reforms. There are, of course, always certain limitations: in a coalition, each party wants to stand out, to demonstrate to their electorate that they are a bit more advanced or that they have a firmer position than the other party. Another limitation in my case was the fact that in all my three terms in office, I had to lead minority governments which depended on the right-wing Dansk Folkeparti.' **(p. 61)**

As implied in Rasmussen's statement, all former heads of government highlight their own vital role as leaders of a (coalition) government in ensuring government cohesion. However, their statements stress that individual leaders pursue different approaches to creating cohesion. Thus, some appear to favour a bottom-up approach, while others prefer a top-down style of government management. Advocating a bottom-up model, Wolfgang Schüssel notes: 'A lone wolf is not a good leader. Leading is more about establishing a team – dedicated to a specific project and flanked by a group of experts, themselves armed with facts, studies and images.' **(p. 44)** Jerzy Buzek argues in a similar way: 'The key point is that this leadership must be modern in character, based on team-building, dialogue and communication, and not on imposing one's own opinion.' **(p. 240)** Jan Peter Balkenende emphasises that, in the Netherlands political leadership generally means involving all stakeholders in a consensus-oriented manner, based on the tradition of the Polder Model. He also emphasises that 'leadership is about sound analysis of socio-economic developments, long-term thinking, generating new ideas, giving hope for the future, seeking cooperation with all stakeholders in the tradition of the Dutch Polder Model and listening to young people'. **(p. 215)** This resonates with Rasmussen, who outlines an idea of leadership that envisaged winning consent from all stakeholders. Similarly, François Fillon argues that leadership 'could perhaps also be about transcending the narrow boundaries of Left and Right'. **p. 108)**

In contrast to the proponents of a bottom-up model, Gerhard Schröder says: 'I think [implementing reforms] is only possible from the top down, rather than from the bottom up. Why? Take a look at how democratically elected governments work. If you try to set a process in motion from the bottom up, with the ultimate decision preceded by a long, drawn-out discussion, then the question is whether this will yield an acceptable result, or whether the issue will simply be talked to death.' **(p. 131)** He certainly draws on his own experience with the German Alliance for Jobs. Over the course of three years, this was an attempt to reach a tripartite agreement on substantial labour market reforms between trade unions, employers' associations and the government. After not having yielded significant results, the Alliance for Jobs was replaced by the Hartz Commission in 2002 and the government adopted an approach with more emphasis on top-down arrangement.

Despite their different views on how to create government cohesion in an effective way, Schröder and his fellow former heads of government agree that leadership is about being willing to risk an electoral defeat: 'You cannot expect a politician to lose an election deliberately. I understand this – I did not want to either. However, political leadership today means being willing to risk losing an election, if the country's future is on the line. Ultimately, the question is not whether someone will voluntarily give up public office or pursue a policy that is sure to produce the same result; you cannot expect that. It is really about whether there comes a time when a government has to say that this is necessary. If it means losing the next election, then that is the price that has to be paid for holding a position of national responsibility.' **(p. 132)** Statements similar to the one by Schröder were made by François Fillon, Georgios Papandreou, Anders Fogh Rasmussen and Wolfgang Schüssel.

Indeed, some heads of government even challenge the very notion that policymakers responsible for tough and painful reforms can ever be re-elected, unless at least some benefits of reforms become visible before the next elections. In this respect, Jan Peter Balkenende notes that his government's 2006 election victory was largely a result of people's admiration for his reform agenda: 'In the summer of 2006, after a long period of criticism by journalists, academics and the public, the mood started to change. People began to say: "We have criticised that Balkenende II government, but we have to admit that the choices they made were necessary." Then the criticism changed into a kind of admiration for what we had managed to do. That was the reason, in fact, why the Christian Democrats won the elections in 2006, after years when we were always second in the polls.' **(p. 216)** In contrast, Iveta Radičová and José Luis Rodríguez Zapatero outline the difficulties reforming governments face when they strive to be re-elected before reform results become visible. Thus, Radičová notes: 'I do not know if I would go so far as to say that my government lost power because of the reforms we introduced, but I am very near to saying it. I just have to remind myself of the social stratification and the lack of trust among the population in Slovakia. [...] One of the main reasons why it is so difficult to keep the majority in parliament after introducing reforms is that the results of the reforms only become visible much later.' **(p. 260)** Drawing on his own experience, Zapatero emphasises that reform governments cannot win re-election 'if there is a major crisis. [...] I think that a crisis of the type Spain and other European countries had to face in recent years, bringing with it such extensive reform attempts, will cause two or three governments to step down. Citizens vote for changing governments to see if things will change.' **(p. 287)** Regarding the labour market, however, most international observers, for instance from the OECD, state that the Zapatero government has not been very engaged in pushing through substantial reforms. Tony Blair took a very different approach: 'In the hundred years of our history, Labour had never won two full terms before; and my government won three, basically – in my view – because this was our position.' **(p. 303/304)**

Jan Peter Balkenende and Mario Monti both allude to the fact that their careers outside politics had helped them to be more courageous when it came to the implementation of reforms. As Balkenende puts it: 'I think my background was rather helpful, when it came to the rules of the political game. Most prime ministers had been a minister first, but I became prime minister "out of nowhere". My background was in academia – I was working with the think tank of my political party and was professor at the Free University Amsterdam. I believe this was an advantage: I came to politics with very strong convictions about the long-term prospects for our society. What kept me busy, in fact, was not all the criticism I had to face, but the question of how we could make the Netherlands stronger and what was needed in the long run.' **(p. 208)**

Finally, it is important to bear in mind that leaders are also human beings, subject to normal emotions and moments of weakness. For example, some former heads of government allude to the need to be ready to survive moments of savage criticism or isolation. Jan Peter Balkenende remembers the moment when his reforming government came under fire, with the biggest of many demonstrations at the Museum Square in Amsterdam: 'I had to stay in hospital and was confronted with huge criticism, not only from the collective bargaining parties, but also from the media.' **(p. 209)** Wolfgang Schüssel recalls a feeling of loneliness in the midst of a party convention: 'I sat at the party convention, my wife next to me, listening to 50 or 60 different speakers, intervening personally several times. I defended my reform proposal and was harshly criticised, especially by union members, but I stuck to the reform agenda.' **(p. 43)**

3 Consultation and compensation – important issues in stakeholder management

The interviews with former heads of governments clearly underline that failure to build alliances in support of LMBP reforms is the single most important reason for the failure of the reforms. Indeed, one of the most important lessons interviewees have learned from unsuccessful reform attempts is that major reform efforts are unlikely to succeed in the face of strong opposition. As Jan-Peter Balkenende puts it, rather soberly: 'I think there is only one issue that we could not carry out, and that was the issue of employment protection legislation. It was not possible to introduce a significant reform in this field because of the unions and the political opposition.'**(p. 203)** Commenting on his government's failure to deliver on the promise made in the 2007 election campaign to introduce a single employment contract, François Fillon admits that perhaps they were 'not courageous enough' in the face of fierce opposition from the unions. Similarly, he stresses that his government failed on the reform to introduce the *revenue de solidarité active*, the so-called RSA and on raising the retirement age to 65, because of what he describes as President Sarkozy's lack of courage to face the opposition. Other interviewees did not even take the risk of learning from unsuccessful reform endeavours. Instead, they mention that they would have also liked to implement reforms in areas other than the one they had originally targeted, but that it had been clear from the outset that any attempt to do so would not have been successful because of severe opposition from those who might, potentially, have lost out through the reform.

Some former heads of government therefore suggest that it is important to 'pick your battles', stressing that reform ventures are carefully chosen at an early stage in the life of a government. The point is made particularly well by Anders Fogh Rasmussen, when he explains why his government did not take on reforms to halt the trend rise in disability pensions and the high rates of sickness absence: 'The main reason why it was not at the top of our agenda was not necessarily that we did not feel the need or urgency to get a substantial part of the working-age population off these benefits, but that there was very strong resistance from all kinds of stakeholders. Sometimes, you do what you can do. It is very similar to the tasks I faced during my time as NATO Secretary General: you have to select your battles carefully.' **(p. 58)**

3.1 The usefulness of compensating those losing out from reform is highly disputed

Most interviewees agree that, to avoid vocal factions to sway public opinion in a way that hampers reform efforts, governments must engage with parties negatively affected by reforms and offer compensation. However, they also agree that any form of compensation must be temporary. In addition, they suggest that compensation should only be granted to specific, clearly defined groups. This can, of course, prove rather difficult at times. As the former Austrian Chancellor Wolfgang Schüssel states: 'I always argued in favour of granting exemptions to groups of workers with known low life expectancy, if it was possible to establish who these groups were, but if there was a feeling that this was simply a pretext for a general reduction in the retirement age, I thought we should resist.' **(p. 38)** Iveta Radičova expressed the same view.

Significantly, in Anders Fogh Rasmussen and Gerhard Schröder we have former heads of government fundamentally opposed to the idea of any form of compensation for those losing out from a reform. Schröder states that compensation 'has little to do with practical policy' **(p. 137)** and Rasmussen says: 'Regarding compensation, our reaction was: "Yes, we will cut your benefits, but in exchange we will give you a job or an education." That is the essence of the concept of active labour market policies.' **(p. 64)** However, the interview with Rasmussen also suggests that there might be indirect forms of compensation that can be offered in lieu of more straightforward ways. Thus, extended periods of transition for the introduction of pension reforms, as implemented in Denmark, can be regarded as a special type of compensating the losers, as they enable the younger age cohorts to adjust their life plans gradually according to the reforms introduced, while those who would suffer the most from an immediate implementation, the cohorts close to retirement, will not be affected at all by the reform. Tony Blair boils it down to the following point: 'I am going to reform it for future claimants. But I cannot touch past or existing claimants.' **(p. 307)** While addressing the same issue, the government of Jerzy Buzek took a different approach: 'As far as the compensation mechanisms are concerned, our reform included bridging pensions, which were finally also implemented. The bridging pensions were intended for those who might have lost the right to early retirement through the reform, but who had worked in conditions which could, according to current medical advice, justify earlier withdrawal from the labour market.' **(p. 237)**

Instead of directly compensating those who suffer a negative impact, Tony Blair proposes trying to find allies within their ranks who are more open-minded: 'You have got to have agents of change. Since the change is usually hotly contested, it is far better to have the voice of someone working within the system than a politician. [...] In addition, there are some trade unions on the more moderate side, who would say: "Look, what we have got to do as trade unions is adapt to the new world; it is right that we do. This is better for the long-term interest of our members."' **(p. 306)**

3.2 Consultation is seen as a key means to ensure that reforms are implemented and sustainable

Most interviewees stress the overall importance of consulting major stakeholders, and in particular union representatives, to ensure the widest possible approval of reforms. Jan Peter Balkenende, for example, notes: 'There must always be room for compromise, for adjustments. That is, in fact, a key element of democracy. Democracy is not only a matter of having the majority; it is also about listening to the minority, and this is part of the whole political game. We have always shown a great willingness to listen. If, for instance, we had said: "We have the majority in parliament in the second and first chamber, so we can do whatever we want" – if that had been our approach, we might, I think, have achieved some results. It would, however, have led to enormous difficulties later on, because you also need union support in the planning of long-term strategies. I do not think it is very wise to focus on implementing reforms that are currently on your agenda just because you have a majority, without taking account of all the other elements.' **(p. 210/211)**

While not being embedded in an environment with a similar tradition of social dialogue as his Dutch counterpart at the time, François Fillon explains: '[...w]hat we mainly tried to do, or what I tried to do as Minister of Labour and Social Affairs, and then as Prime Minister, was to relaunch a social dialogue in France. We wanted to normalise the debate between the collective bargaining parties in the way other European countries operate. France does, after all, have a very weak and conflict-based tradition of social dialogue.' **(p. 98)** Estonia, which did not have a long-standing tradition in the area, started with comprehensive consultations, when Andrus Ansip initiated his labour market reform: 'This was a legislative process where all stakeholders were involved right from the beginning. The consultations lasted for a year and eventually the main principles of the new law were laid down in a tripartite agreement between employers, employees and the government. Such a refined and inclusive legislative process had not been too common in Estonia before.' **(p. 82/83)**

Of course, consultation with the social partners and social dialogue can take on various degrees of intensity and influence on policymaking depending on the country-specific traditions and the level of 'institutional embeddedness'. Jerzy Buzek provides a telling case with a new legal framework for the Tripartite Commission, consisting of representatives of government, employers and trade unions: 'My government took the decision to put in place its legal framework by introducing legislation on the Tripartite Commission for Socio-Economic Issues. Until then, its work had been regulated by a government decree. With the new law, we furnished the Tripartite Commission with binding rights, which obliged the government and the public administration to consult it on all draft laws, including the draft budget, as well as demands that the Tripartite Commission agrees on salary increases for public administration, minimum wage levels, as well as pension increases.' **(p. 238/239)**

Many heads of government also agreed that engaging in consultation processes with the most important stakeholders is key to ensuring the sustainability of a reform. Asked about measures which needed to be taken to ensure that a reform lasts, François Fillon said: 'My initial response would be to strengthen social dialogue. If a reform is backed by a broad social consensus, it is very difficult for any successor government to return to that subject.' **(p. 109)** Anders Fogh Rasmussen states: 'The best recipe to ensure a reform's sustainability is the establishment of wide-ranging political consensus. In fact, we are talking about reforms that are supposed to yield long-term effects. When we implemented the 2006 pension reform, we made every effort to get the broadest political support possible to ensure that the reform would not be reversed after the next election, in case we lost.' **(p. 63)**

However, former heads of government do not only see consultation with key stakeholders as a vehicle for ensuring the legitimacy and sustainability of reforms, but also, as Wolfgang Schüssel emphasises, as a rational and calculated means to prevent what could turn into costly strikes. **(p. 37)** In a similar vein, the former heads of government of Austria, Denmark and Spain stress the importance of maintaining healthy personal relations with union representatives as part of the wider game of successfully governing a country.

Nevertheless, Jan Peter Balkenende also points to limits concerning cooperation with the unions. He suggests that 'there must also be a moment when, after listening to the opposition, you have to proceed, because time is limited. You have to be determined to forge ahead, do things quickly and speed up matters against the background of criticism. You must not let the unions take you hostage; if they develop unacceptable positions – let us say because their plans are too expensive or too narrow in their focus – there can be a moment when you, as the head of government, say: "Well, in that case this is it."' **(p. 211)**

For reasons that resonate with the arguments put forward by Schüssel and Balkenende, some former heads of government, namely Gerhard Schröder and Iveta Radičová, question the importance of reaching consensus with social partners in a much more fundamental manner. Radičová, in particular, seems to attach little or no importance to dialogue with the social partners because 'The Slovak Labour Code is indeed an ideological and political instrument – part of the dramatic performance and under its spell, so to speak, as well as a symbol of the fight between entrepreneurs/employers and the trade unions/employees. From 2001 onwards, successive governments have made changes and carried out reversals to the Labour Code. Left-oriented governments, because of their official agreement with trade unions, usually change the Labour Code according to the requests of trade unions when they are in office. My government had no agreement with the trade unions, none at all. Our intention was never to play on either side but to increase wages and to increase the number of jobs.' **(p. 263)** Indeed, Radičová seems to regard both unions and employers as obstacles to reform, which may reflect the specific circumstances of Slovakia as a transition economy, where the old Communist-era unions were part of the state apparatus and where there was no genuine employer confederation.

Tony Blair alludes to specific issues which make trade unions tough to deal with. This could also help explain why the leaders' discussions of stakeholder considerations focus much more on trade unions than on employers' associations: 'The unions are a very, very difficult factor. [...They] tend to defend their interests extremely strongly. Many people in progressive politics consider the unions a political movement, but they are, of course, also an interest group. Distinguishing between those two things is terribly hard sometimes.' **(p. 306)** Mario Monti has a nuanced view and thinks the need to consult trade unions depends on the specific content of the specific reform – core labour market issues or associated systems: 'If it is about changing labour contracts, I think it is important to come to an agreement – or at least an understanding – with the social partners. If it is more about the accompanying safety nets, provided largely by public finance, the consent of social partners may be less important. [...] I would also say that when a reform is made because of a macroeconomic problem, such as taking away indexation, it could be very helpful that decisions are taken with a high degree of centralisation. However, if a reform is, for example, made to introduce a more disperse and decentralised correlation between productivity and wages, then a more decentralised decision-making process is preferable.' **(p. 180)**

For the case of Italy, he has a particular concern: 'I think Italy has always been one of the countries in Europe with excessive consultation processes and where the unions have been having, until recently, a somewhat unhealthy political relevance. In 1970 a government (led by Prime Minister Mariano Rumor) even felt the duty to resign because the unions had declared a general strike. It is quite unorthodox, in my view, that the life of a government should not be decided in parliament, but rather suspended on a peculiar "vote of confidence", or "non-confidence", expressed by one group within the population, dependent workers and their organisations.' **(p. 181)** Zapatero expresses similar views: '[...] [I]f a reform meets open, determined, firm and unified opposition from the unions, the government's actions lose their legitimacy. Resistance by the unions substantially reduces the political power of reform processes, at least in Spain. The unions may not be important actors at the opinion-making stage, but they are important actors when it comes to invalidating reforms they do not like – that is the reality.' **(p. 283)**

Gerhard Schröder appears to reject any calls for engagement with social partners as it would resonate rather uneasily with his top-down approach to implementing reforms. These are his words: 'In my experience, if you are trying to carry out an ambitious programme of reforms that are sure to cause difficulties for certain groups, including those that might be expected to support you, your party, the unions, your coalition partners – you are unlikely to succeed, if you start off by engaging in a broad-based debate, with every minor aspect of reform being endlessly discussed and picked apart. You therefore cannot simply say to your party and the unions: "Let's discuss what needs to be done." The result will always fall far short of what is needed.' **(p. 131)**

4 Crucial communication in various arenas

The interviewees confirm the vital importance of communication in successful reform implementation. However, they largely agree that a strong narrative is at the heart of a successful communication campaign, they are divided in their opinions on the way in which stakeholders should be engaged, with some suggesting a catch-all approach, while others are in favour of a focused strategy. Many have also had the depressing experience that it can be much more difficult to communicate the link between a reform and its benefits, even *ex post*, than to establish the connection between a reform and its costs. They therefore have little to say about how to communicate the virtues of reforms effectively to mobilise those who actually benefit from the reforms from an early stage.

4.1 A strong and simple narrative is decisive with regard to successfully implementing reforms

Those interviewed for this book believe that communicating a reform is first and foremost about building a strong narrative. As the former Dutch Prime Minister Jan-Peter Balkenende puts it: '[... i]t is key to build a strong narrative. We based our argument on the need to safeguard public services for future generations. Time after time, we emphasised the threat of demographic change. We stressed that remaining on the same path would slowly erode our public services, that we needed to do things differently in the interests of our children and our children's children.' **(p. 206)** For Tony Blair a similar argument was one reason for the success of New Labour: '[...] it was obvious to people that the world had changed, that you could not have the policies of the 1970s back.' **(p. 303)** And he said subsequently: '[...] if the world around you is changing fast, you have to change, too.' **(p. 304)**

Indeed, Balkenende rather accurately describes what European heads consider a 'strong narrative': it should suggest that the envisaged reforms will contribute to the building of a brighter future for everybody and make clear that any disadvantages resulting from the implementation of reforms would only be temporary in nature and result in a greater public good and a better society, however that may be defined, later on. As Balkenende notes: 'Conceptualising and carrying out reforms is about making clear why the reforms are necessary: be it for financial, demographic or any other reasons. However, hope must also be an aspect: make it clear that the changes you advocate will eventually lead to higher labour participation and will create more chances for people. It is always important to spell out that it is not only a matter of reducing services but also building up something new. If it only involves taking away services without giving hope, then I can imagine people will lose trust – it is therefore important that your view of the future includes hope.' **(p. 213)** Tony Blair's words resonate with that: 'Look, there are positive things happening as well with what you regard as negative.' **(p. 307)** He calls the combination of positively and negatively perceived reform elements a 'centre-ground approach'. '[... y]ou had to have flexibility in your labour market. On the other hand, you also had to have certain guaranteed basic rights for people.' **(p. 303)** This could be viewed as the British variant of flexicurity, a notion that is implicitly or explicitly visible in every interview.

While heads of government may consider a strong and simple narrative decisive with regard to successfully implementing reforms, the interviews underline that unsuccessful reform attempts also require their own rather specific narratives, which can ameliorate potential political damage. Thus, one of the more prominent lessons heads of government seem to have learned from unsuccessful reform attempts is to blame another party for any failure. Thus, François Fillon seems to blame the French President for blocking his reform agenda, while Iveta Radičová holds international organisations responsible for reform failure. **(p. 259)** Jan-Peter Balkenende, in turn, identifies unreliable political partners, namely his coalition partners, the Social Democrats, as responsible for the failure of reform endeavours **(p. 211)**

4.2 Heads of government see as much merit in adopting a catch-all communication approach as in targeting specific audiences, such as young people or the unions

Former heads of state and government agree that one of the key problems connected with the implementation of LMBP reforms is the mismatch between the general acceptance of the need for reforms and the lack of acceptance of the personal costs they will bring. Thus, citizens tend to appreciate the need for reforms and their potential for long-term improvement of the economy and the greater public good, but they are less keen on suffering from any adverse effects stemming from reform efforts in the short term. This point is made particularly clearly by Jan Peter Balkenende, when he notes: 'Generally [...] it is very difficult to explain the benefits of reforms at a micro-level. Four years after you have embarked on a reform package, or even sooner, there will be a general election. In the Netherlands, when you ask people whether they are satisfied with their lives, about 85 per cent reply "yes". However, if you ask people whether they are satisfied with The Hague – with politics – everybody is very critical. That is a strange situation, because there must be a kind of link between decision-making in The Hague and your personal life, but people do not feel that way. When you present a cohesive, convincing analysis, people will admit: "Yes, I understand that we have to do something, but not now and not for me." That is the big problem.' **(p. 213/214)**

In light of the difficulties of translating abstract public support for reforms, in general, into very tangible support for a specific reform endeavour, the interviewees underline the importance of seeking appropriate channels for communicating reforms. However, they also point to the problems that may arise from reform messages being channelled through potentially biased media. Gerhard Schröder therefore argues that it would be ideal for any European head of government engaged in the implementation of LMBP reforms to be granted more direct TV time **(p. 134)**, providing the opportunity to reach as many citizens as possible and thus effectively pursuing a catch-all communications approach. Indeed, Schröder suggests: 'I have always wished that I could have had 45 minutes of airtime on television, once a week after the evening news, to explain to people why all of this was necessary. That was, unfortunately, not possible, though. The problem with what we call "political communication" – informing the public about our policies – is that it takes place through the media, except during election campaigns. [...] And, as a politician, you are not able to do that to the extent you would like, since the journalists' perspective always finds its way into the message. That is how it is in a democracy.' **(p. 134)**

Wolfgang Schüssel echoes some of Schröder's sentiments, but he points to the even more fundamental challenge of disseminating government reform messages more generally. Referring to the difficulty of communicating a reform and its aims to the wider population, Schüssel notes that one aspect of his communications strategy had been quite interesting: 'Before my term, the Chancellor and Vice-Chancellor used to hold separate press conferences after the weekly cabinet meeting. As Chancellor, I always gave a joint press conference with my coalition partner, Vice-Chancellor Riess-Passer. Immediately after the cabinet meeting we explained to the press what had been discussed, what had been decided, and we explained purpose and content. Everything was open for questions. This was completely new: open communication where everyone knew that questions were welcome and would be answered. As a result, the press had to write about our ambitions even when they were sceptical. Some journalists were often critical, but they had to write about our plans and decisions. By the way, even the present government has kept this tradition.' **(p. 41)**

In contrast to Gerhard Schröder and Wolfgang Schüssel, the other heads of government interviewed for this book, appear less concerned with reaching as many citizens as possible and instead advocate a more targeted approach to communicating the merits of a reform. Anders Fogh Rasmussen, for example, emphasises the importance of communicating LMBP reform plans to younger generations, who are most likely to benefit from the positive long-term effects of a reform: '[...] we made a great effort to appeal to the younger generation. Opinion polls indicated that the young were very much more in favour of the reforms to the Danish pension system than the older generation was. This influenced our decision to have long introductory periods, which meant that we could tell people that they would not be affected: "The entry age for VERP will not be raised before 2019; so you have plenty of time to adjust your retirement and pension plans." The fact that the reform only affected those in favour of the reform anyway proved to be decisive.' **(p. 63)** Perhaps not surprisingly, in communicating their reforms, the majority of heads of government focused on the unions as a means to gain, or further bolster, their support. For José Luis Rodríguez Zapatero developing a good communications strategy means collaborating with the unions, as it is they 'who shape opinions eventually'.

4.3 Successful reformers use feedback from the key stakeholders with a view to modifying the thrust of reforms and selling the modifications to the general public

Several interviewees underline that engagement with stakeholders should involve elements of consultation, as part of which their concerns are heard and digested, and that, as a result of consultation, some modification of reform proposals, and thus an element of 'learning by doing', may materialise. Iveta Radičová, Gerhard Schröder and Jan Peter Balkenende **(p. 207)** highlight politicians' need to remain open for corrections when designing reforms and communicating them to the public and specific stakeholder groups. As Radičová highlights: '[...] you always have to be open to the need for corrections, because – for one thing – it is not possible to measure the effects of synergy before reform processes have actually started. If you launch three or four reforms at the same time, you cannot know how they interact and you cannot know, plan, measure, analyse all the effects that reforms have on society. There must, therefore, be an opportunity to make corrections. That is why it is always necessary to explain reforms, and to allow question marks to remain alongside certain measures, where appropriate, ensuring that they can be modified at a later point in time. [...] Reality keeps changing, and so do successful reform designs. They constantly need to be adapted to a changing reality.' **(p. 259)**

Gerhard Schröder notes the importance of not only communicating the need to modify a reform package, but also putting the modification in a positive light. Thus, he argues: 'During the last phase of my term as Chancellor, the word *Nachbesserung* (correction) became something of a dirty word, and it was a huge mistake on the part of our communication efforts to allow that to happen. Correcting mistakes should really be regarded as a good thing. Why? When you are implementing a reform programme like Agenda 2010, things never work out exactly as planned. If the theoretical model proves to be unworkable, or the goals you have set cannot be achieved, you have to make modifications. Reform is an ongoing process that requires adjustments to changed circumstances, no matter what the cause of those changes is – external shocks or whatever else. If a government says that there is a problem that it needs to correct, if a government actually admits that some aspect of its plan has not worked out – the appropriate response should be: "Yes, you finally get it!" In a democracy, people should not be afraid of politicians who say: "I have made a mistake, and I am going to fix it." The ones they should worry about are those who never make mistakes, or who think they do not. The idea of correcting a mistake to be considered negative was one of the craziest things which happened during my term in office.' **(p. 136)**

Chapter 4
Epilogue – Learn from the past to be prepared for the future

Evolving socio-economic trends have always had a significant impact on labour markets, as well as benefit and pension systems. Stagnant economies and soaring unemployment in the 1970s prompted scholars and politicians alike to advocate, and engage in, measures reducing labour supply, such as early retirement and working-time reductions. What seemed like a good idea at that time turned out to be a major hindrance for economic and labour-market improvements only two decades later, and policymakers continue to struggle with doing away with these outdated approaches until this day. During the 1990s, the advantages and challenges of globalisation called for enhanced flexibility in the labour market ever more openly, while it was necessary, at the same time, to improve employment security for workers in an increasingly uncertain world. The 'flexicurity idea' was implemented in different ways in the 1990s and 2000s.

The mere fact that we consider these matters now makes it clear that the challenges labour markets, as well as benefit and pension systems are exposed to change over time and that policies have to be continuously created, implemented and adapted in order to properly react to these challenges. Even for the very few countries that have experienced a decline in unemployment, financial stabilisation of the social security system and effective prevention of poverty – all at the same time – there has been no such thing as an 'end to reforms'.

1 New challenges prompting the next wave of reforms

The interviews contained in this book cover reform episodes from the last 20 years. Over this period, the most common catalysts for reform were the need to improve competitiveness, to increase labour market participation of underrepresented groups such as female, low-skilled or older workers and to make pension and other social security systems financially viable. While many countries need to go even further down these routes, new challenges, prompting new reform approaches, have emerged. We regard four areas as especially important for future development: (i) growing disparities in the labour market, (ii) the digital revolution of the economy, (iii) increasing numbers of migrant workers and (iv) ongoing challenges posed by demographic change.

1.1 Growing disparities in the labour market

Current European labour markets are characterised by rising disparities. Inequalities in earnings and incomes have increased in virtually every EU member state since the mid-1990s. A lot of academic work has explored the manifold factors contributing to this trend (cf., for instance, OECD 2011a, Vaughan-Whitehead 2011, Dabla-Norris et al. 2015). They include globalisation, skill-biased technological change, changes in work organisation, different productivity levels between exporting companies and firms focused on domestic markets, declining trade union membership and dwindling coverage of collective agreements, to mention but a few. Many of these trends are hard to stop, let alone reverse. While modest levels of income inequality can be efficiency-enhancing and conducive to economic development, inequalities above a certain threshold have the reverse effect. Recent studies by the IMF and the OECD have shown that today's levels of inequality harm not only those adversely affected but also economic growth overall (Ostry et al. 2014; Cingano 2014). The main challenges for labour market and social policy makers are therefore that these inequalities are addressed: they should be reduced to sustainable levels and their negative impact must be curbed.

Wealth inequality has an important impact on the labour market exacerbating the consequences of earnings inequality. Unevenly distributed wealth, in conjunction with imperfect capital markets and risk-averse individuals, can negatively affect the opportunities for upward mobility. In some countries, a lack of assets poses a serious obstacle to individuals to acquiring higher education or better occupational qualifications.

Increased disparities can also be observed in the relations between employees. Traditionally, workers have organised themselves in trade unions around common goals. In recent years, the large industrial trade unions have struggled to cater for the increasingly heterogeneous needs and demands of their (potential) members. It has become more difficult to find collective interests and to group people who share them accordingly. Consequently, in a number of countries, trade unions face declining memberships. At the same time, new trade unions emerge or certain existing ones rediscover their powers. They typically focus on small occupational groups still characterised by homogenous interests and with members who hold jobs in economically and socially sensitive areas, such as public transport or medical care. Examples include air traffic controllers in France or train drivers as well as physicians in Germany. This gives rise to new inequalities: their strong bargaining power is in contrast to the diminishing assertiveness of traditional ones, which leads to uneven wage agreements. In addition, smaller trade unions tend to ignore the potential impact their actions have on the whole economy. If any of the new unions have the power to shut down certain parts of public life, this is especially detrimental, and politicians have to find constructive ways to deal with them.

1.2 The digital revolution in the economy

How seriously the introduction of new digital technology will influence economies and societies is the 'million euro question' of our time. The digital revolution has the potential to pervade every aspect of our private and professional lives, both in positive and negative terms. In the labour market, digital technology has the potential to further detach human labour from routine tasks that can be codified in algorithms and carried out by computers and robots. Digital technology may thus substitute for human labour that primarily consists of routine tasks and lead to unemployment in those areas. At the same time, it can complement laborious tasks and make working processes more efficient, for example when analytical or interactive problems account for the best part of a specific job and increase the demand for workers in such occupations. In this way, the use of digital technology will produce both winners and losers. Scientists are, however, still undecided about the magnitude of this effect. Estimates across countries range from 9 to 47 per cent for the proportion of today's jobs that can, in principle, be replaced by digital technology (Frey and Osborne 2013, Pajarinen and Rouvinen 2014, Bonin, Gregory and Zierahn 2015). In any event, the digital revolution can be viewed as an additional driver of structural change, with associated job losses and gains unevenly distributed across industries. Such developments can also lead to an increased polarisation in the labour market, where highly skilled, as well as low-skilled, workers – all with jobs involving interactive tasks – profit, while routine jobs, often held by the middle classes, both in industry and the services, are increasingly becoming obsolete. Labour market policies will in future have to account for these shifts.

Digital technology has a number of additional consequences for people's working life. It enables a growing number of employees to work in places other than company buildings, including from home. The merging of work and private life can be regarded as a blessing or a curse. While some people certainly enjoy the increased flexibility and power over their daily schedules, and recognise that this provides new job opportunities which had not existed before, others feel pressured and suffer from a state of constant agitation and stress. Remote work enables a looser employer-employee relationship, not only in terms of distance, but also in terms of the contractual framework. In industries such as IT services or business analytics, work on specific tasks is increasingly contracted out on a freelance basis, without the need for the parties entering into a broader employment relationship.

So far, the labour market has not adapted to these developments. In many countries self-employed and freelance workers are not by default covered by standard social security systems. While, traditionally, these groups may have had incomes well above average, ensuring that they had the means for adequate private insurance, this does not necessarily hold for the 'digital freelancers'. Ignorance, or the mere lack of sufficient resources, may leave them uninsured.

1.3 Growing numbers of migrant workers

Enlarging the European Union and subsequently abolishing barriers to free movement, in conjunction with existing and new economic disparities within the EU, have led to increased flows of migrant workers. The accession of ten Central and Eastern European countries to the EU has produced substantial East–West mobility. More recently, as a reaction to the severe economic crisis in the Mediterranean countries, a smaller, but still significant, flow from the South to the North can be observed (Barslund and Busse 2014). Currently, mobile EU citizens do not face any formal restrictions, when they want to work in another member state. Labour mobility is one of the four core freedoms constituting the EU's Single Market. Being mobile is not only beneficial from an individual or a company perspective, i.e. finding a job that does not exist at home and filling a vacancy with the most qualified worker is positive, but also from a macroeconomic point of view. Workers moving from countries in economic turbulence to those with buoyant conditions can serve as a stabilising mechanism, ameliorating macroeconomic imbalances between member states.

However, many real-life problems exist in fostering European labour mobility. Migrant workers often lack the necessary language skills for a successful labour market entry in their chosen destination. Due to different educational and training systems, as well as divergent traditions of occupational profiles, it is hard for companies to assess the qualifications, knowledge and skills of foreign jobseekers. Differences in social security and tax systems, as well as unfamiliar administrative arrangements, might deter workers from wanting to move in the first place or impose serious obstacles to having a successful career in the new country. Lastly, xenophobic tendencies can be observed to be on the rise in a number of European countries.

Naturally, all these barriers also exist – and often in much more serious ways – for workers coming from outside the EU. In addition, immigration laws are still very different across member states and the movement of third-country nationals between EU member states is still severely limited. The inflow of refugees and asylum seekers is another huge challenge that has to be faced by all involved with labour market policy and social security systems today. Effective and cost-efficient integration of foreign workers – be they from another member state or from a third country – should be a paramount goal.

1.4 Ongoing demographic challenges

By now, the sources, as well as the consequences, of demographic change in Europe are well known. Life expectancy has steadily increased since the end of World War II, following an almost linear trend. At the same time, for many countries birth rates have substantially decreased. Taken together, these developments lead to both shrinking and ageing populations and labour forces, culminating in rising dependency ratios, where a decreasing proportion of active workers and entrepreneurs have to support growing numbers of fellow citizens in retirement.

Policymakers across Europe started to deal with these issues in the 1980s, and many reforms in this area have already been implemented. However, several recent developments have brought demography to the forefront of public debate again. Many EU countries had begun to reshape their pension schemes and also their public balance sheets in the early 2000s, or even before then, to make them financially sustainable, but when the economic crisis hit Europe in 2008, public debt soared to unprecedented levels, quickly wiping out the cushions that had been prepared to deal with demographic change. In contrast to the situation before 2008, politicians now have to face demographic challenges with less financial room for manoeuvre.

Furthermore, the pivotal point for the financial viability of public pension systems is the time when the generation of baby boomers starts to retire, which is beginning about now and which will become fully effective around 2025. Even the countries that had already engaged in substantive reforms earlier have only secured sustainability of their systems up to this point. It is doubtful that the old 'recipes' for pension reform will suffice this time round. A further decrease of public pension replacement rates entails the threat of soaring old-age poverty, because the take-up and the return on investment of private pensions have been disappointing so far.

Finally, the various crises that have hit EU member states since 2008 have made it obvious that fully funded private pension schemes as alternatives to public pay-as-you-go systems have their own pitfalls. Permanently low interest rates induced by expansionary monetary policy have substantially reduced accrued pensions in such schemes. According to some economic models, the period of low interest rates might be ongoing over the foreseeable future, even if central banks begin to increase policy rates in the light of recovering economies (cf. Bernanke 2005, Danthine 2013). If, on the other hand, the expansionary monetary policies of recent years should lead to soaring inflation, the entitlements in fully funded schemes will be wholly exposed to devaluation while pay-as-you-go systems are immune to rising prices.

Demographic change also affects the labour market. The median age of workforces is steadily rising across Europe. In view of early retirement schemes disappearing, companies have to adapt workplaces in order to meet the needs of ageing staff. In addition, innovative approaches are required to avoid the productivity of older workers declining. Lastly, in a small number of European countries, advanced demographic change combined with a buoyant economic environment leads to shortages of skilled labour in general, which can be exacerbated by a lack of young workers entering the labour market.

2 Crucial areas for future reform

These trends call for various political actions for which, in the majority of cases, governments are responsible. The social partners, however, also play an important role in shaping policies, mostly through consultations, but of course they also reach collective agreements and take their own initiatives. In the following section, we present five areas that are crucial for the successful management of labour markets and social security systems today and in the foreseeable future. It is not our aim to be prescriptive, but to point politicians in the direction of reforms in areas which are essential for labour markets to thrive and social security to be reliable.

2.1 Countering labour market segmentation

Many labour markets within the EU are characterised by a two-tier structure. On the one hand, there is a majority of workers who enjoy stable, indefinite employment contracts, which are typically associated with fairly generous social security coverage and easy access to further occupational training. They are protected by effective dismissal regulations and enjoy regular wage increases and favourable working conditions, often governed by collective agreements. On the other hand, one can observe a growing proportion of workers in unstable employment relationships, for example, fixed-term contracts, temporary agency work, zero-hour contracts or self-employment in one-person businesses. Such jobs also tend to be associated with unfavourable working hours, and limited access to social security provisions and occupational training opportunities. This type of work can be precarious: people who work under such conditions face a higher risk of losing their jobs and normally have a higher proportion of unemployment periods in their careers than comparable workers in the upper tier. Over a life time, being stuck in such a situation can lead to poverty in old age.

The labour market is increasingly divided into 'insiders' and 'outsiders' and this is also reflected in societal structures. While older workers are much more prominent in the upper tier, younger workers more often only manage to find a job in the lower tier. Migrant workers, too, tend to be over-represented in the lower tier. Transitions between the two segments are normally difficult to achieve.

In many countries the rise of the two-tier structure is a direct consequence of efforts to overcome 'eurosclerosis', i.e. increasingly inflexible labour markets during the 1980s and 1990s. For a politician, it is difficult to increase flexibility because this immediately reduces job security. In contrast, the potential benefits will only accrue over the longer run and are somewhat less tangible in terms of improved job opportunities and a more dynamic economy. Many governments have therefore chosen to improve flexibility by deliberately creating two-tier labour markets through 'deregulation at the margin', which leads to a plethora of labour contracts with sub-segments of employment relationships under different regulatory frameworks. The deregulated margin of the labour market has, however, become increasingly larger, while we witness a substantial fall in the number of traditional contracts. Thus, one important aim of employment policies is to tear down the walls between insiders and outsiders without simply returning to the state of the 1990s and falling into the 'eurosclerosis' pitfall once again. Smart suggestions on how to achieve this have already been offered, for example the notion of creating single open-ended contracts. In such a contract, the degree of employment protection increases with individual job tenure. Such contracts would cater both for the needs of companies for flexibility at the beginning of an employment relationship and the needs of workers for security when they have been in the same job for a longer time.

'Precarious' work in the lower segment of the labour market is often also associated with low pay. In countries where there is no minimum wage for all workers, where the minimum wage is not properly enforced, where it is too low or does not even exist, a phenomenon can be observed that was long thought to be a thing of the past: the so-called 'working poor'. They constitute a group of people who cannot make a decent living in spite of having a full-time job. It is an important goal for politicians to reduce the number of the working poor to an absolute minimum and to refrain from taking any political measures which could force more workers into such a situation. It will be crucial to develop a mix of policy measures that enable workers with low productivity to find a job and to make ends meet at the same time. Another important issue in this respect is the provision of upward mobility. While low-paying jobs certainly provide an entry into the labour market to workers who had previously not been part of the work force, they should not become an impermeable obstacle to a potentially successful career. Rather, they should serve as stepping stones into better-paid jobs. Policies should support such a path. Currently, there are various low-pay 'traps', often caused by adverse tax-benefit and social security regulations.

2.2 Improving labour market dynamics

The lack of dynamism in the labour market is a severe impediment to lowering unemployment in general and especially to achieving a swift recovery after a crisis. A crucial prerequisite for a smoothly functioning labour market is an efficient job-matching process. Successful matching of workers, with their individual sets of qualifications, skills and knowledge, to companies with job vacancies depends on a number of factors. Public employment services play an important role: they act as information brokers for workers and companies alike. In providing active labour market services, they help workers in acquiring necessary skills. They also play their part in providing incentives that induce the unemployed to be pro-active in looking for work. Politicians are required to gear public employment services towards accelerating and improving the quality of job matching. For a number of countries this will entail a paradigm shift for public authorities to move from dealing with the administrative and bureaucratic aspects of unemployment towards supporting job seekers in finding employment. There is a vast range of policies necessary to drive such a radical change, from retraining of staff in the public employment service to the provision of efficient job-broker facilities. Appropriate labour market policies should adhere to the principle of activation with sufficient support and incentives for the job seekers. In addition, it has to be acknowledged that labour markets, especially for the more vulnerable groups, have a strong regional dimension. Consequently, public employment services have to cooperate and to coordinate their work in local municipalities and in regions, in order to be able to extend the horizon of job seekers beyond their home town or region. Today, job matching does not stop at a country's borders. In an increasingly integrated European Single Market it becomes commonplace, at least for certain segments of the workforce, to look for jobs in another country. While European institutions providing employment services exist, there is still room for improvement in terms of accessibility, range of job offers and wealth of information. National public employment services have started to engage in bilateral cooperation and this should be further encouraged.

Another important aspect for improving labour market dynamics is the transition from job security to employment security. Traditional labour market institutions are more geared towards providing job security –protection against dismissal being the strongest example. They aim at securing the specific job of a worker. Initially, this is beneficial for a worker in a relatively stable employment environment. It creates an incentive for workers to invest in job-related or, more broadly, firm-specific, skills: becoming more productive further stabilises the employment relationship. In rapidly changing economies, however, such regulations can be detrimental to employment prospects over the longer term. Structural change has become an important feature of today's economies. It is likely that the digital revolution will considerably accelerate what sometimes seems to be a chaotic turnover of jobs, companies and industries. Certain types of skills and knowledge will become outdated, or even plainly obsolete, while others will become more relevant to success in the digital economy. The same is true for different types of jobs: some will vanish, others will be newly created, and over the whole spectrum the mix of tasks that add up to a job will shift from routine work to analytical and interactive tasks.

Thus, a shift from increasingly illusory job security towards employment security will be necessary. This essentially means that workers can lose their jobs but that the labour market framework and public support will help them find new jobs in the shortest timeframe possible. Active labour market policies aimed at quick and efficient matching, at skills development and at a decent living standard during periods of unemployment play a central role. Ideally, they promote a preventive approach, assisting workers to find a new job even before they are laid-off by their company. Assessing the employability of individual workers on a regular basis might be a helpful method to achieve a smooth transition between jobs.

2.3 Providing adequate social security, as well as basic income security

In an increasingly uncertain world, social security plays an ever more important role. However, the financial viability of benefit systems has come under severe pressures. In many countries, the financing of social security still depends on taxes and contributions generated by labour income – traditional types of labour, that is. Such systems are susceptible to soaring unemployment, as was the case in many European countries during the crisis. They also face declining resources, if increasing proportions of income are not generated through traditional types of labour. Exactly this occurred with the rise of non-standard employment and the pan-European trend of a shift from labour to capital income. It can be expected that the new types of labour associated with the introduction of digital technology will exacerbate this trend. As an additional consequence, the proportion of economically active people without proper social security will increase if the systems do not adapt. Thus, political actors would be well-advised to look for ways to relieve traditional labour from having to bear the brunt of financing social security and to provide adequate access and coverage for those in non-standard employment.

A huge issue will be the question of how to include migrant workers in social security systems and under which circumstances they should be entitled to draw benefits. It is the advantage of residence-based entitlements that the regulations are a simple and transparent rule and that they also support the idea of a European citizenship. Politically, however, this is a trade-off against newly arrived foreign job seekers able to draw benefits without ever having contributed to the host country's social security system.

Apart from providing social security, guaranteed provision of a basic income is one of the most important functions of the welfare state. Having a minimum living standard that goes somewhat beyond pure physical needs enabling to participate in social, educational and cultural activities are pan-European goals, even though attitudes towards the generosity of such a socio-cultural minimum differ widely across and within countries. The relevance of such a minimum has become even more important in view of the crisis, when the ongoing economic slump in a number of countries has generated legions of long-term unemployed. However, basic income security has to be carefully designed in ways that also preserve incentives and provide assistance through labour market policies which help people to actively look for new jobs. Furthermore, it is important not only to encourage people receiving basic income security to enter the labour market but also to ensure a gradual improvement in terms of working hours and earnings. If this prospect of upward mobility can be made credible, it serves as an incentive on its own to take up work in the first place.

2.4 Adapting to an ageing population

Against the backdrop of the topics discussed in this book, an ageing population has important implications for both pension systems and labour markets. The fact that the adjustment of pension systems has already been at centre stage of reform activities in Europe over the last 15 years is no justification for twiddling one's thumbs now, so to speak.

During the first wave of pension reforms that started at the end of the 1990s, a common theme was to advocate more private fully funded pension schemes to supplement reduced public pensions. During the financial crisis and the subsequent economic slump, which was compounded, for savers, by low interest rates, it has become apparent, however, that fully funded private pension schemes are no less immune to economic challenges than pay-as-you-go systems are to demographic issues. Interest rates close to zero have diminished returns to funded schemes, reduced private pensions today and severely limited accrual rates for private pensions of tomorrow. In view of these developments, it is hardly surprising that workers are reluctant to enrol in such schemes.

Occupational pension schemes play vastly different roles in various European countries: while they are the central pillar for pension provisions in some, in others they only play a marginal role. Every country has its own specific combination of public pay-as-you-go systems, occupational pensions and fully funded private insurance schemes. It will be important to adjust that mix in such ways that the specific risks of the different pillars are brought into a balance. Pay-as-you-go systems are more prone to suffer from demographic risks, while the return of funded schemes depends on capital market developments and inflation rates. Balancing these risks will make pension systems more resilient even in the long run.

Another crucial issue for the next wave of pension reforms will be the division of the burden carried by workers and by pensioners. When having to cut pension income and increase contributions, it is essential that there is a fair distribution between these two necessary evils – otherwise public support for the system may be lost. Countries that mainly use contributions based on labour income will also have to think about tapping other sources of income to finance their pensions. Other options include financial support through taxes in the areas of income, environment, consumption and wealth, or the addition of new groups of contributors, such as the self-employed or civil servants. Such measures will broaden the contribution base and will both be felt to be fairer and enhance sustainability. Furthermore, pension systems have to be made accessible to new types of workers. Finally, politicians will have to ask themselves if pension systems could be reformed in a way that would prevent the growing danger of old-age poverty.

Demographic change does not only affect pension systems, but also the age structure of the workforce. An increasing proportion of older workers prompts individuals, companies and the government to adopt measures to maintain their employability. This is all the more important as most European governments have started retracting early retirement schemes introduced over the past few decades. It is important for companies and policies to provide incentives for workers to invest in their own skills at a relatively early age, say around 40, in order to pave the way for maintaining employability later in life.

Apart from reducing benefits and increasing contributions, the financial viability of public pension schemes can also be improved by putting up the actual retirement age. Increasing the statutory age, while steering clear of early retirement schemes, would be the bluntest way to achieve this. However, such a one-size-fits-all approach cannot deal with differences in individuals' health and personal preferences. Allowing a period of several years for a flexible transition into retirement would avoid these problems. Regulations concerning the retirement age could be linked to evolving life expectancy and equipped with financial incentives which would gear retirement decisions in a way that was politically desirable.

2.5 The future role of social partners

Workers – regardless of their type of contract – have a number of interests that are typically best catered for if they are handled collectively. These interests include adequate wages, working time, physical safety and security conditions, as well as fair play in case of termination, in-house education and training, income guarantees beyond public regulations in case of sickness, invalidity, old age or job loss, to name just a few. Taking proper account of these issues is also in the interest of employers. It lowers the transaction costs of negotiations, provides legitimacy and avoids conflicts in the work environment. On the political level, it is highly beneficial to have representatives of workers and companies with a real mandate to negotiate social interests and to consult on social policy.

In that sense it might even be fair to say that trade unions with their system of members' approval of negotiated results comes closer to real-time democracy than Western parliamentary systems. All these aspects proved to be very successful in the last century and could be of major importance in the 21st century, too. A serious concern, however, is the decreasing number of members of trade unions (and also employers' associations). In some countries, this trend is hidden by the fact that trade unions have a legal basis for their authority, but for a sustained role and overall legitimacy, this can hardly be sufficient. Trade unions should reach out to new workers and provide new, attractive forms of membership. A promising approach could be that they act more like a service provider, with membership benefits immediately visible. Government regulation could support such an approach by allowing trade unions to negotiate certain benefits exclusively for their members. In some European countries trade unions are moving towards profession-oriented rather than 'industry-territorial' organisations. Newer, emerging trade unions are generally much smaller and address the interests of a more homogeneous group, in contrast to the large traditional unions, where increasingly heterogeneous interests evoke centrifugal forces among their members. We also witness the first unions of self-employed and freelance workers in Europe, for example 'HK/Privat' in Denmark.

In some countries, trade unions have a legal status which enables them to block reforms, even when a reform is based on a parliamentary majority vote. In these cases, the legal framework for social partners needs to be reformed through fair consultations and negotiations, before any other reform can be undertaken. In the UK, for example, these reforms were made well before the Blair government came into office and reformed social security. In France, these reforms were recognised by the Fillon government as imperative, but they were only partly implemented, as described in his interview. In Germany and most other EU countries, the trade unions had, and still have, no formal status to block reforms, but they can de facto make or break the electoral effects of reforms favoured by political parties, in particular Socialists and Social Democrats. Political parties and politicians should inform themselves carefully to what extent trade unions represent all workers or whether they just represent those with historically acquired rights.

The role of employers' organisations is also challenged, but less questioned, because these organisations are different in nature. Firms, enterprises and companies join forces for economic and political reasons – their role in social issues is focused on the collective bargaining process with trade unions and, at a macro-political level, on addressing the costs of the welfare state. Beyond that, they represent interests found concerning entrepreneurial climate, innovation, education, taxes and infrastructure, but they do not represent the broader population involved in general social reforms. As such, the organisations of employers do not suffer as much from declining membership, and in times when economic growth is high on the agenda, they are much-respected stakeholders. But for the role of social partners in social policy reforms, the role of trade unions is more critical than the role of employers' organisations. This does not mean that employers should be left out of these processes – on the contrary, recent history, for example in Germany and the Netherlands, has telling examples where trade unions and employers' associations took the initiative and the responsibility to design and see through social policy reforms on issues where public policy had failed or had simply lacked the necessary tools. Governments are well-advised to encourage and to welcome united action from trade unions and employers' organisations. However, governments should never be hostage to their claims or interests – in the end, the general interest, and in particular the interest of future generations, should prevail.

3 Resulting challenges along the process dimension

As this epilogue shows, neither the need nor the options for reform have run out – quite the contrary. New challenges call for new approaches towards adjusting, inventing or abolishing institutions in the labour market and in benefit and pension systems. This entails a number of consequences for the process dimension of reforms as well.

It is in the interest of politicians that the social partners preserve their relevance as intermediaries, where they have played important roles so far, or that they strengthen their significance in other countries where this is not yet the case. A deepened formal or factual embeddedness of trade unions and employers' associations is beneficial in terms of reform communication, implementation and administration, as the examples in this book have shown.

For most countries the budgetary situation has significantly worsened during the crisis. Annual deficits have soared leading to record levels of public debt. While low interest rates have helped to curb even further increases in indebtedness, difficulties are likely to persist when it comes to achieving sustained budgetary surpluses in order to quickly return to pre-crisis debt levels or even below. In general, the financial resources for new reforms have significantly decreased. This does not only apply to reforms that focus on increased spending. With regard to a number of structural reforms described in this book, governments were able to cushion the short-term negative consequences by adopting a two-handed approach: structural reforms were complemented by expansive macro-policies or by directly compensating the losers, e. g. through transition periods. In view of empty coffers, such policies will be harder to implement rendering the politics of reform even more difficult.

New challenges will also arise with regard to the administrative capacity that is necessary to plan and to implement reforms. There are three reasons for this: Firstly, because of increased international connectedness and accelerated structural change, it is likely that new developments will emerge more quickly and that political actors will have to react more swiftly. Secondly, due to increased fluidity in economy and society, subsequent adjustments of already implemented reforms will be necessary more often and more quickly. Thirdly, the reform challenges ahead will require genuine changes of entire systems more frequently whereas in the past gradual adjustments within existing systems have been more common. For instance, many pension reforms over the past years have tweaked certain parameters within the system such as retirement age, benefit levels, contribution rates etc. Future reforms in this area as described above are likely to call for more innovative approaches, such as the inclusion of previously uninsured groups or capital income as part of the contribution base. In total, administrative capacity will be required to be more innovative, faster and more flexible. Improving these dimensions will be a crucial prerequisite for policy-makers to succeed in implementing reforms.

While the topics and the environments for reform processes certainly change over time, the underlying political mechanisms that influence the size, the scope, the implementation and, ultimately, the success of reforms remain largely the same. Against this backdrop, we hope to have provided a thorough assessment of the success factors of past reforms and, at the same time, to have presented a highly relevant set of insights and ideas policy makers can draw on if they endeavour to engage in shaping labour markets, as well as benefit and pension systems, and thus to master the challenges ahead.

Bibliography

Abriac, D., R. Rathelot and R. Sánchez (2009) 'L'apprentissage, entre formation et insertion professionnelle', *Formations et emploi* (INSEE)

Alesina, A., S. Ardagna and F. Trebbi (2006) 'Who adjusts and when? On the political economy of stabilizations', *IMF Staff Papers*, Mundell-Fleming Lecture 53, pp. 1–49

Allegre, G., M. Cochard and M. Plane (2012) 'Quels effets du "contrat de génération" sur l'emploi et les finances publiques?', *Notes de l'OFCE*, No. 23/26 (July)

Andrews, D., A. Caldera Sánchez and A. Johansson (2011) 'Towards a better understanding of the informal economy', *OECD Economics Department Working Papers*, No. 836 (OECD, Paris)

Andrews, D. and F. Cingano (2014) 'Public policy and resource allocation: Evidence from firms in OECD countries', *Economic Policy*, 29 (78), pp. 253–96

Arts, W. and J. Gelissen (2002) 'Three worlds of welfare capitalism or more? A state-of-the-art report', *Journal of European Social Policy*, 12 (2), pp. 137–58

Atkinson, A. and J. Micklewright (1991) 'Unemployment compensation and labor market transitions: A critical review', *Journal of Economic Literature,* 29 (4), pp. 1679–727

Auer, P. (2000) *Employment revival in Europe: Labour market successes in Austria, Denmark, Ireland and the Netherlands* (ILO, Geneva)

Baranowska, A., M. Gebel and I. E. Kotowska (2011) 'The role of fixed-term contracts at labour market entry in Poland: stepping stones, screening devices, traps or search subsidies?' *Work, Employment and Society*, 25 (4)

Barbetta G. (1993) 'Defining the nonprofit sector: Italy', *Working Papers of the Johns Hopkins Comparative Nonprofit Sector Project,* No. 8 (Johns Hopkins Institute for Policy Studies, Baltimore)

Barslund, M. and M. Busse (2014) *Making the most of EU labour mobility* (Centre for European Policy Studies, Brussels)

Bassanini, A. and R. Duval (2006) 'Employment patterns in OECD countries: reassessing the role of policies and institutions', *OECD Economics Department Working Papers*, No. 486 (OECD, Paris)

Beck, P. (1979) 'The electoral cycle and patterns of American politics', *British Journal of Political Science,* 9 (2), pp. 129–56

Bell, D. and D. Blanchflower (2011) 'Young people and the Great Recession', *IZA Discussion Papers,* No. 5674, April

Bentolila, S., J. Dolado and J.F. Jimeno (2008) 'Two-tier employment protection reforms: the Spanish experience', *CESifo DICE Report*, Vol. 6, No. 4, Munich

Bentolila, S., J. Dolado and J.F. Jimeno (2012) 'The Spanish labour market: a very costly insider–outsider divide', *Vox*, 20 January

Blanchard, O. and J. Tirole (2003) *Protection de l'emploi et procédures de licenciement*, Conseil d'analyse économique, Report No. 44

Blundell, R., C. Crawford and W. Jin (2014) 'What can wages and employment tell us about the UK's productivity puzzle?' *Economic Journal*, 124

Boeri, T. and P. Garibaldi (2007) 'Two tier reforms of employment protection: a honeymoon effect?' *Economic Journal*, 117 (521), pp. 357–86

Bonin, H., T. Gregory and U. Zierahn (2015) *Übertragung der Studie von Frey/Osborne (2013) auf Deutschland* (Zentrum für Europäische Wirtschaftsforschung, Mannheim)

Bonoli, G. (1997) 'Classifying welfare states: a two-dimension approach', *Journal of Social Policy,* 26 (3), pp. 351–72

Bonoli, G. (2005) 'Time matters: Postindustrialization, new social risks, and welfare state adaptation in advanced industrial democracies', *Comparative Political Studies* 40 (5), pp. 495–520

Boundless (2015) 'The history of the welfare state', *Boundless Political Science,* 2 February 2015; available at https://www.boundless.com/political-science/textbooks/boundless-po litical-science-textbook/social-policy-17/the-welfare-state-105/the-history-of-the-welfare-state-558–6935/

Bourguignon, F. (2011) *Comité national d'évaluation du rSA,* Rapport final, December

Boyer, R. (2000) 'The French welfare: an institutional and historical analysis in European perspective', Working Paper No. 2000–07 (CEPREMAP, Paris)

Bredgaard, T., T. Larsen and P.K. Madsen (2005) 'The flexible Danish labour market –– a review', *CARMA Research Papers,* No. 2005:01 (Aalborg University)

Brewer, M. (2008) 'Welfare reform in the UK: 1997–2007', *Institute for Labour Market Policy Evaluation (IFAU) Working Papers,* 2008:12, Uppsala

Bunel, M., C. Emond and Y. L'Horty (2012) 'Evaluer les réformes des exonérations générales de cotisations sociales', *Revue de l'OFCE,* No. 126, pp. 59–103

Burda, M. and J. Hunt (2011) 'What explains the German labor market miracle in the Great Recession?' *Brookings Papers on Economic Activity,* Vol. 42, No. 1, pp. 273–335

Cahuc, P. and S. Carcillo (2011) 'The detaxation of overtime hours: Lessons from the French experiment', *IZA Discussion Papers,* No. 5439 (Institute for the Study of Labour, Bonn)

Cahuc, P., S. Carcillo and T. Le Barbanchon (2014) 'Do hiring credits work in recessions? Evidence from France', *IZA Discussion Papers,* No. 8330 (Institute for the Study of Labour, Bonn)

Cahuc, P. and F. Kramarz (2005) 'De la précarité à la mobilité: vers une sécurité sociale professionnelle', Rapport au ministre de l'Economie, des Finances et de l'Industrie et au ministre de l'Emploi, du Travail et de la Cohésion sociale, *La documentation Française,* Paris

Caliendo, M. and J. Hogenacker (2012) 'The German labor market after the Great Recession: Successful reforms and future challenges', *IZA Journal of European Labor Studies,* Vol. 1, pp. 1–24

Calmfors, L. and J. Driffill (1988) 'Centralisation of wage bargaining and economic performance', *Economic Policy,* pp. 13–61

Cappellini, E., T. Ferraresi, D. Marinari and N. Sciclone (2014), 'Il lavoro dopo la legge Fornero', *lavoce.info,* 21 February

Carbonnier, C., B. Palier and M. Zemmour (2014) 'Tax cuts or social investment? Evaluating the opportunity cost of the French employment strategy', *LIEPP Working Papers,* No. 31 (Sciences Po, Paris)

Chlon-Dominczak, A. (2004) 'Pension reform in Poland', in *Reforming public pensions: sharing experiences of OECD and transition countries* (OECD, Paris)

Cingano, F. (2014) 'Trends in income inequality and its impact on economic growth', OECD Social, Employment and Migration Working Papers, No. 163

Codogno, L. (2009) 'Two Italian puzzles: are productivity growth and competitiveness really so depressed?', in M. Buti (ed.) *Italy in EMU* (Palgrave Macmillan)

Costain, J., J.F. Jimeno and C. Thomas (2010) 'Employment fluctuations in a dual labour market', *Documentos de trabajo,* No. 1013 (Bank of Spain, Madrid)

Dabla-Norris, E. et al. (2015) *Causes and consequences of income inequality: A Global Perspective*, IMF Staff Discussion Note 15/13 (International Monetary Fund, Washington, D.C.)

Danish Government (2013) *Denmark's national reform programme 2013* (Danish Government, Copenhagen)

Davì, C. (no date), 'Perspectives on social welfare: the Italian case', *Social Work and Society International Online Journal,* available at http://www.socmag.net/?p=592

Douglas, H.E. (2009) *Science, policy, and the value-free ideal* (Pittsburgh University Press, Pittsburgh)

Dyson, K. (2005) 'Binding hands as a strategy for economic reform: Government by commission', *German Politics,* 14 (2), pp. 224–47

The Economist (2014) 'A golden opportunity', *The Economist, Special report: Poland* (28 June 2014)

The Economist (2013) 'Europe's reluctant hegemon', *The Economist, Special report: Germany* (5 June 2013)

Eichhorst, W. (2012) 'The unexpected appearance of a new German model', *IZA Discussion Papers,* No. 6625 (June)

Eichhorst, W. (2013) 'What can we learn from Germany's dual vocational training model?', IZA Newsroom (26 June)

Esping-Andersen, G. (1990) *The three worlds of welfare capitalism* (Princeton University Press, Princeton)

Esping-Andersen, G. (1999) *Social foundations of postindustrial economies* (Oxford University Press, Oxford and New York)

European Commission (2012) 'The 2012 ageing report: Economic and budgetary projections for the 27 EU Member States (2010–2060)', *European Economy,* No. 2

European Commission (2009) 'The 2009 ageing report: Economic and budgetary projections for the EU-27 Member States (2008–2060)', *European Economy,* No. 2

Eurostat (2015) 'Monthly minimum wages in euro varied by 1 to 10 across the EU in January 2015', *Eurostat Newsrelease,* 35 (26 February)

Fallesen, P., L.P. Geerdsen. S. Imai and T. Tranaes (2014) 'The effect of workfare on crime: incapacitation and program effects', *IZA Discussion Paper* 8716 (Bonn, December)

Fernandez, R. and D. Rodrik (1991) 'Resistance to reform: status quo bias in the presence of individual-specific uncertainty', *American Economic Review,* Vol. 81 (5), pp. 1146–55

Ferrera, M. (1996) 'The "Southern Model" of Welfare in Social Europe', *Journal of European Social Policy,* 6 no. 1, pp. 17–37

Finn, D. (2011) 'Welfare to work after the recession: from the new deals to the work programme', in Holden, C., M. Kilkey and G. Ramia (eds.), *Social Policy Review 23: Analysis and Debate in Social Policy* (Policy Press, Bristol)

Finn, D. and B. Schulte (2008) 'Activation policies in Great Britain', in Eichhorst, W., R. Konle-Seidl, and O. Kaufmann (eds.), *Bringing the jobless into work? Experiences with activation schemes in Europe and the US* (Springer Verlag, Berlin), pp. 297–344

Fornero, E. (2013) 'Reforming labor markets: reflections of an economist who (unexpectedly) became the Italian Minister of Labor', *IZA Journal of European Labor Studies,* 2 (20)

Frey, C. B. and M. A. Osborne (2013) *The future of employment: How susceptible are jobs to computerisation?* (University of Oxford, Oxford)

Galasso, V. (2010) 'Advancing pension and labour-market reforms', in OECD (ed.) *Making reform happen: lessons from OECD countries* (OECD, Paris)

Geerdsen, L.P. (2006) 'Is there a threat effect of labour market programmes? A study of ALMPs in the Danish UI system', *Economic Journal*, 116 (July), pp. 738–50

Gerhart, B. and S. Rynes (2003) *Compensation: Theory, evidence, and strategic implications* (Sage Publications, Thousand Oaks, CA)

Góra, M. (2001) 'Polish approach to pension reform', *OECD Private Pensions Systems* No. 3 (OECD, Paris)

Haggard, S. and S. Webb (1993) 'What do we know about the political economy of economic policy reform?' *The World Bank Research Observer*, Vol. 8 (2), pp. 143–68

Haggard, S. and S. Webb (eds.) (1994) *Voting for reform: Democracy, political liberalization, and economic adjustment*, published for the World Bank (Oxford University Press, Oxford)

Head, B. (2008) 'Three lenses of evidence-based policy', *Australian Journal of Public Administration*, 67 (1), pp. 1–11

Hemerijck, A. (2013) 'Changing European welfare states and the evolution of migrant incorporation regimes', Background paper reviewing welfare state structures and reform dynamics in a comparative perspective (IMPACIM, VU University Amsterdam, COMPAS) available at https://www.compas.ox.ac.uk/fileadmin/files/Publications/Research_projects/Welfare/IMPACIM/IMPACIM_Changing__European__Welfare_States.pdf

Hijzen, A. and S. Martin (2013) 'The role of short-time work schemes during the global financial crisis and early recovery: a cross-country analysis', *IZA Journal of Labor Policy*, 2, pp. 1–31

Hijzen, A. and D. Venn (2011) 'The role of short-time work schemes during the 2008–09 recession', *OECD Social, Employment and Migration Working Papers*, No. 115 (OECD, Paris)

Hofer, A. (2007) 'The severance pay reform in Austria', *CESifo DICE Report* 5 (Munich), pp. 41–8

Hughes, A. and J. Saleheen (2012) 'UK labour productivity since the onset of the crisis – an international and historical perspective', *Bank of England Quarterly Bulletin*, Q2, pp. 138–46

ILO (2008a) 'Greece', Actuarial projections as of 31 December 2005 of the national pension schemes IKA for private sector workers and OGA for agriculture workers, *Report of the National Actuarial Authority* (ILO, Geneva)

ILO (2008b) 'Greece', Actuarial projection results of the national pension schemes of OAEE as of 31 December 2005, *Preliminary Technical Note to the National Actuarial Authority* (ILO, Geneva)

ILO (2008c) 'Greece', Actuarial projection results of the national pension scheme of public servants as of 31 December 2005, *Preliminary Technical Note to the National Actuarial Authority* (ILO, Geneva)

Jong, P. de (2007) 'Recent changes in Dutch disability policy' (APE, The Hague)

Jurajda, S. and K. Mathernova (2004) 'How to overhaul the labor market: political economy of recent Czech and Slovak reforms', *CERGE-EI Discussion Papers* 126 (CERGE, Prague)

Kaluzna, D. (2009) 'Main features of the public employment service in Poland', *OECD Social, Employment and Migration Working Papers*, No. 80 (OECD, Paris)

Koning, P.W.C. (2009) 'Experience rating and the inflow into disability insurance', *De Economist* 157, pp. 315–35

Koutsogeorgopoulou, V., M. Matsaganis, C. Leventi and J.-D. Schneider (2014) 'Fairly sharing the social impact of the crisis in Greece', *OECD Economics Department Working Papers* 1106 (OECD, Paris)

Lauringson, A., K. Villsaar, L. Tammik and T. Luhavee (2011) 'Impact evaluation of labour market training', *Estonian Unemployment Insurance Fund* (Tallinn)

Lepage-Saucier, N., J. Schleich and E. Wasmer (2013) 'Moving towards a single labour contract: pros, cons and mixed feelings', *OECD Economics Department Working Papers* 1026

Levy, J. (1999) 'Vice into virtue? Progressive politics and welfare reform in continental Europe', *Politics & Society*, Vol. 27 (2), pp. 239–73

Lodovici, M. (2000) 'The dynamics of labour market reform in European countries', in: Esping-Andersen, G. and M. Regini (eds.) *Why deregulate labour markets* (Oxford University Press, Oxford), pp. 30–65

Madsen, P.K. (2013) 'Shelter from the storm? – Danish flexicurity and the crisis', *IZA Journal of European Labor Studies*, pp. 2–6

Martin, J.P. and S. Scarpetta (2012), 'Setting it right: employment protection, labour reallocation and productivity', *De Economist* 160, pp. 89–116

Martinot, B. (2015) 'Il faut rénover un dialogue social à bout de souffle', *Les Echos*, January

Matos, C. (2010) 'Unreformed or hybrid? Accounting for pension arrangements diversity in the EU', *Forum for Social Economics*, Vol. 39 (1), pp. 43–51

Mulgan, G. (2005) 'Government, knowledge and the business of policy making: the potential and limits of evidence-based policy', *Evidence & Policy*, Vol. 1 (2), pp. 215–26

Natali, D. and M. Rhodes (2004) 'Trade-offs and veto players: reforming pensions in France and Italy', *French Politics*, Vol. 2 (1), pp. 1–23

National Actuarial Authority (2011) 'Financial evolution of the pension system for the public sector 2008–2060', *Technical notes*, January 2011

National Actuarial Authority (2010) 'Financial evolution of the pension system for IKE-ERAM, OAEE, OGA 2008–2060', *Technical notes*, December 2010

O'Brien, P. (2013) 'Policy implementation in Italy: legislation, public administration and the rule of law', *OECD Economics Department Working Papers* 1064 (OECD, Paris)

Ostry, J., A. Berg and C. Tsangarides (2014) 'Redistribution, Inequality and Growth', IMF Staff Discussion Note, February 2014

Ourliac, B. and C. Nouveau (2012) 'Les allègements de cotisation sociales patronales sur les bas salaires en France de 1993 à 2009', *Document d'études* 169 (DARES)

Pajarinen, M. and P. Rouvinen (2014) *Computerization threatens one third of Finnish employment*, ETLA Brief 22 (ETLA – The Research Institute of the Finnish Economy, Helsinki)

Praxis (2011) 'Sustainable financing possibilities for the Estonian social security system', *Mimeo* (Tallinn)

Reenen, J. van (2004) 'Active labor market policies and the British new deal for the young unemployed in context', in Card, D., R.Blundell and R.B. Freeman (eds.), *Seeking a premier economy: the economic effects of British economic reforms, 1980–2000* (NBER, University of Chicago Press)

Rinne, U. and K. Zimmermann (2013) 'Is Germany the North Star of labor market policy?', *IZA Discussion Paper* 7260 (March)

Rosenstock, L. and L. Lee (2002) 'Attacks on science: the risks to evidence-based policy', *American Journal of Public Health*, Vol. 92 (1), pp. 14–18

Rosholm, M. and M. Svarer (2004) 'Estimating the threat effect of active labour market programs', *IZA Discussion Paper*, No. 1300, available at http://www.econstor.eu/bitstream/10419/20566/1/dp1300.pdf

Saint-Paul, G. (2002) 'Macroeconomic fluctuations and the timing of labour market reforms', *CEPR Discussion Paper* No. 3646 http://www.cepr.org/active/publications/discussion_pa pers/dp.php?dpno=3646

Sapir, A. (2006) 'Globalization and the reform of European social models', *Journal of Common Market Studies,* 44 (2), pp. 369–90

Schmidt, M. (2005) *Sozialpolitik in Deutschland – Historische Entwicklung und internationaler Vergleich* (VS Verlag für Sozialwissenschaften, Wiesbaden)

Sonsbeek, J.-M. van and R. Gradus (2011) 'Estimating the effects of recent disability reforms in the Netherlands', *Tinbergen Institute Discussion Papers*, No. 121/3 (Amsterdam)

Stiglbauer, A. (2006) 'Wie "dynamisch" ist der österreichische Arbeitsmarkt?' *Wirtschaftspolitische Blätter,* 53, pp. 143–60

Stolfi, F. (2008) 'The Europeanization of Italy's budget institutions in the 1990s', *Journal of European Public Policy,* 15 (4), pp. 550–66

Stolleis, M. (2013) *Origins of the German welfare state: Social policy in Germany to 1945* (Springer, Berlin and Heidelberg)

Svarer, M. (2007) 'The effect of sanctions on the job-finding rate: evidence from Denmark', *IZA Discussion Papers,* 3015 (Institute for the Study of Labour, Bonn)

Teulings, C.N. (2014) 'Unemployment and house price crises: lessons for fiscal policy from the Dutch recession', *IZA Journal of European Labor Studies,* 3 (20)

Toharia, L. and M. Malo (2000) 'The Spanish experiment: pros and cons of flexibility at the margin', in G. Esping-Andersen and M. Regini (eds.) *Why Deregulate Labour Markets?* (OUP, Oxford)

Tompson, W. (2009) *The political economy of reform: Lessons from pensions, product markets and labour markets in ten OECD countries* (OECD, Paris)

Vaughan-Whitehead, D. (ed.) (2011) *Work inequalities in the crisis: Evidence from Europe* (International Labour Organization, Geneva)

Venn, D. (2012) 'Eligibility criteria for unemployment benefits: quantitative indicators for OECD and EU countries', *OECD Social, Employment and Migration Working Papers* 131 (OECD, Paris)

Vork, A. (2009) 'Labour supply incentives and income support systems in Estonia', *Institute for Labour Market Policy Evaluation Working Papers,* 31 (IFAU, Tallinn)

Walwei, U. (2013) 'Times of change: what drives the growth of work arrangements in Germany?' *Journal for Labour Market Research*, July 2013

Weishaupt, J.T. (2011) *Social partners and the governance of public employment services: trends and experiences from Western Europe* (ILO, Geneva)

Zimmermann, K. (2014), 'Germany's minimum wage: a costly experiment', IZA Newsroom, 4 April 2014

all documents are published by OECD Publications, Paris

OECD (2015a) *Economic policy reforms 2015: going for growth*

OECD (2015b) *Economic surveys: Italy 2015*

OECD (2015c) *Economic surveys: United Kingdom 2015*

OECD (2014a) *Connecting people with jobs: activation policies in the United Kingdom*

OECD (2014b) *Economic surveys: Denmark 2014*

OECD (2014c) *Economic surveys: Germany 2014*

OECD (2014d) *Economic surveys: Netherlands 2014*

OECD (2014e) *Economic surveys: Poland 2014*

OECD (2014f) *Economic surveys: Spain 2014*

OECD (2014g) *Employment outlook 2014*

OECD (2014h) *Mental health and work: United Kingdom*

OECD (2013a) *Economic surveys: Austria 2013*

OECD (2013b) *Economic surveys: France 2013*

OECD (2013c) *Economic surveys: Greece 2013*

OECD (2013d) *Economic surveys: Italy 2013*

OECD (2013e) *Economic surveys: United Kingdom 2013*

OECD (2013f) *Employment outlook 2013*

OECD (2013g) *Mental health and work: Denmark*

OECD (2013h) *The 2012 labour market reform in Spain: a preliminary assessment*

OECD (2013i) *The political economy of reform: lessons from pensions, product markets and labour markets in ten OECD countries*

OECD (2012a) *Economic surveys: Denmark 2012*

OECD (2012b) *Economic surveys: Estonia 2012*

OECD (2012c) *Economic surveys: Germany 2012*

OECD (2012d) *Economic surveys: Netherlands 2012*

OECD (2012e) *Economic surveys: Poland 2012*

OECD (2012f) *Economic surveys: Slovak Republic 2012*

OECD (2012g) *Economic surveys: Spain 2012*

OECD (2012h) *Employment outlook 2012*

OECD (2011a) *Divided we stand: why inequality keeps rising*

OECD (2011b) *Economic surveys: Austria 2011*

OECD (2011c) *Economic surveys: Estonia 2011*

OECD (2011d) *Economic surveys: Greece 2011*

OECD (2011e) *Economic surveys: Italy 2011*

OECD (2010a) *Economic surveys: Germany 2010*

OECD (2010b) *Economic surveys: Poland 2010*

OECD (2010c) *Economic surveys: Slovak Republic 2010*

OECD (2010d) *Economic surveys: Spain 2010*

OECD (2010e) *Jobs for youth: Greece*

OECD (2010f) *Reviews of labour market and social policies: Estonia*

OECD (2010g) *Sickness, disability and work: breaking the barriers – a synthesis of findings across OECD countries*

OECD (2009a) *Economic surveys: Italy 2009*

OECD (2009b) *Jobs for youth: France*

OECD (2009c) *The political economy of reform: lessons from pensions, product markets and labour markets in ten OECD countries*

OECD (2008a) *Economic surveys: Denmark 2008*

OECD (2008b) *Growing unequal? Income distribution and poverty in OECD countries*

OECD (2008c) *Jobs for youth: United Kingdom*

OECD (2008d) *Sickness, disability and work: breaking the barriers – Denmark, Finland, Ireland and the Netherlands*, Vol. 3

OECD (2006) *Employment outlook 2006*

OECD (2005a) *Ageing and employment policies: Austria*
OECD (2005b) *Employment outlook 2005*
OECD (2003) *Employment outlook 2003*

Index